FACTION AND FAITH

Politics and Religion of the Cornish Gentry
before the Civil War

FACTION AND FAITH

Politics and Religion of the Cornish Gentry before the Civil War

Anne Duffin

UNIVERSITY
of
EXETER
PRESS

First published in 1996 by
University of Exeter Press
Reed Hall, Streatham Drive
Exeter, Devon EX4 4QR
UK

British Library Cataloguing in Publication Data
A catalogue record for this book is
available from the British Library

ISBN 0 85989 435 5

Typeset in 10/12pt Caslon
by Kestrel Data, Exeter

Printed and bound in Great Britain by
Short Run Press Ltd, Exeter

For my mother and father
with love

Contents

List of Illustrations

List of Tables

Acknowledgements

I began work on the Cornish gentry in 1984 as a postgraduate at the University of Exeter. I remain indebted to the British Academy for the Major State Studentship which funded that research, and to the Institute of Historical Research, London, for awarding me a Scouloudi Research Fellowship which allowed the completion of my Ph.D. thesis. The Institute's seminars and common room were a great source of inspiration and friendship. I am also grateful to the Caroline Kemp Benevolent Fund and to the Sir Arthur Quiller Couch ('Q') Fund for helping to finance some of the additional research. I would like to thank Professor Ivan Roots, my Ph.D. supervisor, for his sustained interest in my work, his unfailing support, encouragement, guidance and friendship, and for his invaluable comments on the manuscript of the book. Others who have generously shared ideas and information are Dr Jonathan Barry, Mr James Derriman, Professor Anthony Fletcher, Dr Ronald Hutton, Dr John Morrill, Professor Conrad Russell, Dr Andrew Thrush and Dr Mark Stoyle. I am grateful to the staff of all the record offices and libraries I have used for their kindness and courtesy. Particular thanks are due to Mrs Christine North and the staff of the Cornwall Record Office who have steadfastly assisted, advised, and encouraged me over the last twelve years—and helped me to retain my sense of humour. I am extremely grateful to Sue Rouillard for drawing the maps for the book, and to Sean Goddard and Mike Rouillard for taking and developing most of the photographs. Dr John Critchley, former Head of the Department of History and Archaeology, University of Exeter, has also been very supportive. I have many long-suffering friends who have tolerated with good humour my reclusive tendencies while this book was in production, and I would like to thank especially Mrs Kate Bon and Mrs Maria Coonick for their telephone hotlines of support. My parents have always encouraged me and have provided me with both practical and moral support, for which I am deeply grateful, and this book is dedicated to them. It is the fate of a spouse always to come last in a list of acknowledgements, but my husband, Edward Austin, has made this book possible in so many ways. He has lived with the Cornish gentry for as long as he has been married to me, and he has come to know them intimately. For his support, interest, enthusiasm, constructive criticism, and assistance in editing the book, I thank him.

Preface

In summer 1642 Sir Bevill Grenvile of Stow was one of the most active Cornish gentlemen in raising support for the King. In September he raised a regiment, and four months later, at the Battle of Braddock Down, near Liskeard, he led his men in a charge so wild that, in his own words, it 'strook a terror' in the enemy. In May 1643, at the Battle of Stratton, near his home in north Cornwall, Grenvile led those same men to victory in an uphill charge with only swords and pikes. He was killed on 5 July at the Battle of Lansdown, Somerset.[1]

In contrast, the leading Cornish Puritan, Sir Richard Buller of Shillingham in St Stephens by Saltash, spent summer 1642 trying to raise support for Parliament in Cornwall. In September, he fortified and attempted to hold a number of towns in the east of the county. However, in early October, upon the approach of Sir Ralph Hopton, Grenvile and 3,000 royalist soldiers, Buller and his men retreated to Plymouth, where they joined with the Devon parliamentarians. Buller died in Plymouth in November 1642, and (with royalist acquiescence) his body was brought home to Saltash for burial.[2]

Fifteen years before, Grenvile and Buller had been political allies. Both were members of a faction led by Sir John Eliot of Port Eliot and William Coryton Esq of West Newton Ferrers, and they had worked together to oppose the interests of the Duke of Buckingham and of the Cornish faction which supported him. One of the central questions addressed in this book will be what made men like Buller and Grenvile support the Eliot–Coryton faction in the 1620s and early 1630s, and why they took opposing sides in 1642. This will raise a number of other questions, including what were the issues which united and divided them, and whether those issues changed during the period.

In her 1933 book, *Cornwall in the Great Civil War and Interregnum*, Mary Coate attributed the Cornish gentry's political decisions primarily to the influence of localism. She emphasized elements of the Cornish character, such as 'natural conservatism', 'legal-mindedness', 'a strong personality', 'a spirit of adventure', and 'local patriotism', together with family tradition and the retention of a semi-feudal society. She maintained that despite social and ideological differences, the most important determinant of allegiance was origination from the same county.[3]

Coate broke new ground, working political and social analysis into a narrative of Civil War events. She was a forerunner of the 'county community school', which twenty years later, led by Alan Everitt, defined and developed the concept of localism. Everitt described England in 1640 as 'a union of partially independent county-states', and echoed Coate in his claim that 'the lives of most provincial people were not simply polarized around the ideals of Cavalier and Roundhead, but rather around local rivalries and loyalties'.[4] Clive Holmes and Ann Hughes have since shown that national and local politics were not mutually exclusive, but were deeply integrated, particularly through the gentry's local and national office-holding. These offices provided the dual role of representing the government in the locality, and the locality at the centre.[5]

In considering central–local relationships and allegiance it is important to appreciate that the gentry of all counties were members of a number of 'communities' and interest groups, national and not solely topographical, and that the 'membership' and influence of these groups shifted over time. Consequently, allegiance was a matter of a delicate balance which could and did alter quickly and unpredictably in response to new pressures. This view was proposed by Ivan Roots in 1970, and has since been developed by Ann Hughes, who has shown, for example, that gentlemen from an area dominated by a certain type of agriculture, or religious practice, may have had more in common with those of an adjacent county practising the same type of agriculture, or of the same religious beliefs, than with gentlemen from their own county.[6]

The following pages will attempt to draw out the different social, political, and religious interests which influenced the actions of the Cornish gentry. It will try to show that while many of these interests had a specifically Cornish focus, they were rarely exclusively so. The principal issues which affected and concerned Cornish gentlemen in this period, notably coastal defence, non-parliamentary taxation, and religious change, all had a national impact. The local response to those issues over the period often involved non-Cornishmen, in the Privy Council, in Parliament, and at Court. Consequently, outsiders were drawn into local affairs, and Cornish gentlemen found ways of dealing with local problems in a wider, national context.

This is a study of the gentry, and more specifically of the greater gentry, in the period leading up to and including the outbreak of the English Civil War. The absence of local government records has dictated the nature of the work, forcing a reliance on gentry collections and central government records. Consequently, the book focuses upon certain greater gentry families—the county elite—although there is analysis of minor gentry where appropriate and where records survive.

1

Cornwall and the Cornish Gentry

A County Community?

In the early seventeenth century Cornwall was relatively isolated by virtue of its geographical position, physical features and poor communications. A peninsula, lying at the far south-western tip of England and bordering on the Atlantic Ocean and the English Channel, the county occupies an area of 1,365 square miles, and is approximately one hundred miles long. Forty-five miles wide at its broadest point along the Devon border marked by the River Tamar, it is only six miles wide at its narrowest point between Hayle and Marazion. The coastline is rugged, and inland Cornwall is dominated by the moorland with its great granite tors running through the centre of the county. This rugged scenery impressed John Norden, the cartographer, in 1584:

> The Countrie is full of hills, Rockes, and craggye mountaynes . . . The rockes are high, huge, ragged, and craggie, not only upon the sea-coaste, the Rockes wherof are verie high, steepe, and harde, and are as a defensive wall againste the continuall furious assaultes of the prevayling Ocean on all sides . . . But also the Inlande mountayns are so crowned with mightie rockes, as he that passeth throwgh the Countrye beholdinge some of theis Rockes afar off, may suppose them to be greate Cyties planted on the hills.[1]

Three main roads linked Cornwall with Devon. Taking the road from Okehampton involved crossing the Tamar at Polston Bridge, and travelling on through Launceston, Camelford, Padstow and Truro. From Tavistock, the county could be entered near Calstock, and the journey made through Liskeard, Lostwithiel and Grampound. Alternatively, a coastal road from Plymouth passed through Looe, Fowey, St Austell and Tregony, and on to Penzance and Land's End. Most roads were little more than muddy tracks, unsuitable for wheeled traffic. However, whilst Richard Carew Esq of Antony, the historian, found the roads 'in the Easterne part of Cornwall

1

uneasy, by reason either of their mire or stones, besides many up-hils and downe-hils', he considered that 'the Westerne are better travaileable, as lesse subject to these discommodities'.[2]

There was undoubtedly some feeling of racial difference amongst the Cornish, inspired by their Celtic heritage. However, this should not be over-emphasized, particularly for the gentry. Although the Cornish language was spoken by some inhabitants in the far west well into the seventeenth century, this was exceptional. John Chynoweth has shown that by 1485 no more than half of the county's inhabitants could speak the language. Further, in the 1580s Norden wrote that in all but the two far western hundreds, Penwith and Kerrier, 'it is in manner wholly English'. Carew, also writing at the end of the sixteenth century, said that most could not speak a word of the language, which had been 'driven . . . into the uttermost skirts of the shire'. The administration of the Sacraments in Cornish at Feock, near Truro, in 1646 was for the benefit of the older members of the congregation—there is no indication that the younger communicants could not understand English. It is, however, impossible to determine how many Cornish gentlemen actually spoke the language in the early seventeenth century, and no extant gentry documents are written in Cornish.[3]

Despite poor physical communications, and regardless of any feelings or manifestations of racial difference, many Cornish gentlemen were interested in and aware of events at the centre. A growing desire for news was met by the rapid expansion of the news industry and the generally greater availability of news (particularly through personal correspondence) in the first half of the century.[4] Cornish family collections contain few official newsletters dated before 1640, but most contain personal letters reporting both national and international affairs. The volume of correspondence increased considerably after about 1620, with a far greater number of letters covering the events of 1638–42 than any previous period. The Rashleigh of Menabilly papers, for example, contain three letters relating to the Scots Wars of 1638–40, one of which (written by Jonathan Rashleigh's brother-in-law, John Sparke) reported the King's arrival in York and rumours of Scottish demands for a Parliament. The same letter contained news of the outbreak of war between France and Spain.[5] Similarly, William Honnywood Esq of Kent included in a letter of 15 March 1639 to his brother-in-law, Francis Buller Esq of Shillingham, news of the recent Battle of the Downs:

> on friday and satterday last there was a cruell fight betwixt the Spaniards and Hollander itt is as yett variously reported how many ships weare lost on both sides but doubtles the Spaniards had much greater losse then the duch.[6]

London was the principal centre of news, and many letters were written by Cornish gentlemen on visits there to attend Parliament, on business, or while staying at an inn of court, and sent to family or friends at home. Exeter was another centre of news for Cornwall. For example, in March 1636, Bevill Grenvile Esq of Stow reported to his father that 'I met at Exeter the news of the new lord Treasurer and of my lord of Essex his parting with his lady; but she deserv'd to be cast of if the report be true'.[7] The benefit of these letters was not restricted to the recipient: they were often circulated amongst family, friends and neighbours, and the information they contained spread further by word of mouth. In May 1639, for example, Grace Grenvile informed her husband, Bevill, who was with the King in the north, that 'I sent your letters and papers of news to your frends as you directed and I have sent you now a letter from my cosen Morice'.[8] So, news gathered in London was often spread amongst a wide network of people in Cornwall, acquainting them with current events, and enabling them to place their own local concerns into a wider, national perspective.[9]

Conversely, many gentlemen were an invaluable source of news and information to the government. As well as carrying out instructions, the role of a local governor included informing the government of local events and feeling, and of any problems, actual or potential, in the county. Further, because of Cornwall's important strategic position, local intelligence was crucial, particularly during a time of war. During the late 1620s, when England was at war with Spain and France, frequent communications were sent from Cornwall to London reporting the actual and rumoured activities of both countries. In March 1626 John Bonython Esq of Carclew, deputy governor of Pendennis castle, notified Secretary Conway of reports from various Portuguese, French and Spanish ships concerning Spanish preparations for an invasion. Further, in May eighty large ships were sighted off the south coast of Cornwall and were thought to be Spanish. News of this was sent in turn from the mayor of Penryn to the mayor of Truro, to the mayor of St Austell, to the constables of Fowey, to Sir Ferdinando Gorges at Plymouth, and finally to Secretary Conway.[10]

The duchy of Cornwall provided the government with a unique link with the locality. Established by royal charter in 1337, the duchy was vested in the first son of each monarch from birth, reverting to the monarch if the first son died. However, in 1502 and 1612, upon the respective deaths of Arthur, Prince of Wales, and Henry, Prince of Wales, the next surviving son was named Duke of Cornwall.[11] The duchy owned seventy-eight manors throughout the county, and had an interest in a number of boroughs. By the early seventeenth century there were twenty-one

Cornish boroughs, fourteen of which had been created between 1547 and 1584, each sending two MPs to Westminster. Eight towns had been annexed to the duchy by its founding charter, and were situated upon a duchy manor. Of these, Launceston, Liskeard, Lostwithiel and Helston were enfranchised before the Tudor period, while Grampound, Saltash, Camelford and Bossiney were Tudor creations. In addition, West Looe, St Ives, Tregony, St Mawes, Newport, East Looe and Fowey had been annexed in 1540, and the duchy's links with St Mawes had been strengthened by financing the construction of St Mawes castle, and maintaining the garrison there during the Elizabethan period. Newport had been enfranchised in 1529, and the rest gained borough status between 1547 and 1571. The duchy exercised electoral influence in the boroughs through the Prince's Council, which had been established in 1610 when Prince Henry reached the age of sixteen. The Council was disbanded upon Prince Henry's death in November 1612, and was revived in 1616 when Henry's younger brother, Prince Charles, was granted the title and lands of the Duke of Cornwall.[12]

Through the stannaries, the duchy administered the Cornish tin industry, which, according to James Whetter, employed approximately 3 per cent of the population. The greatest concentration of mining activity was in west Cornwall, and David Cullum has found evidence of engagement in tin mining in over 10 per cent of rural inventories from this area (and in more than one-third of inventories from St Just-in-Penwith) in the early seventeenth century. Many inventories revealed participation in tin mining in conjunction with farming. Tin mining tended to attract younger men, and Cullum considered it likely that the inventories reflected a cyclical arrangement whereby the younger men of a farming family would have engaged in tin mining and would have switched to farming as they grew older.[13]

The tin industry was organized into four stannaries: Foweymore, Blackmore, Tywarnhaile, and Penwith with Kerrier. Each had a court to deal with disputes between tinners, who were exempted from the jurisdiction of the common law courts by certain privileges, granted for the 'good and orderly Managing of the said Commodity . . . their good Government . . . [and] to Encourage them in the search of Tin'. The lord warden was the chief judicial officer of the stannary courts, and delegated responsibility to the vice-warden (always a prominent local gentleman) and to the stewards of each court. Most cases were heard by a steward and a jury of six tinners, and the ultimate punishment was imprisonment in the stannary gaol at Lostwithiel. Occasionally a Convocation or Parliament of tinners met to discuss important stannary issues and to devise new, or revise old, stannary laws. The lord warden or vice-warden presided, and each stannary was represented by six stannators (usually gentlemen) chosen by the mayors and corporations of Launceston, Lostwithiel, Truro and Helston.[14]

The stannaries was ostensibly a local organization, established to ensure the smooth-running of the lucrative tin mining industry.[15] However, the lord warden was also high steward of the duchy. Assisted by the vice-warden and numerous stannary and manorial officials, he controlled an extensive network of political patronage. The lord warden had played a central role in the Tudor duchy administration, but was excluded from the Prince's Council by Prince Henry in 1610, and again in 1616 by Prince Charles.[16] This precipitated competition between the Council and the lord warden for political influence, particularly in borough elections.

William, 3rd Earl of Pembroke was lord warden from 1604 until his death in 1630, when he was succeeded in the office by his brother, Philip, Earl of Pembroke and Montgomery. Until 1627, Pembroke's vice-warden was William Coryton Esq of West Newton Ferrers in St Mellion parish; he was ousted by the Duke of Buckingham for political reasons, and was replaced by John Mohun Esq of Boconnoc. Coryton had regained the position by 1630, and remained in office until 1646. Throughout the period Coryton exerted his influence as vice-warden on behalf of the lord warden's electoral interests and against those of the duchy. The duchy's political power base in Cornwall was therefore split, and consequently its influence declined; by 1640 it was almost extinguished, while the rival influence of the stannaries remained strong. The interests of the duchy and of the stannaries were therefore conflicting, and the fact that the lord warden and vice-warden were duchy officials did not signify allegiance to it.[17]

From 1587 the office of lord warden was associated with that of lord lieutenant, and between 1604 and 1642 the Earls of Pembroke were also lords lieutenant of Cornwall. In February 1642, while retaining the lord wardenship, Pembroke was replaced as lord lieutenant by Lord Robartes. The lord lieutenant was responsible for the military defence of the county, and for mustering and training the local militia. However, because both Earls of Pembroke were absentee office-holders, the militia was organized by deputy lieutenants, who were leading local gentlemen, appointed by the lord warden.[18] Maritime government, for matters such as seizure of enemy shipping and collection of wreckage, was the duty of two vice-admirals, Francis Bassett Esq of Tehidy for the northern shore, and Sir James Bagg of Saltram, Devon, for the southern shore.

For administrative purposes the county was divided into nine hundreds, grouped into four divisions, and 205 parishes. The divisions were East (East and West hundreds), North (Trigg, Lesnewth and Stratton hundreds), South (Powder and Pyder hundreds), and West (Penwith and Kerrier hundreds).[19] Gentry JPs administered justice at county and divisional levels, and delegated to high constables in the hundreds, who in turn gave orders to parish constables. The responsibilities of JPs increased considerably during the late sixteenth and seventeenth centuries, but the office appears to have remained desirable, particularly for its prestige.[20] The position of sheriff was, however, much less desirable, and by the early seventeenth century many gentlemen went to great lengths to avoid it.[21] The sheriff was not permitted to leave the county during his year of office, and was unable to sit in Parliament. He was responsible for summoning juries at assizes and quarter sessions, for organizing the election of knights of the shire, and for supervising the county gaol. Since the creation of the lieutenancy, he had lost control of the county's defence, and his only remaining military power was the right to call out the *posse comitatus*.[22]

Like the rest of England, Cornwall was predominantly agricultural, and approximately half the population was engaged in agricultural activity. Pasture farming was most common, for 60 per cent of investment was in cattle and sheep, although in the sixteenth century there had been a trend towards the enclosure and reclamation of land for tillage, especially corn cultivation:

> The middle part of the Shire (saving the inclosures about some few Townes and Villages) lieth waste and open, sheweth a blackish colour, beareth Heath and Spirie Grasse, and serveth in a maner, onely to Summer Cattel. That which bordereth upon either side of the Sea, through the Inhabitants good husbandrie, of inclosing, sanding, and other dressing, carrieth a better hue, and more profitable qualitie. Meadow ground it affoordeth little, pasture for cattel and sheepe, store enough, corne ground plentie.[23]

Corn, although subsidiary to cattle, remained a fundamental element of the Cornish agrarian economy throughout the seventeenth century.[24]

The manorial system still operated, but was in decline. Every tenement or farm was leased as part of a manor (where the landlord would usually have been either a local gentleman or the duchy) and the most common form of tenure was the lease for lives. Manorial courts were still held, and manorial customs observed, but 'feudal' services were rarely demanded.[25] One apparent exception was at Stow, where in 1641 Sir Bevill Grenvile (described by Clarendon as 'the generally most loved man' in Cornwall[26]) instructed his wife to

> Make it knowne to all my neighbours and Tenants of the west side of our Parrish that I shall take it ill if they grind not at my mill, and lett the Tenants

6

of Northlegh know that if they do it not, as they are bound, I will put them in suite.[27]

After agriculture and tin mining, fishing was the third largest industry in the county, occupying (again according to Whetter) about 2 per cent of the population. Fishing was primarily an urban-orientated occupation, based in ports such as Newlyn and Mousehole, Looe and Padstow. As with tin mining, Cullum has found evidence of fishing in conjunction with farming in rural communities, although rural fishermen appear to have worked only for a wage or for a share of the catch to supplement their farming incomes. Local waters were rich in fish (especially pilchards and herrings), and fish exports were important to the Cornish economy. Pilchards were exported to France, Spain and the Mediterranean countries; hake and conger to Spain and the Mediterranean; and ray to Brittany. There was also some Cornish interest in the Newfoundland cod fisheries, although considerably less than in the larger Devon ports. Of the 200 boats which left the west country for Newfoundland each year, never more than ten were Cornish.[28]

Other economic activities, of less importance, were copper mining and the cloth trade. Copper was initially mined in the county towards the end of the sixteenth century, and the ore shipped to south Wales for smelting. However, the industry did not thrive, because of overwhelming competition from Sweden. The cloth trade operated on a relatively small scale, mainly in central and eastern Cornwall. Some small country weavers wove yarn for the local market, but most yarn and cloth was exported to Devon. This trade was conducted through the east Cornwall wool markets, particularly those at Liskeard and Launceston, and increased considerably during the century.[29]

The Cornish Nobility

In 1602 Carew lamented the lack of a Cornish nobility, remarking that:

so for Noblemen I may deliver in a word, that Cornwall at this present enjoyeth the residence of none at al. The occasion whereof groweth, partly, because their issue female have caried away the Inhabitance, together with the Inheritance, to Gentlemen of the Easterne parts: and partly, for that their issue male, little affecting so remote a corner, liked better to transplant their possessions neerer to the heart of the Realme. Elder times were not so barraine.[30]

By the late 1620s the position had altered, and Cornwall possessed two peers, born, bred, and resident in the county. These two, Richard, 1st Baron Robartes of Truro, and John, 1st Baron Mohun of Okehampton, had very different backgrounds, and each had acquired his peerage in a very different way.

Richard Robartes was the only son and heir of a wealthy Truro merchant and usurer. Like his father, Richard traded in wool and tin, but in 1598 married Frances, daughter and coheir of John Hender Gent of Boscastle, which brought him into gentry circles. Sheriff of Cornwall in 1614, he was knighted in November 1616, paying £12,000 for the honour. One contemporary observer remarked, 'Richard Roberts, a rich Cornishman, who covets a knighthood, has lent the King £12,000 without interest; more such Robertses wanted'.[31] In 1620 Robartes bought the manor and advowson of Lanhydrock, near Bodmin, where he built a family seat, described by Pevsner as 'the grandest [house] in Cornwall and certainly the grandest [house] of its century'.[32] Created a baronet in July 1621, Robartes was raised to the peerage on 26 January 1625 when he purchased the title Baron Robartes of Truro from the Duke of Buckingham for a further £10,000. In June 1626, when Buckingham was impeached by the House of Commons, the ninth article accused him of forcing Robartes to purchase his peerage, and Robartes confirmed this charge in his own deposition. Buckingham challenged the allegation, claiming that the title had been procured at Robartes' own request, and that he had previously offered substantially more for it.[33] Frances Robartes died in 1626, and her husband in April 1634: both were buried at Lanhydrock.[34]

Richard was succeeded by his son John, born in 1606. John received a Puritan education from his mother, before matriculating at Exeter College, Oxford, in 1625. He was influenced there by the Calvinist theologian and rector of the college, Dr Prideaux, with whom his mother corresponded about his education.[35] In April 1630 Robartes married Lucy, second daughter of the leading Puritan, Robert Rich, 2nd Earl of Warwick. His connection with Warwick continued when, between May 1646 and April 1647, he married his second wife, Letitia Isabella, daughter of Sir John Smith of Bidborough, Kent, and whose mother was Isabella, daughter of Robert Rich, 1st Earl of Warwick, and sister to the 2nd Earl.

Robartes took his seat in the Lords on 13 April 1640, at the opening of the Short Parliament.[36] Between 1640 and 1642 he was allied with other Puritans in Parliament in promoting godly reform in the Church of England, although he did not favour the abolition of episcopacy.[37] In 1642 he took up arms for Parliament, as colonel of a foot regiment in Essex's army, and in 1644 became a field-marshal. He encouraged Essex to enter Cornwall in 1644, advising him of the advantages to be gained from

Plate 1. John, 1st Lord Robartes

securing the county, believing that his own presence would win many Cornishmen for Parliament. This resulted in the calamitous parliamentarian defeat at Lostwithiel at the end of August, following which Robartes and Essex escaped to Plymouth in a fishing boat, leaving their troops to surrender.[38] A few days later Robartes was appointed governor of Plymouth, and continued in that office until April 1645 when the Self-Denying Ordinance forced him to resign. Robartes returned to the Lords and joined Essex's faction, which advocated a Presbyterian settlement, and was opposed to the New Model Army.[39] During the Interregnum Robartes withdrew from national affairs, but he assumed a prominent role in central government after the Restoration. In 1679 he was created Viscount Bodmin and Earl of Radnor. He died at his London home in 1685, and was buried at Lanhydrock.[40]

John Mohun was born at the family seat of Boconnoc in about 1592, the second but first surviving son and heir of Sir Reginald Mohun and of his second wife Philippa, daughter of Sir John Hele of Wembury, Devon. John was educated at Exeter College, Oxford, matriculating in 1605 at the age of thirteen. He graduated three years later, and was admitted to the Middle Temple in 1611. In about 1617 he married Cordelia, widow of Sir Roger Aston of Cranford, Middlesex, and daughter of Sir John Stanhope of Shelford, Nottinghamshire. Mohun served as MP for the family borough of Grampound in 1624 and 1625, and was added to the Cornish commission of the peace in May 1625. During the mid and late 1620s, with Sir James Bagg of Saltram, Devon, Mohun led a Cornish gentry faction which owed allegiance to the Duke of Buckingham. Through service to Buckingham in Cornwall, and through Bagg's influence with the Duke, Mohun was created Baron Mohun of Okehampton on 15 April 1628. Cordelia died in October 1639 and in December Mohun succeeded his father as 2nd Baronet. Lord Mohun died on 28 March 1641, and was succeeded by his son and heir, Warwick.[41]

Warwick Mohun was born in 1620. Nothing is known of his education, but like his father he married exogamously, his wife being Catherine, daughter of one Wells of Twyford, Hampshire.[42] He represented Grampound in the Short Parliament of April 1640, and took his seat in the House of Lords in May 1641.[43] He had absented himself from the House by February 1642, stating that the tumults in Westminster made him fear for his safety.[44]

That summer Mohun was one of the most active commissioners of array in Cornwall, raising support for the King. In the early autumn he rode to Oxford, where the King granted him a joint commission with Sir Ralph Hopton, Sir John Berkeley and Colonel Ashburnham to command the western forces.[45] However, Clarendon wrote that:

Plate 2.   John, 1st Lord Mohun of Boconnoc

Plate 3. Sir Reginald Mohun Bt of Boconnoc

The lord Mohun (who had departed from York from the King with all professions of zeal and activity in his service) had from the time of the first motion in Cornwall forborne to join himself to the King's party, staying at home at his own house, and imparting himself equally to all men of several constitutions, as if he had not been sufficiently informed which party to adhere to.

According to Clarendon it was only after the parliamentarians had been driven out of Cornwall, and he heard that the King had not been defeated at Edgehill in October 1642, that Mohun set out; further, he claimed that it was commonly believed that Mohun had intended to ride for London and Parliament if he had not found the King in a good position.[46] Clarendon's account of Mohun's actions and motives bears no relation to other reports, and was probably derived from personal dislike, since Clarendon lost no opportunity of vilifying him in later years.[47] Mohun resigned his commission in September 1643, and in 1644 sat in the Upper House of the Oxford Parliament (called by Charles to vote supply for the spring campaign). Mohun surrendered to Fairfax at Bodmin in February 1646 and compounded for his estate for a fine of £2090.17s.10d.[48]

A third peer, Charles Lord Lambert, was active in Cornwall during the 1620s and 1630s. Lambert, who succeeded his father in 1618 as 2nd Baron Lambert, was born in Ireland in 1600, and was educated at Cambridge. In 1625 he married Jane, daughter of Richard, 1st Baron Robartes, and sister of John; he represented Bossiney in the Parliaments of 1626 and 1628–29. Lambert was appointed governor of County Cavan and the town of Kells in 1627, took his seat in the Irish House of Lords in 1634, and sat on the Irish Privy Council. He raised a regiment of 1,000 foot in November 1641 to suppress the Catholic rebels, and became a notable commander. Jane Lady Lambert died in 1655 and her husband in 1660; both were buried in St Patrick's Cathedral, Dublin.[49]

Lord Lambert's position in Cornish affairs is difficult to establish. He was resident possibly from the end of 1623, and certainly from 1626, until at least 1633–34 (and probably until 1636), and he was very active during that period.[50] It was clearly through the Robartes connection that he represented Bossiney in two Parliaments. In 1628 Lambert was involved in a subsidy dispute in Pyder hundred. A fierce quarrel erupted between Nicholas Borlase and Edward Coswarth, the two subsidy commissioners for that hundred, because Coswarth refused to enter Lambert's name in the subsidy book. Borlase reported the matter to the Privy Council, but Lambert claimed that this was vindictive, as he had previously taken examinations against Borlase 'who is a recusant and a dangerous fellow'. He insisted that he was exempt from the subsidy in Cornwall, as he was

Irish by birth, and was already paying subsidies in Ireland. He owned no land in England, and was resident in Cornwall only with a view to settling a dispute with his father-in-law concerning his marriage portion.[51] His position in Cornwall was not as transient as he suggested, however. He was added to the Cornish commission of the peace in November 1623, and remained on it until at least 1636. He was an oyer and terminer commissioner for the Western Circuit for a decade from 1624, and in November 1628 was appointed a commissioner for the execution of martial law in Cornwall.[52]

The Cornish Gentry

Both Richard, 1st Baron Robartes, and John, 1st Baron Mohun, were essentially members of the Cornish gentry class. Apart from their recently acquired titles, there was little to distinguish them from other prominent Cornish gentlemen, and the county, rather than the Court, remained the principal focus for their activities. The term 'gentleman' was, however, flexible and vague, and there is no general agreement on what did (or did not) constitute a gentleman. Further difficulty has arisen because seventeenth-century society was very fluid, especially where the minor gentry merged with better-off yeomen, tradesmen and professionals. These groups shared many characteristics, and their members inter-changed their positions relatively easily and frequently, often making differentiation difficult. An individual would commonly style himself in different ways depending upon the occasion, or to assume a higher rank than his neighbours considered appropriate. 'Gentlemen' sometimes demoted themselves for tax avoidance, whereas those of lower status often styled themselves as gentlemen in lawsuits, when matriculating at a university, or when drafting their wills, hoping to gain more respect and prestige. As a result of this variable self-ascription, official records can be unreliable, and should be treated with caution. Therefore, while a statistical analysis of the gentry class is possible, this can provide only a general picture.[53]

These problems have caused historians to disagree over the sources and criteria which should be used in 'counting' gentlemen.[54] In analyzing the size and composition of the Cornish gentry in the mid-seventeenth century the following sources were used: the knighthood composition lists of 1631–32, the lay subsidy rolls of 1641, the protestation returns of 1641, and various lists of sheriffs, JPs, and deputy lieutenants. Members of the gentry have been taken to be all those styled 'baronet', 'knight', 'esquire' or 'gentleman' in any two of these sources. Further, all families which provided JPs, sheriffs or deputy lieutenants have been included, as have

14

well-established, independent cadet branches.[55] By this method 321 Cornish gentry families were identified, which constituted slightly less than 1.5 per cent of the total population, based upon a total population of about 98,000.[56] The number of gentry families is relatively low compared with elsewhere, although the proportion of gentry in the county is perhaps more typical. For example, in Lancashire, 763 gentry families constituted about 3 per cent of the population; in Kent 700 gentry families made up 2 per cent of the population; and in Yorkshire 641 families existed, although this was less than 1 per cent of that county's inhabitants.[57]

It has already been established that early modern gentlemen can be placed into four broad categories: baronets, knights, esquires and gentlemen. Those in the first three categories can be termed the 'greater gentry' as they tended to be the wealthiest and most powerful in the county, and generally held the most prestigious offices. Mere gentlemen can be classed as the 'lesser gentry'. Offices held were likely to be more minor, such as high constable of a hundred, and the activities of this group tended to be confined more to their own neighbourhood. As most MPs, deputy lieutenants, JPs, sheriffs, and members of national commissions were drawn from the greater gentry, that group, through access to central government, would normally have had greater awareness of national events and issues than would the lesser gentry.

TABLE 1
The status of the heads of gentry families c.1641

Status	Numbers	Percentage
Baronet	4	1.5
Knight	11	3.5
Esquire	81	25.0
Gentleman	225	70.0

Table 1 shows that approximately 30 per cent of the Cornish gentry constituted the ruling élite. It is often possible to discuss with certainty

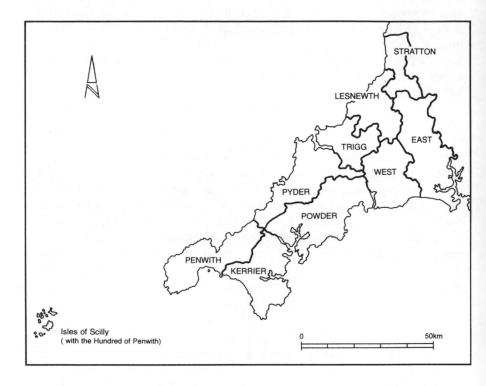

Map 1. The Hundreds of Cornwall

the views and activities of the greater gentry alone; this is partly because they generated a large amount of official correspondence, and partly because far more of their personal correspondence survives than that of the lesser gentry. Therefore, many references to 'the Cornish gentry' necessarily refer to the greater gentry only.

From Table 2 it is clear that the hundred of East contained substantially the highest number of greater gentry families, followed by Powder, and then by Kerrier and West. Considering the predominance of office-holding and communication with central government among the greater gentry, the residence of such large numbers is likely to have placed these four hundreds in a relatively strong position.

16

Table 2
Distribution of greater gentry by hundred

Hundred	No. of heads of greater gentry families
East	23
West	12
Stratton	6
Lesnewth	2
Trigg	10
Pyder	11
Powder	13
Kerrier	12
Penwith	7
Total	96

The hundreds of East and West would have been particularly influential, for between them they contained one of the two peers, all four baronets, and six of the eleven knights. In addition, communication links with Devon, and with London, were better from East than from any other part of Cornwall. The standing of East hundred was further enhanced by the location at Launceston of the county assizes. The assizes did not simply fulfil a legal and administrative function, but were also a major social event attended by the county elite.

The contrast between the situations and lifestyles of the greater and lesser gentry is well illustrated by wills and inventories. This is highlighted in the nature of endowments made to younger sons, and in the size of portions left to daughters. Evidence from Cornish wills suggests that it was fairly common for members of the greater gentry to leave to each of their daughters a portion of £1,000, usually to be paid on coming of age or on marriage. Ezechiell Grosse Esq of Golden, a usurer, was rather more stringent in his terms: his daughter Elizabeth was to receive £1,000 when she reached the age of 21 years, or earlier if she married but only with her mother's consent.[58] In contrast, where heads of lesser gentry families could afford to leave their daughters a portion, these were much smaller. For example, in his will of 1642, William Coode Gent of Morval, one of the more prosperous lesser gentlemen, left only £300 to each of his three daughters.[59] Further, whereas the lesser gentry tended to leave younger sons either a small money portion, or nothing, it was customary for the greater gentry to make a landed endowment. For example, although in his will of 1619 Richard Carew Esq of Antony, the historian, left most of his estate to his son and heir, Richard, he devised to his younger sons,

George and Wymond, a small amount of land and the Maker tithe.[60] An interesting exception occurs in the will of Sir Francis Vyvyan of Trelowarren. He left his estate and the captainship of St Mawes castle to his son and heir, Richard, and £1,000 to each of his two daughters. However, he revoked an earlier devise of land to his second son, Robert, and left him £500 instead because he had become apprenticed to a 'silkman' in London, and 'money is more fitting for merchants than land'.[61]

Wills and inventories also illustrate differences in the possessions of greater and lesser gentlemen. The will of William Coode Gent mentions basic goods and chattels only, whereas Ezechiell Grosse Esq bequeathed to his wife all her clothes, jewels and ornaments, and left his books to his son Charles. An inventory taken in 1643, after the death of Sir Richard Carew Bt, listed his clothes (£20), cash (£200), plate (£62.18s.), jewellery (£131.10s.), civet (musk perfume) and civet cats (£58.13s.), silver silk cloth and taffeta (£17.1s.4d.), and books (£6), in addition to an extensive range of household and farm goods.[62]

Various means were possible for families to rise to the gentry class or within it. In Cornwall a number of merchants acquired gentry status by purchasing landed estates, and then consolidating and improving their positions through advantageous marriages. The rise of the Robartes family by this means has already been described; the Rashleighs also acquired status in this way. The Rashleighs' elevation from the merchant class to the greater gentry was rapid, occurring between the late 1580s and about 1610. The family originated from Devon and became established in Fowey around 1520, when Philip, a younger son, became involved in trade there. A turning point in the family's fortunes came with the increased availability of land after the dissolution of the monasteries. John Rashleigh, grandson of Philip, then of Coombe, purchased Bodmin Priory in 1567 and the lands of Menabilly in 1573, and went on to increase his fortune through trade and expeditions against Spain. His son, also John (1554–1624), continued to trade on a large scale, and had an interest in the Newfoundland cod fisheries. It was during his lifetime that the transition in the family's status took place.

By the late sixteenth century the Rashleighs had become the leading family in Fowey, playing a dominant role in its trading activities, owning much of the property in the town, and exercising considerable influence in local politics. John Rashleigh represented Fowey in the Parliaments of 1589 and 1598, was sheriff of Cornwall in 1608, and took office as a JP from that year. He consolidated the family estates, and in 1600 built the mansion of Menabilly, to which the family moved from their town house in Fowey. John Rashleigh had made a good marriage to Alice Bonython of Carclew, a member of a medieval Cornish gentry family, and their

. children also married into established gentry families, further consolidating the family's position. Jonathan, the son and heir, married Anne Bassett of Heanton Punchardon, Devon, in 1614 and his second wife was Mary Harris of Radford, Plymouth. Alice, the eldest daughter, married Nicholas Sawle Gent of Penrice, St Austell, in 1595. Her sisters Elizabeth and Deborah married Francis Vyvyan Esq of Trelowarren and John Sparke Gent of Plymouth respectively. Indeed, the family had become so integrated into gentry society by the beginning of the seventeenth century, that Carew remarked:

> Where I may not passe in silence, the commendable desserts of Master Rashleigh the elder . . . for his industrious judgment and adventuring, in trade of merchandise, first opened a light and way, to the townesmens new thriving, and left his sonne large wealth, and possessions; who (together with a dayly bettering of his estate) converteth the same to hospitality, and other actions fitting a Gent well affected to his God, Prince, and Countrey.[63]

Hence, whereas John Rashleigh had styled himself as 'merchant of Fowey' in his will of 1578, his son Jonathan described himself in his will as 'of Menabilly, Esquire'.[64]

The Carlyon family of Tregrehan rose from the yeomanry to the gentry at a similar time. Between 1565 and 1616, Walter Carlyon, yeoman, of St Blazey and his son William (described as husbandman in a deed of 1597) gradually purchased property at Tregrehan.[65] On their respective deaths in 1616 and 1615, they still owned only two-thirds of Tregrehan, which was occupied in the mid-seventeenth century by William's son, Walter. However, the last-mentioned Walter's son, William, was more ambitious than his forbears. He left Tregrehan to farm at Lansallos, and in 1652 married Mary, daughter of Thomas Rowe Gent of Endellion. Through this marriage the Carlyons acquired extensive property and, more importantly, a rise in status. In the marriage settlement, William Carlyon styled himself 'gentleman'.[66]

There were other ways of acquiring gentry status. Ezechiell Grosse the elder (born 1564) trained as an attorney at Lyons Inn, but upon his return to Cornwall was chiefly employed as steward for Sir George Cary, later Lord Hunsdon. The lands of Francis Tregian, the recusant, had passed to Hunsdon in 1587–89, following confiscation by the Crown; but in 1607 Francis Tregian the younger made a desperate attempt to regain the family estates by purchasing them from Lady Hunsdon, now a widow. In Tregian's efforts to recover his family lands, he borrowed £3,000 from Grosse (who exploited his position as steward) and sold Golden Manor to George Spry of St Anthony-in-Roseland, who was himself indebted to

Map 2 (see also facing page). Cornish Parishes

Hundreds
in Cornwall

STRATTON
LESNEWTH
TRIGG
PYDER
EAST
WEST
POWDER
PENWITH
KERRIER

Morwenstow
Kilkhampton
Poughill
Stratton
Launcells
Marhamchurch
Bridgerule
Poundstock
Whitstone
Forrabury
St Gennys
Jacobstow
Week
St Mary
North
Tamerton
Trevalga
Otterham
St Giles in
the Heath
St Juliot
Lanteglos by
Camelford
Lesnewth
Warbstow
North
Petherwin
Boyton
Virginstow
Tremaine
Tintagel
Minster
Treneglos
Tresmeer
Werrington
Davidstow
Egloskerry
St Stephen by
Launceston
Launceston
St Teath
Advent
St Clether
Laneast
Trewen
St Thomas
by L
Endellion
South
Petherwin
Lawhitton
St Minver
Michaelstow
Altarnun
Lewannick
St Kew
St Breward
St Tudy
Lezant
Blisland
North Hill
Egloshayle
St Mabyn
Temple
Stoke
Climsland
Helland
St Neot
Linkinhorne
Warleggan
South
Hill
Bodmin
Cardinham
St Cleer
Calstock
St Ive
Callington
Braddock
Liskeard
St Mellion
St Dominick
St Winnow
St Pinnock
Menheniot
Quethiock
Pillaton
Landulph
Boconnoc
Lanreath
St Keyne
Landrake
Botus
Fleming
Duloe
St Erney
St Veep
Pelynt
Morval
St Germans
St Stephens
by Saltash
Lanteglos
by Fowey
St Martin
by Looe
Sheviock
Antony
Lansallos
Talland
St John
Maker
Rame

The Hundreds of Trigg,
Lesnewth, Stratton,
East and West.

0   10   20km

Grosse. Tregian was unable to meet his debt, and in 1612 was forced to give Grosse another manor in compensation. Spry too found himself unable to repay Grosse and was obliged to sell Golden to him. Grosse gradually acquired the whole Tregian estate, and in 1631 the Crown confirmed the possession of Golden to Ezechiell Grosse, grandson and heir of the first Ezechiell, now styling himself 'Esquire'.[67]

Grosse was involved in financial and land speculation throughout Cornwall, and his papers contain large numbers of bonds which illustrate the extent of his usury in both topographical and social terms.[68] He was wholly unscrupulous in all his dealings, and single-minded in the pursuit of his own aggrandisement. Grosse was unlikely to have gained many friends amongst the established Cornish gentry since he had exploited and impoverished their neighbours in his rush to establish himself. Therefore, although the family can be counted amongst the greater gentry in the mid-seventeenth century, and although Ezechiell Grosse the younger made an excellent marriage in 1631 to Margaret, daughter of William Coryton Esq, and their daughter Elizabeth married Francis Buller Esq (grandson of Sir Richard), the family never became fully integrated into Cornish gentry society.

The Enys family of Enys in Mylor parish declined in both status and wealth; in the first half of the seventeenth century financial difficulties forced John Enys Gent and his son Thomas (also Gent) to sell most of their lands. In 1642 they were between £400 and £500 in debt,[69] and they became dependent on Samuel, a younger merchant son, who revived the family's position. In 1646 he returned from Spain, where he had made his fortune, and purchased the remaining estate from Thomas. Samuel educated and apprenticed six of his brother's children,[70] and gradually repurchased the family lands and bought other land, considerably extending the estate.[71] The family was unusual in experiencing a fall in status and wealth; there is more evidence of families rising into or within the Cornish gentry in this period.[72]

Gentry Origins

Many Cornish gentry families, including the Arundells, Bassetts and Carews, claimed Norman descent. Indeed, Richard Carew remarked that:

> The most Cornish Gentlemen can better vaunt of their pedigree, then their livelyhood; for that they derive from great antiquitie, (and I make question, whether any shire in England, of but equall quantitie, can muster a like number of faire coate-Armours) . . .[73]

Calculation of patterns of antiquity is problematic because of the uneven spread of evidence. Using Vivian's *Visitations of Cornwall* it is only possible to be certain of the origins of slightly less than half the gentry families. Further, a much higher proportion of greater gentry origins are known than of the lesser gentry.

Table 3 shows that a considerable proportion (47 per cent) of the Cornish gentry had medieval origins. This figure is low when compared with the 80–90 per cent of Kentish gentry with pre-Tudor pedigrees, but is relatively high when compared with the 39 per cent of Yorkshire gentry, 36 per cent of Lancashire gentry, and 17 per cent of Lincolnshire gentry who claimed medieval descent.[74] The proportion of greater gentry with medieval lineage is higher still (56 per cent). This shows, as may be expected, that much of the power in the county was held by well-established families, although there were fewer greater gentry families with medieval origins than in Lancashire (72 per cent) or Cheshire (80 per cent), for example.[75]

Table 3
The origins of the gentry

Gentry origins[76]	Overall %	Greater gentry %	Lesser gentry %
Medieval	47	56	32
Early 16th century	22	22	22
Later 16th century	27	20	39
17th century	4	2	7

Despite the rise of merchant and other families into the gentry, the proportion of newcomers was exceptionally low (4 per cent), compared with Kent (about 12 per cent), Lancashire (27 per cent) and Suffolk (36 per cent). This can be explained partly by the imbalance of the figures. Many who assumed gentle status would have ranked initially amongst the lesser gentry, for whom fewer statistics are available. Further, approximately 27 per cent of gentry families as a whole, and 39 per cent of the lesser gentry, became established in the Elizabethan period, which was apparently when the most rapid expansion occurred, probably because of new trading opportunities. It is possible therefore that the pace of expansion had slackened by the early seventeenth century.[77]

Gentry Wealth

Cornish gentry wealth has been calculated through use of the 1641 lay subsidy roll. This source is incomplete: not all gentlemen are listed, and the lists for East, north division, and about half the hundred of Stratton are missing. Also, some of the lists for other hundreds are damaged. The assessments of approximately 70 per cent of the 321 gentry families are known, with a slight bias in favour of the greater gentry. Further, the source should be used to determine relative wealth, rather than absolute wealth, because the gentry were greatly under-assessed throughout the period.[78] The Royalist Composition Papers are an alternative source for wealth assessment, but have been challenged as unreliable, since in many cases royalists understated their wealth, possibly assisted by sympathetic local officials. Further, the Composition Papers show royalist wealth only, and therefore are unlikely to provide an accurate picture of gentry wealth as a whole.[79]

Table 4
The wealth of the gentry

Subsidy assessment[80]	Probable wealth	Overall %	Greater gentry %	Lesser gentry %
Less than £5 in land	up to £250 pa	40	11	52
£5–£9 in land	£250–£500 pa	21	38	14
£10–£19 in land	£500–£1,000 pa	6	19	1
£20 & over in land	over £1,000 pa	3	9	0
Unknown	?	30	23	33

Table 4 shows that (by such criteria) the Cornish gentry were not particularly wealthy. In 1641, only eight gentlemen, or 3 per cent of the gentry, enjoyed a landed income exceeding £1,000 per annum. This corresponds with the figure for Lancashire, which Blackwood considered 'remarkably small', and is significantly less than the 7 per cent of Warwickshire gentry and the 11 per cent of Yorkshire gentry in this bracket.[81] The eight Cornishmen were Sir Richard Buller, Sir Francis Godolphin of Godolphin, Sir Francis Vyvyan of Trelowarren, John Arundell Esq of Trerice, Hugh Boscawen Esq of Tregothnan, Ezechiell Grosse Esq, Jonathan Rashleigh Esq, and Charles Trevanion Esq of Caerhayes. The Godolphin wealth had been acquired through tin, Grosse became wealthy by usury, and the Rashleighs had made their fortune through trade. Nineteen other gentlemen (6 per cent) had a landed income exceeding £500 per annum.

An examination of 'low' and 'rich and middling' gentry in Cornwall, relative to other counties, improves the county's position enormously.

Table 5
Gentry wealth compared with other counties

County	Annual landed income £250–£999 (%)	Annual landed income £250 & under (%)
Lancashire[82]	12	48
Yorkshire[83]	36	53
Warwickshire[84]	31	63
Cornwall[85]	27	40

Table 5 shows that Cornwall had almost as high a proportion of 'rich and middling' gentry as Yorkshire and Warwickshire, and two and a half times as many as Lancashire. Further, Cornwall possessed a smaller proportion of poor gentry (i.e. with an annual landed income of £250 or less) than any of the other counties shown. Therefore, although Cornwall was not an exceptionally rich county, it was not exceptionally poor either. Nearly 30 per cent of the gentry as a whole, and approximately 57 per cent of the greater gentry, can be classed as 'rich or middling', comparing favourably with other counties.

Chynoweth concluded that in the Tudor period also, 'Cornwall was not a particularly poor county'. He found that in the period 1522–46 'some sixty to seventy' Cornish gentlemen were assessed at £20 per annum or more and 'more than 40 per cent' at less than £10 per annum. This compares with only eight gentlemen assessed in the higher bracket, and with 60 per cent in the lower, in 1641. These figures suggest that Cornish gentry wealth was in decline, but the notorious under-assessment of the gentry for subsidy purposes in the later period probably accounts for much of the discrepancy.[86]

Gentry Education

Between 1560 and 1640 England experienced an 'educational revolution': a great expansion of educational opportunities open to all but the very poor. There was a rapid increase in the number of grammar and other schools, where pupils were prepared for entrance to a university, an inn of court, or both. Cornish gentry education has been analyzed through the matriculation registers for Oxford and Cambridge.[87] Some students, however, attended a university without matriculating; between 20 per cent and 30 per cent of undergraduates at both Oxford and Cambridge did not matriculate, some to avoid paying fees. Others matriculated but declared themselves as of below gentry status so as to pay less. Conversely, some gentlemen matriculated but never attended.[88]

Between 1595 and 1665 468 Cornish gentlemen experienced higher education. Of the 336 gentlemen who registered at a university, 305 (91 per cent) went to Oxford and 31 (9 per cent) to Cambridge. Further analysis shows that 194 (58 per cent) registered at Exeter College, Oxford.[89] The next most popular colleges were Broadgates Hall, Oxford, with 21 gentlemen (6 per cent) and Queen's College, Oxford with 16 gentlemen (5 per cent). Trinity was the most popular Cambridge college, though with only eight gentlemen. Of those who registered at a university, 82 (24 per cent) graduated, while 55 (16 per cent) gained further degrees. So, Cornishmen showed a marked preference for Oxford University, and a high proportion patronized Exeter College, widely known as the 'West Country college'.

Over the same period, 260 gentlemen entered one of the inns of court. Most popular was the Middle Temple which had 114 Cornish entrants (44 per cent). Considerable numbers also entered Lincoln's Inn and the Inner Temple: 71 (27 per cent) and 56 (22 per cent) respectively. Nineteen (7 per cent) entered Gray's Inn. In total, only 40 of those who entered an inn were called to the Bar.[90]

It is difficult to determine the impact of higher education on gentry thinking, particularly as the influence of education cannot be distinguished easily from those of status, wealth, marriage and other variables. John Morrill has stressed the danger of over-emphasizing the educational sophistication of country gentlemen. In his view, the majority sought only a 'veneer of polite learning' from their time in higher education, and did not avail themselves of the opportunities to explore new political, social, and religious ideas. Similarly, Alan Everitt has maintained that the gentry's 'brief years' of formal education were 'an interlude, principally designed to fit them out for their functions in their own county'. Some historians have also suggested that the regional bias of the Oxbridge colleges and the inns of court would have resulted in students mixing primarily with their own 'countrymen', so that feelings of localism would have been strengthened.[91]

While each college and inn may have had its own regional bias, none excluded students from other areas. Nor was it likely that gentlemen would have interacted socially with those from their own county only. Although the Middle Temple had a strong southern and south-western bias, its members came from counties as far apart as Cornwall and Gloucestershire, and by no means all came from that region. Further, 56 per cent of Cornishmen educated at an inn attended one of the other inns strongly connected with other areas of the country. Indeed, Wilfred Prest, in his study of the inns of court in this period, found no evidence of exclusive provincial commitment or identification.[92] Equally, the Cornish university experience should not be dismissed merely because of the preference for Exeter College, Oxford. It seems likely that regional influences were stronger in the universities than at the inns, but by no means exclusively so. Over 40 per cent attended Oxford colleges other than Exeter, or alternatively went to Cambridge.

Although it might appear that feelings of localism would have been strengthened by higher education, it is more likely that it would have broadened an individual's social and intellectual horizons, through introductions to contemporaries from other counties and through developing awareness of current issues. Attendance at an inn would have been particularly beneficial because of its location in London and the inns' close connections with Whitehall and Westminster. Further, many gentlemen viewed academic study very seriously, and considered that university education played a crucial part in developing intellectual capacity, enabling contribution to government and to family prosperity. Indeed, Clarendon commented that by spending time at a university, the better quality gentlemen 'would be much better prepared to serve him [the King] and their country'.[93]

Some gentlemen held an enlightened view of the value of education and travel. In January 1605 Richard Carew Esq applied to Viscount Cranborne for a warrant to send Richard Erisey (his nephew), Richard Grenvile (his ward), and one of his own younger sons, to the University of Leiden, 'where I hear they may profit in learning the arts and languages, and other fit qualities'.[94] Carew had gone to yet greater lengths to ensure a thorough education for his heir, Richard, who later described his educational experiences in a treatise:

In my tender youth I was by my Father put to School, and so continued for nine or ten years to learn Latine according to the common teaching of ordinary Schoolmasters, by the Rules of Lillies Grammar. Afterward I spent three years in the University of Oxford, and three years more in the Middle Temple, one of our Innes of Court. From thence I was sent with mine Uncle in his Ambassage beyond the Seas, unto the King of Poland, whom when we came to Dantzig, we found to have been newly gone from thence to Sweden, whither also we went after him.[95]

Soon after his return, Carew's father sent him to France with Sir Henry Nevill, ambassador to Henry IV, 'that there I might learn the French Tongue'.

As a result of his extensive education and foreign travel, Richard Carew junior developed enlightened views on these matters. In the same treatise, he dismissed the traditional method of learning languages through grammar, advocating conversation and translation in both directions as more effective. He claimed that his father had learned a number of languages through reading alone, and in his own travels he had frequently communicated by speaking Latin because of his ignorance of other languages.[96]

A series of letters concerning the university education of Richard Grenvile of Stow, son and heir of Bevill Grenvile Esq, illustrate the importance Bevill attached to a thorough education. Richard matriculated at Gloucester Hall, Oxford in April 1638, aged seventeen. At Easter 1637 Bevill wrote two letters to Degory Wheare, principal of Gloucester Hall, concerning his son's proposed admission, which he considered 'a greater trust then if I comitted my whole estate into your hands'.[97] Bevill explained that he was unable to leave Richard a large estate, but believed that through a good education he was giving him the opportunity to gain one.[98] Wheare was instructed that Richard should spend three years at Gloucester Hall, during which time he should attain 'a fluent latine tongue and not loose his Greeke'. He was to be made a good scholar and kept strictly to courses which would achieve that end. His father gave him a monetary allowance sufficient to maintain him in the 'style of a gentleman', but not to 'invite him to excesse or prodigallitie'. He was permitted to enjoy 'decent and gentile recreations' such as fencing and dancing, as long as they did not hinder his studying.[99] He must certainly 'shun drinking houses and drunken companions as poyson'.[100]

Evidently, Bevill Grenvile believed that a university education offered real advantage. He confessed to being a very poor example, as during his time at Oxford (Exeter College, 1611–14) he had over-indulged in the 'sweet delights' of reading poetry and history, to the exclusion of other subjects. As a result, he had since found himself 'greatly defective', particularly in the management of weighty affairs. So strongly did Bevill feel this sense of missed opportunity that he said he would have given a limb that it were otherwise.[101] He urged his heir not to make the same mistake:

. . . it is true some benefitt you may reape out of all Authors, but not out of all alike, and the university is specially appointed for the teaching of those harder and more difficult Artes which are not to be had elsewhere . . . if you imploie not your time while you are there in Attayning the more Academicall Artes, you will have no advantage at all over those which never went farther then their owne home. I therefore . . . do earnestly desire that for my satisfaction you awhile suspend the frequenting of Human Authors, and seriously fixe upon Logick and Philosophy till you have attayned some perfection therin.[102]

Contemporary accounts suggest that time spent at a university often proved to be of greater academic value than at an inn. Conversely, intellectual and social horizons would probably have been broadened more by residence at an inn. Gentlemen entered the inns of court for various reasons. For many, it was the natural conclusion to their education. A legal training was considered useful preparation for life in a litigious society and for holding office as sheriffs and as JPs. Prest is not convinced that many gained sufficient knowledge of the law for either function, but has suggested that the most important role of the inns was introducing country gentlemen to London society and broadening their horizons.[103] Unlike the universities, the inns offered no tutor system, and so left students free to pursue their own interests: to attend schools of dancing, fencing and music, to go to plays, to listen to sermons and political gossip, and to attend Court. Prest has claimed that in the early seventeenth century the law was 'intermeshed with politics'. Many members of inns served as MPs (by 1640 more than half of the House of Commons resided at an inn), the halls of the inns and the Temple Church were frequently the venue for Commons committees, while the Westminster courts were in close proximity to St Stephen's Chapel.[104]

Clarendon implied that there was a strong link between membership of an inn and political awareness when he advocated spending time at an inn 'where many of the Nobility, and the best Gentry of the Kingdom, spend some part of their Youth together in conversation, by which they know the general State of the Kingdom, and much of the Temper and Humour of the People'.[105] Indeed, situated between the City and the Court, the inns were ideally placed to hear news from Parliament, Court and Fleet Street. John Grenvile Esq of Stow entered Lincoln's Inn in November 1619. In a letter of July 1621 to his brother Bevill, he showed awareness of the issues of the day, and reported that

My lord of Oxford is sent to the Tower for a preremptorye answere he gave the kinge upon a late examinatione before the cowncell, my Lord of Essex went latley to the Lowcuntries, and is sente for backe againe, as it is reported. The Kynge begins his progress this day . . .[106]

So, through his stay at Lincoln's Inn, John developed his sense of political awareness and sent news to Cornwall. Therefore, the benefit of an individual's education at an inn could be reaped not only by himself, but by family and friends in the locality. Clarendon also commented that 'the Inns of Court were always looked upon as the Suburbs of the Court itself'.[107] Many students were influenced by the Court in their dress and behaviour, and sought patronage and personal advantage there. For example, Richard Vyvyan Esq of Trelowarren played a central part in the Middle Temple masque at Christmas 1635, performed in honour of Charles Louis, Elector Palatine.[108]

Gentry Marriage

This angle which so shutteth them in, hath wrought many interchangeable matches with eche others stock, and given beginning to the proverbe, that all Cornish gentlemen are cousins.

This was Carew's perception of the marriage patterns of his fellow gentry at the end of the sixteenth century. It suggests that Cornishmen chose their brides mainly from within their own county, and implies an introspective and 'incestuous' community. Carew's view was echoed by Daniel Defoe a century later, and has been used by Everitt to support his belief in 'the insularity of local communities and the tenacity of local attachments' in the mid-seventeenth century.[109] The principal source for gentry marriages is Vivian's *Visitations of Cornwall*. Only about 45 per cent of gentry marriages are known, substantially more for the greater gentry than for the lesser.

Table 6
Gentry marriage patterns

Origin of bride	Overall[110] %	Greater gentry %	Lesser gentry %
Cornwall	60	53	72
Devon	29	33	22
West Country	2	2	2
Elsewhere	9	12	4

Nearly 60 per cent of gentlemen married Cornish brides, which largely supports Carew's statement.[111] This compares with over 70 per cent of Lancashire gentry marriages within the county, 60 per cent in Lincolnshire, and 42 per cent in Herefordshire.[112] However, perhaps more significant is that 40 per cent did not marry Cornishwomen, and that nearly 30 per cent of known marriages were to Devonian brides. Indeed, given Carew's statement, and the geographical isolation of the county, the figure for non-Cornish marriages is perhaps surprisingly high.

An even higher proportion of greater gentry married outside the county: 33 per cent married Devonians and 12 per cent married outside the West Country, usually to London or Home Counties brides. Conversely, a higher proportion of lesser gentry (over 72 per cent) married within the county. These trends reflect (and would have reinforced) the different social and political horizons of the greater and lesser gentry.[113]

A marriage outside the county would have established or developed a family's links with another region, and would have ensured a free flow of news and information from that area, as was the case between the Bullers of Shillingham and the Honnywoods of Kent. In a letter of 1639 to his brother-in-law, Francis Buller, William Honnywood related news of the Battle of the Downs, and enclosed a bill of exchange for a loan of £200 from Buller.[114] The two families had a shared interest in the Montgomeryshire estate of Varchall, although the nature or source of this is unknown. A series of letters from Thomas Rogers, steward of the Welsh estate, either to Francis Buller or to Thomas Robins, Buller's steward in Cornwall, reveals that, with Honnywood, Buller was very active in the administration of the Welsh estate, and spent a considerable amount of time there.[115]

When a prospective marriage alliance was under review, status, wealth and landed estate were major considerations. Writing in or before 1634 to Mary Arundell of Trerice, Grace Grenvile of Stow discussed the attributes commonly considered desirable in a prospective husband. The letter concerned the proposed marriage of Ann, daughter of John and Mary Arundell, and John, eldest son of Charles Trevanion Esq, which was celebrated at Newlyn in Pyder on 8 December 1634. Grace was evidently responding to a request for her opinion of the match, and of the size of the dowry required by the Trevanions, and stated

. . . We cannott thinke that the west of England can affoorde you a better or more convenient motion then this of Mr Trevanion. The family is noble, the estate greate, the young gent of good disposition, and that which in my opinion is not the least considerable, is the neerelesse of his habitation, wherbye you

31

shall still have at hand the Comfort of so deserving a child as your worthy daughter.[116]

Clearly practical considerations were not incompatible with human factors.[117] Indeed, despite the clear importance of status and land, and the relatively high rate of marriage within the county, marriage for many Cornish gentlemen (if not most) does not appear to have been the cold, remote 'low-keyed and undemanding institution' described by Lawrence Stone.[118] The sermon given by the Reverend Charles FitzGeffry at the funeral of Anne Rashleigh, first wife of Jonathan Rashleigh Esq, emphasizes marital love, although couched in terms of the Puritan ideal:

As particularlie her conjugal love, her sweet and amiable conversation in wedlock, living with her beloved without anie impairement of love, so much as with a looke, much lesse with anie unbeseeming word. In so much that who knew her might read in her real commentarie on the Apostles rules for wives behaviour towards their husbands. Manie doe read and know them, shee did both know and performe them.[119]

The correspondence between Bevill and Grace Grenvile of Stow contains frequent exchanges of love and affection; and they usually addressed each other as 'My Best Friend'. Grace evidently had full control of household, estate, and financial management during her husband's absences. For example, in 1621 he instructed her to

have a care that the People want no provision & lett my co: Tremayne take up Oxen & sheepe enough, to serve all the yeare . . . [and to] . . . make all the haste you can to thresh out your corne for feare it be spoiled & observe how many bushells it is . . . [Also] . . . lett Charles the joyner make a board for the Parler assoone as you can, as plaine & cheape as possible he can make.[120]

In her letter of April 1628, Grace expressed anxiety about the poor state of the family's finances. She had apparently been endeavouring to collect outstanding debts, but with limited success. The letter shows her to be a competent and able financial manager:

I have entreated earnestly for 60 which must be payd away as soone as I have it, there was above 80 due before your going & have payd 20 and better, & I shall dayly have use for money to keepe the house besides what is to be payed.[121]

Bevill and Grace also shared an intellectual relationship. The responsibilities entrusted to Grace were not confined to household affairs: she also supervised the children's pre-university education.[122] Further, Bevill provided Grace with a steady flow of news from London society and Parliament, keeping her well-informed of the issues of the day. The couple frequently engaged in vigorous dialogue about national affairs, as in her replies Grace stated her opinions and concerns about Bevill's political activities. In his will Bevill displayed his liberal attitude and great affection towards his wife, appointing her sole executrix, and leaving her for life the whole Stow estate, with all the chattels, 'as a remembrance of my love to her'. He also adopted a liberal attitude with his daughters, by stating (unusually) that their portions were to be paid at the age of twenty years, or sooner if the sum could be raised conveniently. No mention was made of payment upon marriage.[123]

The Grenviles may have been exceptional, but many of the same characteristics were evident in other Cornish gentry marriages. For example, William Coode Gent appointed his wife, Anne, as his executrix. Both Francis Gregor Gent and his son John, of Trewarthenick, also left to their wives their houses and household goods and furniture, and Francis referred to his 'loveing wife' Honor, while his son referred to 'Anne Gregor my lovinge and deare wife'.[124]

There were still, however, marriages based on social and financial considerations alone, where the wife was subservient. Many gentlemen severely restricted the movements of their widows, and made provisions to guard against remarriage. For example, in his will of 1620, Richard Carew Esq listed lands which his wife was to hold on condition that she remained a widow and fulfilled all the agreements he had made. Further, as late as 1665 Sir Richard Vyvyan showed his intention to maintain strict control over his daughters' marriages. He left them portions of £1,000 each, payable within two years of marriage, but should they marry without consent, they were to receive a mere £50 each.[125]

Gentry Networks

Carew said that the Cornish gentry:

> keepe liberall, but not costly builded or furnished houses, give kind entertainement to strangers . . . are reverenced and beloved of their neighbours, . . . They converse familiarly together, and often visit one another. A Gentleman and his wife will ride to make merry with his next neighbour; and after a day or twayne, those two couples goe to a third: in which progresse

33

they encrease like snowballs, till through their burdensome waight they breake againe.[126]

The Grenvile family lived in eastern Cornwall (at Stow in Stratton hundred) and their friendship network was extensive. Bevill Grenvile had a wide network of friends, which extended over time and reflected shifts in his political views. Within Cornwall, in the 1620s his friends ranged from Sir John Eliot of Port Eliot in the hundred of East, to John Arundell Esq of Trerice in Pyder, and John Trefusis Esq of Trefusis in Kerrier. Besides sharing political sympathies and factional allegiance, Grenvile and Eliot enjoyed a close friendship. In 1626, for example, Grenvile directed that his third son be called John, with Eliot as godfather.[127] By the mid-1630s Grenvile's former factional enemy, Sir William Wrey of Trebigh in St Ive (East hundred), appears to have become another friend, and in 1636 Bevill expressed his sorrow at Wrey's absence from his father's funeral, since

> no man in the world should have been gladder of your company then myselfe, neither is there any place where you can have better welcome then to my house, wherof I hope you do not doubt.[128]

At around the same time Grenvile's friends also included Sir Nicholas Slanning, governor of Pendennis castle, and son-in-law of his former enemy, Sir James Bagg. In a letter of c.1641, Grenvile promised to visit Slanning as soon as he was able, and remarked that

> You are Sir environ'd with many rare felicities & I wish them Centupled, but I only grutch you one which is neighbourhood to my Ancient, most dear & noble friend of Trefusis because I cant share it with you.

Plainly, Grenvile had friends throughout the county.

Grenvile's friendship network extended into Devon and beyond. Five of the six overseers named in his will were Devonians, and only one, John Arundell Esq, was Cornish. Of the other five, Antony Denys of Orleigh was Grenvile's brother-in-law, and the remaining four were apparently friends. One of these, Richard Prideaux of Thuckborough, had strong connections with the Cornish Prideaux family of Padstow, and represented Bodmin in the Short Parliament of April 1640.[129] A letter from Grenvile to Prideaux, dated 8 February 1635, after the latter's marriage, suggests that their friendship stemmed from Prideaux's periods of residence in Cornwall:

Plate 4. Sir Bevill Grenvile of Stow, 1636

It was your lov'd company made me love this country . . . reflect a little upon our barren North, which hath in former times pleas'd you, and when you can be best spared then afford a little time to make these parts happie . . .[130]

Grenvile's two most notable friends from beyond Cornwall and Devon were Sir Edward Seymour of Bradly, Wiltshire, grandson of Protector Somerset, and Sir William Waller of Kent. In each case, even allowing for linguistic excesses, there was deep mutual affection and regard. In 1640, for example, Seymour promised to visit Stow shortly, as 'I cannot long live without your society, in which ther is soe much cheerfullness as it sweetens all misfortunes, and makes them none wher you are'. Replying, Grenvile said that Seymour's pen made 'a musick when it strikes next to that of the spheres, & has no less enchanting power over me'.[131] Grenvile and Waller exchanged similar declarations, and Waller also provided hospitality for Grenvile's son when he was in Oxford.[132] It is ironic that Waller should have led the parliamentary forces at the Battle of Lansdown where the royalist Grenvile was killed.

The Rashleigh family's friendships were centred around the family home of Menabilly, near Fowey. However, they were also connected with families in east and west Cornwall (Carew of Antony and Godolphin of Godolphin, for example), and with some Devonian families.[133] The Devonian link was strengthened by Jonathan Rashleigh's marriages.[134] Many of Rashleigh's friendships appear to have been based upon family or business connections, although not exclusively, and often the two were combined. Much of Rashleigh's correspondence was with members of his wives' families, or with his brothers-in-law and their families. In all there are numerous and frequent references to financial matters.

Jonathan Rashleigh had extensive financial interests. It is likely that this was partly due to his trading activities, but he was not a usurer like Ezechiell Grosse, and lent money only to family and friends. For example, in April 1633 Rashleigh was asked for a loan of £500 by his brother-in-law, John Harris Esq of Radford, and in May, his cousin, John Harris of Hayne, requested a loan of £150. In February 1638, Richard and Oliver Sawle, Rashleigh's nephews, desired to borrow £20 each from their uncle.[135] From a business relationship, Rashleigh appears to have developed a friendship with his future son-in-law, Peter Courtney Esq of Trethurfe. In the formative stages of their friendship, Rashleigh encouraged the speedy repayment of a debt:

in which doinge you shall approve your selfe a true accountant & incurage me heerafter to send you such goods as you do not fayle me in payment . . .

thus hoping to be better acquainted with you for present I rest your loving friend . . .[136]

The Grenviles and Rashleighs were members of the greater gentry, and a study of lesser gentry families would probably show different trends. These case studies demonstrate that for the greater gentry at least, the county boundary was no barrier, and in the choice of both friends and marriage partners it was transcended easily and frequently. This suggests that while the preservation of a local identity was important, the greater Cornish gentry were neither as insular nor as narrow-minded as they have been portrayed.[137]

2

The Religious Landscape: Papists, Puritans and Arminians

Cornwall and Devon jointly comprised the diocese of Exeter, and were subject to the jurisdiction of the Bishop of Exeter. Within the diocese, Cornwall formed a separate archdeaconry which, in turn, was divided into eight deaneries. The archdeacon dealt with diocesan administration, 'managed' the clergy, and held his own courts. Careerists perceived the office as a useful stepping-stone, and it was also coveted for the income it generated.[1] Indeed, it was so desirable that competition for it provoked a fierce dispute in 1629.[2] In contrast, the position of rural dean was unfashionable and troublesome, and generally rotated annually, by election, between the clergy of each deanery. A ninth deanery, St Buryan, exempt from diocesan jurisdiction, had the freedom to admit clergy to its livings without reference to the bishop.[3] So, Cornwall was relatively removed from the centre of ecclesiastical administration in Exeter.[4] This may explain, in part, why Cornwall was affected rather less by the major religious upheavals of the period than other counties. It may also help to account for the persistence of Calvinist doctrines there after the proscription of Calvinist teachings from the mid-1620s, although the moderate and conciliatory policies of Joseph Hall, Bishop of Exeter 1627–41, also protected the county from the full force of anti-Calvinism. Within this religious landscape there existed a small but notorious group of Roman Catholic recusants, and a thriving and extremely vocal group of Puritans.

Cornish Catholics

Using the 1641 lay subsidy rolls, it has been possible to identify and locate many Cornish recusants, since recusant gentlemen were charged a double subsidy, and those who were not otherwise liable to pay were charged an 8*d*. poll tax. In Cornwall, as elsewhere, Roman Catholicism was a nuclear religious practice, concentrated around recusant gentry families prepared to shelter priests in their homes. Most recusants lived in the centre of the county, particularly in the hundreds of Lesnewth, Pyder, Powder and Kerrier, although only certain parishes in each of these hundreds contained recusants, usually those close to the home of a recusant gentleman. The Trevillians of St Clether were the nucleus of the recusant community in Lesnewth; indeed, St Clether was the only parish in that hundred where recusancy was recorded in the 1641 subsidy roll. Pyder contained by far the largest number of recusants in the county, with a particularly large group in the parish of Mawgan-in-Pyder, encouraged no doubt by the presence there of Sir John Arundell of Lanherne. The Catholic Borlase family in Newlyn-in-Pyder would also have been influential. In Powder, the principal recusant family was Tremayne of St Kew, although the Arundell influence probably extended to part of this hundred too. The very few recusants in Kerrier were concentrated around a minor branch of the Trevillian family in Stithians parish.[5]

A letter of 17 December 1625 from the deputy lieutenants of Cornwall to the Earl of Pembroke reveals much about the extent of recusancy in the county, and about Protestant gentlemen's views on Catholics. Fears of Catholicism would have been heightened in the previous August by the government's order for a full mobilization of coastal defence forces, prompted by the danger of an invasion from the continent.[6] Consequently, the deputies expressed immense satisfaction at the King's command to disarm all recusants, as they were fully aware 'of the dangerous contageon that may grow in this kingdome by those kind of Jesuited Papists more to be feared then the Pestilence'. The deputies stressed the need to remove 'the abhominacon of Idolitry', which Robin Clifton has said was possibly the most appalling feature of Catholicism to Protestants. About the situation in Cornwall, the deputies declared that

> for our partes we have true cause to give God praise that our Country hath very few of this sorte And those that are we conceave are not any way to be feared for their power . . . [although] . . . we cannot but acknowledge to our griefe that of late time those prophane recusants have somethinge increased both in number and acion cariadge here in theise partes of the kingdome.

They estimated there were approximately two hundred recusants, of whom they had found only one in possession of arms: John Trevillian Esq of St Clether, whose drum, musket and corslet were accordingly confiscated.[7] The 1641 subsidy roll records a total of sixty-eight recusant heads of households, which probably broadly equated with the JPs' figure for individuals.[8]

The most influential recusant was Sir John Arundell of Lanherne, whose father, in Elizabeth's reign, had been arrested for recusancy and his protection of Catholic priests. He was, for example, a friend of the Jesuit missionary, Cuthbert Mayne. Moreover, two of his sisters, Dorothy and Gertrude, had entered the convent of the English Benedictines in Brussels.[9] In 1603, imprisoned in London for his recusancy, Arundell asked leave of Secretary Cecil to return to the West Country.[10] The following year he was discharged.[11]

On 9 February 1606, Nicholas Prideaux Esq, JP, informed the Privy Council of accusations made by one Richow Penvose against her brother-in-law, John Penvose, yeoman.[12] She alleged that Penvose was a recusant ('maried and united to the recusants of this countrie'), a servant to Sir John Arundell of Lanherne, and an 'intelligencer' for recusants, travelling to and from London for this purpose. In September or October 1605, upon Penvose's return from London, she had informed him that his cattle were soon to be confiscated for the King as a penalty for his recusancy, to which Penvose had replied: 'let him drive them quicklie for he shall not be longe kinge'. Since Penvose had spent the late summer and autumn of 1605 in London, this naturally aroused suspicion of pre-knowledge of the Gunpowder Plot. Penvose was questioned closely concerning the matter but strongly denied any such words or knowledge, and suggested that the allegations were malicious, since at that time a lawsuit was pending between him and his brother Michael (Richow's husband). If John were to die, the disputed tenement would pass to Michael. Nicholas Prideaux tended towards this view, since Richow had waited four months before reporting the incident.[13]

John Trevillian was at the centre of a major incident in October 1628, which arose from a conversation between John Prideaux Esq of Trevorder, his wife Anne, and Martin Nansogg, Bishop Hall's chaplain. The two men had been discussing the likelihood of a Catholic uprising in the event of a successful invasion of England, when Mrs Prideaux had interjected that 'theare is Mr Trevillyan he is a lusty man, if all the papists weare such men as he wee had then cause to feare', and that Trevillian had tried to persuade her to convert to Catholicism, for

yf shee weere a papist shee would be a good woman, & he did hope shee would turne before shee dyed, & yf shee would not be a papist, shee should dye befor shee was willing.

Trevillian had apparently gone on to say that Mrs Prideaux and her husband must convert within the month or their throats would be cut. He had further declared that Protestants should expect worse days and greater persecution than in Queen Mary's reign, and that 'Queen Tibb' (Elizabeth

I) was 'as arrant a whore as ever breathed, and that she was kept by Essex, Leicester, and others'. He had also referred to the singing of a psalm within a Church of England service as a 'Geneva Gygg' (a reference to Calvinism), and had claimed that the Protestant Bible was composed of 'Lyes and Tales'.[14]

Nansogg reported all this to Bishop Hall, who asked Sir Richard Buller to investigate. Buller and three fellow JPs (Sir Reginald and John Mohun and Charles Lord Lambert), sensing so much implied danger to King, Church, and commonwealth, reported to the King that Trevillian was a 'recusant-convict . . . the greatest of that faction in the West'. They went on to give Trevillian's reported words, asserting that 'he is a close, reserved man, and weighs his words before he lets them fall', so that there was probably 'much more in his heart than on his tongue'.[15]

Mrs Prideaux further deposed that

> shee heard by one Marshe of Padstow that one Mr Burlace of Newlyn tooke the byble out of the viccar of Mercyans hand one smalridge & spurned at yt with his foote.[16]

As a result, Nicholas Borlase Esq was prosecuted. However, he sought revenge against Lord Lambert (John Lord Robartes' brother-in-law), one of the JPs involved in the examination of witnesses against him, by exploiting his own position as a subsidy commissioner to insert Lambert's name in the subsidy book. Lambert informed Secretary Conway of this injustice, and the reason for it. He went on to say that Borlase

> hath alwaies bine reputed for a papist, who hath not receyved the Comunyon in his owne parishe church, nor elsewhere that hath bine knowne this two yeeres at the least; and seldome cometh to church, but when prayers is almost done, and was at the Bishops last visitacon, presented for a Recusant, as the mynister of the parishe where he lives hath often infourmed mee. And I assure your Lordship he is a dangerous fellow as any in those partes.[17]

The Puritan Community

From the mid-sixteenth century until the late 1620s Calvinism was the dominant doctrine of the Church of England: the majority of clergy and probably most educated laymen were steeped in Calvinist theology. Shared acceptance of the Calvinist doctrine of predestination, a common hostility to Rome, and a zeal to spread the gospel, combined with the King's commitment to unity within the Church, held together a broad Protestant alliance during James I's reign. Puritans formed part of this alliance, since they shared Calvinist predestinarian beliefs and most were members of the established Church. They tried to reform the Church of England in a 'godly' way from within, for example by placing Puritan clerics in benefices under their control and increasing the emphasis on preaching the Word. Therefore it is not easy to distinguish Puritans from other Protestants, at least until the late 1620s when the Jacobean Protestant alliance (under strain since the last years of James' reign) was shattered by Charles I's promotion of anti-Calvinist churchmen and the proscription of Calvinist teaching and writing.[18]

Anti-Calvinists (often labelled by contemporaries and historians by the more doctrinally specific term, Arminians) rejected the Calvinists' emphasis upon predestination and upon preaching as the means to salvation, and most did not share their antipathy towards the Roman Catholic Church. Rather, they believed in free grace for all through prayer and the sacraments, which (following their ascendancy in the late 1620s) led to a new emphasis upon the altar, and (particularly after Laud's appointment as Archbishop of Canterbury in 1633) to the removal of communion tables to the east end and railing them in, the introduction of new ceremonies, and an emphasis on the beauty of holiness. Anti-Calvinists also stressed the importance of order in divine worship and played up the historical links between the Church of England and the pre-reformed Church.[19]

The continued attachment to Calvinist doctrines by many in Cornwall after the suppression of Calvinist teaching extends the problem of identifying Puritans. However, certain characteristics distinguish Puritans. For example, they stressed the fundamental principles of Calvinism, especially the beliefs that they were assured a place amongst the elected saints, and of the exclusivity of the godly. Puritans also emphasized the preaching of the Word as the principal means of salvation, and stressed the need for personal Bible study, prayer and meditation. Through these they claimed an intense personal relationship with God, which made them deeply aware of sin and redemption. They emphasized the importance of strict godly moral discipline, both on a personal level and within the household. Puritans opposed ceremony, idolatry and the use of vestments. Throughout the period they were the strongest advocates of rigorous measures against papists. Using these criteria, though the label 'Puritan' should not be applied lightly, it is possible, principally through wills, sermons, dedications and correspondence, to identify an overtly Puritan group in Cornwall with national connections in the first half of the seventeenth century.

During the Elizabethan period Cornish Puritans had never been more than a minority group, based in eastern Cornwall. The Supplication presented by Puritans to the 1586 Parliament showed that there were only twenty-nine preachers in Cornwall, and most of these were in the eastern half. A.L. Rowse attributed this to the fact that eastern Cornwall was English-speaking by this period, and that preaching was more difficult in western Cornwall where Cornish was still spoken.[20] By the early seventeenth century, however, language appears no longer to have been a factor, and the strength and topography of Puritanism were largely determined by gentry influence.

The gentry's use of advowsons (the right of presentation to a living), taken alone, is not a reliable source for the identification of Puritans. In some cases it is clear that Puritan gentry installed clergymen of their own views to livings under their control: for example, Sir Anthony Rous of Halton placed Charles FitzGeffry at St Dominick, and Sir Richard Buller installed John Fathers at St Stephens by Saltash. These two clergymen published sermons which demonstrated their Puritan beliefs and outlook, but for the majority of clergymen (who did not publish) there is insufficient evidence to be certain of their beliefs. These difficulties are compounded by the fact that the Crown, the Bishop of Exeter, and the dean and chapter of Exeter controlled a large proportion of Cornish livings.[21]

Preambles to wills generally expound religious beliefs, and are therefore a useful source for identifying Puritans. For the period 1600–60, 366 Cornish gentry wills have been analyzed in an attempt to identify Puritans and their topographical distribution. The results of this survey should be taken as impressionistic because of flaws in the source material, but they are nonetheless useful if combined with other sources. Some wills for known Puritans are unobtainable, and others reveal surprisingly little or no Puritan dogma. Preambles must be treated with caution, since some wills were composed by a scribe, often the local clergyman, and certain common formulae recur. Nevertheless, many preambles contain idiosyncratic statements clearly revealing personal beliefs, and even those in standard form must surely have represented the views of the testator to some extent. Therefore, on the premise that Puritans placed special emphasis upon assurance of election and the exclusivity of the godly, and following Anthony Fletcher's method of identification, three features in preambles were taken as indicative of likely Puritanism.[22]

The first indicator was demonstrable confidence in predestination. This was expressed in a number of ways, most commonly in the form of a statement that the testator was 'trusting assuredly', 'not doubting', or 'steadfastly believing' that he would inherit the kingdom of God. Some Puritans articulated more precisely belief in their own election and the exclusivity of the godly. Edward Trelawny Esq of Bake in Pelynt parish, for example, believed that upon his death his soul would 'without spott fly to the place of perpetuall rest prepared from all eternity for gods elect', while Richard Pinch Gent of Poundstock anticipated being 'amongst the Juste that dye in the Lord'.[23] Degory Chamond Esq of Launcells displayed supreme confidence in his own election, based on Biblical faith:

> by gods moste holye worde (w[hi]ch never fayleth) through his holye spirit fullye assured of free p[ar]don & Remisson of all my sinnes of his free mercye w[i]thout any deserte of myne & through the death & me[r]its of our onelye saviour & Advocate Jesus Christ to be Accepted amongst his electe & chosen, to have the fruition of his dietye . . .[24]

A few, like Thomas Laughern Gent of St Erme, went further still and expressed assurance that God would 'Receave my soule into his glorie And place it in the companie of ye heavenlie Angells & blessed Saints'.[25] Thomas St Aubyn Esq of Helston was certain that he would reign with Jesus and 'enioye the companie of Archangells Angells the holy martires and p[ro]ffetts and the Rest of the holye quire of heaven', while Robert Harris Gent of Lostwithiel expected to 'possesse a place w[i]th Abraham Isacke and Jacobe in the kingdome of heaven'.[26]

In the 366 wills analyzed, 89 (24 per cent) of the testators stated a belief in predestination in one or more of these ways. Of these, 9 (10 per cent) mentioned their assurance of joining the angels and saints in heaven, while only 5 (6 per cent) used the term 'election'. Further, 21 (24 per cent) lived in East hundred, 18 (20 per cent) in Powder, 14 (16 per cent) in Kerrier, and 9 (10 per cent) in West. The remainder were spread between the other five hundreds in relatively small concentrations.

A further indicator was a stated belief in physical resurrection, where the testator expected body and soul to be reunited on the Day of Judgement. In his will of 1620 Sir Anthony Rous of Halton committed his body to the earth

> Nothinge doubtinge but accordinge to the article of my faith at the great day of the gen[er]all resurrection when wee shall appeare before the iudgem[en]t seate of Christ I shall receive the same againe by the mightie power of God wherew[i]th he is able to subdue althinges to himself not a corruptible mortall & weake body as now it is but an incorupttible immortall & perfecte bodye in althinges like unto the glorious boddie of my Lord and Saviour Jesus Christ.[27]

Others who expressed similar expectations included Hugh Boscawen Esq of Tregothan, Nicholas Sawle Esq, Sir Alexander Carew Knight of Antony, John St Aubyn Esq of Clowance, John Harris Esq of Lanreast, Thomas

Trefusis Gent of Constantine, and Hannibal Gamon, rector of Mawgan-in-Pyder and chaplain to Lord Robartes.[28] In all, 29 (8 per cent) of the 366 testators referred to physical resurrection. Of these, 10 (35 per cent) lived in Powder hundred, 6 (21 per cent) in East hundred, and 3 (10 per cent) in each of the hundreds of West, Kerrier, and Lesnewth. All but two of the 29 also made an overtly predestinarian statement.

A third indicator was emphasis on personal sin, or contempt for sinfulness and corruption. Most of the eighty-nine wills expressing predestinarian beliefs and all of those anticipating physical resurrection included such expressions. Ambrose Manaton Esq of Trecarrel in South Petherwin, for example, praised God 'for giveing me this and many other tymes a sence of my many and greevious sinnes against him and his blessed commandements'.[29] However, such expressions are more difficult to isolate as they were usually incorporated into one of the other categories, as in Sir Anthony Rous' will above.

Twenty-seven gentlemen expounded all three elements in their wills. Of these, 9 (33 per cent) resided in Powder, 6 (22 per cent) in East, and 3 (11 per cent) in each of West, Kerrier and Lesnewth. Ninety-two wills contained at least one indicator. Of these, 21 (23 per cent) lived in East, 19 (21 per cent) in Powder, 14 (15 per cent) in Kerrier, and 10 (11 per cent) in West. It is noticeable that in all these analyses, using both broad and narrow criteria, East and Powder contained the largest numbers of Puritans, followed by Kerrier and West. These same four hundreds, which adjoined each other along the south coast, also contained the largest number of greater gentry families and the largest number of wealthy gentry.[30] If this pattern is accurate, there would appear to be a connection between these relatively powerful and wealthy hundreds, which were united by their dominance of Cornish trade, and the incidence of Puritanism.

Only four of the 366 testators mentioned and bequeathed Bibles.[31] In his will of 1619, Richard Connock Esq of Calstock left 'all my Bibells and Prayer bookes' to his wife. Although gentry ownership of a Bible does not necessarily indicate Puritanism, Connock made a number of bequests of religious pictures to Puritan friends and relatives. He gave Sir Thomas Wise of Sydenham and Mount Wise (near Plymouth) the choice of a picture of Abraham sacrificing Isaac (which, he said, hung in the dining chamber at Calstock) or a picture of the Philosopher. Whichever Wise declined was to go to Wise's first cousin, Sir Richard Buller. Lady Wise was to have a picture of St John the Baptist (which also hung in the house) and Lady Buller was bequeathed a picture of cruelty demonstrated by all ages. A picture of St Jerome was left to Connock's nephew, Emmanuel Langford Esq of Liskeard. Connock also possessed a number of musical instruments, and he bequeathed his best virginals (which he claimed had once belonged to Queen Elizabeth) to his godson and great nephew, Richard Vyvyan Esq. The preambles to the wills of Richard Vyvyan's father (Sir Francis) and his grandfather (Hannibal) suggest Puritan beliefs. The preambles are almost identical and may have been written by a scribe (although this is not acknowledged), or may simply reflect shared views. Both 'steadfastly believed' 'that Christ had redeemed them from 'the Tyranny of Sathan', and committed their bodies 'to be buried in some decent and comely manner (without any pompe or extraordinary charge or expenc[e]s).'[32]

It is curious that Wymond Carew Esq of Antony, son of the historian, bequeathed in 1632 to his Puritan brother, Richard, the sermons of the Arminian Bishop Lancelot Andrews. Wymond's other bequests included 'Kinge his sermons' and 'all my prayer bookes', together with his extensive collection of Hebrew works and history books. Carew was a Fellow of King's College Cambridge and styled himself as such in his will; his considerable library reflected his scholarly position. He acquired his fellowship in 1626, the year of Buckingham's appointment as chancellor of Cambridge University, holding it until his own death in 1632. During that period Cambridge Calvinism was suppressed and the university was subjected to close royal control, so Carew himself may have subscribed to Arminianism, or may have included Arminian works in his library for scholarly purposes or for appearance's sake. Although from a Puritan family, Wymond's own religious view is difficult to establish. The preamble to his will contains no element of Puritanism; he merely beseeched God to receive his soul.[33]

In the preamble to his will of 1646 Roger Gayer Gent of Minster commended his body to Christian burial 'in full hope of the Resurreccon thereof at the last day', which suggests that he was a Puritan. This impression is strengthened by Gayer's bequest to his son-in-law of 'Mr Brightman's works on the Revelacon'. Thomas Brightman (1562–1607) was a celebrated preacher, known for his disaffection from the established Church. The message of his radical book *Apocalypsis Apocalypseos* was that the Pope was anti-Christ, doomed to destruction, and that after a long period of persecution European Protestants would enjoy 'the most glorious and triumphant times of peace and union'. Translations of this work were printed at Leiden in 1616 and London in 1644, so Gayer may have possessed the most recent edition.[34]

Puritans generally advocated simple funerals, not least as a final demonstration of humility, and their wills often contain appropriate instructions. However, during the seventeenth century there was a growing trend away from the expensive, elaborate and impersonal heraldic obsequies of the Elizabethan era and towards less expensive and more personal funerals. This prompted a fashion for night burials, avoiding the daytime ceremony and attendant expense, allowing expressions of affection regardless of status, and providing a sentimental atmosphere in which to mourn the deceased. Hence, although requests for simple or nocturnal burials may suggest Puritanism, alone they are insufficient.[35]

In his will dated 1650, Ambrose Manaton Esq, having emphasized his sinfulness, requested a very simple night-time burial. He committed his body to the earth

> desyring that my Corps may be interred in South Petherwyn church neere my Ladyes without any coffin in a Linnen sheete and that in the night tyme in a private way without any mourning cloathes by any.[36]

If these instructions were followed, Manaton's funeral would have been very simple, even by night burial standards. It was unusual for a gentleman to be buried in a shroud alone, and although (unlike in a daytime funeral) the cost of mourning clothes for a night burial was not provided by the deceased's estate, it was nonetheless accepted practice for mourners to wear black.[37]

Hugh Boscawen Esq of Tregothnan, a staunch Puritan, in his 1636 will expressed confidence in his salvation and committed his body, his 'soul's prison', to the earth, certain of its future resurrection. Accordingly he desired that his body 'be decently interred' in a Christian manner in the north aisle of St Michael Penkevil church, 'without any vaine pompous or popish ceremonies'.[38] Following their respective predestinarian statements, Ezechiell Grosse Esq requested burial in a Christian manner 'without pomp or vayne ostentacon', and John Kempthorne Esq of Tonacomb asked 'to be buryede comely and christyanlye, w[i]thout pompe pride or anye vayne ceremonye'.[39] Similarly, Thomas St Aubyn Esq, having expressed confidence of his salvation and of sitting with the angels, requested 'noe soleme nor great funerall for my Buriall', and John Tremayne Gent of Lametton, St Keyne, hoped that his 'vile carkes' would be buried 'w[i]thout sup[er]stitious ceremonies'.[40]

A number of Puritan writers expressed disapproval of funeral sermons on the basis of potential popish interpretation. They alleged an implicit suggestion that the deceased would benefit from the sermon, which could be equated with intercessionary prayers for the dead. Nonetheless, funeral sermons held special appeal for many Puritans, who craved sermons of all kinds, and sometimes requested in their wills that one be preached for them. Seventeen of the 366 wills examined contain sermon requests, but this is not representative of the actual number preached. Sir Anthony

Rous' will, for example, does not request a sermon, but one was preached nevertheless.

Twelve of the seventeen sermon requests did not specify a preacher, but referred to 'him who shall preach', or to the minister, while the other five identified a particular preacher. Of named preachers, four were the incumbent of the testator's parish, and the fifth of the adjoining parish. Thomas St Aubyn Esq, for example, bequeathed 10 shillings to the vicar of Helston, Robert Jago, for a funeral sermon. It is likely that Jago shared St Aubyn's Puritan beliefs since he remained in the living throughout the 1640s, and in 1646–48 was paid additional sums for preaching in vacant livings following the ejection of royalist clergy. In her will of 1627 Thomasine Buller, widow, of Shillingham, left 10 shillings for a funeral sermon to Matthew Drake, who had been presented to the living of St Stephens by Saltash two years earlier by her son, the Puritan patron, Sir Richard Buller. In addition, in his 1633 will John Edy Gent of Bodmin requested a sermon from John Saunders, vicar of Bodmin (although Saunders died in 1635, two years before Edy).[41] Ambrose Manaton Esq was unique among the 366 testators in specifying the text for his funeral sermon. He desired that 'at some convenient tyme after [his night burial] on the Lords day [a minister would] preach on this blessed parcell of Scripture vizt Blessed are they that dye in the Lord for they rest from their Labours'.[42]

Published funeral sermons provide an insight into Puritan lifestyles and households, although, by their occasion and nature, they tend to eulogize their subjects and should therefore be read accordingly. Charles FitzGeffry, Puritan rector of St Dominick from 1603 until his death in 1637, published three of his own funeral sermons: those for Sir Anthony Rous and Rous' second wife Lady Philippe in 1622, and that for Mrs Anne Rashleigh of Menabilly in 1631.[43] Hannibal Gamon, rector of Mawgan-in-Pyder from 1619 until his death in 1651, and yet more radical than FitzGeffry, published the sermon he had delivered at the funeral of Lady Frances Robartes of Lanhydrock in August 1626.[44] Each sermon was divided into two parts, the second and shorter of which discussed the life of the deceased. The first part fulfilled the main purpose of the sermon: to remind the congregation of the frailty of human life and to exhort them to prepare for their own deaths.

FitzGeffry praised Sir Anthony Rous for the fair and just execution of his public duties, as a JP and previously as vice-warden of the stannaries. He had resisted corruption, and had been bold in ensuring that justice prevailed. To illustrate, FitzGeffry remarked that:

I know that in his office of Vice-warden-shippe, he often desired to have some

Divine a spectator and arbitrator of his proceedings, taking my selfe sometime in stead of others, to bee present at the scanning and censuring of cases, desiring to decide all matters by the best rule of religion and conscience.[45]

FitzGeffry commended Lady Rous for her exemplary conduct as a wife, mother and step-mother, and for the way in which she had supported her husband in his public duties, and also applauded Mrs Rashleigh for similar qualities.[46]

In their hunger for preaching, Puritans liked to hear at least two sermons every Sunday, and also attended weekday sermons or lectures whenever possible. Rous had attended Church regularly:

his timely repair thither shewed his zeale for that which was to be performed there: being more early at the Church, then many of his inferiors in age and place (and these neerer unto the Church) were out of their Chambers.

Indeed, 'distance of place, distemper of Weather could not with-hold him' from a sermon, and he had incurred his last illness on a cold, frosty morning when travelling by boat to a Saturday lecture at Saltash.[47] Further, Rous had supported and entertained godly British and European ministers, who would probably have preached to the household at Halton:

If they were painefull and conscionable in their Calling, he highly regarded them . . . How acceptable to him were the feet of those, who brought the glad Tidings of Peace? From Scotland, Ireland, and the Netherlands, have they come, that have dranke plentifully of his favour and bountie.[48]

Mrs Rashleigh had shown that she was 'a Disciple indeed, a true believer' by 'constantly repayring to the Temple . . . not onlie on the Lord's day, but on the Lecture-day, and by her attention and devotion in the Temple'.[49] Lady Robartes too had taken great delight in listening to 'conscionable and searching' sermons, in both Cornwall and London. Indeed, she stated that attendance at sermons had been the only pleasure she had derived from visits to the capital.[50]

Household godliness was central to Puritanism, and all four of the deceased had spent several hours daily in prayer, Bible reading, and meditation. Lady Rous, in the true manner of the Elect, had 'kept her selfe unspotted from the World, and the spots that appeared to God and her Conscience, she was carefull to wipe away by daily Prayer and Repentance'.[51] Further, all four subjects had attempted to impart to their children and servants the knowledge and insight they had acquired from their own devotions. Mrs Rashleigh, 'embracing religion herself . . . was

49

careful to propagate it to her children, and to diffuse it over her whole familie'.[52]

Lady Robartes had been a major influence upon the religious thinking of her children, especially John, the heir, and had taken pains

> to plant the feare of the Lord in their hearts, to fit them with worthy Matches out of Religious Families, to adorne her onely Sonne with the Richest endowments of Grace and Learning.[53]

She had corresponded with Dr Prideaux of Exeter College, Oxford, concerning her children's education. Prideaux, vice-chancellor of Oxford University, rector of Exeter College and regius professor of divinity, regularly lectured on the Calvinist tenets of conversion, predestination, perseverence, and the certainty of salvation, and argued against Arminian principles. Gamon claimed that Lady Robartes' letters were 'worthy to be kept as a Monument of her truly Noble Spirit and Godly Desire . . . to have the fruit of her Body become the fruit of the Spirit'.[54] Further, she had extended her witness and influence beyond her immediate family to the neighbourhood of the family seat at Lanhydrock, and to that of their town house at Truro. Many had received 'spiritual Helpe and refreshment' by

> conversing with Her in the choicest passages of sanctification. For shee had the Art to uphold holy conferences about the perplexities of conscience, Relapses into sin, and Remedies against the same: Shee had the skill to beget many ioyfull Meditations of mortifying Grace and everlasting Glory.[55]

Sir Anthony Rous also had ensured that his children acquired the essentials of Puritan doctrine at an early age by sending them to teachers renowned for their godliness and learning. Later,

> sparing no cost for their breeding [they were educated] in the most eminent places of the Land, in the Universities and Innes of Court, that they might like himselfe prove profitable to Church and Commonwealth.

To round off their education with experience, he had encouraged them to travel abroad, although only to countries 'whence they might returne home free from the tainture of irreligion and superstition'. To reinforce this teaching, Rous had ensured that his own behaviour was exemplary, and had provided his children with a book of useful Bible passages and notes.[56] FitzGeffry's comments are supported by those of Francis Rous, Sir Anthony's son, in his dedication of *The Art of Happiness* to his father:

it cannot but be a comfort to you, to see some increase from above, where your careful Education hath planted and watered below; in which you have far exceeded the usual providence of Fathers, that ordinarily looks no farther then the body, pride, and earth.[57]

Sir Anthony and Lady Rous were both commended for displaying the Puritan virtues of hospitality and charity to people of all social levels. FitzGeffry described Sir Anthony as

A constant and famous House-keeper, for at least forty yeares continuance . . . his house for many yeares was the center of charity and hospitality, wherein met the lines of poore and strangers, drawne from a large circumference round about him.[58]

Lady Rous had been friendly and courteous towards her neighbours,

observing truly the Apostles precept for Humilitie, Equalling herselfe to those of lower estate, whereby she gained their love, and yet lost nothing of her Reputation: they honouring her more for her Meekenesse, then others for their Greatnesse . . . Glad when she had oportunitie to doe good unto any: making her Closet as an Apothecaries shop, for the poore Neighbours in time of their sicknes.[59]

Similarly, Mrs Rashleigh had shown contempt for her earthly status (compared with her second birth in the Holy Spirit), and had done many good works, exhibiting charity to the poor, particularly widows and orphans, and like Lady Rous, had nursed the sick.[60] Charity, humility and contempt for worldly values were considered essential for all Puritans, but the provision of medical care for the poor was exclusively a female duty.[61]

FitzGeffry asserted that Sir Anthony had shown great forgiveness, 'an especiall fruit of Election'. However, the 'crown' of Rous' virtues was his perseverance in all his other virtues, a sign of Grace, so that 'wee may therefore safely pronounce him saved'.[62] Lady Rous had also exhibited so many godly virtues that FitzGeffry declared: 'I doubt not to pronounce her blessed, she resteth from her labours, her good Workes follow her, and she keepeth continuall Sabbath in Heaven'.[63] Gamon referred to Lady Robartes as 'this Elect Lady', indicating that that there was ample evidence to show that she was assured eternal life. He also credited her with the essential virtues of perseverance in Grace and good works, and concluded by proclaiming the certainty of her salvation.[64]

Published funeral sermons also reveal connections and friendships between certain gentry and clergy, and for Cornwall they illuminate the

Puritan community. FitzGeffry's connections with the Rous family dated from the late sixteenth century when he was a contemporary of Sir Anthony's sons, Francis and Richard, at Broadgates Hall, Oxford. In 1596, while at Oxford, FitzGeffry's poem, 'Sir Francis Drake, his Honorable Lifes Commendation and his Tragical Deathes Lamentation', was published, prefixed by commendatory verses to the Rous brothers. Seven years later Sir Anthony presented FitzGeffry to the living of St Dominick. FitzGeffry dedicated Sir Anthony's funeral sermon to his grandson and heir, William Rous, the new patron of the living.[65]

In the dedication FitzGeffry evoked a sense of a Puritan community in Cornwall. He extolled William's great godly heritage and commended his marriage to Mary Robartes, daughter of the prominent Puritan, Sir Richard Robartes of Lanhydrock:

> Your Match into a worthy House (the wealthiest of the West) cannot so much advance you (if not exceed) the worth of your owne House.[66]

FitzGeffry also referred to his sermon at the funeral of Richard Carew Esq, 'that other starre of our West', who had predeceased Rous by four days.

Further, FitzGeffry's dedication of Lady Rous' sermon to her son, John Pym, whom FitzGeffry described as 'my most honoured friend', suggests that the Puritan community extended beyond the county boundary. Pym, later to become leader of parliamentary opposition to Arminianism and to government policies generally, was Lady Rous' son by her first marriage to Alexander Pym, and had grown up with the Rous brothers in the Tamar Valley. The Pym–Rous connection was further strengthened when Pym's sister Jane, daughter of Alexander Pym, married Robert Rous of Landrake, Sir Anthony's second son. Further, the marriage in 1604 of Philippe, daughter of Sir Anthony and Lady Philippe Rous (Pym's half-sister), with Humphrey Nicoll of Penvose in St Tudy added another dimension to the Pym–Rous alliance. Humphrey and Philippe's son, Anthony Nicoll, was MP for Bodmin in the Long Parliament (1640–48) and a close ally of his uncles, John Pym and Francis Rous. The Rous family also had connections with Devon Puritans through the marriage of Elizabeth, daughter of Sir Anthony Rous of Halton by his first wife, with Sir John Northcote of Newton St Cyres. Northcote was known for his austere lifestyle and his strictly Puritan-style dress.[67]

FitzGeffry also had strong links with Fowey in Powder hundred, where he was born in 1575 and bred. Many of its inhabitants appear to have shared his Puritan outlook, including the two principal families, the Rashleighs of Menabilly and the Treffrys of Place. In an undated letter,

Bevill Grenvile represented to 'the wife of the Chancellor of the Diocese' the grievances of the inhabitants of Fowey, 'some of w[hi]ch are worthy gent and my good frends' against their 'verrie worthless Vicar'. Grenvile was in Fowey on business, and having previously lived near the town (at Tremeer) he was able to reinforce the inhabitants' complaints. He confirmed that the vicar was

> a person so void of Edifiable parts as . . . utterly unable to contribute helpe unto, or any way further, the work of salvation . . . [and] . . . wholy possessed w[i]th the spiritts of obstinacy and ignorance.

Grenvile further explained the town's wish

> to have a lecturer at their owne charge. They desire not to do their owne minister any wrong, nor will take a penny of his means from him, but because of his unworthines they desyre to have a worthyer to do som part of his duty, without cost to him at all. The man they have chosen is Mr F[itz]G[effry].[68]

The letter is likely to have been written in 1625, as in May of that year, Edward Basill, vicar of Fowey, received from the Bishop of Exeter orders 'concerninge the readinge of divine service, preachinge and catachisinge in his parish church'. Whatever the outcome of this matter, Mr Basill retained his living, since he signed the protestation in 1641 as vicar of Fowey.[69]

There is no record of FitzGeffry's appointment as Fowey's lecturer, although other evidence, not least his close relationship with the Rashleighs, suggests that he was. He demonstrated allegiance to Mrs Rashleigh on 17 February 1629, by dedicating to her a sermon entitled *A Preparative to Repentance*, preached before the House of Commons on the occasion of the general fast on Ash Wednesday. William Coryton, who lived in St Mellion, the adjoining parish to St Dominick, had proposed FitzGeffry as one of the preachers for this day.[70] As shown above, FitzGeffry (rather than the vicar of Fowey, Mr Basill) preached Anne Rashleigh's funeral sermon in 1631 and showed a deep knowledge, not only of her character, but also of her behaviour in church. Further, in a memorandum of November 1637, concerning a dispute with Sir Reginald Mohun, Jonathan Rashleigh recorded FitzGeffry's role as mediator. He mentioned that FitzGeffry had visited his house in Fowey and that they had dined together at the house of another gentleman in the town (most likely John Treffry Esq).[71]

The impression of FitzGeffry's appointment is strengthened by a letter he wrote from Fowey to Lord Robartes on 24 March 1634. This gives a detailed account of a thunderstorm which had caused considerable damage in Fowey earlier that year. FitzGeffry, residing in the town, 'lay waking at that time, my chamber window being right opposite to yt Pinnacle of ye Church w[hi]ch suffered'. FitzGeffry interpreted the storm in providential terms as 'that warninge-peece from heaven', and was puzzled that the only injury was to Mrs Rashleigh's maid servant, 'whom for this seaven yeares I have knowne to bee of sober, modest, religious conversation'. FitzGeffry's complaint to Robartes of a shortage of time due to 'my manifold imployments' reinforces the impression that he was lecturer of Fowey as well as rector of St Dominick. Further, FitzGeffry's correspondence with Robartes (brother-in-law to FitzGeffry's patron William Rous), and his remembrances to Lady Robartes and to her kinsman, Sir Nathaniel Rich, enhance the impression of a Puritan community in Cornwall with national connections.[72]

Hannibal Gamon, son of a London goldsmith, was born in about 1582 and, like FitzGeffry, was educated at Broadgates. He was presented to the living of Mawgan-in-Pyder by Elizabeth Peter, on the assignment of the Catholic recusant, Sir John Arundell of Lanherne, who owned the advowson. The identity of Elizabeth Peter is uncertain, but she may have been Elizabeth, wife of the radical Puritan Hugh Peter (who was born in Fowey, the son of Martha née Treffry of Place, Fowey, and later Fairfax's chaplain). Gamon clearly had connections with the Peter family, since in his will of 1650 he made bequests to his 'daughters-in-law' Grace and Ann Peter, daughters of Thomas Peter, Puritan vicar of Mylor (in Kerrier hundred) and brother of Hugh. In 1631 Hugh Peter dedicated a pamphlet entitled *Digitus Dei or Good News From Holland* to his nephew by marriage, John Treffry Esq, and his own great-nephew by marriage, John Trefusis Esq, and 'to all that have shot arrows agaynst Babels Brats, and wish well to Sion wheresoever', which adds to the picture of Fowey as a centre of Puritanism.[73]

Gamon also became associated with the Robartes family and dedicated Lady Frances Robartes' funeral sermon to her eldest son, John, later Lord Robartes. In the dedication he counselled the twenty-year-old heir to the Robartes fortune:

Abandon then I beseech you in the name of Christ, all iniquitie, yea abominate the sweetest sin, to which your youthfull affections are most endeared, else you will never be able to encline and enlarge them to the pursuit and practise of so excellent and Glorious a Grace as the Feare of the Lord.[74]

Gamon and John Robartes became close friends, and Gamon was later

Robartes' chaplain and established an extensive library of Puritan tracts at Lanhydrock.[75]

In August 1628 Gamon preached at the Launceston assizes, probably at the invitation of the sheriff, Jonathan Rashleigh. The sermon, entitled *God's Smiting to Amendment, or Revengement. With Preservatives against Revolting*, was later published and dedicated to Rashleigh and 'the vertuous Gentlewoman his wife'. The dedication was full of Puritan phraseology:

> For the end of God's electing, calling, justifying, and correcting mercy is this, that we should be holy . . . [and] . . . it is motive enough unto me for the edition of this Sermon preached in your Shrievalty, that herein I honour none, but the true convert with the title of a true beleever, and good proficient in God's schoole of affliction.

The sermon itself took the form of a full-bodied attack on 'popery', reciting various offences committed against the state by Catholics, including the Spanish Armada and the Gunpowder Plot.[76]

Other sermons and dedications contribute to the picture of a Puritan fraternity in Cornwall and beyond. John Fathers, vicar of St Stephens by Saltash from 1629, was patronized first by Sir Richard Buller and then by his son Francis, to whom he dedicated a sermon in 'publick acknowledgement of what I owe unto your Family, for my first induction into a Pastoral charge'.[77] In 1638 one Roger Bickton reported Fathers to Laud for 'many offences punishable by the Justice of the high commission court'.[78] Apparently Fathers had stated that he would confess if questioned, although this would result in his certain dismissal. The articles listing Fathers' particular offences are missing, and the outcome of the case is unknown, apart from Laud's reply that the case should be pursued in the Court of High Commission. However, Fathers evidently retained his position, since in 1641 he took the protestation oath as vicar of St Stephens by Saltash, and in the same year wrote, in that capacity, to Sir Richard Buller regarding the arrival of the new minister of Saltash.[79] Fathers went on to support the parliamentarian cause, and in 1648 dedicated a printed sermon entitled *The Strife of Brethren and a Treaty for Peace* to Thomas Lord Fairfax.[80] However, in that year he was ejected from his living, and in another sermon, *The Accompt of a Ministers Removall*, gave some indication of the reason for his ejection (probably his Presbyterianism):

> In the beginning of this Parliament wee admired to see how England was turned Arminian, and how neere it was got of a sudden unto Rome, wee have now more cause to wonder, how Rome is come into England, and how England

is turned Libertine, Pelagian, Socinian, Antinomian, Antiscriptarian; yea it hath had so many turnings, as that turning unto Christ by repentance and humiliation, is now turned out of doores . . . we know not whether the tyranny of Bishops, or treachery of seducers, have done London, England, most hurt: for the one kept from us the power of godlinesse, the other hath beguiled us even of the forme of it.[81]

Through marriages and friendships the Bullers were at the hub of a Puritan network in east Cornwall and beyond. They entertained godly family and friends at Shillingham and visited them in their homes. The Buller papers contain letters of thanks for 'courteous entertainment' from (amongst others) Richard Moyle of Bake, Thomasine Calmady (née Buller) and Sir William Courtenay of Saltash.[82] Further, in 1619 Sir Richard Buller received this invitation from Sir Anthony Rous:

I should fynde myselfe much beholdinge unto you & yor Lady yf you booth would do me the favor to dyne att Halton tomorrowe: wher I do assure you boothe of my hartie wellcome. And you shall fynde ther Sir Rycharde Roberts & his Lady whom I fynde very willinge of yor companye.[83]

Sir Richard Buller's marriage in 1601 with Alice, daughter of Sir Rowland Hayward, alderman and lord mayor of London, extended the Bullers' network. On 28 September 1632 John Hayward implored his brother-in-law, Buller, to visit and support him during an impending case in the Court of High Commission:

Since your going, I have beene very much troubled in ye High-Commission Court, by my Lo[rd] of Canterbury. I doe finde both my Lo[rd] himselfe, and his man Mr Baker, to bee made very strongly against mee: by what meanes, I doubt not but you may guesse. Other busines there is a course of Law and Courts of Justice for: but as for that Court,—I dare write nothing of it, least my letter should mis-carie.[84]

Hayward reinforced the point by writing again on 1 October, and telling Buller, 'on [your company] I doe esteeme the issue of all my businesses cheifly to depend'. Buller agreed to leave for London, even at the neglect of his own affairs.[85] The Bullers also forged an alliance with the staunchly Puritan Honnywoods of Elmstead, Kent. Sir Richard Buller's sister, Margaret, took as her second husband (and became the second wife of) Sir Thomas Honnywood. Sir Thomas' first wife had been renowned for her godliness, and had held private days of humiliation. Links between the two families were further strengthened in 1625 when Sir Richard's heir, Francis, married Thomasine, Sir Thomas Honnywood's daughter.[86]

A close relationship existed between the Bullers and the Wise family of Mount Wise (Plymouth) and Sydenham, Devon, who lived across the Tamar and shared a Puritan outlook. Richard Connock's bequests to Sir Richard Buller and Sir Thomas Wise have already been noted. Buller and Wise were first cousins: Sir Thomas' mother, Mary, was a sister to Sir Richard's father, Francis. Sir Thomas Wise sat in the Long Parliament with Sir Richard Buller and his two sons, and seems to have been guided by them politically.[87] Buller and Wise sent their respective heirs, Francis and Thomas, to the Puritan Cambridge college, Sidney Sussex (Wise matriculated in 1619 and Buller in the following year), and a deep friendship developed.[88] Thomas Wise referred to Francis Buller in correspondence and in his will as 'my best friend', and Buller became guardian of Wise's children after his death in 1641. Wise's widow married twice more: first to John Harris of Radford (Devon) and Lanrest (Cornwall), and second to Jonathan Rashleigh, both of whom Wise had mentioned in his will as friends.[89] Wise also mentioned in his will as friends the Puritan Rolle brothers, sons of Robert Rolle of Heanton Satchville, near Okehampton, Devon. Samuel Rolle, the eldest, was Wise's brother-in-law, and had major interests in Callington.[90]

The Rolles, a zealously Puritan family who followed an austere lifestyle, had further connections with Cornish Puritan families. In 1621 Grace, daughter of Robert Rolle and sister of Samuel, became the second wife of Sir Richard Carew. Ten years later Grace's sister Joan married Sir Richard's son and heir (from his first marriage), Sir Alexander Carew. Margaret Rolle, another sister, married Hugh Boscawen Esq in 1622. Their son and heir, also Hugh, married Margaret, daughter and coheir of the prominent Lincolnshire Puritan and parliamentarian, Theophilus (Clinton), 4th Earl of Lincoln. Hugh's first cousin, Robert (son of Sir Samuel Rolle and Margaret Wise), married Arabella, another daughter and coheir of the Earl of Lincoln.[91]

The Church of England and the Impact of Anti-Calvinism

William Cotton, Bishop of Exeter from 1598 until his death in 1621, began his episcopate in controversial and reformist mood. In 1600 he issued a statement on 'Common disorders in the Diocese of Exeter'. He reported 'a dangerous increase of Papists about the coast and country', and a profusion of 'Profane Atheists'. At Launceston, for example, a horse's head had been brought to church for baptism, and afterwards the bell had been tolled for the death of the head. Cotton also complained of abusive behaviour towards ministers, and of the increase of schism ('Few or none come to Church to pray to God for her Majesty . . . but they will follow rattle headed preachers from town to town'). Disorderly behaviour, such as bigamy, incest and grave-robbing, was also rife. Cotton therefore requested the assistance of an ecclesiastical commission, 'for my diocese . . . is so far from London, and as large as almost any in England', and characterized by 'intolerable wildness and wickedness'.[92]

Cotton clearly intended to appear resolute in the suppression of papists and Puritans, and acquired a reputation as an ardent opponent of Puritans in particular.[93] In 1606 Cotton made the exaggerated claim that

> I had reformed by the help of that Commission many factious preachers, and reclaimed many Papists. Within these 10 days I have brought 8 or 9 recusants to the Church; and within one year I hope to clear my diocese of that Popish faction, as I have done of the peevish.[94]

However, although the Commission (which sat from 1602 to 1609) alarmed Puritans, who tried to have it revoked, it made little real impact on either nonconformity or Catholicism, and dealt mainly with such issues as marital deviations.[95]

Further, during the 1604–5 subscription crisis Cotton was conciliatory towards Puritans.[96] He organized a conference with leading Puritans in the diocese, and devoted much time over the next year to encouraging acceptance of the Thirty Nine Articles by those 'who privately dissented from the present state and government of the Church'. As a result of Cotton's efforts, about seventy moderate Puritan clergymen eventually subscribed, and the Bishop was obliged to deprive only four radical Puritans of their livings, and to suspend another three.[97]

Cotton's family circumstances also suggest some tolerance (at least) of Puritanism. His wife, Mary, had godly inclinations, and was perceived by Puritans in the diocese as an intermediary between themselves and her husband. Mary's brother-in-law was Jaspar Swift, a Marian exile, whose son, also Jaspar, Cotton appointed to the archdeaconry of Cornwall in 1616 (although he resigned later that year).[98] Further, Cotton's son, also William, married Elizabeth, daughter of John Hender of Botreaux Castle, Minster, Cornwall. Hender's religious disposition is unknown. His will showed no signs of Puritanism, but his other daughter, Frances, married Richard Robartes and was the great Puritan matriarch described by Gamon in her funeral sermon of 1626. Hender's will (made and proved in 1611) named 'the Right Reverend father in God William Lord Bishopp of Exon' and John Robartes as overseers, while William Cotton junior and Richard Robartes were named executors.[99]

There was much personal animosity between Cotton and Matthew

Sutcliffe, dean of Exeter, not least because the latter had expected to be nominated to the see. Sutcliffe lost favour with James I (whose policy was one of peace, moderation, and unity in Church and State) by his strong and active opposition to Catholicism, and his encouragement of Puritan projects for the colonization of Virginia and New England. Sutcliffe clearly had connections with Cornish Puritans, since in 1620 Sir Anthony Rous named him an overseer of his will, and bequeathed him 50s in gold to make a ring 'in remembrance of mine affection'. In 1621 Sutcliffe was imprisoned for a short time for speaking openly against the Spanish marriage project.[100]

Valentine Carey was appointed to the see of Exeter in 1621 through the combined influence of his cousin, Lord Hunsdon, and the (then) Marquis of Buckingham. It is likely that Carey owed Buckingham's patronage to their shared anti-Calvinist views. Carey had been appointed a Fellow of St John's College, Cambridge, in 1599.[101] The college had an anti-Calvinist bias and produced some of the first English Arminians. According to Nicholas Tyacke, 'The best-known of these . . . was Valentine Carey, future Bishop of Exeter'. In 1620 the Arminian Lord Maynard (of St John's) referred to Carey 'and the rest of our good friends of St John's'. Further, in 1625, while Carey was Bishop of Exeter, he was described by the Arminian Richard Montagu as 'doctrinally sound' and 'one of the firmest against our [Puritan] faction'.[102]

While accompanying James I on his expedition to Scotland in 1617, Carey was forced to rescind his commendation of a deceased person's soul to the mercies of God. However, Carey continued to believe in the necessity of such commendations, and in the importance of confession to a priest. He advocated ritualism, and described the surplice as 'the armour of light'. He perceived his mission as Bishop of Exeter to be the enhancement of the clergy's status, and he sought to undermine the exclusive Puritan community which he perceived as frustrating this aim.[103] As shown above, Carey responded resolutely to Bevill Grenvile's criticisms of the vicar of Fowey and the town's request for a lecturer, by sending 'Orders to be observed by Mr Basill vicar of Fowy concerninge the readinge of divine service, preachinge and catechisinge in his parish church made 22 May, 1625'.[104]

Evidence from churchwardens' accounts suggests that Carey's anti-Calvinism may have had some effect upon Cornish churches by 1625. In that year at St Neot the King's arms were painted and framed, the ten commandments and the degrees of marriage were painted and placed on the church wall, one table of scripture was written in the middle chancel, and others on the higher side of the roodloft.[105] Further, anti-Calvinists placed great emphasis on the major Christian festivals and feast days,

59

especially Christmas, Easter and Whitsun, and favoured the more frequent celebration of communion, ideally once a month. Liskeard churchwardens' accounts reveal a trend towards holding more communions each year from 1625, with a corresponding increase in expenditure. Between 1615 and 1624 annual communion expenditure there was between £3 and £4, and communion was celebrated generally on Whit Sunday, Christmas Day and Easter Day, and occasionally on All Saints Day. The number increased between 1625 and 1632, with annual expenditure rising from £5 to £9.[106] Poughill increased its communions from three to four per year from 1625, introducing celebrations at Whitsun and All Saints Day, which had not featured previously.[107]

However, Carey's overall impact on Cornwall was very limited, and he seems to have had no effect upon the strength of Puritanism. This was largely because Carey was even more remote from Cornwall than other Bishops of Exeter. He resided in London and attended Court regularly, making only annual visits to his see, each autumn. He died after only five years in office, on 10 June 1626.[108]

Joseph Hall, a Calvinist, was appointed to the bishopric of Exeter in 1627 at a time when the King was filling most important sees with anti-Calvinists. Hall was one of only three evangelical Calvinists nominated to bishoprics after 1625, and his appointment owed much to the influence of the Earl of Pembroke.[109] Buckingham fiercely opposed Hall's nomination, but was in France (besieging the Isle de Rhé) at the time it was announced, and his letters opposing it arrived too late to prevent confirmation of the appointment.[110]

Hall had been appointed chaplain to Henry, Prince of Wales, in 1607, attended James I on his visit to Scotland in 1617, and in 1619 was selected as a delegate to the Synod of Dort (which discussed and condemned Arminianism) because of his Calvinist views. He continued to stand by the Calvinist doctrine propounded at the Synod, and later declared that he would

> live and die in the suffrage of that reverend synod, and do confidently avow that those other opposed opinions cannot stand with the doctrine of the Church of England.[111]

Hall regretted that within a few years of his return from the Synod, the Church of England had begun 'to sicken of the same disease which we had endeavoured to cure in our neighbours', and he consistently attacked Arminianism and advocated Calvinist principles, both from the pulpit and in his writings.[112]

In a dedication to the diocese of Exeter, soon after his appointment,

Hall declared his determination to protect his people from 'sins of practice' and 'errors of doctrine':

> Against both these I have faithfully vowed my utmost endeavours. I shall labour against the first, by preaching, example, censures . . . Against the latter, my pen hath risen up in this early assault.[113]

In the Jacobean tradition of the bishop as a 'preaching pastor' Hall preached regularly at different churches in his diocese.[114] He maintained that all religious questions could be solved by consulting the Thirty Nine Articles, and advised members of his diocese to 'leave all curious disquisitions to the schools'.[115] Hall enforced discipline in the diocese through his court of audience, where he censured immoral clergy and laity for drunkenness, brawling and other 'scandalous' behaviour, but he never greatly persecuted Puritans.[116]

Hall adopted a Jacobean-style policy of conciliation towards Puritans. He made unity and conformity amongst the clergy of Exeter diocese a priority, and later enforced as few Laudian measures as possible. During his first three years at Exeter, Hall's policies were firmly supported by Cotton's old adversary, Matthew Sutcliffe (still dean of the Cathedral), who was now actively anti-Arminian.[117] Hall said that upon finding

> some factious spirits very busy in that diocese I used all fair and gentle means to win them to good order, and therein so happily prevailed that saving two of that numerous clergy . . . they were all perfectly reclaimed; so as I had not one minister professedly opposite to the anciently received orders (for I was never guilty of urging any new impositions) of the church in that large diocese.[118]

Despite the moderation of his policies, Hall was initially regarded with suspicion by Puritans, who felt that he did not sufficiently condemn popery. On 6 February 1629 Hall wrote to Sir John Eliot (whom he had seen a few days earlier) requesting his support. Hugh Cholmley, Hall's chaplain and close friend, had dedicated to him a work asserting 'the true being and visibility of the Roman Church', and the Puritan pamphleteer, Henry Burton, had responded by publishing an attack on Cholmley and Hall. In this, Hall said that Burton was

> labouring to possesse the world w[i]t[h] an opinion, that I went about to helpe popery over the stile. . . therein suggesting very maliciously that Mr Cholmly, & my selfe . . . have sure some plot in hand of restoring Popery to England, or England to Popery.[119]

Hall had given Eliot a pamphlet full of his 'zealous defiances of Popery', and sought Eliot's assistance in preventing Burton's accusations becoming a parliamentary matter. Eliot responded positively, and replied that

> it was noe small part of the happiness I receav[e]d from y[ou]r hands to be presented w[i]th those lines w[hi]ch (besides the knowne character of your worth) import a vindication of y[ou]r truth against all scandall & aspersions.

He said that he had not heard the matter raised in Parliament, but if he did he would attend to it. There is no mention of Burton's accusations in the proceedings of Parliament for the rest of the 1629 session.[120]

Anti-Calvinists were also suspicious of Hall:

> for some that sat at the stern of the Church had me in great jealousy for too much favour of Puritanism . . . complaining of my too much indulgence to persons disaffected, and my too much liberty of frequent lecturings within my charge.[121]

Laud placed him under surveillance, and complaints of Hall's activities reached the Court, so that he 'was three several times upon my knee to his Majesty to answer these great criminations'. However, he remained firm in his beliefs and 'plainly told the Lord Archbishop of Canterbury, that rather than I would be obnoxious to those slanderous tongues of his misinformers that I would cast up my rochet'.[122] Indeed, Hall was vindicated in Laud's annual reports to the King on the state of the diocese. In 1634 the Archbishop was forced to admit that

> For Exeter, where, according to many complaints that had been made here above, I might have expected many things out of order; I must do my lord the bishop this right, that for your majesty's instructions, they have been carefully observed.[123]

Laud's reports on the diocese of Exeter for 1635–39 were similarly complimentary to Hall.

During the 1630s Hall laid greater emphasis upon the restoration of church fabric, an element of Laudian policy on which Calvinists and anti-Calvinists could agree, than upon the relocation of altars. The altar policy was central to Laudianism, but hated by many. In his 1636 survey of the churches in his diocese Hall encouraged improvements in the condition of church buildings, flooring and seating, but made little comment on the position of communion tables.[124] This emphasis is reflected in Cornish churchwardens' accounts. Three sets of accounts survive which cover the whole period: Camborne in Penwith hundred, and Liskeard and St Neot, both in the hundred of West. In Liskeard average annual expenditure on church fabric increased three-fold in the 1630s as compared with the 1620s (from around £8 to about £25), and in Camborne and St Neot it approximately doubled over the same period (£3 to £8 and £3.10s. to about £6.5s. respectively). For Poughill parish church in Stratton hundred the accounts for the crucial years 1631–37 are missing, but in 1638 expenditure on church fabric was noticeably higher than in 1630.[125]

The Laudian altar campaign placed great emphasis upon cathedrals setting the example for parish churches. Hall never enforced the altar policy rigorously, and the communion table in Exeter Cathedral was placed altarwise relatively late, possibly in response to Laud's metropolitical instruction of 1634.[126] Sir Reginald Mohun had already, however, in 1629, provided a new carved oak communion table for Boconnoc church, which was situated in the grounds of his house. In 1634 he gave to the church of Lanteglos-by-Fowey a similar table, with a rail, inscribed 'The gift of Baronet Mohun to the Parishe, 1634'. The Mohuns had formerly lived in this parish at Hall, which they still owned. It is possible that the Mohuns were amongst the few anti-Calvinists in Cornwall, although their earlier sycophancy to Buckingham and the King suggests that they may have perceived compliance with the Laudian altar policy as a means of winning (or retaining) favour at Court.[127]

In 1636 seats were removed from the chancel at St Neot and repositioned at the lower end of the church at a cost of 5s.3d., although there is no record of a rail being erected.[128] Further, it appears that at Poughill the chancel was cleared and the communion table repositioned in 1639–40. The 1640 accounts record the payment of 2d. to John Pope for 'making cleane of the chanchell', and the provision of bread and drink for help in 'setting up of the benches about the chancell'. However, since these benches were presumably to seat communicants, they would not have received at a rail.[129]

Liskeard acquired a new communion table in 1636 with two new forms to 'set about' it, bringing the number of forms 'in the chancel for the communicants at the communion table' to sixteen. In the same year a chancel door was purchased, and the churchwardens repaired the cover of the silver communion cup, and had a new 'globe' put on top. An abnormally large quantity of matting was also bought for communion purposes in 1636, 1638 and 1640. This activity followed the appointment of a new vicar, Peter Cowling, in February 1635. However, the purchase of many new seats for the church and chancel in 1638–40, including those for 'ye south syde Alley of ye Chancell' and 'the seate wherein Mr Vinsent sitts in ye Chancell lecturor', together with the forms for communicants, suggests that although a new emphasis may have been given to the sacrament from 1636, the chancel was not cleared completely and no rail was erected.[130] Nicholas Lower of Clifton, in Landulph parish, donated an elaborate silver gilt chalice to his parish church in 1631, possibly reflecting anti-Calvinist sympathies.[131] Further, Tywardreath obtained two flagons in 1637; and Lesnewth and Kilkhampton parish churches each acquired a new chalice and paten in 1638.[132] However, there is no indication of the communion table being repositioned nor of any associated activity in Camborne, St Breock (accounts from 1637) or Padstow (accounts from 1638).

The increase in expenditure on communions in Liskeard from 1625 has already been noted. There appears to have been a further impetus in the 1630s, since from 1633 the figure increased steadily, rising to £11 in 1636, and reaching £14 in 1640, with communion being celebrated additionally on Palm Sunday, Sheeve Thursday (Maundy Thursday), Easter Eve, and on various other dates throughout the year. In addition, in 1637 communion for the sick in their homes was recorded for the first time, and was further mentioned in 1638 and 1639. Together with the repair of the chalice and expenditure on items associated with communion, this new emphasis on the sacrament adds to the impression of Laudian influence in Liskeard.[134]

Evidence from other churches is less conclusive, however. Before 1630 between four and seven communions were celebrated annually in Camborne. Little regard was shown to the major Christian festivals, Easter Day being the only feast celebrated regularly. In the 1630s the number of communions reduced, but a pattern was established of celebrating communion four times a year at the major festivals: Christmas, Easter, Whit Sunday or Trinity Sunday, and All Saints Day.[135] At St Neot throughout the period there were four communions annually on the major feast days, and communion expenditure remained constant at £2 to £4.[136] It is difficult to be certain about expenditure patterns for Poughill, but the figures for 1638–40 are in the same range (£1–£2) as in the 1620s.[137] In Padstow (where accounts exist only from 1638) communion was celebrated monthly, but the only major feast to be celebrated regularly was Easter, and Christmas was not celebrated at all.[138]

Cornish clergymen appear to have conformed in the wearing of vestments throughout the reigns of James I and Charles I. All churches with extant accounts possessed at least one pair of surplices throughout the period. It seems that in all cases they were worn, since annual stipends were paid for washing them, although not all parishes were assiduous in repairing or renewing them. Liskeard and St Neot renewed and repaired

Plate 5. Chalice presented by Sir Nicholas Lower to Landulph parish church, 1631

their ministers' and clerks' surplices fairly regularly. Liskeard, for example, bought a new one for the clerk in 1622, and a new pair (presumably for the vicar) in 1625. They were repaired in 1626, 1631, 1632 and 1633, and another pair was made for the new vicar, Mr Cowling, in 1638–39. Poughill, however, may well have been responding to Laudian pressures when it paid £1.3s.9d. in 1637–38 for a new pair of surplices and for mending the old. The previous ones had been made in 1626 and there is no record of their repair.[139]

Camborne may also have been encouraged to improve its church linen in the 1630s. The churchwardens paid £1.3s.6d. for 10 yards of holland cloth to make new surplices in 1633 and for mending old ones (apparently over twenty years old and mended only once). A similar amount was paid in 1638 for another pair. Further, in 1637 the pulpit cloth was mended, and in the following year was lined with 4 yards of lace and embroidered with silk thread. Similarly, lace was sewn onto the old pulpit cloth in Liskeard in 1631, and in 1637 the churchwardens of St Breock paid £4.11s.4d. for a new one and a bag for its storage. In 1639 they bought a cushion for the vicar to kneel on in the pulpit.[140]

Anti-Calvinists emphasized the importance of the annual perambulation of boundaries, traditionally at Rogationtide (around Ascension Day). Boundaries were particularly important because they affected levels of tithes and church rates, which Laud was determined should be paid to the church rather than to patrons of livings. The parishioners of Liskeard perambulated annually on 'Ascension Eve' throughout the reigns of James I and Charles I, and were provided with 'bread and drink' and the children with apples. In St Neot the parish bounds were viewed, significantly, in 1637 and 1638 only, on which occasions bread and beer were provided. Camborne did not respond to this Laudian policy and the parishioners did not view the boundaries at all in the 1620s or 1630s.[141]

Perhaps the most noticeable effect of Laudian policies in Cornwall was in the decoration of some churches, as had happened at St Neot in 1625. In Liskeard in 1634 a painter was paid for drawing the King's arms and for writing sentences of scripture on the church wall, and further work was undertaken in the chancel in 1637. Two years later a sentence of scripture was inscribed on the south side of the church, and the table of marriages was purchased.[142] At Poughill in 1638 the King's arms were painted and erected in a timber frame, sentences of scripture were painted in the church, the ten commandments were renewed on the church wall, and the pulpit was 'coloured'. The King's arms at Feock church also are dated 1638.[143] However, Puritans may not have objected to these measures, since even the church of St Stephens by Saltash, with its Puritan rector, John Fathers, and his Puritan patron, Sir Richard Buller, paid a painter £10 in 1639 for writing the sentences of scripture, the King's arms and the ten commandments by the font.[144]

Anti-Calvinists also advocated increased expenditure on church music, but there is little evidence of it in Cornish churches. There was a fifteenth-century organ in St Ives parish church, which was removed and destroyed in 1648. Padstow also possessed an organ and spent several shillings annually on its maintenance. There are no Padstow accounts before 1638 so it is not known when the organ was acquired, although it had been dismantled by 1651 when the organ pipes were listed in the church goods. Ralph Michell, vicar of Padstow from 1633, was one of the first to be sequestered in Cornwall, and 'suffered as much as possible'. His church was quickly brought into line, and the 1646 churchwardens' accounts record 'carryeing ye common praier Books to Truroe' and the purchase of the Directory of Public Worship (the only surviving example of this in Cornwall).[145]

Hall refrained from enforcing the reading of the 1633 Declaration of Sports (a re-issue of James I's Declaration, seen as contradictory both of traditional Sunday observance and of Calvinist teaching) and never denounced any clergyman for refusing to read it. The St Neot and Liskeard accounts record the purchase of the Book of Sports in 1634, but this is no proof that it was read in either church, and there is no mention of it in any other set of accounts.[146]

Laud advocated closer control over lectureships and preaching, and in particular the replacement of Sunday afternoon sermons with catechizing. However, with Hall's support local lectures continued and thrived in parts of Cornwall, Penzance being a notable example.[147] Hall declared himself

ever ready to encourage those whom I found conscionably forward and painful in their places, and willingly giving way to orthodox and peaceable lectures in several parts of my diocese.[148]

Throughout this period, in addition to their own lecturer, Mr Vincent, the churchwardens of Liskeard regularly paid outside preachers for giving a sermon, several of which took place 'on a sabbath day' and 'on Whitsunday in the afternoon'. This picture is reflected in the borough's mayors' accounts, where disbursements were made regularly to named individuals 'who preached here'. Of identifiable preachers, most were from neighbouring parishes, such as Duloe, St Martin-by-Looe, St Pinnock, Braddock, St Neot and St Wenn. The sermon bell was rung regularly at Liskeard on sermon Saturdays, and in 1637 the churchwardens paid £10.10s.2d. for a new pulpit.[149] The sermon bell was also rung frequently at Padstow, and Camborne also paid outside preachers.[150]

Plate. 6 (see also facing page). The 1636 pulpit, Liskeard parish church

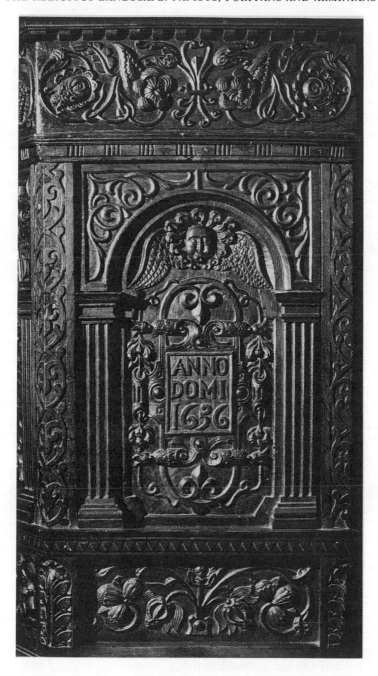

Hall inherited as archdeacon of Cornwall William Parker, a popular incumbent since 1616, who was remembered by a number of the Cornish gentry in their wills. John Hender Esq (to whom Bishop Cotton was overseer) bequeathed to Parker 40*s*. in gold to make a ring. In 1622 Nicholas Sprey Gent of Bodmin bequeathed 'To my worshipful & long acquainted friend Mr William Parker Archdeacon of Cornwall a gilt silver bowl for a remembrance, whose Love and assistance (general to all) I desire to my posterity'. Sprey also named Parker as one of the overseers of his will.[151]

Hall's chaplain, Martin Nansogg, (who had attached himself to Hall when his bishopric seemed certain) coveted the archdeaconry of Cornwall. Nansogg also claimed Buckingham's support in this ambition, so Hall promised him the archdeaconry upon Parker's death. However, Nansogg grew tired of waiting for the office to become vacant, and tried to force the issue by claiming that the archdeaconry was already vacant because Parker had made 'a private resignation . . . to another man; though never legally published or exhibited'. Hall was uncertain about this, but Nansogg persisted, claiming that financial compensation would 'win him [Parker] to be content with the act'. Hall succumbed, but Parker's allies in the chapter advised the Bishop of the invalidity and nullity of Nansogg's appointment, and they refused to install him.[152]

Hall then received reports of 'certain foul miscarriages of Mr Nansogg's tongue' against him and his family. When these claims were substantiated Hall declared 'that I would henceforth take off my hand from him, and be a stranger to him'. Nansogg responded by writing (in Hall's words) 'the most insolent letter that I think hath been written by a chaplain to his pretended lord', upon receipt of which Hall revoked the grant of the archdeaconry of Cornwall to Nansogg.[153]

Nevertheless, Hall successfully maintained a general unity amongst his clergy until spring 1640, when a split occurred over the canons, and particularly the sixth canon, or *Et Cetera* Oath, passed by the convocation of clergy after the dissolution of the Short Parliament, and by which all clergymen were obliged never to 'consent to alter the government of this church by archbishops, bishops, deans and archdeacons et cetera, as it stands now established and as by right it ought to stand'. Since the canons were intended to reinforce Laudian innovations in worship, and all the clergy present at the convocation were obliged to take the *Et Cetera* Oath, the position of the Calvinist bishops was seriously undermined. Bishop Hall claimed never to have administered the Oath to the clergy of his diocese, but admitted that 'the happy sense of that general unanimity and loving correspondence of my clergy' had nevertheless been broken.[154]

There can be little doubt that Hall's stand against the infiltration of anti-Calvinism into the Church of England was greatly weakened by the canons. He considered church government by bishops to be of paramount importance, and in 1639 had published a treatise entitled *Episcopacy By Divine Right, Asserted*, dedicated to Charles I, and lamenting recent attacks upon episcopacy. Further, early in 1641, Hall made a speech in the House of Lords in defence of the canons, emphasizing the need for authority in the Church, and the suppression of popery and separatism; and in May of the same year he spoke in support of the secular power of bishops.[155]

Despite the survival of only three full sets of accounts, the impression given is that Cornish churches did experience the effects of anti-Calvinism, although to varying degrees. Differences between the churchwardens' accounts for Liskeard and St Neot compared with those for Camborne suggest that the impact of anti-Calvinism was more pronounced in the east than in the west, although a firm conclusion is difficult to ascertain. Nevertheless, evidence from the accounts and other sources suggests that in Cornwall, as in Warwickshire, the impact of anti-Calvinism was 'muted'. In both counties this was at least partly due to the protection of a moderate bishop, Hall of Exeter and Thornborough of Worcester.[156] Hall's moderate policies, combined with the distance of the county from Exeter, and, perhaps more significantly, from London, shielded the county and slowed the pace of change considerably. Indeed, the overwhelming impression is one of creeping Laudianism, softened by a moderate and conciliatory bishop, against a backdrop of passive Puritan resistance. There is no indication that Puritanism was suppressed in Cornwall during the 1630s. The Puritans' acute awareness of dangers from the centre was heightened by events such as John Fathers' clash with Laud, and by contacts with Puritans like the Haywards from outside the county. Godly organization remained strong and vibrant, so that in 1640 Puritans were in a position to seize new opportunities for political and religious reform.

3

The Political Landscape: Harmony and Faction 1600–1638

Early Harmony

In Cornwall the first two decades of the seventeenth century were characterized by relative political harmony. Political activity did not engender conflict or faction at a local level. As elsewhere, county elections were uncontested, and where there was competition for the two prestigious county seats, an arrangement was reached between rival candidates before the election.[1] Borough elections were generally determined by the influence of gentry patrons and various Court interests. The most powerful Court patrons in the opening decade were Robert Cecil, who was created 1st Earl of Salisbury in 1603, and William, 3rd Earl of Pembroke, lord warden of the stannaries. Of the two Salisbury was dominant. In October 1601 Jonathan Trelawny of Trelawne presented Cecil with two burgess-ships, probably those for East and West Looe, and in November 1605 Edward Coswarth also offered Salisbury the disposal of a burgess-ship. In December 1609 John Hender Esq of Botreaux Castle in Minster parish sent Salisbury a blank indenture for the new vacancy at Bossiney.[2] Salisbury died in 1612, but Pembroke benefited little from this. Two years previously much of the lord warden's political power in the duchy had been usurped by the newly formed Prince's Council, which included members of the Prince of Wales' household and the Prince's solicitor-, attorney- and receiver-general, but which excluded the lord warden. The Prince's Council was disbanded on Prince Henry's death in November 1612, but was revived upon Prince Charles' assumption of the dukedom of Cornwall in 1616, and became very active in exercising electoral influence in Cornish boroughs.[3]

The elections for the Addled Parliament of 1614 saw duchy officials, Crown office-holders and courtiers returned in twenty Cornish boroughs. For example, Sir Robert Naunton (secretary of state) was elected at

Camelford and Sir Henry Vane (cofferer to the Prince of Wales) at Lostwithiel. Local duchy officials were also returned, such as Sir Francis Vyvyan, governor of St Mawes castle (elected for St Mawes) and Richard Connock, duchy auditor (returned by Bodmin and Liskeard, and sat for Liskeard). However, since these elections took place during the inter-regnum of the Prince's Council it is likely that most of these men were returned through the influence of the Crown or local gentry patrons rather than that of the duchy.[4]

By 1620 the Prince's Council had established firm control over the duchy's electoral patronage. On 1 December the Council sent instructions to the duchy havenor, William Roscarrock, and the feodary, Richard Billings, regarding the proposed return of thirteen nominees for Cornish boroughs at the forthcoming election. They were warned: 'See you perform this service with all care for his highness expects not to be disappointed'.[5] Only four of the nominees were returned for the specified boroughs: Sir John Walter, the Prince's attorney-general, by East Looe; Sir Robert Cary, an officer of the Prince's household, at Grampound; Newport returned Sir Edward Barrett; and Launceston Thomas Bond, who had local connections. A further six of the nominees were returned by Cornish boroughs other than those specified, while Bossiney additionally elected the duchy auditor, Thomas Gewen (a Cornishman) who had not been nominated.[6] So, the concentration of the duchy's political patronage in the Prince's Council had resulted in considerable success: the Prince now controlled eleven Cornish seats, a quarter of the county's total representation.

In 1620 John Arundell Esq of Trerice went to great lengths to secure a county seat. He placed Richard Carew Esq (his nephew) and John St Aubyn Esq of Clowance (his brother-in-law) at his family borough of Mitchell, and came to an arrangement about the county seats with Bevill Grenvile Esq, apparently allowing the more experienced Grenvile to have the senior knight's place. Arundell then sent Nicholas Burton 'to sounde howe Will Currington [Coryton] woulde stande towards him'. Coryton had already decided to stand, and had

bespoken manye voyces for himselfe; but finding his cosen Arrundell to have the same designe he woulde set downe, and throwe all his voyces upon his sayd kinsman: J[ohn] A[rundell] that woulde not be behinde in courtesie, the next day made him the like offer, which he refused and theye both agreed that JA showld stand.

Coryton told Arundell that he would 'possess his freindes that himselfe [Arundell] intendeth to stande, and by that meanes be suar to howlde them'.[7]

After this arrangement was reached, Sir Reginald Mohun informed Arundell of his own intention to stand for the county, and asked for Arundell's 'voyces and assistance'. Arundell exploited the arrangement with Coryton to block Mohun's aspirations, by professing that he would willingly step down and assist Mohun if it were not for his own obligations towards Grenvile and Coryton. Arundell had, however, been assured by Sir Reginald that if John Mohun, his son and heir, stood for the county, he (Sir Reginald) would support Arundell against him.[8]

At the next election, in 1624, Coryton was returned as senior knight of the shire, probably on a reciprocal basis, with Bevill Grenvile as his partner. Coryton's position as Pembroke's vice-warden of the stannaries may also have assisted his election, since in the same year Pembroke began to reassert his political influence in Cornwall, and to develop his patronage network there and elsewhere.

On 1 January 1624 the Prince's Council again wrote to William Roscarrock with a list of thirteen nominations for the same Cornish boroughs as in 1620. Five nominees were elected by the named boroughs.[9] A further two nominees were returned, although not for the specified boroughs, and Sir Francis Cottington (secretary to the Prince of Wales), who had not been nominated for a Cornish borough, was returned for Camelford in place of the nominated Sir John Suckling (comptroller of the household).[10] With likely support from the duchy auditors, Thomas Gewen (Bossiney) and William Hockmore (St Mawes), the Prince's Council controlled a maximum of ten Cornish seats.[11]

Five boroughs (West Looe, St Ives, Camelford, Newport and Grampound) did not elect any duchy nominees. West Looe elected Pembroke's client, George Mynne, together with Sir James Bagg of Saltram, near Plymouth. Bagg, vice-admiral of south Cornwall, was a client of the King's favourite, the Duke of Buckingham, lord high admiral of England, and it is likely that Bagg's election was due to the influence of Sir Bernard Grenvile, who lived at neighbouring Killigarth in Talland parish.[12] Newport chose Sir John Eliot of Port Eliot in St Germans, also patronized by Buckingham, and Grampound returned two local men, Sir Richard Edgcumbe of Mount Edgcumbe and John Mohun Esq, both supporters, if not clients, of Buckingham.[13] Further, John Coke, commissioner for the navy and Buckingham's candidate, was returned at St Germans through the influence of Valentine Carey, the Arminian Bishop of Exeter (Coke's brother-in-law), with Eliot's assistance. Pembroke's client, Sir John Stradling, was returned for the other St Germans seat.[14] Hence,

Plate 7. William Coryton Esq of West Newton Ferrers: his effigy on the monument commemorating him and his wife, St Mellion parish church, 1651

although the electoral influence of the Prince's Council remained strong in 1624, it was challenged by the rival influences of Pembroke and Buckingham.

Pembroke's political activity had previously been determined by his equal hatred of the Duke of Buckingham and of Spain. When Prince Charles and Buckingham returned from the Spanish marriage negotiations in October 1623 advocating war with that country, Pembroke's initial reaction was to support the Spanish match so as to undermine Buckingham. However, in January 1624 the Privy Council engineered a 'reconciliation' between Pembroke and Buckingham: from this point the two rivals maintained a fragile truce, and Pembroke actively supported Buckingham's war policy.[15] Coryton followed Pembroke's lead in the 1624 Parliament, and on 1 and 2 March advocated a speedy breach of the treaties for the Spanish marriage and the opening of hostilities. He wanted 'the great business expedited', and favoured an early conference with the House of Lords to discuss the matter.[16]

Sir John Eliot, MP for Newport in 1624, owed his knighthood (of 1618) and his position as vice-admiral of Devon (1619) to Buckingham's patronage. In addition, he owed his recent freedom to Buckingham. In November 1623 Eliot had been imprisoned in the Marshalsea for his part (as vice-admiral of Devon) in the case of the pirate, Nutt.[17] Eliot requested Buckingham's assistance in securing his liberty, and on 23 December the Duke proposed to the Privy Council that Eliot should be released. In a letter of 28 February 1624 Eliot made a clear statement of his gratitude and loyalty to his patron (even allowing for linguistic and stylistic excesses):

> as I am devoted whollie unto your service, I shall ever covett that which maie be most for your advantage, and for myselfe retaine noe other ambition than the honor of the imploiment and your lordship's favor . . . This expression I have made of my desires to shew how fullie I am your creature, and that your word in all things maie dispose me.[18]

Eliot gave Buckingham his full support in the coming Parliament. On 1 March, in the debate on the breach of the Spanish treaties, Eliot introduced the notion that it was imperative for England to attack Spain so as to pre-empt an invasion, and urged the speedy departure of a fleet.[19]

On 12 April 1625, less than a month before that year's county election, John Arundell of Trerice wrote to Sir Richard Carnsew, expressing interest in standing as knight of the shire, and requesting

> the continuance of an ancient custom of yours, I mean for your helps and assistance of voices when occasion shall require in the choice of the knights

76

of the shire, hoping I shall find you the same man and the same friend. Wherein I desire your best furtherance, both for myself and my friend, especially for the public good which I prefer before mine own.[20]

Arundell was not elected, but his 'friend', Charles Trevanion, was returned. Arundell's reference to the 'public good' suggests that he and Trevanion may have been standing as anti-Buckingham candidates. Further, it is possible that Arundell's earlier dealings with Coryton had drawn him into Pembroke's circle, and that he and Trevanion were Pembroke clients. Instead of Arundell, however, Trevanion's partner was Sir Robert Killigrew, governor of Pendennis castle, and Buckingham's client.[21]

Buckingham's was the dominant interest in the Cornish borough elections of 1625. Killigrew placed another Buckingham client, Sir Edwin Sandys, at the Killigrew family borough of Penryn after Sandys failed to win a county seat in Kent.[22] Further, Buckingham wrote personally to the officials of Mitchell on behalf of Sandys' son, Henry, who was duly returned by the borough.[23] Sir Richard Weston, chancellor of the exchequer and a supporter of the Duke, was returned by Callington, and Weston himself influenced the return of Sir Francis Cottington at Bossiney.[24] Sir Henry Vane, Buckingham's client, was doubly returned for Lostwithiel and Carlisle, but chose to sit for Carlisle.[25] However, Sir Reginald Mohun, one of the Duke's Cornish supporters, was returned and sat for Lostwithiel, and Mohun's son, John, was elected for the family borough of Grampound. Edward Thomas, an employee of John Mohun, was returned for West Looe on Mohun's influence.[26] Sir John Eliot was again returned for Newport, Sir James Bagg was chosen by East Looe, and Sir John Coke was again elected at St Germans. Pembroke's interest was apparently little represented, although William Coryton was returned for Liskeard, and Sir James Fullerton was elected for St Mawes.

On 1 April 1625 Sir John Eliot professed to Buckingham that he was 'wholie devoted to the contemplation of your excellence'.[27] Eliot supported Buckingham throughout the 1625 Parliament, although his confidence in his patron's integrity was severely shaken by events at the end of the first session. On 8 July, although Parliament had already voted the King two subsidies, Sir John Coke (as Buckingham's agent) proposed a motion for additional supply to pay for the Cadiz fleet. This was unprecedented. At the request of Sir Humphrey May, who perceived Eliot to be 'a gentleman whom he thought more powerful with the Duke and knew to be affectionate to the public', Eliot intervened and spent two hours trying to dissuade Buckingham from requesting further subsidies.[28]

Eliot employed a range of arguments, including the fear such a request would arouse in the country; the potential damage to the King's honour (particularly since so few MPs remained in London due to the plague); and Buckingham's own safety. However, the Duke insisted that those subsidies already granted were given out of affection to the King, whereas the new subsidies were needed for the King's business. Further, the absence of MPs was their own responsibility, and 'their neglect must not prejudice the state'. Finally, the King's honour depended upon the success of the fleet; this would be impossible unless the fleet departed soon. Eliot retorted that it was unlikely that Parliament would vote further supply, and if it did the King would suffer a yet greater loss:

> alienation of the affections of the subjects who, being pleased, were a fountain of supply without which these streams would soon dry up.[29]

Buckingham was adamant that the motion for supply must proceed, regardless that success might be unlikely: it was to be 'lodged . . . merely to be denied'.[30] From this Eliot concluded that Buckingham was engineering a confrontation between the King and the Commons and seeking to undermine the system of parliamentary taxation. This forced Eliot to reconsider his position regarding his patron:

> It gave that gentleman [Eliot] some wonder with astonishment who, with the seal of privacy, closed up those passages in silence, yet therein grounded his observations for the future that no respect of persons made him desert his country.[31]

Despite his new concern about the Duke's motives, Eliot twice spoke in Buckingham's defence on 6 August, during the Oxford session.[32] He urged MPs not to place all blame for naval maladministration upon the Duke as lord high admiral, but rather to consider the shortcomings of the navy commissioners in preparation of the Cadiz fleet:

> But it dare my conscience clear and vindicate that noble Lord who has had some aspersions laid upon him and that if there has been any abuse in the fleet, it is not his fault; for there is a commission for the furnishing of this navy which is no new thing . . . And therefore the commissioners, if any, faulty.[33]

The Emergence of Factions

Sir James Bagg had been trying to undermine Eliot's relationship with Buckingham so as to usurp Eliot's position as Buckingham's chief agent in the west for some months. Buckingham appointed Bagg as prestmaster and victualler for the Cadiz fleet, which was assembling at Plymouth. On 18 April 1625 Bagg reported that 'Sir John Elliot is displeased hee was not soly imployed [as prestmaster] and therefore could not be invited to assist'.[34] Buckingham's preference of Bagg in this office almost certainly would have offended Eliot, particularly since Plymouth was in his own vice-admiralty. However, it was insufficient to cause a breach between Eliot and the Duke: Eliot's actions during the 1625 Parliament clearly demonstrate that the patron-client relationship remained intact.

It seems likely that Eliot's trust in his patron was undermined more by Buckingham's attitude towards Parliament at the end of the first session than by his appointment of Bagg. This did not have an immediate effect since Eliot defended the Duke in the Oxford session in August, and at Christmas he entertained Secretary Conway's son at Port Eliot, Conway being a Buckingham client.[35] However, by the opening of the new Parliament on 6 February 1626 Eliot had transferred his allegiance to Pembroke, who had turned against the Duke again since the 1625 Parliament. The impression of Eliot spending the autumn and winter of 1625–26 considering his position is supported by Bagg's report to Buckingham of March 1626 that Eliot had been 'in a distraccon howe to devide himself, betweene yor Grace and the Earle of Pembrooke, But to whom he hath wholy given himself yor lordshipp can Iudge'.[36]

Pembroke's renewed opposition to Buckingham prompted him to exert his full influence in the 1626 elections. In his March letter Bagg described to Buckingham how Pembroke had exploited his power as lord warden of the stannaries to place some of his clients in Cornish parliamentary seats, and had instructed Coryton (as vice-warden) to obtain places on his behalf. Coryton, who was himself returned for the county, had placed Sir Robert Mansell at Lostwithiel, Sir Francis Stuart at Liskeard, William Murray at Fowey, and Sir Clipsby Crew at Callington. Pembroke had also placed other clients in non-Cornish boroughs where he had influence: for example, Dr Samuel Turner at Shaftesbury and Sir James Fullerton at Portsmouth. Other Pembroke clients named by Bagg included John Thoroughgood and Michael Oldsworth (the Earl's two secretaries), Sir Benjamin Rudyard, Sir Thomas Lake, Sir Dudley Digges, Sir Maurice Abbott, and Sir Walter Erle. Bagg asserted that the Duke should 'knowe the instruments yor enymye' so that he could 'iudge whether the principalls be yor freinds'.[37]

Bagg reserved particular vitriol for his rival, Sir John Eliot, now a client of Pembroke. He claimed that Eliot 'can neither paye yow yor dues, or deserve yor past favours'. More damagingly, Bagg suggested Eliot's involvement in an anti-government plot:

his carriage as much tende to the depravinge of the present government &
crossinge his most sacred Ma[jes]ties princely and iust demands, comannds &
desires, as yor lo[rdshi]pps Ruine.

Significantly, in March 1626 Bagg used the words 'faction' and 'party'
for the first time to describe Pembroke's clients. This suggests that
they had become more organized and united, and were working together
as a team with specific aims. Further, Bagg's description showed that this
was not simply a local faction based in one county, but a national 'party'
with national aims. Bagg's letter placed Cornishmen who supported this
'party', and Cornish boroughs which were used by it, in a national
context.[38]

Fewer Cornish boroughs returned Buckingham clients in 1626 than in
the previous year, although the Duke's influence in the county remained
strong. Sir James Bagg was again returned for East Looe, Sir Reginald
Mohun for Lostwithiel, and John Mohun's agent, Edward Thomas, by the
Mohun borough of Grampound. Sir Edwin Sandys was again elected by
Penryn, and Sir Richard Weston by Bodmin, both through Sir Robert
Killigrew's influence. Killigrew himself was returned at Tregony.

The Parliament of 1626 was characterized by its insistence upon the
redress of grievances (meaning the removal of Buckingham) before voting
supply. The new threat of war with France, for which Buckingham was
held responsible, united the Duke's opponents, and the attack was led by
the Earls of Arundel and Pembroke and their respective clients. Three of
Pembroke's clients—Eliot, Coryton and Walter Long—launched the
offensive by highlighting the effects of Buckingham's seizure of the
French ship, the *St Peter*.[39] These three also joined with Dr Turner
(another Pembroke client) in putting the question whether it was good
that all decisions rested with the Duke's 'single counsel', meaning that a
more effective Privy Council would reduce the Duke's power. On 11
March Dr Turner raised six queries which widened the attack on
Buckingham and set the agenda for the House of Commons proceedings
against the Duke. Four days later Coryton defended Turner when the
King ordered an investigation into his conduct.[40]

The attack on Buckingham gathered momentum on 18 April when Eliot
proclaimed that 'the whole kingdom suffers under the too great power of
[one] man', and Sir Dudley Digges (who had also transferred allegiance
from Buckingham to Pembroke since 1625) proposed that the Commons
should lay aside all other business until the question of the Duke had
been resolved.[41] Six days later Coryton named the principal cause of the
grievances:

We must upon necessity lay the fault upon some body. Upon the King we cannot, seeing his care and great wisdom; upon the Council we cannot, but on no body but the Lord Admiral.[42]

When the charges against Buckingham were being drafted, Coryton defended his fellow Cornishman, Lord Robartes, who was accused of purchasing an honour from the Duke. Coryton maintained that 'Lord Robartes refused to pay any money'. Consequently the ninth article of impeachment against Buckingham charged him with forcing Lord Robartes to buy his peerage for £10,000.[43] On 8 and 10 May the Commons presented their charges against Buckingham to the Lords. Digges delivered a preamble to the charges, and Eliot concluded the presentation with a summing up speech.[44] Eliot marvelled that Buckingham had continued in high office for so long, and significantly attributed this to his construction of a 'party':

> To that end, therefore . . . he made a party. He made a party in the court, a party in the country, a party in almost all the places of government, both foreign and at home.[45]

The following day the King imprisoned Eliot and Digges for their speeches to the Lords concerning Buckingham's impeachment, and particularly for the charge that the Duke had been responsible for James I's death—which implicated Charles also.[46] Coryton spoke in defence of both, and on 17 May (with Digges released) proposed 'that we may go on to clear Sir John Eliot for as much as we know'. The following day Eliot's close friend, Bevill Grenvile, MP for Launceston, wrote to his (Grenvile's) wife:

> I hope S[i]r Jo: Eliot shall be there too . . . though the King hath lately sent him to the tower, for some wordes spoken in the Parl[ia]m[en]t. But we are all resolved to have him out againe, or will proceed in noe business.[47]

As Grenvile anticipated, parliamentary pressure forced the King to release Eliot on 20 May. On that day Grenvile joyfully reported to his wife, 'we have Sir Jo: Eliot at liberty againe; the house was never quiet, till the King released him'.[48]

Charles dissolved Parliament on 15 June 1626. Buckingham then launched a nationwide purge against his leading opponents, and rewarded his friends. From July, the Duke ensured his own dominance in Cornwall by suppressing Pembroke's power as lord lieutenant and lord warden of the stannaries. This was achieved by Pembroke's promotion to lord steward and the offer of a marriage contract between Pembroke's heir (aged seven) and Buckingham's daughter (aged three).[49] Members of Pembroke's faction were treated less leniently. Eliot and Coryton, the two Cornishmen involved in the impeachment attempt, were both removed from the commission of the peace.[50] In October Eliot also lost the vice-admiralty of Devon, while Coryton was deprived of his deputy lieutenancy and lost the vice-wardenship of the stannaries to John Mohun of Boconnoc.[51]

Charles and Buckingham wasted no time in pursuing and punishing Eliot, whom they perceived as one of their most dangerous enemies.[52] On 1 July 1626 the 'commissioners for the Duke's estate' drafted a memorandum proposing the appointment of an admiralty commission to investigate Eliot's conduct as vice-admiral of Devon. The memorandum proposed that the commission should be staffed by 'gent[leme]n of worth, spirit, and integrity in the country who are well affected to my lord'. Those recommended were Sir James Bagg, Sir Bernard Grenvile of Killigarth and John Mohun, together with Devonians Sir George Chudleigh, Sir William Strode, Sir William Poole, John Drake Esq of Ashe and Mr Kiste.[53]

Grenvile and Mohun were close allies of Bagg, and, like him, courted Buckingham's favour. In return for their support, Bagg promoted both (and particularly Mohun) with Buckingham, while simultaneously plotting Eliot's and Coryton's downfall. On 22 September 1626, when writing to the Duke about collection of the benevolence in Cornwall, Bagg proclaimed that 'Grenvile: Mohun: and some other of my freinds, have exprest their harty affeccon and Loyalty to his Ma[jes]tie'. He thanked Buckingham for pressing Pembroke to replace Coryton with Mohun as vice-warden of the stannaries, and urged the Duke to persevere in this cause, since Mohun was 'able and willing to do your service'. Bagg further urged Buckingham to act quickly to deprive Eliot of his vice-admiralty, 'for in my poore opinion I hold it convenient yor grace should in all thinges express yor dislicke of yt ungratefull villien Elliott'. A month later, the Privy Council, before examining the evidence, ordered Eliot's removal from the vice-admiralty, and Buckingham rewarded his supporters by dividing the office between Bagg and Sir John Drake.[54] It is clear from Bagg's letter that by September 1626 Bagg, Grenvile and Mohun shared common goals. They also shared common enemies—Eliot and Coryton. Further, Bagg's reference to other 'friends' suggests the evolution of a faction.

Less than a month later, when suggesting 'loyal' collectors for the forced loan, Bagg again recommended to Buckingham's 'most especiall favour':

My noble freind Mr John Mohun who studies nothinge more then to honor yow, and to advantage his Ma[jes]t[ie]s commands; And as his will is resolved w[i]thout changing to doe both, soe is his power not short to p[er]forme it w[hi]ch can be no waye more strengthened, then by yor Grace his directinge the chiefe care of his Ma[jes]t[ie]s affaires in that county [Cornwall] to his hands & managinge, whose wisedome I am a pawne for.

Bagg again thanked the Duke for advising Pembroke to appoint Mohun as his new vice-warden ('w[hi]ch I presume his L[ordshi]pp hath done'), and reminded Buckingham of Mohun's desire for 'an Englishe honor'.[55]

Although Eliot and Coryton had been removed from their offices by October 1626, they retained a strong presence in local politics. In April 1627 Bagg complained to Buckingham (concerning the forced loan) that in Cornwall 'in generall all Lend, savinge Elliot, Corrington, Arondell and their associates and faction'.[56] Here, for the first time, Bagg firmly associated John Arundell of Trerice with Eliot and Coryton, and referred to their 'faction'. This tends to suggest that Eliot and Coryton had responded to the suppression of Pembroke's influence, their own loss of office, and the political ascendancy of Bagg, Grenvile, Mohun, and their 'friends' by assembling, or formalizing, their own 'faction'.

Eliot and Coryton had worked together (and against Buckingham) since February 1626. Both had suffered personal humiliation and loss of power and prestige as a direct result of Buckingham's purge. Arundell's political association with Coryton dated back to their electoral arrangement of 1620.[57] Further, Arundell's concern for 'the public good' in 1625 when requesting the county seats for himself and 'his friend' Charles Trevanion, hints at an anti-Buckingham stance. These pre-existing political associations, together with shared opposition to Buckingham (at least from February 1626), provided the basis for factional development and action. It is clear from Bagg's account that in 1627 this faction focused its political activity on forced loan refusal.[58] This suggests that for Eliot, Coryton and Arundell at least, loan refusal was not solely or perhaps even primarily ideological, but also provided a platform for political opposition to Buckingham.

For Coryton particularly, loan refusal was an expression of bitterness about his removal from office. In his *Relation* of his appearance before the Privy Council in April 1627, Coryton stressed that his refusal was based upon the unlawfulness of the loan. However, his true feelings are apparent from numerous references to the conduct of 'good and honest' local governors, and to his own exemplary behaviour while in office. He claimed that he had, in several offices, 'with as much payne, and industrye served the kinge, as any man of my qualletye within the kingdome'.[59]

On 27 June 1627 Buckingham revealed the names of other Cornish loan refusers who were, by implication, members of the Eliot–Coryton faction. The list was headed by Sir Richard Buller, Ambrose Manaton Esq of Trecarrel, and Nicholas Trefusis Esq of Landue in Lezant parish (all from the hundred of East). Other refusers were Humphrey Nicoll Esq of Penvose in St Tudy (John Pym's brother-in-law), Francis Courtney of Lanivet, and John Scory Gent, all allegedly 'men of yll affecktions'.[60]

Buller, a Puritan, was undoubtedly a member of the Eliot–Coryton faction, but denied that he had refused the loan.[61] Manaton, another Puritan, was described by Buckingham as 'a meere creature of Corringtons'. Trefusis was Coryton's nephew, and (according to Buckingham) said that 'he will doe as Elliott, Buller and Currington doth'. Further, when questioned by Sir Bernard Grenvile and Sir William Wrey (both assiduous collectors), Trefusis had answered that 'he would doe as Mr Bevill Greenfeild and Mr Nicolls did'. From this Bagg had concluded that Trefusis was 'not guided so much by an perticuler reason to himself, but by the example of others'.[62] If these reports are accurate, for some factional loyalty may have been an even stronger motive for loan refusal than hatred of the Duke.

Despite protestations of innocence, Buller was summoned before the Privy Council, removed from the commission of the peace and ousted from his deputy lieutenancy.[63] Trefusis also appeared before the Council, and he and Manaton too were removed from the commission of the peace. Buckingham ordered that the removals be performed 'before the assises, that so the people may obsearve there disgrace'.[64] Nicoll, Courtney and Scory were also summoned before the Council. This, proclaimed Bagg, would make 'those westerne people' aware that it was not only Eliot and Coryton who would 'lye by the heeles for my Lords sake'.[65]

One refuser who, curiously, was neither summoned nor punished was Bevill Grenvile. He was the son and heir of Sir Bernard, a supporter of Bagg, but was himself a close friend of Eliot. He was on poor terms with his father, but may have escaped punishment as a favour to Sir Bernard; he was also not a JP. His letter of 23 August to Eliot and Coryton during their imprisonment, referring to 'the honest knot', demonstrates collective political feeling. The letter also shows that by this stage the forced loan had become such an important and divisive issue that an element of martyrdom had entered into refusal:

I canot but out of the fullness of my griefe be verrie Passionate at your long suffering, from which there hath not wanted the prayers of many good men to redeeme you, but whence it growes that I am thus long left at home, when now of late also more of the honest knot are fetch'd away, drives me into wonder and amazement, no man hath with more bouldness declar'd his resolution in this perticular then my selfe, which nor fire nor torture can divert me from, while in myn owne heart I am satisfied that it belonges unto the duty of an honest Englishman so to do . . . I present my service to you and my co[usin] Trefusis . . . Pray remember my service and love to my co[usin] Nicoll.[66]

Bagg did not perceive Cornish loan refusers to be isolated. He suspected a conspiracy between the Eliot–Coryton faction and the Puritan Earl of Warwick, who was also a refuser. In April 1627 Warwick was in Plymouth preparing to lead his own fleet against Spain, and Bagg's suspicions were aroused by Warwick's fraternization with Eliot and his associates:

The Earl is lodging in the house of one Jennings, Eliot's friend; & as soon as he put foot ashore, his invited familiars were, that pattern of ingratitude, Eliot, malicious Corrington, & a man no less true to his friend, Sir Ferdinando Gorges . . . you may discearne the lord of Warwicks wayes, w[hi]ch breed muche wonder in those parts; that he elects & invites those to be his friends.[67]

On 23 May 1627, after Eliot and Coryton had been summoned to London for their forced loan refusal, Bagg tried to implicate them further by claiming that they and Sir Ferdinando Gorges had been the only men to visit and give service to Warwick, 'who little loves your Grace'.[68]

Once Eliot was imprisoned for loan refusal the inquiry into his conduct as vice-admiral of Devon was resumed. In September 1627 William Davyle, solicitor to the admiralty, reported that despite the inactivity of certain commissioners, 'S[i]r Barnard Greenfeild, Sir James Bagge, and Mr Mohun are as forward in ytt, as anye freind my lord hath'.[69] In November the same three lost no time in expressing their joy at Buckingham's safe return from La Rochelle. Bagg wrote on behalf of them all to welcome the Duke home, and described Grenvile and Mohun as two gentlemen who would lay down their lives and fortunes at the Duke's feet, but claimed that Mohun would best serve the Duke 'in a lordlike way'.[70]

In a letter to Buckingham dated 20 December 1627, Bagg introduced new language and added a new dimension to the factional dispute. Bagg's letter concerned Eliot's petition to the King from the Gatehouse, in which Eliot justified his forced loan refusal in historical, legal and constitutional terms. Bagg claimed that although the petition was addressed to the King, it was really directed at a much wider audience:

I mett this petition wanderinge (amongst the subiects) directed to (or rather against) my soveraigne; . . . I held it dangerous to roame upp & downe among

the (many headed) people, in these times made discontented by him [Eliot],
and his complices . . . least such a petition (not the transcript but the originall)
marchinge under the colours of humilitye & allegiance, rekindle that fire of
discontent & murmure, in those unquiett spiritts which were of his [Eliot's]
opinion.[71]

Since Eliot's petition was an attack upon the forced loan, it would have
been aimed at those gentlemen and freeholders who qualified for payment.
On this basis, Richard Cust has argued that Bagg's definition of the 'many
headed people' went far beyond normal contemporary understanding of
the term, and included respectable freeholders and yeoman farmers, thus
indicating that Bagg feared involvement in politics by anyone of below
gentry status. Dr Cust further believes that Bagg shared the King's and
Buckingham's abhorrence of 'popular' participation in politics, and their
belief that a balanced political system and social hierarchy depended upon
the full exercise of royal authority and the royal prerogative.[72]

Bagg was certainly echoing the views of Buckingham and the King.
What is uncertain is whether these were Bagg's own views, or whether he
simply adopted the 'popularity' issue to win favour at Court. Bagg had
already shown himself to be both sycophantic and corrupt; he was prepared
to go to almost any length in his quest for personal power and wealth.[73]
Dr Cust himself has described Bagg as 'spectacularly obsequious . . .
the worst type of corrupt, court-backed local tyrant', who supplied
Buckingham with 'a constant stream of malicious, and often false, gossip'
to discredit his enemies.[74] With this background, Bagg's motives in
espousing fashionable Court ideology must be open to question. Bagg
knew that, as a result of Eliot's behaviour in the 1626 Parliament, the
King perceived Eliot to be a potential leader of the 'ill affected' and of
the 'multitude' in a conspiracy to undermine the monarchy.[75] Thus, by
accusing Eliot and his 'complices' of arousing 'discontent' among 'unquiet
spirits' against a loan demanded by the Crown, Bagg would have been
aware that he would inflame the King's fears of plots and conspiracies and
confirm his worst suspicions about Eliot. Further, by employing language
used at Court, Bagg gave his message extra clarity and authority. So,
through manipulative use of language and by exploiting the King's fears
of 'popularity', Bagg simultaneously undermined Eliot and enhanced his
own position.

The 'popularity' issue was raised again in March 1628, during the
election for Cornish knights of the shire. For the first time the county
election was contested, reflecting the increasingly entrenched factional
divisions amongst the gentry. John Mohun Esq and Sir Richard Edgcumbe
stood as Buckingham's candidates, and Eliot and Coryton stood against

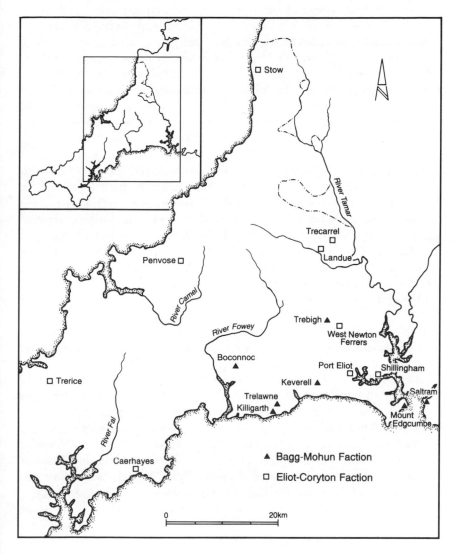

Map 3. Distribution of Cornish Factions, c. 1627

them. Each faction rallied its supporters. Those most active for Eliot and Coryton were John Arundell, Bevill Grenvile and Charles Trevanion. The political association of these five gentlemen was not new. Bagg had linked Arundell with Eliot and Coryton in April 1627 (although Arundell's connections with Coryton dated back much further); Grenvile was a close

87

friend of Eliot and had allied with the Eliot–Coryton faction in forced loan refusal; and Trevanion had been proposed for a county seat by Arundell in 1625.[76] The list of signatories on Eliot's and Coryton's election indenture was headed by Arundell, Grenvile and Trevanion, with Humphrey Nicoll (John Pym's brother-in-law) who had acted with this faction in loan refusal. Other signatories included a number of Puritans who were connected with members of the faction: William Rous Esq of Halton in St Dominick (Nicoll's nephew, John Pym's step-nephew and Lord Robartes' son-in-law), Thomas St Aubyn of Helston (whose brother, John, was Arundell's brother-in-law), Richard Carew (Arundell's nephew), and John Moyle Esq of Bake in St Germans (Eliot's neighbour).[77]

Bagg named seven gentlemen who were active for Mohun and Edgcumbe. These were Sir Reginald Mohun, Sir Bernard Grenvile, Sir William Wrey of Trebigh in St Ive, John Trelawny Esq of Trelawne (John Mohun's brother-in-law and Sir Reginald Mohun's son-in-law), Edward Trelawny Esq of Bake (John's younger brother), Walter Langdon Esq of Keverell near Looe, and Richard Trevanion Esq of Gorran.[78] All were forced loan commissioners, and it is likely that they had proved the most active in collection and the most loyal to the Crown.[79]

Eliot and Coryton had no Court influence to assist their campaign, and the normal channels of communication with many of the county gentry were blocked by the factional divide. Coryton, the first to seek election as shire knight, sought support for his candidature from members of the Bagg faction, probably in an act of provocation. On 8 February, at a meeting in Liskeard, Coryton asked Sir Reginald Mohun, Sir Bernard Grenvile, and Sir William Wrey for their voices. He told them that he had suffered for his country, but that he knew of nothing which might render him unworthy of a knight's place. They refused to support him, as he had no doubt anticipated.[80] Bevill Grenvile canvassed the most influential voters in the county by letter, but the Eliot–Coryton faction now focused its activity upon winning wider support. They turned to ordinary 40-shilling freeholders, whom the Bagg faction labelled 'the vulgar'.[81] In their appeal, Eliot and Coryton emphasized their recent sufferings for their country, especially loss of office and imprisonment for forced loan refusal.[82] Coryton also distributed his 'ticket' to remind freeholders of the election, and to require their attendance and voices:

> These are to give you notice that the day for the election of our shire knights is at Lostwythiell on Mondaye the tenth of March by eight of the clocke in the morninge, that the freeholders ought to be there to give there voyces, those that have forty shillings yerely of inheritance . . .[83]

Coryton tried to get the 'ticket' read in all parish churches, which would have guaranteed maximum publicity throughout the county, and would have added authority to Coryton's candidature.[84]

In their campaign the Bagg faction wrote to Eliot and Coryton, urging them to withdraw their candidature in the interests of the county. They told Coryton that the King would look unfavourably upon a county which elected those who had incurred the King's disapproval:

> Now how gracious you and Sir John Eliot are, you know, and how many ways his Majesty hath expressed his displeasure against you. And His Majesty will conceive your election to be an affront to his service; and so we shall draw the displeasure of the King upon us.[85]

The Bagg group also threatened Coryton, and said that if he refused to withdraw they would oppose him 'by all possible means'. They wrote to Jonathan Rashleigh and to other gentlemen, and to various freeholders, warning of the dangers of voting for such 'unquiet spirits' as these. They advised all gentlemen and freeholders to take care to elect men of 'moderation and gravity'.[86]

Grenvile, Arundell and Trevanion arrived at the election, each with five hundred men 'at their heels'. Bagg complained to Buckingham that by this conduct, and by lodging the supporters in towns together, Grenvile, Arundell and Trevanion had created an unlawful assembly. Further, they had prevented a free election, since 'by theire so comming together [they] through feare doe constraine or exclude those that Indifferentlie thought to give their Voices to the Election'.[87] Bagg seized upon this behaviour to remind the Duke of the dangers implicit in Eliot's and Coryton's election:

> their country carr[i]age must breed a beleefe in you that yf they returne w[i]th power, they will act as they have had longe intention.[88]

Members of the Bagg faction insisted that they had not attended the election, although they admitted, as deputy lieutenants, that they had summoned the trained bands to appear on their behalf.[89] However, it was reported that the deputies were acting upon the instructions of the lord lieutenant, Pembroke, who had ordered them 'to call the colonels, captains, and the trained bands, all armed, to be present at the election'. If this report were accurate, Pembroke was acting directly against his former clients' interests, perhaps to prove to Buckingham that he had distanced himself from them.[90] However, regardless of military intervention, four or five thousand at the election gave their voices for Eliot and Coryton, who were duly returned: 'their pretence of suffering for their country had stolen away the hearts of the people' claimed their opponents.[91]

On 20 March, two days after Parliament met, letters written by the Bagg faction during the campaign were read in the Commons at Coryton's request. A committee was appointed to consider the faction's electoral behaviour, and the nine ringleaders were summoned to appear before the House. Eliot, Sir Edward Coke and Sir Robert Phelips spoke in favour of these proceedings, but Sir Richard Grenvile (MP for Fowey, son of Sir Bernard and younger brother of Bevill) claimed that 'those speeches proceeded from malice'. It is unclear whether Sir Richard supported the Bagg faction, or whether he was defending his father. He certainly did not share his brother's allegiance to the Eliot–Coryton faction.[92] However, the ringleaders neither appeared nor commenced the journey to London immediately. Instead they petitioned the Commons, maintaining that their intention had been to keep the election free, and 'to avoid faction amongst the gents, and a great expense to the freeholders'. They admitted 'electing' Edgcumbe and Mohun at a private meeting, and justified this by claiming that

> it is usuall in devon and Cornwall for the deputy lieutenants and iustices to assemble for easinge the countrye, and for avoydinge faction to agree which amongst them shall stand.[93]

On 12 May Eliot's friend, Sir Robert Cotton, reported from the committee for the Cornish election. The nine had been found guilty of prejudicing the free election on three counts. The first was abuse of power. They had taken it upon themselves to be governors of the county, and had held an assembly at which they had 'elected' Edgcumbe and Mohun. They had also employed the King's posts to carry their letters against Eliot and Coryton. The second count was spreading scandal against Eliot and Coryton, accusing them of being 'unquiet spirits'. The third was menace, particularly by their threats against Coryton, and by having summoned the trained bands to appear at the election.[94] The nine were also found guilty of contempt of the House on three counts. First, they had wrongly addressed their petition 'To the Right Worshipful Mr Speaker'. Second, they had failed to appear at the time appointed by the House, and had chosen their own time to appear. Finally, their excuse for not attending immediately—that they had to stay to hang a man condemned by martial law—was considered an insult to the House.[95]

By this stage four of the named men, Walter Langdon, John and Edward Trelawny, and Sir William Wrey, had arrived in Parliament. Sir Edward

Giles, MP for Totnes, defended them on the ground that they were 'mere country gentlemen', unaware of the customs of the House. However, Sir Thomas Wentworth retorted that well they might be 'plain country gentlemen', but he was certain that 'they were set on this bad work by some more active spirit than their own'. He demanded, therefore, that they be called in and asked who had drafted the letters and the petition, and 'whether they had not other more active counsels to advise them'.[96] Accordingly the four were called to the bar of the House, one by one. Wrey and Edward Trelawny pleaded ignorance: they did not know who had drafted the letters or the petition, but had merely signed the documents. John Trelawny claimed that he too did not know who had drafted the documents, but that the scribe had been one Peter Hendon, Lord Mohun's clerk. However, Langdon revealed that the letters had been drafted by Lord Mohun, John Trelawny (Mohun's brother-in-law) and himself. Langdon further confessed to drafting the petition, but claimed that the incorrect address was the result of 'mere ignorance', since he had never been a 'Parliament man'.[97]

The following day the four apologized to the House for their behaviour and contempt, and MPs debated the appropriate punishment. There was a general sense that, in Secretary Coke's words, they did not have the 'principal doer' there.[98] Mr Sherwill reminded MPs that 'this business was not alone carried by these gentlemen, but Sir James Bagg [now MP for Plympton] had a hand in it'. However, Bagg's loyalty to his faction did not extend to risking his own person, and he promptly declared that he was ready to sign any charge against the Cornishmen. Sir Edward Giles blamed Mohun, now elevated to the Lords: 'The special offender is not here. These are but underlings, and did all but by directions; wherefore no further punishment'. Nonetheless, the House resolved that the four men should be punished in proportion to their guilt. Langdon and John Trelawny, 'the active men', were sent to the Tower at the pleasure of the House, whereas Wrey and Edward Trelawny were committed to the custody of the sergeant-at-arms. It was further resolved that all should be forced to acknowledge their offences at the next assizes, to make an example of them in their own county. This additional punishment appears to have been a direct attack upon Buckingham, Bagg and Mohun and their divisive factional rule: 'these men in the country are great men and wise men. Let us teach them their duty to their country, and not to depend on others, or be led by great men.' However, it is surprising that despite his declaration, Bagg escaped punishment.[99]

The imprisoned men petitioned the King and requested his intervention, claiming that their actions had been in his service. The petition described Eliot's and Coryton's 'dangerous' use of 'popular' pressure to achieve their ends, and their incitement of 'the vulgar'. 'Wee conceaved this pretence of Mr Coriton's, of suffering for his Country to be an unworthy way, tending to the alienating of the people's hearts from our Gracious Soveraigne', they claimed. Reference was made to the King's *Declaration* at the dissolution of the 1626 Parliament, in which he had stated that 'the House was then abused by the violent passions of some few members'. Since Eliot had been one of those 'few members', the Bagg group had considered it their duty to 'advise our country gent[lemen] to beware of giving their voices for our shire knights unto men of unquiet spirits'. Further, since Eliot and Coryton had been removed from all their offices since the dissolution of the 1626 Parliament, and

> conceiving that they stood in his Ma[jes]t[y']s disfavo[u]r, because he did not hold them worthy to beare any office under him: wee did not thinke fitt to chuse these men for our shire knights, fearing wee might draw our whole county into the disaffeccon of his Ma[jes]tie.[100]

Cust has highlighted this petition to demonstrate that the new Court ideology, so readily embraced by Bagg, was now being espoused by these local governors:

> Perhaps the most interesting aspect of this statement was the way in which it demonstrated that the local governors were coming to be influenced by the 'new counsels' mooted at Court. The reference to the King's *Declaration*, the concern with the threat of 'unquiet spirits' and the recognition that the demands of 'popularity' were incompatible with the demands of the Crown were just what one might have expected from the Duke's entourage.[101]

However, it is not clear how far the petitioners were convinced of the dangers of 'popularity' and how far they were following Bagg's example of using particular language to win favour at Court. They had worked closely with Bagg, in Buckingham's interest, for two years or more, so it is inconceivable that they would have been unfamiliar with the Duke's political opinions. They had also witnessed the benefits of espousing these views, since Bagg's exploitation of the 'popularity' issue had assisted their own political ascendancy over their local rivals in all but parliamentary terms. Reference to the King's 1626 *Declaration*, and to Eliot's attack on Buckingham, together with the use of emotive words such as 'popular' and 'unquiet spirits', plainly demonstrates awareness of the 'new counsels' at Court. However, more than that, it suggests a shrewd and deliberate assault upon the sensibilities of the King and the Duke. Further, it is possible that the petitioners were assisted in drafting the petition by Bagg or Mohun, both of whom were in Parliament at this time. Both had an acute insight into the prevailing Court ideology, and both were adept at exploiting it for their own purposes.

In their letter accompanying the petition, the Bagg men emphasized their own loyalty and honesty, and warned that their 'sufferings' might discourage the 'best affected subjects'. Further, they claimed that their imprisonment would cause their 'perpetual disgrace' in Cornwall (which would, by implication, weaken the Court interest there), 'unless your Majesty shall be pleased by some good way to repair us in our reputations'.[102] The King responded favourably, and on 26 June, as soon as he had prorogued Parliament, signed a warrant for their release. Langdon was knighted on 29 June, and Wrey and John Trelawny were created baronets on 30 June and 1 July respectively.[103] John Mohun had already received his reward for loyalty: he was created Baron Mohun of Okehampton on 15 April 1628 and took his seat in the House of Lords on 10 May that year.[104]

Following the election defeat, Bagg had promoted Mohun's elevation to the peerage more strongly than ever. On 17 March, for example, he had claimed that a peerage would increase Mohun's (and therefore Buckingham's) influence in Cornwall, and that Mohun would be a useful supporter for the Duke in the House of Lords. 'He is honest', said Bagg, 'and I am a Pawne for his Constancie.'[105]

Mohun's elevation was timely. The following day the Commons launched an enquiry into his conduct as vice-warden of the stannaries. On 10 April Hannibal Vyvyan Esq of Trelowarren, MP for St Mawes and comptroller of the duchy, read a petition in the Commons, first complaining of his own false imprisonment by Mohun, and then listing Mohun's other alleged abuses: 'the said Vice-Warden doth use his power to the great greife of the whole countie of Cornwall'.[106] On 16 April a committee of enquiry was appointed, with Eliot as chairman, and on 27 and 28 May Eliot reported to the House.[107] As soon as Eliot sat down, Coryton reminded the House that he had himself been vice-warden until ousted by Buckingham and replaced by Mohun in 1626. Coryton drew attention to his own exemplary conduct in the office: 'I know this court, and in my time there was no difference between the privileges of the court and the judges at law. And all these complaints here are not for the power of the court, but for the abuses of power.'[108]

Mohun was found to have committed numerous acts of imprisonment and extortion. William Mayowe, mayor of Looe, had incurred Mohun's wrath for imprisoning one Thomas FitzWilliams. Mohun had hurried to Looe with his brother-in-law, John Trelawny, and with Walter Langdon, and had summoned the mayor to appear before him. The mayor had refused, and Mohun had responded by arresting him while he was on his way to church, and then by sending him to Launceston gaol. This act provoked particular local anger since the arrests were made not by the bailiff, but by Mohun's clerk and his servants. During Mayowe's imprisonment Mohun 'stirred up' a number of other suits against the mayor, some without the consent of the persons concerned, so that when Mayowe was released, he was immediately re-arrested upon the other suits.[109]

Mohun had also increased his income by a number of extortions. For example, he had forced 'almost all men in that country to be tinners by writs of privilege', and had appropriated their fees of 3s. per writ. Many of these people had little or no connection with the stannaries, such as one Talvar, who 'only sometimes sold beer to the tinners'.[110] Mohun had also abused the power of the stannary courts to undermine the jurisdiction of other courts. One such case, of particular concern to both Eliot and Coryton, was that of Thomas Dix, 'a reverend minister and preacher'. Dix had been the incumbent of St Germans (Eliot's parish) until 1625, when he transferred to the rectory of St Mellion, under Coryton's patronage. The new rector had sued a parishioner for tithes in the Exeter consistory court; however, the man was one of Mohun's newly created tinners, and the vice-warden ordered Dix to desist, 'or you shall provoke me'.[111] Mohun had also undermined the authority of the stannary courts by assuming all their jurisdiction, rather than merely dealing with appeals.[112]

Most seriously, Mohun was alleged to have summoned the Convocation (tinners' parliament) without the necessary warrant from the lord warden, and to have nominated the stannators himself, rather than giving the mayors of the four stannary towns the customary free choice. During the Convocation Mohun had made a speech which contradicted the recent judges' resolution against the privileges of the stannaries, and he had pronounced that a curse would fall upon any stannator who failed to maintain these privileges. Further, Mohun had employed intimidation and bribery to persuade the stannators to give him £500 for the maintenance of tinners' liberties, the first time Convocation had been asked for money. Mohun had threatened that 'if any man opposed him he would make that man the mark he would aim at'.[113] Eliot was appointed chairman of the committee to draft the formal charge against Mohun, which he read to the Commons on 14 June.[114] Mohun elected to answer in the Lords, but there is no evidence that an examination took place. Indeed, it appears that Eliot and Coryton had spent much of the summer recess seeking further evidence to strengthen their case. On 8 October Mohun complained to Bagg that 'Elliott and Corriton have incessantly roamed upe and downe all Cornwall in inquisition of my Car[r]iag[e] in the vicewardens place'.

Mohun shared the view of his four colleagues in their petition to the King: he was certain that the King would protect him since all his actions had been in the King's service. Nonetheless, he considered it appropriate for Bagg to prepare the ground for him: 'If you will give his Ma[jes]tie a tast[e] of theire envy ag[ains]t me, it will prepare his eare for that w[hi]ch at my cominge upe I shall pr[e]sent him'.[115] The allegations against Mohun were again raised in Parliament on 27 January 1629, but this attack similarly proved abortive.[116]

In July 1628, during an after-dinner conversation, Sir William Courtney reported to Eliot a conversation he had held with Mohun, in which Mohun had expressed the view that

> the state could never be well ordered while ther were parliam[en]ts because in parliam[en]t every man will have his owne fancies & soe nothing can be brought into any certaynty or settlement by that course but that the committing the direction of businesses unto such select men in every county & by their moving the affaires of the County might therby better order & dispose them.[117]

Cust has presented this statement as a striking example of a local governor echoing the views of Buckingham's advisers at Court, and has linked it with Bagg's denunciation of parliaments as being what 'the vulgers cry for, thinkinge that to be the way unto their ends and their libertie, which I greive is soe muche'.[118] Cust has maintained that Bagg and Mohun shared the King's and Buckingham's perception of parliaments as a threat, since they provided opportunities for popular participation in politics.[119] Bagg and Mohun certainly perceived parliaments as a threat, but not necessarily for the same reasons as the King and the Duke. Charles and Buckingham feared that the 'popularity' of parliaments would undermine the monarchy. However, both Mohun and Bagg were unscrupulous and self-seeking, and it is more likely that they considered parliaments to be a threat to their own power in the locality.

For at least two years Mohun's aim had been to acquire complete control of Cornish government. In October 1626 Bagg had informed Buckingham of Mohun's desire for the 'chief care' of the King's affairs in Cornwall, and in May 1628 Eliot had noted in his report that Mohun had been 'ambitious of the sole government of that country'. In advocating county government by a few 'select men', Mohun undoubtedly had himself in mind. Further, Mohun's views on Parliament would have been coloured by his recent experiences: he had failed to win election to one of the influential county seats, and his victorious opponents had directed a parliamentary investigation into his conduct. The outcome of that enquiry threatened to deprive Mohun of his vice-wardenship and to undermine his local power and prestige. So, it was not fear of 'popularity' in itself which concerned Mohun, but the resultant diminution or loss of power in the locality.[120] Further, Bagg's comment to Buckingham, of October 1626, contained language and sentiments which Bagg knew would be well-received by the Duke in the aftermath of the impeachment attempt. The comment was also made at a point when Bagg's faction was in the ascendancy and its enemies suppressed: another meeting of Parliament threatened to reverse that position.[121]

Some borough elections were also decided on a factional basis in 1628. Bagg presented Buckingham with four burgess-ships: one for Plympton, Devon, which Bagg filled himself, and three for Cornish boroughs.[122] Bagg offered the Duke two blank indentures, one for 'Looe' and the other for 'Probus'. The Looe seat was almost certainly East Looe, where John Mohun's influence was strong. Buckingham's choice was probably William Murray, who was returned for East Looe on a separate indenture dated 4 March. On 8 October Mohun wrote to Bagg, who was in London for the Parliament, and asked Bagg to commend his service to Mr Murray, which would appear to confirm the connection.[123] As Probus was not a borough, Bagg presumably meant the neighbouring borough of Grampound, also controlled by the Mohuns. Bagg suggested the nomination of Mr Packer, Captain Heydon or Sir Robert Pye, and Pye was returned for Grampound on a separate indenture dated 7 March.[124]

The fourth burgess-ship was Saltash, where the Duke placed Sir Francis Cottington. This seat had been given to Bagg by the mayor of Saltash in the face of opposition from Sir Richard Buller, the town's recorder, who was returned for the other Saltash seat. After the election the mayor was punished by the Commons for electoral malpractice, and Bagg sought protection for him from Edward Nicholas (secretary to the admiralty) and Buckingham. Bagg's letter to Nicholas illustrates the deeply factional nature of the election:

> I have now written to his Grace in behalfe of the Maior of Saltash against whome there is noe fownded complainte, and the man deserves exceedinge well, is to me a frend, gave me against the opposition of Sir Richard Buller, there Recorder and divers others A Burgesship w[hi]ch S[i]r Francis Cottington hath, and tells the world he is the Dukes servant...oh I wish his charges could be borne to receave from my Lord some speciall countynance that he might glory in his Jorny [to Parliament] and not greeve.[125]

Bagg's faction had also written, unsuccessfully, to the mayor of Callington to commend John Trelawny as candidate for the town.[126] Sir

Richard Edgcumbe, defeated in the county election, was returned for Bossiney, and Mohun's agent, Edward Thomas, was elected for West Looe.

Buckingham's supporter, Sir Robert Killigrew, was returned for Bodmin, but his partner was Humphrey Nicoll, a member of the Eliot–Coryton faction. Other members of that faction elected included Bevill Grenvile (Launceston), John Arundell (Tregony), and Nicholas Trefusis of Landue (Newport). The inhabitants of Newport had first returned Eliot, who had sat for the borough in 1624 and 1625. Since he had already been elected for the county, he proposed Trefusis: 'I desired them to put it upon a neighbour of mine in the country; and he for the first place was chosen with the general consent of all'. The second place was contested between Sir William Killigrew and Piers Edgcumbe Esq of Mount Edgcumbe, and was referred to the committee of privileges, which decided in Edgcumbe's favour. He and Trefusis took their seats on 14 April.[127]

During the 1628 session Cornish MPs, like their colleagues from other counties, were preoccupied with the effects of the recent wars and with the continued presence of pirates off the English coast.[128] Coryton and Eliot were particularly active on defence issues. For example, on 28 March Coryton was appointed to the committee to investigate wrongful billeting in Surrey, and on 3 April he was named to the committee to frame a bill against impressment.[129] On 9 June Coryton complained that the coasts remained unguarded, and that thirty ships had been seized by pirates off the west coast 'since we sat here'.[130] Three days later, in the debate on the Remonstrance, Eliot complained about the lack of payment for billeting in Cornwall in particular:

> In Cornwall one part of the country is so overcharged with divers soldiers that now £6000 is owing to them. Let us move his Majesty to have some assignment out of these subsidies.[131]

Later that day Eliot, Coryton and Arundell were all named to the committee to frame a petition to the King concerning coat and conduct money and payment for billeting.[132]

Defence issues caused MPs to unite in the belief that the government had overridden fundamental liberties and had undermined the law in pursuit of its war policy. They claimed that subjects felt exposed since confidence in property rights and in the law had been shaken.[133] On 22 March Eliot stated:

> The question is of the propriety of the laws: whether there be a power in them to preserve our interests, our just possessions, our lands, our goods? . . .

97

The law makes the distinction between mine and thine . . . Where, then, is property?[134]

The issue of martial law had particularly aroused fear that the common law was to be supplanted and property rights undermined. The continuing presence of armed soldiers in the country (in readiness for an expedition to La Rochelle) deepened this concern. Many soldiers were billeted in private houses, and there was great fear that martial law would be brought in and imposed on civilians.[135] This problem affected many parishes in south-east Cornwall, neighbouring on Coryton's own, and on 22 April he highlighted concerns over the displacement of the common law:

I desire to live under a known law. The common law gives every man his due, and every offence that deserves death is punished by it. This martial law strikes to every subject. We are all soldiers to serve the King . . . Let us know under what law we live, that we may obey it.[136]

In May, the Cornish lawyer, William Noy, MP for Helston, complained of the illegality of martial law in peacetime. The Petition of Right, given royal assent on 7 June, stated that commissions of martial law were 'wholly and directly contrary to the said laws and statutes of this realm', and requested that all existing commissions be revoked and annulled, and that none be issued in the future.[137]

Eliot was beginning to perceive a connection between such attacks on liberty and the advance of anti-Calvinism:

without a change and innovation in our liberties there is no fear of an innovation in religion: and without an innovation in religion there is no fear of a change or innovation in our liberties . . . it is our laws which regulate liberty, and the safety of our liberties which secures religion.[138]

Coryton too connected defence problems with the anti-Calvinist ascendancy and regarded Buckingham as the originator of grievances in both cases:

This great Duke is the grief of the Kingdom. He is admiral of our seas, and general at the land . . . Religion and all is at hazard by his means now.[139]

Coryton was one of the leaders of the attack on Buckingham on 11 June, again associating him with both innovations in religion and recent military disasters:

For our opinion of him in Spain we cannot go less. Papists and Arminians he favours . . . Disasters all belong to him: consumption of men at the Island of Re, neglect of counsel, and our late victual intended for Rochelle transported to Dunkirk. Guarding the seas is all his. Shipping, mariners, and trade all suffer under his command. He that will free him speaks not with my conscience.[140]

Coryton resumed the attack on Buckingham on 14 June, proposing that the Commons should ask the King either to remove the Duke, or to let him stand trial.[141]

Buckingham was murdered at Portsmouth in August 1628; La Rochelle fell to Louis XIII in October, and English soldiers and sailors were disbanded by the end of November. So, by the opening of the 1629 session of Parliament, two of the major grievances of 1628 had been removed. However, since Buckingham's death the King had advanced anti-Calvinism even further, and had promoted those clerics most condemned by the Commons in 1628 for Arminian practices.[142] A group of Cornish MPs were particularly active in opposing these developments, and drew attention to the political implications of Arminianism. Headed by Francis Rous (MP for Tregony, son of Sir Anthony of Halton and step-brother of John Pym), the group included Eliot and Coryton (both of whom had attacked Arminianism in 1628), Benjamin Valentine (MP for St Germans, but not a Cornishman) and William Noy (MP for Helston). Of these, Rous, Eliot and Coryton were the principal speakers.

On 26 January, Rous opened the debate on Arminianism[143] by linking alleged violations of the Petition of Right with recent violations of religious rights:

but there is a right of an higher nature that preserves for us far greater things, eternal life, our souls, yea our God himself; a right of Religion derived to us from the King of Kings, conferred upon us by the King of this kingdom, enacted by laws in this place, streaming down to us in the blood of the martyrs, and witnessed from Heaven by miracles.[144]

He went on to identify Arminianism with 'popery' ('for an Arminian is the spawn of a Papist'), describing it as a 'Trojan horse' which would open the way for 'Romish tyranny' and 'Spanish monarchy'. Rous developed the theme which Eliot had established in 1628, describing the rise of Arminianism as an attack, not only upon religion, but also upon liberty, property rights, and the very existence of Parliament itself:

Either they think thereby to set a distaste between prince and people, or to find out some other way of supply to avoid or break Parliaments, that so they may break in upon our religion and bring in their own errors.[145]

Eliot again denounced the power of the Arminians, and of the writer Richard Montagu in particular, claiming that 'we may be in danger to have our whole Religion overthrown'.[146] Eliot believed that military problems, extra-parliamentary taxation, and the resultant attacks on liberty were intertwined with the advance of Arminianism in a 'popish plot' to impose Catholicism and absolutist government upon England. However, Eliot's anti-Arminianism was not purely political; he held strong Calvinist views, and objected to innovations in religion per se. On 29 January he complained specifically about the introduction of new ceremonies into the Church,[147] and five days later, at the committee for religion, urged the use of 'the truth' as a weapon against the Arminians:

Are there Arminians (for so they are properly called)? look to those, see to what degrees they creep. Let us observe their books and sermons, let us strike at them, and make our charge at them, and vindicate our truth that yet seems obscure; and if any justify themselves in their new opinions, let us deal with them, and then testimony will be needful; our truth is clear, our proofs will be many.[148]

On 27 January Coryton declared that 'the unity of this House is sweet, especially in God's cause', and proposed the formation of a committee for religion.[149] At the meeting of that committee on 3 February he reinforced Eliot's statement of the need to stand firm in 'the truth', which, he claimed, in the form of the Lambeth Articles and other doctrinal statements, had been suppressed.[150]

Though less vocal, Benjamin Valentine and William Noy also attacked Arminianism. On 6 February Noy spoke in support of Eliot's attack upon the Arminian dean of Durham, John Cosin, who had allegedly uttered seditious words against the King—that he was not the head of the Church. Eliot complained bitterly that the case against Cosin had been dropped by the attorney-general, and Noy agreed that it was a serious matter, and that 'Cosens wold have the Church without a head, that is he wold have us have noe Church'.[151] The following day Valentine supported Eliot's complaints against Bishop Neile, and connected anti-Calvinism with recent secular grievances:

That this Bishop hath a chaplain in Grantham, that preached they were all damned that refused the loan, and that he hath made a great combustion in placing the Communion Table there.[152]

Valentine clearly considered the forced loan and the anti-Calvinist altar campaign to be interrelated, and even part of a single plot.

The ascendancy of anti-Calvinism was considered particularly threatening in view of the King's recent attempts to find sources of revenue independent of Parliament. The major financial grievance of the 1629 session was the continued collection of tonnage and poundage, which still had not been voted by Parliament, and the continued imprisonment of merchants for their refusal to pay. On 22 January the Commons was divided about the action it should take in the case of John Rolle, younger son of Robert Rolle of Heanton Satchville, Devon, a merchant and MP for Callington. Customs officers had seized Rolle's goods for non-payment, notwithstanding his plea of parliamentary privilege. Coryton proposed the appointment of a select committee to examine Rolle's statement. Eliot disagreed, but it was resolved that a committee should be named, and Coryton was appointed to it.[153] On 10 February Coryton was named to the committee to examine why Rolle had been subpoenaed to appear before the Star Chamber, and two days later he made an important speech on tonnage and poundage:

> I conceive it is fit the merchants should have their goods before we can think of the bill. Kings ought not by the law of God thus to oppress their subjects. I know we have a good King, and this is the advice of his wicked ministers; but there is nothing that could be more dishonourable to him.[154]

MPs' antipathy towards the twin grievances of Arminianism and tonnage and poundage reached a climax on 2 March, when the King had ordered an adjournment. Holles and Valentine prevented the Speaker from ending the sitting by restraining him in his chair. Eliot stood up (at the back of the House) and threw his papers forward so that the clerk could read them if the Speaker refused his consent. In the ensuing tumult, Coryton struck a fellow MP, and the doors of the Commons were locked. Coryton urged the Speaker to put the question of reading Eliot's paper to the House.[155]

Ultimately Eliot read his declaration, which described 'how Arminianism creeps in and undermines us, and how Popery comes in upon us'. He blamed Neile, Bishop of Winchester, for favouring Arminians, accused the late Duke of Buckingham of having laid the foundations for the rise of Arminianism in England, but laid the greatest blame for the present troubles at the feet of Lord Treasurer Weston 'in whose person all evil is contracted'. Eliot maintained that Weston was the head of 'that great party the Papists', and claimed that all Jesuits and priests looked to him for protection.[156] The venom of Eliot's attack on Weston may partially have been due to Bagg's transfer of allegiance to him after Buckingham's death. Eliot followed his declaration by reading the Three Resolutions, which stated that supporters of Arminianism and those who collected or paid tonnage and poundage would be declared traitors.

Realignment and Reconciliation

The King dissolved Parliament immediately and the next day Eliot, Coryton, Valentine and the five other ringleaders were summoned before the Star Chamber.[157] Both Eliot and Coryton were committed close prisoner to the Tower. Coryton soon weakened, however, and in April petitioned the King for his freedom. Released in June, he was restored to all his former offices, including, by Pembroke, the vice-wardenship of the stannaries, during the next few months.[158] Other members of the Eliot–Coryton faction were also returned to office in 1629, presumably in an attempt to appease them and to dissolve the faction. Sir Richard Buller and Nicholas Trefusis were put back on the commission of the peace on 28 May and 19 December respectively.[159] Buller was also restored to his deputy lieutenancy. However, he was not appeased, and continued to attack the lieutenancy (which remained dominated by the Bagg faction) and to undermine militia reform.[160]

Coryton's re-appointment as vice-warden was challenged in May 1630 by the recusant, Nicholas Borlase Esq of Newlyn-in-Pyder, claiming that he himself had been acting as vice-warden, and that he had been promised confirmation of the office by Pembroke. Borlase petitioned the King, expressing disbelief that the King would have granted the office to Coryton, 'who has so often and notoriously employed his breath to graceless distaste and disservice of his Majesty'. Coryton cross-petitioned, setting out the circumstances of his appointment, and claiming that Borlase had in 'several ways misconducted himself in the execution of that office to the great discontent of the Earl'. The King decided in Coryton's favour, and Pembroke's successor, Philip, Earl of Pembroke and Montgomery, confirmed Coryton's appointment by Letters Patent dated 18 August 1630.[161]

Eliot remained in prison for nearly four years. He and Bevill Grenvile maintained their close friendship and corresponded regularly and affectionately throughout.[162] In July 1631 Eliot requested Grenvile's assistance in a lawsuit with Sir Richard Edgcumbe. The case was due to be heard

Plate 8. Sir John Eliot, painted a few days before his death in the Tower of London, 1632

at the next Launceston assizes, and, with a hint of continued factional enmity between himself and Edgcumbe, Eliot reminded Grenvile of

> the disadvantages I have, if it depend upon the judges, and what incertainties, if not more, are implied in common juries, the presence and practise of my adversarie with his sollicitous adherents and the reputations of their Justice-ships compar'd with my nothing, and that absent, it is not without reason that I seeke the assistance of y[ou]r arme to add some weight unto that number w[hi]ch must take the decision of our cause.[163]

Grenvile obliged and 'sent forth' his 'neighbours' to pack the jury on Eliot's behalf, and the case was decided in Eliot's favour.[164]

Coryton's submission to the King and desertion of Eliot caused an irreconcilable breach between the two, and between Coryton and Grenvile.[165] In January 1632, upon rumours of a new Parliament, Grenvile promised Eliot (who was still in the Tower) that he could be sure of the first knight's place, but that he would certainly not have his 'old partner'.[166] Grenvile soon became seriously worried about Eliot's health, and urged him to reconsider his position:

> I beseech you be not nice, but pursue y[ou]r libertie if it may be had on honourable termes. I will not desire you to abandon a good cause, but if a little bending may prevent a breaking yeald a little unto it, it may render you the stronger to serve y[ou]r cuntry hereafter.[167]

Eliot refused to submit and died in the Tower on 27 November 1632.

Eliot's death, together with Coryton's defection, brought about the end of the Eliot–Coryton faction. However, the connection between other members of the faction was maintained. For example, the relationship between John Arundell and Charles Trevanion was strengthened by the marriage, on 8 November 1630, of Arundell's daughter, Ann, with Trevanion's son and heir, John. Arundell's wife, Mary, sought the advice of Grace Grenvile about the suitability of the match, and Grace replied 'by Mr G's direction' with a hearty recommendation of Trevanion.[168] A year later, Grenvile comforted Arundell over the death of his mother, 'as no man can love you better than I do, so none hath a greater share in any of your griefs than I have'.[169] Further, in his will, made on 10 April 1639, shortly before his departure for Scotland, Grenvile named Arundell as a trustee.[170]

By 1632 the Bagg faction was also disintegrating. Buckingham's assassination in August 1628 had deprived the faction of its focus, although Bagg had astutely transferred his allegiance to Sir Richard Weston, the new lord treasurer, and the rising star at Court.[171] Further, Bagg and John Lord Mohun had become estranged, and at the end of 1632 Mohun accused Bagg of defrauding the King of £30,000 intended for the Rhé expedition, and of the illegal sale of the King's ordnance. Allegations of Bagg's corruption were not new. In the 1628 session of Parliament William Strode, one of Eliot's allies in the Commons, had implied that Bagg had peculated much of the £3,500 billet money, and had proposed that he be called before the House. Bagg had protested his innocence, and had told Buckingham that 'For spite of all enemies it shall be found I have loyally with affection to his Majesty's service served him'.[172]

In 1635 Bagg sued Mohun for libel in the Star Chamber, and Mohun cross-petitioned, making yet more serious allegations, charging Bagg with embezzling the £55,000 which he had received to provide victuals for the King's ships, and asserting that Bagg had supplied the fleet instead with cheap, rotten food which had 'killed four thousand of the King's Subjects'. Bagg had not even paid for the rotten food, but had run up debts in the King's name, many remaining unpaid or having been compounded by Bagg 'to the Grievance of the People'.[173] The King intervened in the case on Bagg's behalf, claiming that he did not want to see him 'unjustly traduced' for acts undertaken in royal service, and that he 'did in those times well accept of those premises so seasonably and cheerfully done unto his Majesty by his servant Sir James Bagg'.[174] The Star Chamber fined Mohun £500 'for undue inquiries into his Majesty's debts'.[175]

In the same year Bagg faced another charge in the Star Chamber. Sir Anthony Pell had spent £13,000 in the King's service, but had been unable to secure reimbursement from Bagg's patron, the lord treasurer, now 1st Earl of Portland. Bagg had suggested that Pell should bribe Portland, using himself as intermediary, and Pell had given Bagg £2,500 for that purpose. However, it soon became apparent to Pell that no progress had been made, so Pell charged Bagg with appropriating the money.[176]

When the case came before the Star Chamber Portland defended Bagg's character. He said that Bagg had been recommended to him by the King 'as one that had so well served, and so largely disbursed great Sums in his Majesty's Service'.[177] Francis Lord Cottington, chancellor of the exchequer and a supporter of Portland (to whom Bagg had given the burgess-ship of Saltash in 1628), and his allies also defended Bagg's actions. However, Archbishop Laud proclaimed 'I have now done with that bottomless bag', and he and his allies supported Pell, so that the Court was evenly divided.[178] The lord keeper's casting vote was for Pell, but for a second time the King intervened on Bagg's behalf and prevented the Court from sentencing him.[179]

By this time Bagg was becoming reconciled with Bevill Grenvile. In 1631 Grenvile had sold Killigarth (a family estate in Talland parish where his father lived) and the advowson of Talland to Bagg for £3,000.[180] It is not clear whether this transaction marked a thaw in their relationship, or whether it was merely the result of financial necessity on Grenvile's part, but by 1636 a reconciliation had apparently taken place. In March 1636 Bevill wrote to his father, Sir Bernard:

> My journey to Ex[eter] was to meet Sir Ja[me]s Bag[g] as he appointed me by his l[ette]re, and there I found both his sonnes in Law and diverse others expecting him, but he came not, neither have I heard of him since. I pray for his happines.[181]

This new accord may have come about as a result of Bevill's reconciliation with his father in 1635–36. Sir Bernard died on 16 June 1636 and Bevill was saddened that this occurred so soon after their accommodation:

> My hope and desire was great that we might have lived longar comfortablie togeather, and I have taken more comfort in his late loving expressions to me then ever I did in any thing in my life.[182]

Bevill wrote to Bagg and told him of Sir Bernard's deathbed request:

> He then tould me it was concerning his Regim[en]t and Depu[ty] Lieu[tenancy] that I would accept of it and execute it, w[hi]ch I had often before refus[e]d . . . He added for reason likewise, that seeing those places had ever been in the hands of my Ancestors ever since the first institution of them, and that the Reg[imen]t lyes about my habitation, and in the heart of my estate, it were unfitt for me to suffer a stranger to come in.[183]

It appears that Bevill had withdrawn himself from politics and county affairs since Eliot's death. He told his father of his 'resolution not to intermeddle with the affairs of the comonwealth' and of 'the disproportion between my disposition and the course of the time'. However, Sir Bernard's persistence, and his appeal to family honour and duty, persuaded Bevill to accept.

The tone and contents of a letter from Bevill Grenvile to Sir William Wrey, written shortly after Sir Bernard's death, make it clear that they, too, had become reconciled. Grenvile expressed his 'great grief' at Wrey's absence from his father's funeral (which had been brought forward because of the negligence of the embalmer). He proclaimed that 'no man in the world should have been gladder of y[ou]r company then myselfe, neither is there any place where you can have better welcome then to my house', and said he hoped to enjoy Wrey's company at his musters. Wrey himself died at the end of 1636.[184]

When Bagg died on 26 August 1638, deeply in debt, the Exchequer took immediate action to seize his property for the Crown.[185] On 10 December his only son and he:r, George, petitioned the King, requesting support and assistance, and attributing his father's debts to Crown service and to the Star Chamber case against Mohun:

> having lived at a high rate to enable himself to serve your Majesty, as he did in the expeditions of Cadiz and the Ile de Rhe, exposing his credit and estate for the advancement of these services, which afterwards begot suits in the Star Chamber with Lord Mohun, wherein, although his faithfulness appeared clearly, yet the charges became his ruin.[186]

On 8 October (acting on an Exchequer writ) the sheriff of Cornwall, Francis Godolphin, held an inquisition at Truro. He ordered the seizure of Killigarth (worth £231.5s.10d. per annum) to help meet Bagg's debt of £22,500.15s.5d.[187] A second inquisition was held at Launceston on 31 March 1640 by the sheriff, Richard Trevill, and an additional charge of £1,480 was attached to Killigarth. This sum related to debts and fraud dating back to 1624, including embezzled money intended for the Cadiz expedition and for naval stores at Plymouth (thus partially substantiating Mohun's claims in the Star Chamber), and embezzled knighthood composition fines, collected locally.[188]

So, during the 1630s the factions which had dominated Cornish gentry politics disintegrated. Coryton's defection, Eliot's death, and Bagg and Mohun's quarrel caused the loss of local leadership. Buckingham's assassination in 1628 and (to a lesser degree) the 3rd Earl of Pembroke's death in 1630 deprived the factions of channels of communication with the Court and Privy Council. Although Bagg quickly allied himself with Sir Richard Weston (Portland), his factional allies did not follow his lead, and Pembroke's successor, Pembroke and Montgomery, appears to have been less forceful than his brother. Coryton (as vice-warden) remained loyal to him, but had himself lost favour with his former allies, and had far less influence in gentry circles than previously. The loss or weakening of these Court connections, together with the absence of Parliament for eleven years between 1629 and 1640, and the disintegration of the factions, prompted realignment and reconciliation amongst the gentry. Some former connections and friendships were maintained, as with Grenvile, ·Arundell

107

and Trevanion, and with the east Cornwall Puritans, Buller, Manaton, Nicoll and Trefusis. However, other alliances dissolved and new friendships were formed. By 1638 Cornish gentry politics and alliances had a very different appearance from a decade earlier.

4

Local Government and Defence
1600–1638

The Commission of the Peace and the Book of Orders

The duties of a magistrate increased considerably during the late sixteenth and early seventeenth centuries, and were potentially onerous. Justices of the peace met four times a year at quarter sessions to enforce law and order, but their responsibilities extended to areas such as control of the poor, regulation of alehouses, enforcing church attendance, and repair of roads and bridges.[1] At the end of the sixteenth century Cornish quarter sessions were held in Bodmin and Truro: in one quarter they would begin at Bodmin and end at Truro, and in the next quarter the order would be reversed.[2] It is not known whether this pattern continued throughout the first half of the seventeenth century, although there is some indication that additional meetings may have been held in other towns, such as Fowey.[3] A detailed analysis of quarter sessions and of magistrates' activity is impossible since no quarter sessions records survive for Cornwall.

As in other counties, the Cornish commission of the peace expanded considerably during the sixteenth century. There were about 12 names on the commissions of Henry VIII's reign, and around 30 on those of Elizabeth's reign.[4] Expansion continued during the reign of James I, with 41 members listed in 1608, peaking with 53 in 1622. This pattern is comparable with, for example, Kent, where the commission increased from 44 members in 1562 to 97 in 1608. The Norfolk commission expanded from 17 to 52 and the Northamptonshire commission from 17 to 37 over the same period.[5]

Between January 1616 and March 1617 James conducted a nationwide remodelling of commissions of the peace to improve efficiency and effectiveness. In the country as a whole there were almost 400 changes, with 209 men appointed for the first time, 142 removed, and 44 re-admitted.[6] Curiously, the sole addition to the Cornish commission between those dates was William Parker, the new archdeacon of Cornwall 'in his due place' in November 1616.[7] However, between May 1617 and May 1625 there was an enormous influx onto the Cornish commission, with 34 new appointments.[8]

There is no indication whether the 34 new appointees were selected by the Privy Council, or whether the Council was guided by local advice, as was the case in Somerset, for example.[9] The reason for such a large number of new appointments in so few years is also unclear. Only 6 of the new magistrates replaced their deceased fathers or other relatives. Sir Robert Killigrew replaced his father, Sir William; Francis Vyvyan replaced his father, Hannibal; William Rous succeeded his grandfather, Sir Anthony; Degory Chamond replaced his father, John; Sir Francis Godolphin replaced his father, of the same name; and John Trefusis succeeded his father, Richard. The rest were completely new appointments, so that by the early 1620s a new generation of JPs had emerged, who had largely eclipsed their predecessors.

Of the 53 names on the 1622 commission, 11 were officers of state and non-resident peers, 3 were clerics from the diocese of Exeter, and 39 were local gentry.[10] Of these 39, 27 had not been members of the 1608 commission: 7 had been appointed between 1608 and 1616, and 20 had been added since 1617.[11]

Appendix 2 shows that there were striking differences between the 27 magistrates who had been appointed since 1608 and the 12 who had survived from the 1608 commission. The new JPs were significantly younger and better educated. Their mean age was 37, compared with 59 for the existing JPs. Seventy per cent of the new appointees had experienced higher education, whereas only one-third of the existing JPs had done so. There was also a Puritan emphasis amongst the new appointees, which was not apparent amongst the existing magistrates. The difficulties in identifying Puritans makes settling firm figures difficult, but almost half the new JPs were likely Puritans, compared with only a quarter of the existing magistrates.

In addition, the new JPs were generally from older established families in the county, and a slightly higher proportion of them married Cornish brides. Slightly more of them also had a landed income exceeding £1,000 per annum, which generally was considered to be the minimum necessary for a JP, but was relatively rare in Cornwall.[12] However, in each case, the differences should not be overstated. Of the 12 magistrates also named in the 1608 commission, 8 resided in west Cornwall and only 4 in the east of the county. In contrast, two-thirds of the 27 new appointees resided in east Cornwall. The net effect was a slight imbalance in favour of the east, whereas in the 1608 commission the balance had slightly favoured the west. However, since the imbalance was relatively small[13] it would seem that in making these appointments the Privy Council desired equal representation for the east and west of the county to facilitate local law enforcement and administration in all areas.[14]

Eight further appointments were made to the commission between 1623 and 1625.[15] The average age of these new magistrates was 31, and 5 of the 8 had experienced higher education. Insufficient is known of their religion or marriage details to draw any firm conclusions. However, only 3 were of medieval origins, and only 2 had a landed income exceeding £1,000 per annum. Three resided in the east and 5 in the west, which slightly redressed the imbalance.

So, the unprecedented number of appointments to the Cornish commission between 1617 and 1625 brought to power a group of men generally young and well-educated, including a considerable number of Puritans. Their arrival on the county bench over such a short period would have transformed the internal dynamics of the commission, and must have affected county politics in some way.[16] Indeed, the emergence of this group, in the period immediately preceding the conflict between the Bagg–Mohun faction and the Eliot–Coryton faction, suggests that it may have been a pre-condition of that conflict. The rapid expansion of the commission did not cause the conflict; rather, a sequence of political events was responsible. However, the expansion gave status and influence to a number of gentlemen who became active in local politics, and provided opportunities for them to meet at quarter sessions.

William Coryton was initially appointed to the commission in 1618, and Sir John Eliot was added in 1621, although both had already enjoyed local power, as vice-warden of the stannaries and vice-admiral of Devon respectively. A number of others, soon to be associated with Eliot and Coryton, were appointed to the commission in the same period. Charles Trevanion was appointed in 1617, John Moyle and Nicholas Trefusis of Landue in 1620, William Rous in 1621, and Ambrose Manaton in 1622. Sir Richard Buller had been added since 1608, but John Arundell had sat on the 1608 commission. Two JPs later to be associated with Bagg (Sir Reginald Mohun and Sir William Wrey) had sat on the 1608 commission, and Sir Richard Edgcumbe was appointed between 1608 and 1616, but five others were appointed from 1617. Sir Robert Killigrew was added in 1617, Walter Langdon in 1618, John Trelawny in 1619, and Edward Trelawny in 1624. Most importantly, John Mohun was appointed in 1625, the year he became an adherent of Buckingham.[17]

By October 1626 the number of local gentry on the commission had fallen from thirty-nine to twenty-two.[18] Sir Thomas Coventry, appointed lord chancellor in November 1625, had made it a priority to control the size of commissions of the peace. He aimed at further improvements in efficiency, desiring smaller commissions filled with active JPs. He purged the commissions, removing those members whom he perceived to be the least active or lacking the appropriate wealth and status.[19] There is no extant Cornish commission list between 1622 and October 1626, so it is uncertain when the purge took place. It is, however, likely that it occurred in December 1625, as in Warwickshire and Sussex.[20]

In many cases the reason for removal was clearly non-political. Three omissions followed the deaths of the incumbents: Christopher Harris died in November 1623, John Rashleigh in 1624, and Thomas St Aubyn in March 1626. At least two magistrates were probably considered too old: Sir Nicholas Prideaux and John Chamond would both have been aged seventy-six in 1626. Further, Thomas Tubb and John Wood probably had insufficient status for the position, while John Roscarrock and Sampson Manaton had relatively low landed incomes. Manaton's younger brother, Ambrose, retained his position, despite failing the wealth qualification, probably because as a barrister he would have possessed relevant skills for the position. The motive for other removals, such as the experienced Sir William Wrey and John Arundell, is unclear. They may have been perceived as inactive, but the absence of quarter sessions records makes this impossible to verify. Only one of those removed, Wrey, had been restored to the bench by 1632, and even this, on 8 July 1629 a week after Wrey had been created a baronet, was politically motivated, to compensate for his imprisonment by Parliament for electoral corruption. This contrasts sharply with the situation in Sussex, where five were restored within a year and seven more in due course.[21]

Following these upheavals, the Cornish commission was then subjected to political interference in 1626–27. Eliot and Coryton were not named on the October 1626 commission. However, they were ousted not by Coventry in December 1625, but by Buckingham in July 1626, following their participation in the impeachment attempt upon the Duke. Buckingham further purged the commission in June 1627, when he removed Eliot's and Coryton's supporters, Sir Richard Buller, Nicholas Trefusis and Ambrose Manaton, for forced loan refusal.[22] Buller was restored in May 1629, Trefusis in December, and Coryton in February 1630. Manaton's restoration is not recorded in the Crown Office Docquet Book, but he was certainly an active JP in April 1631, and named to the 1632 commission.[23] Eliot was not restored, and died in 1632.

Throughout the 1630s the commission of the peace remained relatively stable. There is no indication that the Privy Council's purge of 1637 (when all JPs were commanded to take the oaths of supremacy, allegiance and office, or be removed) had any impact upon the Cornish commission.

Emmanuel Langford Esq of Liskeard appears to have been the sole victim of Coventry's subsequent purge of January to March 1638. During these months Coventry dismissed sixty-seven JPs from twenty-one counties who had failed to appear at the assizes, through age, illness or perceived idleness. Langford is the only recorded Cornish omission in the Crown Office Docquet Book, dated 1 March 1638.[24]

The Book of Orders of January 1631 has been seen by many as the ultimate test of relations between Charles I's government and magistrates. The Book was formerly perceived as an unusually high level of central interference pitched against local government resistance, an instrument of oppression, and part of Laud's and Wentworth's policy of 'Thorough'.[25] However, recent studies by Paul Slack and Brian Quintrell re-evaluating the Book have necessitated a reconsideration of its impact on county government and on relations between the centre and the localities.[26]

They have shown that the Book was not completely new, but in fact had many precedents going back half a century. Its recent origins were in correspondence between the Earl of Manchester and his brother Lord Montagu concerning local government practice in Northamptonshire. Further, the studies show that there was no conflict between the government and the magistracy over the Book's intentions. Assistance from central government was desired and even requested by magistrates in 1629 to help them deal with problems arising from war, harvest failure, plague epidemics, and the collapse of the cloth trade. Indeed, Kevin Sharpe suggests that the Book of Orders 'originated in the war years and the dislocations which they had revealed'.[27]

Slack and Quintrell have also stated that magistrates became less rigorous in their enforcement of the Book only when the associated procedures became burdensome, in 1634–35. By that stage the Privy Council had become preoccupied with the collection of ship money, and appears to have considered implementation of the Book as a lower priority.[28] Significantly, the Book of Orders was the only major policy of Charles' personal rule which was not criticized in the county petitions to the Long Parliament in 1640–41, nor was it listed in Parliament's catalogue of grievances, the Grand Remonstrance of November 1641.[29]

There was not merely one 'Book', but rather three sets of instructions, of which those of January 1631 were the last. The first instructions issued in April 1630 contained measures to deal with vagrancy, poor relief, and epidemics of bubonic plague. A second set was issued in September 1630 'for the preventing and remedying of the dearth of Graine and Victuall'.[30] Several reports were sent from Cornish JPs and from the sheriff to the Council in response to these grain orders. These suggest that the grain shortage, while not particularly severe, had been worsened by exports of grain from Cornwall to other markets for profit, which in turn had caused prices to rise.[31]

The third set of instructions, issued on 31 January 1631 (normally known as the Book of Orders), directed JPs in measures for the control and relief of the poor, and dealt with issues such as vagrancy (in greater detail than the first instructions), alehouses (commonly perceived as sources of disease and disorder), and houses of correction. To guarantee the due implementation of these orders, JPs were to hold monthly divisional meetings, and to provide the sheriff with quarterly reports. The sheriff was to forward these reports to the assize judge, who in turn was to send them to the Council. A royal commission of privy councillors was established to oversee the whole operation.[32]

Cornish JPs, while not the most diligent in the country, were reasonably active in implementing these instructions: between April 1631 and May 1635 they returned twenty-eight certificates. Quintrell calculated that four counties, Shropshire, Sussex, Hertfordshire and Kent, returned between fifty-five and seventy-five certificates, and that Leicestershire, Lincolnshire, Norfolk, Suffolk and Surrey 'were in the top dozen', with thirty to fifty reports each. It must be assumed from this that Cornwall was just below the top dozen counties.[33] Reports from west Cornwall were made on a divisional basis, but those for the east of the county were compiled by hundred, and the hundred of East was itself divided into north and south divisions.

The earliest reports are generally detailed, and suggest enthusiasm for the cause. For example, on 16 May 1631 Thomas Gewen Esq and Tristram Arscott Esq reported their proceedings in the hundred of Stratton during the last three months. They had taken security from all alehouse keepers to ensure that the keepers would not dress or serve any flesh during Lent or other fish days, and had similarly bound butchers not to kill any animals during Lent. In addition, two general searches for 'rogues' had been conducted, resulting in the apprehension and punishment of 'divers idle and disorderly persons'. Sixty-eight poor children (listed by parish) had been bound apprentices. Twenty-four people had each been fined 3s.4d. for 'tippling' in alehouses; four alehouse keepers had been fined 10s. each for allowing this practice; and two men had been fined 15s. each for drunkenness. Two others had been fined £1 each for selling ale and beer without a licence, but William Welles and Zachary Philpe, both of Kilkhampton, and guilty of the same offence, had insufficient money or goods to pay the fine and so had been whipped instead. Others had been fined for non-attendance at church and for 'prophane swearing'. All the fine money had been given to the poor in the parishes where the offences were committed.[34]

Although spasmodic, the JPs' reports remained detailed throughout the four-year period. In some cases the details were even more specific, and were listed parish by parish. For example, on 2 November 1632, in their report on proceedings in Trigg hundred, Charles Lord Lambert and Emmanuel Langford stated that the constables of Blisland had presented one Henry Johns, alehouse keeper, 'for keepinge of ill rule in his house'.[35] In April 1633 Thomas Gewen and Ambrose Manaton reported from Stratton that in the parish of Week St Mary one Andrew Benson had been convicted for drunkenness and had paid his fine of 5s., while one George Frost of Morwenstow had been convicted of the same offence, but unable to pay the fine had been put into the stocks.[36] The last extant report, from Edward Coswarth and Thomas Herle, dated 27 and 28 May 1635, recorded their proceedings in the southern division (Pyder and Powder), but dealt with two subjects only: rogues and vagrants who had been convicted and punished, and poor children who had been bound apprentices, although in each case names were given by parish.[37]

The areas dealt with by the justices remained constant. There was a strong emphasis upon vagrancy and pauper apprenticeship, which was typical of the country as a whole.[38] However, the Cornish certificates, and particularly those from the east of the county, were equally concerned with the punishment of unlicensed alehouse keepers and their patrons, and those guilty of drunkenness, non-attendance at church, and swearing. These were all matters of particular concern to Puritans, and Puritan zeal may account in part for the generally positive response to the Book of Orders in Cornwall. The close association between the Book and Puritanism is underlined by the sabbatarian emphasis of some entries. For example, in October 1633 six people in South Hill parish (East hundred, north division) were punished for 'playing att unlawfull games on the Sabaoth daie', and in the same month one Theophilus Philpe was presented by the JPs of Trigg hundred to the sheriff for 'being in an Alehouse on the Sabbath day and absenting himselfe from his p[ar]ish churche'.[39]

It is perhaps not insignificant that of the twenty-eight reports sent to the sheriff, twenty-two were from the JPs of the more Puritan eastern hundreds, and only six from the western hundreds. Further, eight of the twenty-two eastern reports came from the hundred of East, the most Puritan of all Cornish hundreds.[40] The most active of all JPs was the Puritan, Ambrose Manaton, a former member of the Eliot–Coryton faction and a forced loan refuser. Manaton's name is attached to fifteen reports in all, from the northern division of East hundred (where he lived), Lesnewth, Trigg and Stratton, covering the entire period, dating from April 1631 to May 1635. Thomas Gewen and Emmanuel Langford, the

115

next most active JPs (with eight and six reports respectively), were also Puritans. Some active justices, such as Sir William Wrey and Sir Richard Edgcumbe, were not Puritans, but their activity may be explained by the universal concern amongst the gentry for the preservation of social order.

Cornish Puritan zeal for the Book of Orders may have been influenced by the sermon preached at the quarter sessions of 1630 (and published in 1631) by Charles FitzGeffry, Puritan rector of St Dominick. The published version was entitled *The Curse of Corne-horders: with The Blessing of seasonable selling*, and was dedicated to Sir Reginald Mohun, as head of the bench. Mohun, a likely anti-Calvinist, would not have sympathized with FitzGeffry's Puritan views, a situation which FitzGeffry acknowledged by saying 'I crave not your patronage, but onely acceptance'. The sermon related particularly to the grain shortages of 1630, although grain control was still a matter of concern to JPs in the following year, and in the 1631 dedication FitzGeffry referred to 'Theese two yeeres of dearth'.[41] FitzGeffry condemned those who hoarded corn with the intention of selling it at a higher price, and proclaimed, 'let Ministers (as his Majesty commandeth) ioyne their forces with the Magistrates against this Monster, Avarice'.[42] He told the JPs that

> you have God, the King, the Cleargie, the Country on your sides . . . As blessing shall be on the head of them who sell their Corne willingly, so shall it be on your heads, who cause them, or compell them to sell, who are unwilling.[43]

However, FitzGeffry went on to encourage the JPs to demonstrate the important Puritan virtues of charity and hospitality:

> Hospitality at all times commendable, in these hard times is Royall . . . make your houses Hospitals to the poore . . . Your Over-seers for the poore, in many Parishes, are poore over-seers: It is a worthy worke for a Justice of Peace, in his Parish, to over-see them, and if need be, to be a Deacon, in ministring and distributing to the necessities of the brethren.[44]

This command was equally (if not more) relevant to the Book of Orders of January 1631 (issued before the publication of this sermon), and FitzGeffry later wrote that the sermon had 'found good acceptance among the Godly, and (by Gods gratious blessing) produced good effects from some whose former uncharitablenesse proclamed them ungodly'.[45]

Barnes claimed that in Somerset the office of JP had become so onerous during the 1630s, with the combined effects of the Book of Orders and ship money, that membership of the commission was undesirable. He asserted that local government collapsed with the demands of the Bishops' Wars, but that even had it not done so the 'dwindling numbers of magistrates would have effectively crippled it'.[46] Hughes has shown that in Warwickshire the size of the bench similarly decreased.[47] However, in Cornwall membership of the commission remained buoyant throughout the 1630s.[48] Puritan interest in the responsibilities of magistrates may partially account for the relative stability of the Cornish commission, as evidenced by the responses to the Book of Orders, at least until May 1635. The absence of quarter sessions records prevents analysis of individual activity beyond this date, but from the commissions alone there is no indication that membership became less attractive during the 1630s.

The Lieutenancy and Militia Reform

William, 3rd Earl of Pembroke, was appointed lord lieutenant of Cornwall in May 1604, and remained in that office until his death in 1630, when he was succeeded by his brother, Philip, Earl of Pembroke and Mont-gomery. All deputy lieutenants were senior local gentry who were also magistrates (save for Sir Bernard Grenvile, who was not a JP). Unlike the commission of the peace, the lieutenancy was greatly biased in favour of the east of the county. Deputies were appointed by the lord lieutenant, although between summer 1626 and summer 1628 Pembroke's involve-ment appears to have been nominal only. In 1623 the deputies were Sir Reginald Mohun, Sir Robert Killigrew, Sir Bernard Grenvile, Sir Richard Edgcumbe, Sir William Wrey, Sir Richard Buller and William Coryton. Only Killigrew, as governor of Pendennis castle, represented the west of the county.[49] By summer 1626 Killigrew's name no longer appeared on the list of deputies, and Charles Lord Lambert, John Mohun and Charles Trevanion had been added. Trevanion was now the sole representative of the western half of the county.[50] A likely explanation for the dominance of the lieutenancy by the eastern gentry is that, with the close proximity of Plymouth, a major naval port, there was a greater need for deputies to control military affairs in eastern Cornwall.

The internal dynamics of the Cornish lieutenancy were altered drama-tically in 1626–27. Pembroke's power as lord lieutenant was diminished by Buckingham in summer 1626, when the Duke launched a counter-attack upon his enemies. Coryton was deprived of his deputy lieutenancy by October 1626 (in addition to his place on the commission of the peace); Trevanion was removed from the lieutenancy by Buckingham soon after; and in the following year Sir Richard Buller was ousted from his position as a deputy, allegedly for forced loan refusal.[51] The remaining deputies (with the exception of Lord Lambert) were all members of the Bagg–

Mohun faction, and between 1626 and 1629 opposition to the government's militia policy, and to impressment, billeting, and martial law, became intrinsically linked with factional conflict and political expediency.

One of the first legislative actions of James I's government had been to repeal the 1558 statutes for the taking of musters and the keeping of horses and armour. In 1612 annual general musters and special musters for training were re-introduced, to continue throughout the rest of James' reign. There is no certificate of mustering from Pembroke for Cornwall among the State Papers until 4 May 1613, reflecting the relative inactivity in the militia nationally during the first decade of James' reign. In 1613 fears of a Spanish invasion prompted increased concern over the militia, which led to additional mustering throughout much of the country. As Cornwall was in relatively close proximity to Spain, Pembroke mustered not only the trained bands, but the whole forces of the county. Concern over the militia continued: in the following year Pembroke reported that the deputies had attended to the musters. They had been obliged to defer training until after the harvest, but the foot intended to exercise regularly.[52]

Tension heightened further with the outbreak of the Thirty Years War in 1618, and government intervention in the militia became more pronounced. In a letter to the lieutenancies, the Council stated that the King

> in his princely wisdome . . . observeth that the manner of trayninge & arminge hitherto generally used in this kingdome, is not so exact & serviceable as the Course held by all Strangers, & by his owne subjectes being in forraigne imployment.[53]

Great emphasis was placed upon uniformity in training and arms. For example, in 1618 the Council banned the use of calivers in favour of muskets, and in 1623 issued a new book of training orders. Further, both the Council and the lieutenancy took measures to deal with opposition. Those who failed to appear at musters or to produce the required arms were severely punished, often by imprisonment. For example, Arthur Hill of St Keverne was imprisoned in the Marshalsea for failure to produce sufficient arms at the Helston muster of 1620. In his petition to the Council, Hill claimed that formerly he had been assessed by the deputies to provide one musket and one pike, which he had shown at every muster for the past five years. However, at the last general muster he had been ordered to produce an additional musket and pike, but as this was a new requirement, he had come unprepared. He had been bound over in £100 by Sir Reginald Mohun, the deputy lieutenant, to appear before the Council, which had committed him to the Marshalsea. This swift action had immediate effect, as Hill concluded in his petition that he had now prepared the arms and was ready to perform any other service.[54]

The 'exact militia' policy was not, however, fully developed and implemented until the reign of Charles I. From his accession, Charles was determined to create an 'exact' or 'perfect' militia to improve the nation's defences and to win prestige on the continent. This entailed the implementation of an extensive programme of military reforms, with the aim of producing a well-disciplined, highly trained militia, armed with the most modern weapons available. The government directed that training was to be undertaken at holidays and at other 'convenient' times, and that lord lieutenants were to make efforts to convince those concerned that such drilling and training were enjoyable recreations.

On 28 August 1625 the Council ordered the mobilization of coastal defence forces, fearing a possible invasion from the continent, and in February 1626 eighty-four sergeants were imported from the Low Countries to train the militia in modern continental techniques. Further, the presence of forces in both Spain and Flanders, which were perceived to be directed at England, prompted the Council on 10 July to issue an extraordinary general order for the calling of musters throughout the country, and for placing national defences on full alert.[55]

In response to the August 1625 order 'for the better securinge our coaste by the exacte musteringe' the Cornish deputies were unanimous in their acknowledgement of the King's 'greate goodnes in beinge carefull of our safeties in this the remotest parte of his kingdome'. They declared:

> for our parte we have endevoured by the best meanes wee coulde, with all carefull dilligence accordinge to the same instructions, and have cawsed all the Trayned Bands of our countrie (beinge all foote) to be mustered and Trayned in severall partes in the manner Lymmited in the printed booke.

The deputies had allocated to each company a place for rendezvous at one hour's notice. They had also made plans for assembling all county forces in an emergency, and had ensured that all beacons were prepared for lighting. This letter, written in January 1626, was signed by Charles Lord Lambert, Sir Reginald Mohun, Sir William Wrey, Sir Bernard Grenvile, Charles Trevanion and William Coryton, suggesting that there was still unity amongst the deputies at this stage.[56]

The deputies' response to the extraordinary order of July 1626 was similarly enthusiastic and efficient:

Wee assure your Lordship that with the ordinarye exerciseinge upon holye dayes according to the printed Bookes and moderne forme . . . and the helpe of the Serieants sent downe our men are growne to much more abillitie and dexteritye in the use of their armes . . . and wee are perswaded everye daye will approve them better . . . the Militia or warlike provision of all sorts in this Countey is (as wee conceive) in much readinesse and well ordered to attend the worst adventure that may befall and more able to repell an enimye (with gods blessinge) then in any time paste.[57]

The deputies advised Pembroke that they had imposed the charge of arms upon all who qualified to provide them. However, they maintained that Cornwall was over-charged with arms relative to other counties 'if you have respecte to the quantitye and barrennes of the lande, and now the povertye of the people in general'. They had mustered all the county's forces, company by company, but had decided against holding a general muster of the whole county. The deputies considered that such an assembly might spread the plague then rife in eastern Cornwall, would leave the coasts unguarded, and would exacerbate the great poverty of the county. They further believed that Cornishmen were unwilling to leave their homes whilst soldiers were billeted there, and that a general muster would prove inconvenient at harvest time.[58]

In other respects the deputies showed no reservations, and appeared united in support of the reform programme. For example, they ordered that at every training session there should be 'some peice of small value for the musketteires to shott att with the bullett which [would] . . . make it with a little practise to become pleasant unto them'. This emphasis upon training and enjoyment was, of course, precisely what the government desired. The deputies had also made provision for the storage of powder, match and bullets. They had distributed ammunition between parishes, as an enemy could land at any point on the long coastline, and by the time supply was brought from a central store it could be too late.[59]

The deputies argued that allowing recusants to pay money, instead of providing arms, freed them from the burden of mustering, which other inhabitants were forced to meet. The deputies had therefore devised a scheme whereby Cornish recusants were charged, according to their estates, with providing twice as many arms as others; these arms were to be distributed by the local captain to militiamen who were to serve at the recusants' cost.[60]

In the previous month, however, the deputies had reported to Pembroke the disaffection of the town of Truro. The mayor and burgesses had prohibited the town's company from attending a general muster. They claimed that the town's Charter and Letters Patent, granted by Queen Elizabeth, contained clauses exempting the inhabitants from 'forraigne musters'. Further, Truro was the principal coinage town and tin worth many thousands of pounds was held there. Since Truro was 'dailie subiect to forraigne dangers' (owing to its proximity to the sea and its situation upon a navigable river), it would be unsafe to leave the town unmanned. Besides, the costs of transporting and maintaining a hundred men would be excessive.[61]

The deputies feared that other towns might follow Truro's lead, and indeed Truro's defiance was typical of many towns throughout England. The deputies sent the ringleaders' names to the Council, and claimed that the punishment of these defaulters would set an example. The Council showed none of its earlier zeal, however, and merely ordered Pembroke to find a solution satisfactory to all parties. There is no indication that Pembroke took any action in this case.[62]

From the summer of 1626 unity amongst the deputies began to crumble, and the lieutenancy became engulfed in the bitter factional conflict between the followers of Buckingham and Bagg and those of Eliot and Coryton.[63] This upset the balance of power within the lieutenancy, now dominated by members of the Bagg faction. In this way opposition to militia policy became inextricably intertwined with factional attacks upon the deputies and attempts to undermine their authority.

By July 1629 the Cornish deputies were either afraid or unwilling to carry out the Council's orders regarding the militia. Sir Bernard Grenvile, writing to Bagg, attributed this to 'the fowlenes of sondry ill disposissions poysoned by yt Malevolent faction of elliot'. Although Eliot by this stage was imprisoned in the Tower, Grenvile believed that the activities of his faction, particularly in the 1628-29 Parliament, had fatally weakened the authority of the deputies:

> Ye Leiftenannsey is grown into sutch contempte since the Parlament began as ther bee those that dare to countermawnd what we have on ye lordes commawndes willed to be done.[64]

The deputies' authority had no legal basis, but was founded solely upon the royal prerogative. Their actions were not directed by a legal framework, but were a matter of discretion.[65] This had become a subject of public debate since 1625, and on 24 March 1628 Coryton drew it to the attention of the Commons:

> It is better to live under the hardest law than under any man's discretion; yet it is better to live under discretion than to have laws and either not have

them executed or else have some commands come that hinder or contradict the execution of those laws. I offer to your consideration proclamations that notwithstanding the laws the proclamations contradict them upon a great penalty.[66]

On 27 July 1629 the situation reached a climax. The regiments of Grenvile and Charles Trevanion were being mustered at Bodmin, their custom for many years. When the parish of Launcells in Stratton hundred was called to muster, Tristram Arscott Esq, a resident, presented Grenvile with a petition to the Cornish deputies from the trained bands of the hundred. Arscott, followed by a large crowd, delivered the petition 'at so fitte a time to rayse a mutiney if not a rebellion two regimentes being in armes & in the middest of Mustering'. He claimed to present the petition at the request of the whole neighbourhood, but the parish constables later informed Grenvile that they had been misled, as they had added their signatures only upon Arscott's assurance that he would deliver the petition to Grenvile privately.

The petition complained that Cornwall was more charged with arms than any other county, certainly more than Devon, Dorset, Somerset and Hampshire. The county was also more heavily burdened by the unequal manner in which the charge was distributed, since in many cases fewer arms were demanded from owners of large estates than from those of smaller ones. The petitioners called upon the deputies to put their countrymen first, and listed four main demands. These were that the amount of arms demanded from Cornwall should be reduced, or that the county might at least receive contributions from other counties; that no man be called to muster at such a distance from his home that he be put to great expense; that no-one should be compelled to travel on the sabbath; and that a rule should be published stating that every man should provide arms in proportion to his estate.[67]

The petition undoubtedly reflected genuine concern about the militia reforms, twice referring to them as a 'common greavannce'. However, Arscott's political and factional connections, and the manner in which he presented the petition, led Grenvile to believe that the crisis was the responsibility of his factional enemies. He complained that 'I have bin a deputey Leiftenant 2: or 3: & 30 yeires & never in all this time mett so ill affections as now'. Grenvile informed Bagg of his belief that the 'busey headed Parlament men with who Arscott is a greate sider' (in other words, Eliot's and Coryton's faction) were responsible for the trouble, and reported that Arscott had since ridden to London to gain support from his 'Master', the Earl of Bedford. The Earl of Bedford was one of the Puritan leaders in the House of Lords, and the patron of John Pym, who had strong Cornish connections. The sabbatarian clause of the petition also suggests a Puritan connection, providing a further link with the Eliot–Coryton faction and between that faction and the Bedford–Pym group in Parliament.[68]

Another incident of July 1629 illustrates the level of disintegration of the militia policy in Cornwall. Robert Rous Gent of Wootten in Landrake, a militia captain for twenty-one years, customarily held musters at Landrake Cross.[69] On this occasion he had decided to muster the company in the church as the weather had turned stormy. One William Hawking failed to provide arms, and Rous ordered him to leave the church. Hawking refused, so Rous ejected him. The two churchwardens and two of their kinsmen, John Roberts and William Brookings, exploited the incident to sue Rous in the consistory court at Exeter. Rous was excommunicated, in accordance with the recent Laudian policy of enforcing the 1604 canon against the profanation of churches, and complained bitterly to the Council. He claimed that as Hawkings' action had been 'in the publique view of those western partes', others had threatened to follow his example, and would do so unless speedy action were taken. Indeed, he believed that 'his Majesties service is like to be ruinated, the said countie to be in factions and devisions, his Majesties dutious Officers to be disheartened and consequently all future commands from your honours to be frustrated'.[70]

John Roberts appears to have been the leader of this protest.[71] He had a record of opposition to the 'exact militia', and had previously refused to attend or present arms at a muster at Landulph. He had also encouraged his neighbours to refuse 'through his contemptuous cariage and undecent speaches'. At the next muster Roberts did appear, but without arms. He had also refused to march to Saltash at the most recent muster, giving his pike to a boy who marched in his place. During that exercise, Roberts' pike was broken, but when ordered to bring a new one to the next muster, he refused to appear, and sent a boy with the broken pike. After the first offence, he was pronounced by one of the deputies, Sir Richard Edgcumbe, to be a 'contemner of his Majesties service', and following the Landrake church incident two other deputies, Sir Bernard Grenvile and Sir Reginald Mohun, issued a warrant for his arrest. Pembroke ordered that Roberts should be imprisoned for one year, and that the matter should be heard before the Council, 'for he averred he could not endure such insolencies and misdemeanors especiallie in that daingerous nooke of the land'. However, Pembroke died a few days later, and when Roberts eventually appeared before the Council it merely ordered that 'henceforth he doe dutifully and dilligently (upon all occasions) attend at the Musters as he ought to doe'.[72]

The Council was similarly lenient in its treatment of John Jeffrey and Thomas Bake, the constables of Landrake parish, who had failed to arrest Roberts and who had refused to appear before the deputies to account for their actions. The constables were imprisoned in the Marshalsea for eighteen days, but the Council discharged them since they claimed not to have received the warrant from the deputies.[73]

The Council heard the case of Roberts and the constables on 30 May 1630. Also present were Sir Richard Edgcumbe, Sir Richard Buller, John Arundell of Trerice, William Coryton and Paul Speccott Esquires. The connection of these gentlemen with this particular case is not clear, but the Council evidently appreciated the inter-relationship between the factional conflict and the disintegration of the militia policy in Cornwall, and

> did by a grave and serious exhortation exhort the said Sir Richard [Edgcumbe] and the gentlemen afore named in freindly sort to accommodate and reconsile them and hence-forth to live in freindship and good neighborhood . . . and be most forward to advance his Majesties service and suppress all factions and divisions that may growe among the gentrie and other the inhabitants of the said Countrie.

The Council also ordered that the gentlemen stop at Exeter on their return to Cornwall to ensure that Rous' excommunication was revoked.[74]

By the autumn of 1629 only three deputies were active, namely Sir Bernard Grenvile, Sir Reginald Mohun and Sir William Wrey, all members of the Bagg–Mohun faction. On 29 September, the three asked Captain Robert Bennett of Lawhitton to prepare a list of gentlemen under his command who refused to attend musters. He was to deliver the list, together with his muster roll, to them at Fowey by 14 October in time for the deputies' meeting to certify the musters. However, in a letter of 16 October to his friend, the Reverend Ralph Byrd, Grenvile mentioned this meeting and complained that no-one had attended save Mohun, Wrey and himself.[75]

Grenvile went on to describe the disarray of the militia in his 'diseased cuntry', naming those whom he considered the most active opponents of the government's militia policy in Cornwall. These included Sir Richard Buller (now restored to the lieutenancy), Sir Francis Vyvyan of Trelowarren (a new deputy), John Connock Esq and John Harris Esq, the provost-marshal. Grenvile asserted that

> if theise thinges so pass & o[u]r Cuntry bee still Governed by sutch Deputyes as will rather uphowlde or excuse sutch Malefactors & opposers of ye

124

Kinges & his Cowncells commawndes . . . all [will] cume to speedy ruin as it will if ye deputeys bee not better reformed & better graced . . . all theis disorders ar sprung since ye Humerus actions of ye two late parlamentes.[76]

Like Sir Robert Phelips in Somerset, Buller felt no compulsion to halt his attacks on the lieutenancy once he had been restored to office: on the contrary, he continued the assault from within.[77] Grenvile complained that Buller and Connock had failed to communicate some new instructions from the lord lieutenant, so as to hinder the deputies in the taking of musters. In addition, Nicholas Borlase (the recusant) had refused to provide arms, and had destroyed the constables' book of rates in which his assessment was listed. More seriously, Thomas Gewen, the duchy auditor, had failed to provide arms, and had forbidden his officers to attend musters. This blatant opposition to the militia policy by one of the leading duchy officials in Cornwall, together with the attacks on the lieutenancy from within its own ranks, illuminates the extent of decay in the militia. Further, Buller and Gewen were Puritans, and Connock, Vyvyan and Harris also had godly connections, which appears to reinforce the link between the Eliot–Coryton faction, Puritanism, and opposition to militia reforms.

So, despite some early successes, the 'exact' militia reforms had only a limited impact in Cornwall. One reason for this was a widespread belief there that Cornwall was overcharged with arms relative to other counties. The main reservation voiced by the Cornish deputies to the Council's order of July 1626 was the relative excess of arms charged upon their county, and this was the principal point raised in the 1629 petition of the Stratton trained bands. This was, however, not a new grievance; indeed, Carew had remarked in 1602 that 'The number [of arms] as it standeth, much exceedeth the shires proportion, if the same be compared with Devon and other Counties'.[78] Therefore, it is not a sufficient reason for the collapse of the militia policy by 1629.

The lack of authority and discipline demonstrated by the Privy Council and the deputies in implementing the 'exact militia' programme partially accounted for its failure. However, the authority and effectiveness of both in Cornwall were likely to have been seriously prejudiced by Pembroke's lack of involvement as lord lieutenant after 1626. The role of lord lieutenant for any county was crucial since as a privy councillor he formed the main link between central government and county governors. After July 1626, although Pembroke was nominally lord lieutenant, in practice the deputies (dominated by Buckingham's and Bagg's supporters between 1627 and 1629) were left to their own devices.[79] This allowed factional conflict to engulf the lieutenancy and to undermine its authority.

Factionalism, more than any other factor, hindered the creation of an 'exact' militia in Cornwall.

There is evidence that mustering did continue throughout the 1630s, but the conclusion of peace with France and Spain in 1630 caused the issue to assume lesser importance. Further, the disintegration of the two factions between 1630 and 1632 depoliticized the militia. Correspondence between the deputies and the centre effectively ceased for much of the 1630s and evidence of continued activity remains solely in parish records. For example, the St Neot churchwardens disbursed 1s. in 1633 for carrying the parish armour to a general muster at 'Trecan Yeate', and in the following year they paid 2s. for carrying the parish arms for two days at the general muster.[80] In 1637 the St Breock churchwardens paid 2s.8d. to Thomas Pettegrew and John Eare for carrying the parish arms for two days, and a further 6d. for cleaning it.[81] This level of activity was typical for much of the decade, until 1639 when new demands were made for men and money for the Scots War.

Impressment, Billeting and Martial Law

On 18 March 1625, in preparation for the expedition to Cadiz, the Privy Council issued a list of commissioners for impressing mariners in Cornwall. These were Sir Bernard Grenvile (a deputy lieutenant), Sir Robert Killigrew (governor of Pendennis castle), Arthur Harris (governor of St Michael's Mount) and Francis Bassett (vice-admiral of north Cornwall). Sir James Bagg was appointed prestmaster. Sir Richard Buller and Sir Francis Vyvyan were appointed commissioners later, probably when they became deputy lieutenants. On 18 April, Bagg despatched the press to Cornwall to raise the first 200 men, and in May the Council ordered the impressment of a further 150 in the county. Two weeks later the Council instructed Pembroke (as lord lieutenant) that the commissioners were to impress young, able-bodied men, and were to take no-one from the trained bands. The greatest number were to be impressed from the most populous areas of the county, and were to be conducted by land to Plymouth by 25 May. They were each to be allowed 8d. per day, to be met by the levying of coat and conduct money in Cornwall. In September, shortly before the fleet sailed, the Council needed to levy a further 500 men to replace those who had deserted, become ill, or died while at Plymouth, and stipulated that fifty of these were to come from Cornwall. Twenty tinners were impressed for this service by William Coryton, as vice-warden of the stannaries.[82]

The commissioners did not find it easy to raise such large numbers, as it was extremely difficult to find fit men who were not members of the trained bands, and whose families did not rely upon their labour. Consequently the commissioners often resorted to impressing vagrants and outcasts who would not be missed. Most men would go to great lengths to avoid impressment. For example, in February 1625 the Council was obliged to send a warrant to the vice-admirals and port officials in Devon and Cornwall, ordering them to prevent the departure of any ship bound for the Newfoundland cod fisheries until the normal date of 1 April. The annual fishing voyage to Newfoundland occupied large numbers of mariners, and the Council had received information that the merchants and shipowners had advanced the departure date by a month, so that their crews might avoid the press.[83]

Despite general dislike of impressment, and widespread efforts to avoid it, there was no open opposition in Cornwall to impressment for the 1625 Cadiz expedition. However, the demand for yet more men for the expedition to the Isle de Rhé in 1627, in addition to the continued billeting of soldiers in Cornwall at the expense of the inhabitants, triggered open protest. Further, by this stage many of the gentry and the lieutenancy itself had become engulfed in factional conflict, and it seems likely that factionalism had spilled over into this area of government policy also. Since Bagg was prestmaster, and Sir Bernard Grenvile and Sir Robert Killigrew (both Buckingham supporters) were commissioners, the same opportunities existed for attacking the Bagg faction and government policy simultaneously, as happened with the 'exact' militia.

On 9 April 1627, responding to the severe shortage of mariners, the Council ordered the impressment of all seamen aboard ships in south coast ports. Between August and November 150 men were conducted from Cornwall to Plymouth and Southampton. Further, in October, Bagg was authorized to impress ships in certain ports, including Falmouth, to provide transport to the Isle de Rhé. Aware of the shortage of suitable men, and of local feeling against the policy, Bagg told Buckingham in December 1627 that 'men is a second want, and these parts will hardlie affoord the nomber desired; yet I will doe my best, greevinge as little as I maye the Countrye'.[84]

As with militia demands, Cornish inhabitants believed their county to be overburdened relative to others. In a petition of 1627 to the Privy Council, the inhabitants of Devon and Cornwall joined together to complain that their counties had been much weakened of late,

and in the presses and levyes of men they have bene seldome spared though it bee well knowne that these countryes yeeld more seamen to his Majesties service then any parte of his other dominions. And of these said late imployments have taken up so many as the very fishermen and sand bargemen have not escaped. The idlers which all countryes willingly spare are either allready prest or have thrust themselves as voluntaryes into the late expedicons. There wants nothing to consummate their undoinge but the taking of their husbandmen . . . Their humble and obedient sufferance of these infinite pressures (that wee may not terme them oppressions) gettes them no favour before others, it seems rather to draw upon them new charges in the same kinde.[85]

In April 1628 one Captain William Cooke and some of his officers complained that they had been hindered in the task of impressment by the mayor of Saltash, alleging that he had insisted on the public reading of the warrant in his house, and that 'coming into the streete [he] made an open oration that he did not knowe wheare to find a man [for the press]'. The town constables, Dagcombe and Piper, had pursued a similar course, warning passers by of the press, and urging them to avoid it. In some way, this incident appears connected with the Saltash borough election of the previous month, when the mayor had given a burgess-ship to Bagg (for Buckingham's use) against the opposition of Sir Richard Buller. The mayor was punished by the Commons for electoral mal-practice, and Bagg had sought the Duke's protection for him. Bagg had said that the mayor 'is to me a frend . . . [and] . . . tells the world that he is the Duke's servant'. It is not clear why the mayor opposed impressment whilst supporting Bagg and trying to win favour with Buckingham, but one possibility is that he expected exemption from the press for Saltash in return for his electoral favours.[86]

Before the Cadiz expedition, 10,000 men were billeted in or around Plymouth, 2,650 of whom were placed in Cornwall. The Council appointed Sir Reginald Mohun, Sir Richard Edgcumbe, Richard Carew of Antony, and William Bastard Gent of Duloe as commissioners to assist Sir John Ogle in the control of the billeted men. All four lived in south-east Cornwall, the area most affected by billeting. The Council directed them to do 'all things necessary to secure the country thereabouts from such damage and outrage as otherwise they might be in danger of through the insolencies and disorders of the soldiers'.[87]

The soldiers were inadequately supplied from the outset. In June 1625 Sir John Ogle reported to the Council that 'there is great want in your troopes in generall of those things which are necessary for ye maynteyning of them not only for decency but for health'. He attributed this to the hasty manner in which the soldiers had been sent to their destinations without regard for their personal needs, and he welcomed the news that the commissioners of war had ordered the provision of 'shyrts, shooes, & stockings . . . as alsoe for some breiches' for the soldiers.[88] The following month, the commissioners at Plymouth urged the Council to send money, as their supply was exhausted. They complained that they could not satisfy with words the hungry bellies of the soldiers, nor the empty purses of the hosts; nor could they secure the country from damage.[89] Despite the lack of provisions, Ogle was able to report 'for ye most part a good correspondencye & frendlynes hitherto betwixt ye Country-inhabitant & ye Soldier'. The commissioners had boasted to Ogle that military discipline remained intact, and that they had rarely known a time when 'there hath been so little occasion given for iustice to use the sword'.[90]

Upon the fleet's return in December 1625, the soldiers and sailors were sent back to Cornwall as a 'standing army'. From this moment military discipline and local goodwill started to break down. Many of the gentry rebelled against billeting, especially as they had not been paid, so that the commissioners found difficulty 'in billeting the captaines, officers and soldiers because the rich in manie places refuse it whereby it is imposed on the poorer and meaner sorte'.[91] In April 1626 the Council was compelled to issue instructions to the commissioners to deal with the likelihood of mutiny. They directed that guards from the trained bands be placed strategically to prevent soldiers who were billeted in different places from meeting and becoming dangerous.[92] On 8 June, the commissioners reported that plague had spread to all parishes where soldiers were billeted. They echoed the pleas of those parishes that the soldiers be removed, and also their belief that soldiers were more likely to spread plague than civilians, 'findinge by experience that they can better restraine theire domesticall servants then theire military soiourners from infected places'. The Liskeard churchwardens' accounts for 1625–26 record the purchase of a prayer book 'comanded to bee read containing gods visitation in the time of the plage', and a later entry that year shows payment for two prayer books of thanksgiving 'for the staying of the plague'.[93]

The impact of billeting on the parishes is also apparent from the Liskeard mayor's accounts for 1625–26. The mayor disbursed substantial amounts in hospitality towards the commissioners 'when they sat here about the souldiers', and the officers. The mayor also lent or gave money to billeters, believing that the King would repay the town. For example, the mayor lent Mr Jeffery, the clerk, 35s. 'for billating mony', and paid 2s.6d. 'for releife of Souldiers that lay in Mr Beills house'. Richard Cardue was paid 5s. 'for keeping a sicke souldier that dyed in his howse', and the mayor gave Henry Thorne 3s. to buy a shroud for the soldier who had died in his house. Payment of 10s. can have been little comfort to William Michelmor, however, who kept a sick soldier for three weeks, 'by S[i]r Reynold Mohuns command'.[94] The soldiers were clearly billeted in the church too, as the town's churchwardens' accounts for the same year record payment of 1s. to George Haynes 'to make cleene the church after the soulders laye in it'.[95]

The gravity of the situation prompted the Cornwall and Devon commissioners to send an envoy, Sir George Chudleigh, to the Council to request the urgent removal of the soldiers. On 24 August the Council responded. It praised the commissioners 'for the great care and industry which you have used from time to time in the carriage of this business', and two days later issued instructions for the removal of all soldiers billeted in Cornwall and Devon to other southern counties. To ensure a smooth withdrawal, the Council ordered the commissioners to take a careful muster of all the billeted companies, and to take accounts of the money owed by the King. The commissioners were to raise a week's provisions, either in money or in kind, for the departing soldiers, and were to punish those refusing to contribute by billeting upon them as many soldiers as they saw fit. Further, the commissioners were to purchase clothes for the soldiers and to distribute them as necessary. Most importantly, the Council promised payment for the billeters and for those providing supplies, as £30,000 had been assigned for this purpose from the tin farm.[96] This calmed the situation, but in February 1627 the government made a shrewd move when it cancelled the order for money from the tin farm, and promised that

> for asmuch as the county of Cornwall has shown itself very forward in his Majesty's former & present services . . . for the more speedy satisfaction of that county, the money which shall arise out of the loans to his Majesty of Cornwall (other than those already assigned to Sir Robert Killigrew for Pendennis, and to Sir Francis Godolphin, captain of his Majesty's new fort on St Mary's island, Scilly, and governor of those islands) shall be assigned for the payment of the apparelling, billeting, and other charges of the soldiers and their officers.[97]

This ensured present rather than future payment for services rendered, and provided the deputies with an incentive to collect the forced loan.

Cornwall was free from billeted troops for a year only. In September 1627, 2,000 troops were billeted in Cornwall and Devon in preparation for the expedition to the Isle de Rhé. When the expedition returned at the end of November, 4,750 soldiers were billeted in the two counties, 1,300 of whom were sick or injured. Two hundred died within a week of landing. In addition, 600 sick mariners were billeted in the area. All the soldiers billeted in Cornwall were placed in the eastern half of the county. There were concentrations in Launceston, Liskeard, Bodmin, Lostwithiel and

Fowey, and large numbers were also billeted in parishes along the south coast and in the Tamar Valley. As in 1626, most of the sick soldiers were concentrated in the Tamar Valley and on the Rame peninsula; the largest number were billeted in Saltash. Both Sir William Courtney of Saltash and Sir James Bagg stressed to the Council the pressing need for money and for clothes to avoid further deaths. On 7 December Bagg told Buckingham that he had disbursed all the money he had received, and more besides, in paying the soldiers until the 10th of that month, and in caring for the sick and wounded. He added that if new supply were not received by the 10th, he could do no more. In particular, Bagg urged the supply of clothing for the mariners 'whose wants are such as a man sees their ruine to see them goe so naked to the Sea, and to cloth[e] them will content them'.[98]

After the return of the fleet from Rhé there was no loan money to defray the expenses of the billeters, and the full cost of accommodating and caring for the soldiers fell upon the local population. The continued presence of these defeated, sick, and inadequately clothed soldiers, dependent upon local charity, ensured that Cornish opposition to billeting was sustained.[99] As with militia charges and impressment, it was felt that Cornwall was overburdened relative to other counties. More seriously, many felt that the billeting of soldiers without payment to hosts called the King's honour into question. In a petition from Cornwall and Devon to the Council it was stated that

His Majesty's honor doth . . . suffer much in these penurious wayes of billeting souldiers without money. What say the people will his Majestie make warre without provision of treasure or must our country beare the charge for all England. Is it not enough that wee undergo the trouble of the insolent souldiers in our houses, their robberyes and other misdemeanours but that we must mayntaine them too at our owne cost.[100]

The petition also addresses grievances about impressment, underlining the connection between these issues. Although some of the soldiers were later moved to other counties (paid for by Cornish coat and conduct money) 500 were retained in Cornwall throughout the spring of 1628 in readiness for their departure to La Rochelle.[101] These men were billeted at a rate of 3s.6d. per head, and the Council declared that the immediate cost was to be borne by the county.

St Germans was one of the few parishes exempted from billeting. Eliot's factional opponents exploited this, despite the fact that between April 1627 and January 1628 Eliot was imprisoned in London for forced loan refusal. Sir John Drake drew the case to the attention of Secretary

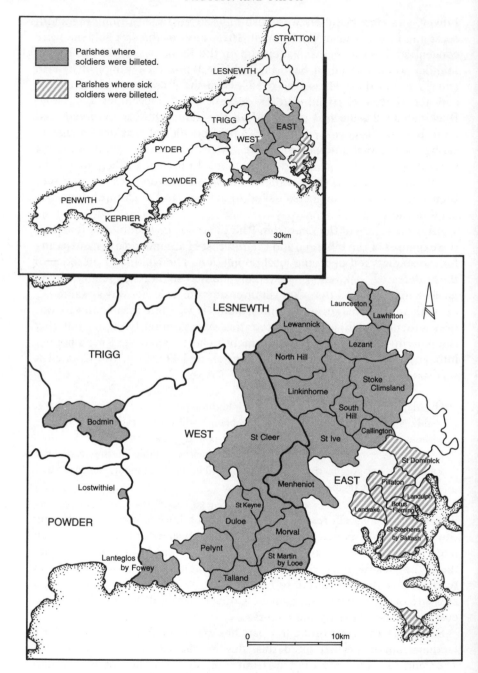

Map 4. Distribution of Billeting, 1627

Nicholas, and said that certain Cornish gentlemen had informed him that St Germans was one of the richest parishes in the county, and they had marvelled at its exemption.[102] Bagg claimed that Eliot 'hath gained [exemption] out of some conceit to popularise himself among his Western friends and faction'. He lamented that by actions of this nature, Eliot and others of his 'mutinous opinion' were winning support from the 'ignorantly disaffected'.[103] Eliot and his allies retaliated in the 1628 Parliament by attacking the practice of billeting and by questioning Bagg's probity in accounting for billet money.

Grievances about billeting were compounded at the end of 1627 when the Council issued a commission to execute martial law upon soldiers billeted in Plymouth and adjacent parts.[104] Bagg evidently supported the martial law policy and boasted to Buckingham that 'there will nothing advantage . . . [the King's service] . . . more then the death of one Runneawaie, and it is better that some perish then that Ruine should betide manye'.[105] Sir Reginald and John Mohun, Sir Bernard Grenvile, Sir Richard Edgcumbe and Sir William Wrey (all members of the Bagg faction) also were active commissioners. When they (with other members of Bagg's faction) were summoned before the Commons in March 1628, they pleaded the need to delay, and claimed that there had been a mutiny amongst the soldiers. They were about to execute some of the ringleaders under martial law in order to make examples of them, and told the Sergeant's messenger that:

> Their Quarter Session was at hand; their country full of soldiers; and their desire to execute martial law upon some of them so far as to hang them for example's sake, caused their longer stay.[106]

Martial law tended to evoke fears of an extension of central authority in the locality, particularly as its use was not confined to the military, but was extended to civilians to force them to take soldiers into their homes. Further, it was feared that once soldiers who were subject to martial law were billeted in a private house, that household would also fall under martial law, and that the protection of the common law would be lost. These fears were expressed in Parliament in 1628 by (amongst others) Coryton and William Noy, MP for Helston. They complained respectively about the erosion of the common law and the illegality of martial law in peacetime. The response to these complaints was the condemnation of commissions of martial law in the Petition of Right as 'wholly and directly contrary to the said laws and statutes of this realm'.

Piracy and Defence of the Coast

Throughout the first half of the seventeenth century Cornish coastal towns were faced with a constant threat from pirates, primarily Turks and Dunkirkers, infesting the coast. The 'Turks' were pirates of many nationalities who operated from the Barbary ports of Algiers, Tunis, Tripoli and Sallee. Barbary-based piracy had been developed by European privateers made redundant by the Franco-Spanish peace of 1598, and peace between England and Spain in 1604; the ships were crewed by Moriscos expelled from Spain between 1609 and 1614. The 'Dunkirkers' were privateers who operated from the Spanish Netherlands, particularly Dunkirk. They were particularly active after the resumption of hostilities between Spain and the United Provinces in 1621. Nationally, between 1616 and 1642 approximately four hundred ships and seven thousand subjects were captured by the Turks. Almost all ships lost were small merchant vessels from London and from south-western ports, and the heaviest losses were of merchants and mariners plying the southern trade routes to Biscay, Spain, Portugal and the Mediterranean.[107]

In Cornwall there was widespread awareness of the problem from the early years of James' reign. In 1607, for example, Liskeard borough gave Bernard Barrett 3s. 'towardes the ransoming of his Brother being taken by the Turks', and in the following year the borough gave 2s.6d. to John and Thomas King, 'w[hi]ch had there tonngues cutt out of there heades and towardes the Ransoming of there Owner and shipp being in prisonne by the Turkes'.[108] In 1613 the St Neot churchwardens donated 2s. to help 'prisoners in Turky', and in 1617 the Camborne churchwardens paid 5s.6d. 'for the ransoming of prisoners taken with the Turks'.[109]

The problem became particularly acute in 1625. On 18 April Bagg reported to Buckingham that the boldness of the Turks caused 'much feare [among] such as live upon the Cornish coast'. In that week alone the Turks had seized a Dartmouth ship and three Cornish fishing boats, and Bagg urged Buckingham, as lord admiral, to dispatch a sea force to combat the pirates and to pacify coastal inhabitants.[110] No action was taken, and in July the commissioners at Plymouth informed the Council of 'the affrightments and dayly terrors, which our marchants, Owners, or fishermen apprehend, by reason of the contynuall infesting of our Coastes by the Turkishmen of warre, or pirates of Sally'. They complained that many merchants and fishermen had been taken into slavery, and that the pirates often raided the coast as well.[111] This had aroused fear, not only among the sea-faring community, but among 'the Country generally'. It had also caused economic decay. Merchants feared for the safe return of the Newfoundland cod fleet, and of other ventures to Virginia and elsewhere. There was also concern about a consequent shortage of essential provisions, particularly local fish, and imported malt, sea coals, and salt, as fishermen and merchants were afraid to put to sea.[112]

On 2 August Bagg again urged Buckingham to take decisive action against the Turks. The Oxford session of the 1625 Parliament had opened the day before, and many MPs were armed with complaints from their constituencies about the ravages of piracy. Bagg advised the Duke that it would be wise to pre-empt the presentation of grievances by taking remedial action.[113] Buckingham promptly dispatched a naval squadron commanded by Sir Francis Stuart to deal with the pirates, but the five ships proved wholly inadequate for the task.[114] Stuart's squadron chased the pirates between Plymouth and Falmouth, but 'could not come near them, the sayd Pyrats being farre better saylers then our English shipps'. Consequently the squadron abandoned the chase, and retreated into Falmouth harbour.[115]

The situation at Looe was particularly acute. On 12 August the mayor of Plymouth drew the plight of the town to the Council's attention:

one poore Maritime Towne in Cornwall call[ed] Loo hath within ten dayes last past lost 80 Marryners and Saylers which were bound in fishing voyages for the deepes, and there have ben taken by the turks within the sayd tyme 27 Shipps and barkes at least, and in them there could not be lesse then 200 persons.

The mayor complained that if the activities of the Turks were not curbed, all West Country merchants and mariners would be forced to withdraw from their occupations, which would utterly ruin many in that area.[116] Six days later the mayor of Bristol reported that the Turks had captured Lundy Island (owned by Sir Bernard Grenvile) with all the islanders, and also had seized inhabitants of the Padstow area.[117] On 25 August Sir James Perrot informed his patron, Pembroke, that the Turks had snatched sixty men, women and children from the church of 'Munnigeesa' in Mount's Bay and had carried them away into slavery.[118]

During the 1625 Parliament Sir Walter Erle, MP for the maritime county of Dorset, and a Pembroke client, moved that tonnage and poundage was normally granted to a monarch for life so that the Narrow Seas might be guarded. However, it was plain that Charles had failed to guard the sea against pirates during the first months of his reign, and should not be granted tonnage and poundage for life until he had fulfilled that obligation. As a result Parliament voted the King tonnage and poundage for one year only. Notwithstanding this, Charles continued to collect the duty without parliamentary consent.[119]

Reports from the following year show that the threat from pirates remained. In May 1626 John Bonython, deputy governor of Pendennis castle, reported that many Turks and six Dunkirkers were lying off the coast. He believed that the Isles of Scilly were likely to be the main target since the pirates were chiefly plying between the islands and the Lizard, and their ships were fully manned.[120] In July one Captain James Duppa urged Nicholas to provide protection for Falmouth harbour,

> which if it be not presently supplied, heer will be noe fishing, if noe fishing, then much misery & poverty in these west parts; the Turks men of warre on both sides of the mount dayly visiting their ports that noe fishermen dare goe forth.[121]

In May 1626 a Turkish man-of-war was captured by Cornishmen and brought into St Ives, in Sir Francis Bassett's vice-admiralty of north Cornwall. Fifteen mariners from Looe had been captured by the ship on 28 April while en route to Newfoundland, and were held as slaves until 10 May. On that day they joined with eight other English captives on the ship, and overcame the forty Turks by slaying eight of them, and imprisoning the remainder in the hold until they reached St Ives. Bassett stated that

> the Turkes never yeelded to them, untill theire shipp strooke agrounde, they were maisters of the holde, and would have blowne upp the Englishe but that the shipp beinge very Leakie, & they who were above not daring to pumpe, the water increased so in the hold, as it wett all theire powder, and so prevented that mischeiffe.

Bassett's hatred of the Turks is apparent from the tone of his request for a commission of oyer and terminer to try them: he complained that 'the waching of these doggs' cost him 10s. a day, and as the ship was of little value, he desired to be free of both as soon as possible. By June Bassett had received the commission, but the additional instructions not to execute the Turks irritated him, as 'they are a great charge for their diet and guard'. In August the Council ordered the transfer of the Turks to Launceston gaol, and ultimately the Turks were exchanged for English prisoners in Barbary.[122]

As lord high admiral, Buckingham had the specific duty to ensure that the Narrow Seas were guarded. The failure of Stuart's squadron, and the continued piratical attacks, therefore called the Duke's competence into question. This point was raised in Parliament in 1626, Eliot being one of the chief accusers, and Buckingham's failure to guard the Narrow Seas

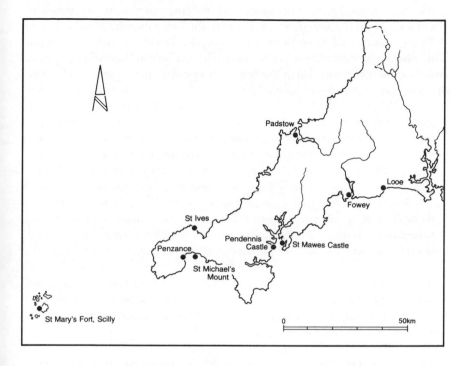

Map 5. Fortifications and Principal Coastal Towns.

was one of the main charges brought against him in the articles of impeachment.

Between 1627 and 1630 there were fewer reports of Turkish piracy. However, merchants and mariners still faced attacks from Dunkirkers and French men-of-war. In November 1628, for example, John Tresahar, the new lieutenant-governor of Pendennis, reported to Conway that the coast around Falmouth was infested with Dunkirkers and French men-of-war, who were taking new ships daily.[123] Further, in August 1629 the mayor of Exeter complained to Pembroke of the constant danger on the western coasts from these pirates. On 4 September 1630 the Camborne church-wardens paid 1s.6d. to Ellinor Smith 'who had a pass to redeem her husband out of Dunkirk', and on 30 March 1631 they paid 6d. to two Irish merchants who had been taken by Dunkirkers.[124]

The situation had worsened again by the mid-1630s. The Turks had resumed their attacks on small vessels and on the coast, again taking captives into slavery. The problem peaked in 1636. In July the JPs advised the King that they had received complaints from coastal towns, and

137

particularly from Looe. The town had recently lost three vessels and twenty-seven mariners, who had been taken into slavery, in addition to the four vessels and forty-two mariners seized in the previous two years. The townsmen complained of impoverishment at the loss of these men and their industry, and also of the cost of supporting the wives and children of those captured:

> and through the terror of that misery whereunto these persons are carried by these cruel infidels, the owners and seamen rather give over their trade than put their estates and persons into so great peril, there being now about 60 vessels and 200 seamen without employment. In other parts the Turks have taken other vessels, and chased others so that they have run on the rocks, choosing rather to lose their boats than their liberty. These Turks daily show themselves at St Keverne, Mounts Bay, and other places, that the poor fishermen are fearful, not only to go to the seas, but likewise less these Turks should come on shore, and take them out of their houses.[125]

Some towns contributed towards the cost of redeeming captives, supported their dependents, and gave alms to the victims themselves on their return home. For example, the mayor of Liskeard included in his accounts for 1636 the following items:

> given to one Londoner that was spoiled by the Turks, 6d; given to a poor man that had his tongue cut out by the Turks, 12d; given to a poor man of Fowey that was spoiled by the Turks, 6d.[126]

In the same year the town's churchwardens disbursed 5s. for the redemption of 'one of Plymstocke out of Turkey' and paid a further 3s.4d. towards the redemption of one William Leane of St Mawes who had been taken by the Turks. Also in 1636, the St Breock churchwardens gave 2s.6d. to John Penticost of Falmouth and 4s. to John Leane of Manaccan and others of St Keverne, all of whom had been taken by the Turks. In the same year, Charles FitzGeffry, the Puritan rector of St Dominick and the likely lecturer of Fowey, preached a sermon urging charity towards captives and their dependents, both in prayer and generous giving, and praised the people of Plymouth for their monthly collections for that cause. The sermon was originally preached in that town and was dedicated to its mayor and brethren.[127]

The situation had become so serious that the government authorized an expedition to Sallee, which set off in February 1637 led by Captain William Rainsborough. The English fleet blockaded the town, which surrendered on 28 July. Three hundred captives were released.[128] On

20 September 1637 Sir Nicholas Slanning, the governor of Pendennis castle (and Bagg's son-in-law), reported to Secretary Windebank that Rainsborough was said to be at Saffi, negotiating peace terms with the King of Morocco, and that Sallee had surrendered. Many English and Irish captives had already returned. Slanning was optimistic that this news would advance the collection of ship money.[129]

The menace of piracy and the fear of Spanish invasion prompted demands for improved coastal fortifications. In December 1625 the inhabitants of Fowey petitioned for the fortification of their 'open and unfortified' town.[130] In January 1626 the deputy lieutenants supported Fowey's case in their correspondence with Pembroke, reminding him that the town consisted of 500 dwellings and was strategically important, being situated mid-way between Falmouth and Plymouth, and in a position to offer protection to any naval vessels heading for or lying in those ports. It was also able to accommodate '200 good ships', and was one of the best outlets for Spain on the south coast of England. The deputies recommended the erection of a small garrison for the defence of the town.[131]

The deputies also recommended the fortification of Looe, 'a prettie Towne consistinge of 400 howses and is now very well builte', because of the numerous and frequent attacks made upon it by the Turks in 1625. They believed that a few pieces of ordnance would be sufficient to protect the town. In addition, the deputies recommended the same for Penzance, which was 'altogether unfortified'. They maintained that the fortification of Penzance would secure the whole of Mount's Bay and much of west Cornwall. The inhabitants had themselves petitioned the Council of War in 1625 for eight pieces of ordnance and a grant of £600 for fortifications, since their town had been burned by the Spanish in 1595, and recently had suffered greatly at the hands of the Turks.[132]

By the mid-1620s the castles of Pendennis and St Mawes (which defended Falmouth harbour), St Michael's Mount, and the garrison on St Mary's, Scilly, were all dilapidated and poorly supplied. The state of each had begun to decline in about 1615, but complaints became far more frequent and vocal from September 1625, when the fleet sailed for Cadiz. It is likely that the impressment and billeting of soldiers in Cornwall in readiness for the Cadiz expedition, together with the presence of pirates in coastal waters, and the government's greater emphasis on the 'exact militia', increased the governors' awareness of the poor state of their garrisons, and of the neglect of their soldiers.

The complaints made to the government by the governor and lieutenant-governor of Pendennis were fourfold: the decay of the castle building, the shortage of ammunition and ordnance, the arrears of pay, and the lack of essential food supplies. In May 1626, John Bonython, the deputy governor, reported that upon his return to the fort he had found that part of the south bulwarks had collapsed.[133] Numerous other letters and petitions complained that the castle did not have a single piece of ordnance mounted, and neither did it possess any ammunition.[134] This was of particular concern because of the strategic importance of Falmouth harbour:

> and for the saftie of his Majesties fleate outewards bound or for the expectance of an ennemy to com for the chanell, they cannot lye better then at falmouth; This forte, naturallie so situated, that were it mande and vitualed is not to be taken. But being as it is, wheare we should have 40 pecis of ordynance we have none; no not one; nor almoste anny amonysyon.[135]

In their petition of September 1625, the 'distressed soldiers of Pendennis Castle' informed the Council of War that they should each have received 8*d.* per day, but that none had received anything for the last two years,

> and being destitute of all other meanes to maintayne themselves, and their poor wifes, and children, are now driven to soe miserable and lamentable estate, as they are almost famished, and ready to perish for want of ordinary sustinance; having already been forced to pawne their bedding, and other their necessary commodities, to buye bread to keep them from starving.[136]

From autumn 1625 and throughout 1626 many petitions and letters were sent to the Council of War and to Conway describing the poor condition of the soldiers at Pendennis, but the situation appears gradually to have worsened. In April 1626, Sir Robert Killigrew, governor of the castle, petitioned the Council of War:

> that yor Lordships would be pleased to take some course that the poore men there (beeing 50 in number) may have their paye, which they have wanted above two years, and are in that lamentable and miserable estate, that had they not liv'd on limpets (a poore kinde of shell fish) without bred, or any other sustinance, with some small release from yor petitioner, thay had all been starved before this time.[137]

Still no money arrived. In January 1627 Killigrew complained to the Council that some soldiers had already died of malnutrition, notwithstanding that he had wearied the Council with sixty-nine petitions over the previous eleven years, requesting the supply of the castle and pay for the men.[138]

A similarly precarious situation existed at the other garrisons. Between 1617 and 1628 Captain Arthur Harris, governor of St Michael's Mount, petitioned the Council for supply and for the repair of the castle. By 1628 there remained only a small store of ammunition at the castle, and Harris reminded the Council of Sir Richard Morrison's findings in the survey of forts made in 1623: that the Mount was a place of 'good consequence' but 'defective in supply and repair'. Morrison had recommended the speedy rectification of this situation, but Harris regretted that he had been struggling for a number of years to procure it.[139] In addition, Sir Francis Godolphin requested money to improve the fort on St Mary's, of which he was captain.

The government eventually responded to the governors' demands, beginning with St Mary's. It is likely that Scilly was given priority because, being situated twenty-eight miles off Land's End, the islands were particularly exposed to enemy attack and occupation, and recently the waters around them had been infested by pirates. Further, in enemy hands Scilly would have represented a threat to the safety of the realm. Therefore, on 3 December 1626 'having taken into consideracion how greatly it concerneth and importeth his Majesty's service, especially in these dangerous tymes, that speedy and effectuall order be taken for the garde and defense of Silly', the Council advanced £770.5s.10d. to Godolphin for the purchase of sufficient supplies to secure the fort.[140] In addition, on 17 January 1627, Godolphin was ordered to add one hundred 'fit and able men', including twelve gunners, to the existing twenty-five soldiers on Scilly, and he was assured that the new recruits would be paid and supplied out of the loans of Cornwall and Devon.[141] The following month, after the King's engineer had visited Scilly, the Council accepted Godolphin's view that new outworks and fortifications were required, and granted him an additional £800 for this purpose.[142] However, the islanders felt that these measures were still inadequate. Ironically, in June 1628 Thomas Bassett informed Godolphin (who had returned to Cornwall) that work on the fort was progressing slowly since the presence of so many ships (friendly or otherwise) around the islands had aroused alarm among the inhabitants.[143]

Supply began to reach Pendennis in March 1627. On 4 March Tresahar acknowledged receipt of ammunition and of carriages for ordnance.[144] Further, on 3 April Killigrew received two warrants. One granted him £638.15s. per annum to pay for fifty extra soldiers, and the other provided 1,177 to Killigrew and Godolphin jointly, for repairs to Pendennis castle and St Mary's fort, and for the erection of new fortifications at Pendennis. All this money was to be raised from the forced loans of Cornwall.[145]

By mid-July work had begun at Pendennis, and on 6 August Killigrew

141

informed Conway of the progress made, and of his proposed alterations to the original plans. He claimed to have saved much money by his economies, especially in the construction of a hornwork rather than a coffer, but he believed that certain additional repairs were necessary (costing £300) to the old fortifications so as to make the new work worthwhile. Otherwise, he maintained, the Council would have spent a great deal of money making the castle strong upon one side, while leaving the other indefensible. Killigrew urged Conway to persuade the Council to finance the additional work from the loans of Cornwall, which, he claimed, the county could well bear. Killigrew added that he had received a visit from Sir Francis Godolphin (a collector of the loan as well as captain of St Mary's fort) who had complained of 'a generall slackness both in the colectors and payers of the loanes', and Killigrew recommended that 'a letter to quicken the contry would do his Majesty good service heere'.[146] By appointing Godolphin a collector, and by making the repairs dependent upon the collection of the forced loan in Cornwall, the Council gave both Killigrew and Godolphin a strong vested interest in the success of this expedient.

Grievances over the state of forts in Cornwall and in other maritime counties, and continued complaints about piracy, were voiced in Parliament in 1628. On 6 June Coryton complained in the Commons that 'There are no forts manned in this time of necessity'. Three days later, following Sir Walter Erle's complaints about Turkish piracy, Eliot reflected: 'It is too much known that the coasts are not guarded, so there must needs be a decay of trade if the seas be not open'. The same day, in the Committee of the Whole House, Coryton stated that thirty ships had been taken off the west coast 'since we sat here', and Eliot added 'This is the want of the Admiral's duty'.[147] On 11 June Sir Nathaniel Rich reported to the House from the sub-committee concerning the Remonstrance:

> The 4th head is the weakness and decay of the forts. They are not strong, want repair, men, and munition, chiefly instanced in Sandown Castle in the Isle of Wight where had they powder they dared not use it lest the ordnance should scare down the fort.[148]

Since by this time supply had been sent to many forts, and since the Remonstrance was primarily a renewed attack on Buckingham, it is likely that Eliot and his allies were (at least in part) exploiting coastal defence issues to undermine further the Duke's position. With the exception of St Mary's fort, Scilly (which was particularly exposed),[149] no further complaints were raised about the state of Cornish coastal defences before 1640. Clearly, the lack of a Parliament reduced opportunities for voicing such concerns, but there is no extant correspondence from the governors to the Council for these years either. Invasion fears would have been diminished by the conclusion of peace with France and Spain in 1630. Further, although piracy remained a problem, particularly in the mid-1630s, complaints on this matter were not accompanied by demands for the improvement of local fortifications, and largely were quelled by the success of the Sallee expedition in 1637.

5

The Impact of Arbitrary Taxation

Privy Seal Loans

In late autumn 1625 Charles I, in urgent need of war revenue, despatched privy seal letters, based on medieval precedents, requesting loans from the most substantial inhabitants of each county:

> the Kings and Queenes of this our Realme upon extraordinary occasions have used either to resort to those contributions which arise from the generality of subjects, or to the private helpes of some well-affected in particular by way of loane.[1]

Although payment was in effect made a test of loyalty, collection was slow and inefficient, and the response from the counties was generally poor. In Warwickshire, for example, requests for loans were 'more-or-less ignored'.[2] However, in Cornwall, despite considerable initial resistance, all the money required appears ultimately to have been paid.

On 14 December 1625 the Privy Council ordered payment of £5,000 from the Devon and Cornwall loan money to the mayor of Plymouth to provide a 'compleate suite of apparell' for each of the soldiers upon their return from Cadiz. Of this, £2,000 was to come from Cornwall.[3] However, the same day, Secretary Coke, reporting to Secretary Conway the gradual return of the fleet, expressed grave concern for the welfare of 'this unfortunate armie and fleet that cometh home' since

> Sir James Bagge writeth plainly that the gentlemen of those parts wil in no wise bee drawn to anie contribution or to anie ingagement in matter of monie.[4]

Sir Francis Godolphin of Godolphin and William Coryton were appointed collectors of Cornish privy seal loans. Godolphin, governor of St Mary's fort, Scilly, was given responsibility for the western division (Powder, Pyder, Kerrier and Penwith), and Coryton for the eastern division

(East, West, Stratton, Trigg and Lesnewth). Godolphin was not entirely at ease with his position, and on 27 December revealed to Jonathan Rashleigh Esq of Menabilly that

> finding one [privy seal letter] directed unto your selfe, my respects prompts mee to accompanie it with these lines unto you, to signifie how unpleasing it is to mee to bee imployed in this kinde and yett dare not but undergoe the Commande for his Majestie's service.[5]

Nevertheless, both Godolphin and Coryton were assiduous in their duties, making personal appeals, explaining the nature of the emergency, arranging for payment at the next quarter sessions, and compiling lists of refusers.[6] Coryton, amongst others, had advocated the opening of hostilities with Spain during the 1624 Parliament,[7] which may explain his commitment to the task.

At the end of 1625 Coryton listed all those in the eastern division who had not paid, with their excuses. All those asked in Lesnewth had paid, but twenty-five in the other four eastern hundreds had not. Many reasons were given, all common excuses for tax avoidance. Six were listed merely as not having paid, eight pleaded poverty, and three indebtedness. Two, Thomas Wyvell Esq of St Stephens by Saltash, the sheriff, and William Wills Gent, the mayor of Saltash, claimed exemption through their offices. Two others said they had received and had paid privy seals in Devon, and in two further cases the seal had allegedly never been delivered (in one instance because of mistaken identity, and in the other because the intended recipient had been absent from the county). One person had since paid.[8]

Given all these excuses, it is remarkable that by 30 January 1626 Coryton had paid £970 from the eastern division to the mayor of Plymouth, and that later in the year all 141 persons from whom loans had been requested had complied. Cornish loans totalled £3,190, the most common payment being £20, although some of the wealthier inhabitants paid £30 or even £40.[9] There were clearly special local circumstances which overcame initial resistance and ensured payment of privy seal loans in Cornwall when the response from most other counties was so poor. These are likely to have been the presence of billeted soldiers in the county from the end of 1625 and consequent awareness of the need to clothe and provision them, and perhaps also to maintain order. Since Cornish privy seal loans had been allocated specifically for clothing the soldiers, local taxpayers would have witnessed the soldiers' need, and would have had an interest in the success of the measure. Billeting therefore appears to have been the key to ultimate payment.

The Benevolence

The privy seal loan was nationally so unsuccessful that after a few months it was abandoned and replaced in July 1626 by a benevolence, another form of non-parliamentary taxation. The benevolence had medieval precedents, and was based on the precept that the monarch was entitled to call for additional supply from his subjects when the security of the realm was threatened.[10] Initial letters from the King and Privy Council on 7 July ordered all local governors to meet with subsidymen, to persuade them to contribute, and to collect the money. However, no incentive was provided for payment, and no coercive powers were given to assist collection. The expedient was short-lived, and was generally unsuccessful.

In Cornwall it seems that only five JPs attempted to collect the benevolence—Charles Lord Lambert, Mr Harris, John Trefusis, William Rous and Richard Erisey. On 7 October they informed the Council that they had complied with the instructions of 7 July, and had assembled at Bodmin, each assuming responsibility for different parts of the county. They had then written to the 'principall gentlemen and of moste sufficiencye' and had notified them of the time and place of the county meeting for collection. At that meeting they had encouraged payment, 'usinge the best of our perswasions for the advancement of his Majesties service'. However, the gentry had answered that

> their burthens were manye, their charge greate, their abillities little, and money extreame scarse, soe as they were not able to give in that manner but if itt shall please his Majestie to sumon a Parliament they wilbee readye by sale of their goodes, or what else they hadd in a Parliamentarye waye to give satisfaccon to his Majesties desires. The like answere (haveinge conferred with the particular parishes) were receyved of them, protestinge that if they had but two kyne they would sell one of them for the supplye of his Majestie and ye Kingdomes occasions in a Parliamentarye course.[11]

As in other counties, a single meeting for all taxpayers limited opportunities for individual acts of persuasion. Further, the Cornish defence of the need for parliamentary approval of taxation was similar to that raised by other counties, such as Nottinghamshire and Essex. Such a defence was apparently considered necessary because of the implication in the initial instructions that the benevolence was an alternative to parliamentary taxation, which seemed to challenge the future of parliaments generally.[12]

There is no record of payment but the response to the JPs' attempts at collection suggests an appreciation of the importance of parliaments to the localities. Nascent factionalism may also have influenced this response.

Eliot's and Coryton's role in the impeachment attempt upon Buckingham in the Commons in June 1626 had cost them their local offices that summer. Recall of Parliament would have been in their interests, enabling them to continue the attack on the Duke. On 22 September their chief enemy, Bagg, implied their involvement in resistance to the benevolence:

> This country and the gentlemen that were interested as comissioners for the contribucion followe the example of the east. Grenvile: Mohun: and some other my friends, have exprest their harty affeccon and Loyalty to his Ma[jes]tie. But by the ill example of others, their intendments were destroyed.[13]

There is, however, some uncertainty about this account, since primarily it was a blatant attempt by Bagg to promote his own supporters at the expense of his enemies, and there is no further evidence of Grenvile's and Mohun's activity in this service. It is possible that Bagg was simply misrepresenting genuine countywide resentment to encourage the King and Buckingham in their belief that Eliot was a potential leader of a conspiracy against the monarchy.[14] Bagg's motives must further be questioned because in the same letter he urged the Duke to promote John Mohun's appointment as vice-warden of the stannaries in Coryton's place.

The Forced Loan

The failure of the benevolence convinced Charles of the disloyalty of many local governors, and of the need for greater coercion in non-parliamentary taxation. In September 1626 it was decided to levy a forced loan from all taxpayers, and to make payment a conclusive test of loyalty to the King. Commissioners (JPs and others) were given detailed instructions about collection (including the individual persuasion of lenders), and coercive powers to deal with refusers.[15]

In October Bagg introduced a factional dimension to Cornish loan collection. He advised Buckingham to select as loan commissioners 'such gentlemen as stand best affected to his Majesties service, and suche as by their owne examples will guide others unto the same'. Bagg provided a list of suitable candidates for Cornwall and Devon (now missing), and particularly recommended the services of John Mohun 'who studies nothinge more then to honor yow, and to advantage his Majesties commands'. Bagg also requested a peerage for Mohun, and advised the Duke of the progress of the admiralty commission into the affairs of 'that ungratefull villain' Eliot, so underlining the factional nature of the letter.[16]

Select commissions of the type recommended by Bagg proved

147

impractical because of the need to cover the whole of each county, and commissions instead named all JPs, with some additions. As shown in Appendix 3, forty-five Cornish loan commissioners were appointed. This number included all twenty-two local gentry JPs, together with the twelve great officers of state and clergymen who were also members of the Cornish commission of the peace. Bagg was the only non-Cornish loan commissioner who was not also a JP for the county, but his appointment is not surprising. In addition, ten local men who were not JPs were named. Of these, Sir Bernard Grenvile and Sir William Wrey had proved loyal deputy lieutenants and were close associates of Bagg. Richard Lord Robartes was the only indigenous Cornish peer, and Francis Bassett was vice-admiral of north Cornwall. Bevill Grenvile and Humphrey Nicoll would have filled gaps at Stratton and Trigg respectively, but there is no clear reason for the other choices.[17]

No approach was made to the counties until early 1627. On 16 February the Cornish loan commissioners reminded the Council of the heavy burden of billeting borne by the county since 1625. Cornwall had actually been freed from billeted troops at the end of August 1626, when the Council had responded to local complaints by ordering the removal of soldiers to other southern counties.[18] However, the billeters clearly remained unpaid. When requesting the loan from former billeters the loan commissioners had received a common answer:

> that in their hearts, they are most dutifully ready to subscribe to the said loane, so as they may receave a defalcacon of the Money due from his Majestie, for billeting of souldiers: otherwise they professe themselves utterly unable to lend the proporcons directed.[19]

The Council responded favourably to this request, and to similar representations from Pembroke and from Sir George Chudleigh, treasurer and paymaster for the loan in Devon and Cornwall, and agreed that Cornish loan money should be earmarked for the payment of former billeters.[20] This major concession greatly advanced the service in Cornwall, and on 4 March John Tresahar, deputy governor of Pendennis castle, reported that the commissioners had held meetings throughout the county, and had met little resistance.[21]

An illustration of the interrelationship between loan payment and billeting is provided by the case of John Scory of Lanlivery, who was listed as a refuser in June. On 14 August Thomas Hoblyn, the collector for Powder, pleaded Skory's case with the commissioners and treasurer of the loan for Cornwall, stating that Skory's refusal had been through indebtedness. He was now prepared to pay provided that he could subtract

148

the billeting money due to him from the amount he owed.[22]

Some Cornish loan money was also allocated to finance the urgent repairs to Pendennis castle, and to St Mary's fort, Scilly. This gave the governors, Sir Robert Killigrew (a commissioner) and Sir Francis Godolphin (a commissioner, as well as treasurer and paymaster of the loan in Cornwall from May 1627), a great incentive for industrious collection. Writing to Secretary Conway on 6 August, Killigrew explained the need for additional repairs to Pendennis, and asked Conway to

> order the payment of this mony out of the loanes of Cornewell, which it will well beare . . . As I was sealing this letter Sir francis Godolphin came heather from the receivers who tels me he findes a generall slackness both in the colectors and payers of the loanes a letter to quicken the contry would do his Majesty good service heere.[23]

So, it seems that application of Cornish loan money to billeting payments and to repairing the forts, both matters of great local concern, provided an incentive for some collectors. It was also an important influence upon the attitudes of many taxpayers, and is the most likely explanation for the obedience of the majority.

Bagg frequently reminded Buckingham that his own supporters were the most fervent loan collectors, and was quick to alert the Duke to the refusals of his enemies:

> in generall [in Cornwall] all Lend; savinge Elliot, Corrington, Arrondell and their associates and faction . . . I hope his Majestie wilbe pleased to make those that thus disaffectionately disserve him examples for tymes to come.[24]

There is no other evidence of Arundell's non-payment, but Eliot and Coryton were the two most prominent Cornish loan refusers: indeed, Coryton has recently been described as 'perhaps the most stubbornly awkward of all refusers'.[25] On 27 April 1627 Eliot and Coryton were summoned before the Council, and appeared the following day. From this date until 2 January 1628 both were imprisoned in London for their dissent.[26]

Both Eliot and Coryton claimed that their refusal was based upon the unlawfulness of the loan. During his imprisonment in the Gatehouse, Eliot sent a petition to the King, with the declared intention of showing

> that no factious humour nor disaffection, led on by stubbornness and will, has therein stirred or moved him; but the just obligation of his conscience, which binds him to the service of your majesty in the observance of your laws.[27]

Eliot cited various statutes to demonstrate the unlawfulness of the loan. He further maintained that the loan was not free because the instructions for it had been accompanied by the great seal (therefore constituting tacit commands); that by its very nature the loan threatened the liberties of the subject, which had been preserved by monarchs throughout the ages; and that it was likely to set a precedent, if not during Charles' reign, then for the future.[28]

In his *Relation* of his appearance before the Council, Coryton too cited statutes which demonstrated the unlawfulness of the loan. He asserted that he had always 'in all publicque accons where I was in dowbte, sought to god by my prayers; and then searched the statutes', and that 'every honest Justice of Peace which made care or conscience what he did, had . . . [the statutes] ever for his direccon'.[29] Coryton made a number of further references to 'honest' local governors, and stressed his own exemplary behaviour while in office:

> Whilest I had to doe with publicque officees I tooke the Best Care I could to perfforme them as I ought, And I thancke god I had never any Taxe, or Taynte layde uppon me in any suche place, which was knowne to some of them—But nowe I was freed from any suche Imploymente: all my care was to keepe one man (my selfe an honest man) which I should not have done, had I yeilded to paye this Loane.[30]

He was careful to distinguish between privy seal loans (which he had considered legal and had collected assiduously) and the forced loan, again emphasizing his own virtues as an office-holder:

> And for my parte I had bin soe farre from dissaffeccon to the kings service therein, as in that verye thinge of Privye Seales . . . I did the kinge more service then all the countie of Cornewall besides, And that I was collector for the kinge for the Privye Seales, And that I had in severall other offices, with as much payne, and industrye served the kinge, as any man of my qualletye within the kingdome.[31]

The Lords maintained that this loan too was asked freely, and that no-one was compelled to pay, to which Coryton replied, 'I then Marvayled, whie any weare restrayned for not payeinge it'.

The wide circulation of both Coryton's and Eliot's treatises suggests that they did not intend merely to convince the King and the Council of the unlawfulness of the loan, but sought a wider audience.[32] One possibility is that they were motivated solely by a conviction that the loan was ideologically unsound and that it threatened property rights. However, their shared opposition to Buckingham since February 1626 and their recent humiliations and deprivations at his hands make it more likely that they were using loan refusal as a platform from which to express political opposition to the Duke. Coryton's constant emphasis upon his own qualities and loyalty as an office-holder reinforces the impression that, over and above the question of legality of the loan, bitterness at his loss of office was the principal reason for his refusal.[33]

Five loan commissioners refused to pay: Sir Richard Buller, Bevill Grenvile, Nicholas Trefusis, Ambrose Manaton and Humphry Nicoll. These individuals were, by association, members of the Eliot–Coryton faction. Of the five, three (Buller, Trefusis and Manaton) were also JPs, and were summoned before the Council and removed from the commission of the peace for their refusal. Buller was also ousted from the lieutenancy. Nicoll was summoned by the Council, but the outcome is unclear. Grenvile alone was neither summoned nor punished, which caused him 'wonder and amazem[en]t',[34] but was perhaps the effect of his father's influence with Bagg. Instructed to administer the removals from the commission of the peace, Bagg applauded Buckingham's decisive action, which undermined the Eliot–Coryton faction's local power base, and placed control of local government into the hands of his own faction.[35]

Buller was charged with having been 'often invited to the bussines but never appeared nor will he declare himselfe to lend or not'.[36] In July, Buller pleaded that there had been a mistake in his case, claiming that he had never neglected his duties as loan commissioner (except during an unavoidable absence in London) and that he had never refused to pay. Rather, several months previously he had paid part of his loan money, and had engaged himself for the other part. He accompanied this plea with a receipt for £25, the total amount of his loan money, from William Wills (the collector for the hundred of East).[37] Regardless of this plea, and of the amendment of a list of defaulters with the marginal note 'paid' beside Buller's name, he was nonetheless removed from the commission of the peace and from the lieutenancy, almost certainly because of his associations with the Eliot–Coryton faction, and he was not restored to his former position until May 1629.[38]

Generally, the forced loan was successful in Cornwall. This was principally because of the allocation of loan money for the payment of billeters and the repair of fortifications. The government's compromise over billeting payments had a similarly positive effect on loan payment in other affected southern counties, including Devon, Kent, Hampshire and Sussex. Indeed, Cust has shown that the counties to which the concession was made were amongst the most willing payers, and that none experienced the widespread opposition which occurred in Essex and Lincolnshire, for example.[39]

However, in Cornwall the expedient also acted as a vehicle for factional division and for political opposition to Buckingham, and resistance on this basis was strong and determined. All the refusers (or alleged refusers) were associated with the Eliot–Coryton faction, and were almost certainly Puritans. Their legalism has no apparent previous history, which is not surprising since this was the first occasion for their collective action, and seems to have developed as a response to the loan. Whether or not concerns about the legality of the loan were genuine, they provided a respectable facade for attacks upon the Duke. For Eliot and Coryton, the immediate stimulus for these attacks was certainly their loss of office at the Duke's hands. However, their underlying motives were implicit in their reasons for attacking the Duke in the 1626 Parliament, not least for his military failures. These had had an adverse effect on Cornwall, but Eliot and Coryton, as Puritans, may also have interpreted them as divine judgement upon the Duke. Buller, Manaton, Trefusis, Nicoll and (probably) Grenvile shared this godly perspective, which perhaps accounts for their collective action against the loan and therefore the Duke.[40]

Knighthood Composition Fines

In January 1630 the government introduced knighthood composition fines as another means of raising urgently needed revenue, particularly to repay war debts. The fines were based upon another medieval precedent, established in 1227 by Henry III, when he summoned men of a certain landed status to accept knighthoods in times of military necessity, imposing fines upon those who failed to attend. Over the centuries, this practice lost its military connections and became associated with coronations, last used in 1558. Charles revived and extended the procedure, and demanded money from all gentlemen who had enjoyed a landed income in excess of £40 per annum for the three years preceding the coronation, but who had not received the order of knighthood. A fine of two and a half times their subsidy assessment was imposed, increasing in February 1631 to three and a half times the assessment, with a minimum fine of £25 for JPs and £10 for others.[41]

Initially all compositions took place in London but, owing to the distances involved, few payments were made by those from outside London and the Home Counties. Therefore, in June 1630 local commissioners were appointed to supervise the scheme. Their tasks included compiling a list of liable gentlemen; summoning those gentlemen to appear before them to compound; assessing fines; and directing payment.[42]

Four commissions were issued for Cornwall. The first commissioners were John Lord Mohun, Sir John Trelawny, Sir William Wrey and Sir Bernard Grenvile, all former adherents of Bagg and Buckingham, and probably selected for their proven loyalty to the government.[43] However, they demonstrated little enthusiasm for their new task, and on 29 September 1630 the Council reprimanded them for holding meetings for composition at Bodmin alone. The commissioners had probably chosen Bodmin because they all resided in the east of the county, but the Council considered it inappropriate given

> the situation of your Countie, that it lyeth much in length and that by this meanes many must travill farr, and this being a Commission of grace is intended for the accomodacion of the subject as well as for the profitt of the King.

The Council ordered the commissioners to separate and to meet in different parts of the county, 'which would much ease the trouble and charge of those that are to attend you and would expedite the worke, which wee desire might be don with all convenient speede'.[44]

Some changes were made to the list in the second commission, probably to facilitate a more efficient collection of fines throughout the county. Trelawny was omitted, and Sir Reginald Mohun, Sir Richard Buller, Sir Francis Godolphin, Sir James Bagg, Sir John Killigrew and William Coryton were added. All those named in the first and second commissions, with the exception of Killigrew and Coryton, had also been forced loan commissioners for Cornwall. Mohun and Bagg were almost certainly added to strengthen the representation of the government's proven supporters. Godolphin had also proved loyal as an efficient collector of the privy seal and forced loans, and both he and Killigrew resided in the west of the county. Buller and Coryton were less obvious choices, given their residence in eastern Cornwall, and their record of opposition to government policies. However, as shown above, both had been restored to office in 1629.[45]

The Cornish compositions were closely linked to the subsidy assessments. For example, Ralph Keate Gent of St Columb Major in Pyder and Robert Dodson Esq of St Ive in East hundred were both assessed at £5 for the 1626 subsidy, and were both fined at £12.10s. John Lampen Esq of Linkinhorne in East hundred was assessed at £7 in 1626, and was fined at £17.10s. Of the 554 Cornish gentlemen named as liable under the first commission, only 25 (4.5 per cent) compounded, paying a total of £340. This compares unfavourably with 57 of 213 (27 per cent) Oxfordshire gentlemen who compounded, 38 of 300 (12.6 per cent) in Gloucestershire;

153

33 of 112 (29.5 per cent) in Northamptonshire, 81 of 153 (53 per cent) in Leicestershire, and 65 of 104 (62.5 per cent) in Warwickshire. As with the demands of the previous decade, a wide range of excuses was offered by those who did not compound. Many were listed as having 'appeared not' or as refusing; others said that they were willing to pay, but pleaded 'inability', a 'want of money', or indebtedness. A number of gentlemen claimed that they had not been summoned, or that they had been out of the county at the time of the summons, and had not been warned by the constable; and many more pleaded age, sickness, or insufficient land.[46]

One of the most elegant pleas was made by Sir Walter Langdon, who

> being in London on the xxviiith day of June 1628 received a comand to attend his Majestie, and coming before his highnes the next day at Whitehall, his Majestie gave him many gratious words in the hearing of some of the commissioners now present, and his Majestie layd the sword on him in so free and gratious a way, as he is confident his highnes did alsoe therewith freely forgive his not attendance at his Majesties coronacon, he being neither retorned nor sumoned by the sherriffe, yet if he be mistaken in his oppinion he is ready to compound upon notice given.[47]

Langdon had indeed been knighted by the King on 29 June 1628, following his release from the Tower, where he had been imprisoned for his part in the corrupt county election campaign of March 1628 against Eliot and Coryton. Like his factional allies who were named in the first commission, he showed little enthusiasm for knighthood fines, despite his previous fervent loyalty to the government.

All JPs were fined at the minimum figure of £25; they were generally dealt with more fairly than many of their fellow gentlemen. However, initially nine Cornish JPs refused to compound. Since Nicholas Trefusis, Ambrose Manaton and Joseph Bastard had all been assessed at £10 in 1626, they were being fined at the same rate as other gentlemen. However, the standard £25 fine was of benefit to Edward Coswarth, John Moyle, William Rous, Richard Erisey and John Trefusis, since all were assessed at £20 in 1626, and were therefore paying little more than their subsidy assessment in fine. In the main their excuses (listed in Table 7, opposite) appear implausible, but the resistance of JPs to government policy suggests a deep-rooted opposition to knighthood composition fines in the county.[48]

Factional ties had weakened by this stage, but they may still have been a factor in refusal. Manaton and Nicholas Trefusis had been active members of the Eliot–Coryton faction, and had been removed from the commission of the peace in 1627 for forced loan refusal. Moyle and Rous

Table 7
JPs who refused to pay Knighthood Composition Fines[49]

JP	Reason(s) given for refusal
Edward Coswarth of Little Colan (Pyder)	aged 80 years; indebted; received no summons.
Thomas Gewen of Boyton (Stratton)	no reason given.
Nicholas Trefusis of Lezant (East)	not summoned; 'holds noe land of the kinge'.
John Moyle of Bake (East)	not summoned; willing to pay £10.
William Rous of Halton in St Dominick (East)	fear of the sheriff; indebted.
Ambrose Manaton of South Petherwin (East)	not summoned; had no estate.
John Trefusis of Trefusis in Mylor parish (Kerrier)	no lawful summons; did not possess so much land.
Richard Erisey of Grade (Kerrier)	no lawful summons; no lawful return; no land to charge him to compound.
Joseph Bastard of Duloe (West)	much charged with his children; conceived he was not liable.

had also been associated with the Eliot–Coryton faction, although there is no record of their refusal of previous non-parliamentary taxation. Gewen, the duchy auditor, had resisted government militia demands in 1629, but had no history of tax refusal.

If there was an element of collective action, it was specifically directed against knighthood fines, and not against government policies generally. Seven of the nine were soon to be active enforcers of the Book of Orders, and Manaton and Gewen were the most active of all Cornish JPs in that capacity. In so far as the positive response to the Book of Orders can be explained by the zeal of Puritan JPs (such as Manaton and Gewen), and given that at least seven of the nine JP refusers of knighthood fines were Puritans, it seems likely that resistance to knighthood fines was Puritan-led. A possible explanation is that the godly objected to repaying debts for disastrous wars which they therefore believed to be an expression of divine judgement.

Concern about legality may also have been a factor in refusal, and it is significant that both John Trefusis and Richard Erisey imputed a lack of legality in the composition procedure.[50] In February 1631 the Crown's right to distrain was vindicated in the Exchequer Court, after a challenge by Edward Stephens of Gloucester. The second commission of 22 March 1631 was accompanied by a letter declaring the Crown's victory, and the Council's new confidence was reflected in a much firmer approach. They stated that they sent the new commission

> not doubting but such as have hitherto been backward in this service, will now, upon the late declaration in our Court of Exchequer by Councell learned in the Lawes, of our right to theis fines cheerfully conforme themselves to render us our due . . . [and] . . . those who shall nowe refuse to make their Compositions shall hereafter have no other recourse for it but the Lords of our Privy Councell.[51]

This new coercive strategy, supported by the law, had immediate effect. Most liable gentlemen paid on the second commission, which raised £2,543.16s.4d., with £432 outstanding. The third and fourth commissions raised £30 and £150 respectively, making a total of £2,723.16s.4d. from Cornwall.[52]

Offenders were dealt with as warned: on 27 May 1633 Charles Trevanion, and another of his family (Christian name unknown, but probably his son John), and John Trefusis were summoned before the Council for non-payment, and on 12 July Thomas and Edward Hoblyn, John Arundell of Trerice, and Jonathan Rashleigh received the same treatment.[53] So, although recourse to law may have prompted payment by some, it did not persuade John Trefusis to comply, suggesting that for him at least concern about legality masked other reasons for refusal. Trevanion and Arundell had acted together politically since 1625, and were formerly prominent members of the Eliot–Coryton faction. By 1633 that faction had lost its leaders and had disintegrated, but it is possible that these two still collaborated. The likelihood of the other Trevanion being John is increased by the fact that he had married Arundell's daughter, Ann, in 1630.

The Council's new policy was effective. John Trefusis at last paid £100 on 1 June 1634. Thomas and Edward Hoblyn each paid £31 on the day they were summoned (12 July), Jonathan Rashleigh paid £70 on 16 July, and Charles Trevanion paid £124.17s.4d. on 29 July. John Arundell paid £150 on 5 April 1636, and was one of the last Cornishmen to pay.[54]

Dislike of knighthood fines amongst the Cornish gentry crossed former factional divisions. By 1632 both factions had largely disintegrated, but it is unclear how far previous factional allies continued in united political activity. Former members of the Bagg–Mohun faction adopted a relaxed approach to collection. In addition, seven of the nine JP refusers had been connected in some way with the Eliot–Coryton faction and with earlier resistance to government policies; so had Trevanion and Arundell, two of the most stubborn refusers. Therefore, although knighthood fines were not a vehicle for factional conflict in the way the forced loan had been, the nature of resistance appears to have reflected earlier factional associations. Where these were related to Puritanism, that too may have influenced refusal.

Ship Money

Ship money was levied upon the maritime counties in 1634, and upon the whole country from 1635 to 1640. It was a rate rather than a tax, based upon medieval precedents and upon those of 1596, 1603, 1618 and 1626. Each year a separate writ was issued to each county, demanding payment of money to equip a fleet to defend the Narrow Seas in a time of national emergency, when pirates were infesting the English Channel, and a continental invasion was threatened:

> we are given to understand that certain thieves, pirates, and robbers of the sea, as well Turks . . . wickedly taking by force and spoiling [our] ships, and goods . . . have carried away delivering the men in the same into miserable captivity . . . also the dangers considered which, on every side, in these times of war do hang over our heads, that it behoveth us and our subjects to hasten the defence of the sea and kingdom with all expedition or speed that we can; we willing by the help of God chiefly to provide for the defence of the kingdom, safeguard of the sea . . .[55]

The sheriff played a key role in collection. His responsibilities were extremely onerous, and the Council avoided a policy of strict enforcement by exploiting his position. The Council monitored the sheriff's activities closely, and forced him to employ coercive measures against refusers, while itself remaining aloof and appearing only as the arbiter of local disputes which had arisen through the sheriff's actions. The Council ensured the sheriff's commitment to his task by making him personally responsible for paying his quota, even after his year in office had ended. This also minimized the potential ill effects upon the locality, since the sheriff would need to re-integrate himself into local society at the end of his shrievalty.[56]

The Council levied a fixed sum upon each county, which was to be paid to Sir William Russell, the treasurer of the navy. Once a figure had been allocated to corporate towns, the sheriff was responsible for dividing the remainder between the hundreds and the parishes. The Council usually advised sheriffs to rate according to the value of houses and lands within the county, or else to follow other public payments 'most equal and agreeable to the inhabitants'. In the task of assessment, sheriffs generally enlisted the help and advice of the high constables of hundreds, who in turn summoned the petty constables to assist in rating individuals within the parish. The constables were also employed in collection, although ultimate responsibility for this, as well as for assessment, lay with the sheriff.[57]

Table 8
Cornish payment of Ship Money 1634–1639[58]

Writ	Sheriff	Charge £	Arrears £	Rate %
August 1634	Hugh Boscawen	2,204	0	100.0
August 1635	John St Aubyn	6,500	0	100.0
August 1636	Sir Richard Buller	5,500	0	100.0
September 1637	Francis Godolphin of Godolphin	5,500	0	100.0
November 1638	Francis Godolphin of Treveneage	1,700	63	96.3
November 1639	Richard Trevill	5,500	2,700	51.0

Rating disputes were the major difficulty encountered by the first Cornish ship money sheriff, Hugh Boscawen Esq of Tregothnan. This problem was common to all early ship money sheriffs, principally because of the vague and sometimes contradictory instructions issued by the Council. For example, sheriffs were instructed to rate according to property, but to avoid taxing poor cottagers by assessing in their place men with considerable personal wealth but no lands. However, Cornish rating disputes were far less numerous and less disruptive to collection than elsewhere and did not present a serious problem. In November 1634 Boscawen apologized to the Council for his failure to provide an exact account of receipts, which was 'in regarde of sume disagreeings and diffrences in the countye, concerninge the rate'. However, he had called a meeting at Truro for the 30th of that month, where he hoped to settle the rate and to receive some of the money.[59] Notwithstanding these difficulties, it was noted by the King on 1 April 1635 that Cornwall had paid in full, and was the first county to do so.[60]

Boscawen made great efforts to appease the Council: his letters to

Secretary Nicholas and the Council contain strenuous expressions of his desire to oblige. For example, writing to the Council in November 1634, Boscawen maintained that, 'I have no waye neglected the service'. He claimed to have prepared an account of his proceedings for the Council, even before they had requested it; and said that he would 'as often as opportunitye and the necessitye of the business shall so require, give all due satisfaction and make it apeare that I have used my best indeavors to advance and hasten the service'.[61]

Boscawen's successor, John St Aubyn Esq of Clowance, also experienced rating problems. After St Aubyn had fixed the assessment for Penwith hundred, and all but two or three had paid, he altered all the rates of the hundred in response to one man's claim that his parish was over-charged.[62] St Aubyn lived in Penwith, and may have altered that hundred's rate to appease his neighbours, or perhaps to satisfy one particularly influential neighbour. However, St Aubyn was obliged to yield to pressure from the centre, since the Council was more concerned with receiving the full amount than with local rating squabbles. Nicholas maintained that a second assessment would cause delay or 'make men refractory', and that it would be better to have a 'mischief' than an 'inconvenience'. Therefore, he urged St Aubyn to find a quick solution to the problem.[63]

St Aubyn experienced greater difficulty in collecting his quota than had Boscawen, probably because he was told to raise three times as much (£6,500 compared with Boscawen's £2,204). Nevertheless, the Council maintained a very hard line, and on 19 June 1636 accused St Aubyn of being insufficiently coercive. The Council alleged that he had returned distrained goods to their owners, and ordered him to make amends for 'this great fault', or he would 'soon be made sensible of so gross a neglect of duty'. The Council directed St Aubyn that if he were unable to sell distrained goods, he should send them to his Majesty's victualler at Plymouth, ensuring that the distress was sufficient to cover both the sum due and the transport costs.[64]

St Aubyn found his task so arduous that in December 1635 he asked either to be relieved of the shrievalty, or else for the county's assessment for that year to be reduced. He was told that there was no possibility of either until he had collected his full assessment. On 5 November 1636 he completed payment of his quota, after 'much trouble, great opposition, and extraordinary expence of money'. He had been left £50 or £60 out of pocket, and requested from Nicholas a 'reasonable allowance towards the great charge . . . which is heavie for me to beare'.[65] Although the Council had shown no sympathy to St Aubyn, a note written by Nicholas in July 1636 suggests that, in retrospect, it recognized the validity of his case:

Cornwall was too high rated by near half, being three parts maritime places, and those places consisting of poor fishermen, there being no merchants or ships, and there being very little land or inland towns.[66]

Cornwall's assessment was reduced to £5,500 in the writ of August 1636, and was never so high again.

On 10 February 1637 Sir Richard Buller, who succeeded St Aubyn as sheriff, reported to Nicholas his difficulties in raising the levy, because many of 'the principalest gentlemen say they have no money' (presumably a reference to the lack of ready money rather than to poverty). Further, the inhabitants of many parishes were refusing to co-operate in making assessments, and some were suing the constables for wrongful distress.[67] In April Hugh Boscawen, who had zealously and successfully collected ship money during his own shrievalty two years earlier, appealed to Buller on behalf of 'the little poore towne of St Mawes'. He claimed that 'in regarde of the poverty of that place they wer not abell the laste yeer to paye towards the ship rate the Ten pounds assessed on that towne by the Lords of his Majesties Cowncell'.[68] St Mawes was near Boscawen's seat at Tregothnan, and Boscawen apparently considered that having proved his loyalty to the government, it would be advisable to be seen to represent the local interest also.

Buller drafted an account of the particulars of his collection for inspection by the Council, listing, by hundred and by parish, receipts, arrears, and those refusing.[69] As shown in Appendix 4, forty-four individuals are listed as 'persons refusing' of whom twenty-eight were gentry. John Arundell of Trerice owed the largest amount (£5.7s.4d.). Arundell had a history of tax refusal: he had previously been named as a forced loan defaulter (although this accusation cannot be substantiated), and he was one of the most stubborn refusers of knighthood fines. His reason for refusing to pay ship money in 1636–37 is unknown. Edward Coswarth of Colan, who had refused to pay his knighthood fine, is also listed as refusing to make his ship money payment of £3.13s. Buller also listed his own son and heir, Francis, of Morval, for refusing to pay his £1.10s. None of the others listed is known to have been involved in earlier opposition to non-parliamentary taxation.[70] However, the total arrears listed amount to only £119.14s., slightly over 2 per cent of the total £5,500 assessment demanded from the county under the August 1636 writ. By 30 November 1637 Russell had received the full amount due from Cornwall, which suggests that the problems of collection in that year were transitory, and that the refusers were not particularly resolute.[71]

In September 1637 the Council issued a writ for a further £5,500, to be collected by the new sheriff, Francis Godolphin Esq of Godolphin.

Although he collected the entire amount, it was not without difficulty. The inhabitants of Lanlivery pleaded poverty and disability, and told Godolphin that they were 'groaneing under the insupportable pressures both of the former and present Rate for the Shipp'. Their letter was signed by William and Nicholas Kendall and Charles Trewbodye (gentlemen and leading inhabitants of Lanlivery), and by William Collyer (vicar of the parish), with the signs of eight other inhabitants, suggesting that the financial burden affected and concerned all levels of society in the parish. Godolphin had used the subsidy to calculate the parish rate, but (according to the petitioners) on the last occasion in 1628 the subsidy assessors had increased the overall parish subsidy by £9. Since then, eight subsidymen had died, and had not been replaced by other eligible persons. The petitioners claimed that such a high assessment was no longer sustainable, that they were unable to pay, and that the assessment should be reduced accordingly.[72]

Francis Godolphin of Treveneage, sheriff 1638–39, faced greater difficulties in collection than had any of his predecessors, notwithstanding the considerable reduction in the county's assessment to £1,700. On 19 April 1639 Godolphin reported to the Council that £1,240 had been collected so far, although only 'with much labour and trouble, often quickening negligent constables with my strict warrants, and causing many distresses to be taken'. Godolphin feared that in attempting to collect the arrears he would encounter 'great opposition by some of the best sort of this county'. In addition, he had found 'no great willingness in the commonalty to pay it', which he attributed to 'general poverty'.[73]

In his letter to Nicholas of the same date, Godolphin complained further about the constables' behaviour:

> I now find the constables of divers parishes to be at a stand, and to grow careless in the collecting of the arrearages, though I have threatened to bind them over to answer their contempts at the Council board.

He observed that the constables preferred to suffer imprisonment by the sheriff than to appear before the Council, 'out of a hope they have to get some advantage in aftertimes against me or any other sheriff that shall commit them'.[74] Godolphin exerted pressure by instructing his bailiffs to present refractory constables with a bond in £100 for appearance before the Council within fourteen days. If the constable refused to enter the bond, or to pay the assessment, he was to be imprisoned until the bond was sealed or payment made.[75]

Godolphin also reported to the Council that certain towns had claimed inability to pay their full assessment through poverty:

At the general meeting of the county at Truro on 3rd January, divers corporations assessed by you complained much of their poverty and disability, and desired to be relieved by other corporations. Those that complained most and I believe are poorest, were Callington, Camelford and St Mawes . . . I caused the mayors to withdraw to a private room, who conferred about the complaints, but there was no help afforded, each mayor holding his own corporation to be highly assessed.[76]

On 5 February 1639 the mayor and burgesses of St Mawes had petitioned the sheriff, pleading that no individual there was worth more than £20 in real or personal estate, and most no more than £6. The rest, they said, were poor widows, hireling sailors, or fishermen, unable to pay anything. Nevertheless, to show that they were 'most willing beyond our strength to manifest our readiness in the service', they sent the sheriff £1.10s., and begged him to accept it as their full assessment in place of the £4 which had been demanded.[77]

Godolphin was probably the most zealous of the Cornish ship money sheriffs, and was anxious to impress the Council with his obedience and efficiency. He reminded them that he was the first sheriff in the country to make a payment upon the November 1638 writ, and distanced himself from the behaviour of the towns, which were assessed under a separate writ. Indeed, he denied responsibility for their payments:

And so having neglected it I leave them [the recalcitrant towns] to your Honourable consideration praying your Lordships to accept this my service, being the meanest of his Majesties subjects that hath borne that office in this Countie yet most loyall to my Soveraigne.[78]

Godolphin told the corporations that he would return their money to Russell only if it were paid to the constables within the allotted time. If they failed to comply, they would be responsible for returning it, and he would provide no further assistance.[79] The towns nevertheless continued to declare their poverty and inability to pay, which resulted in the £63 shortfall for that year.[80]

However, apart from this small shortfall, the full Cornish assessment had been paid each year from 1634 to 1638–39. Although collection broke down in 1639–40, the Cornish response to ship money was a resounding success for Charles I's government, and Cornwall was one of the nine counties which paid the greatest proportion of their assessments.[81] There is no evidence to support Coate's statement that 'Cornwall knew well the need for increasing the Navy, but it disapproved of ship money as unconstitutional'.[82] No ideological reasons were given for inability to pay, either before or after Hampden's case of 1637, in which the judges upheld the constitutional validity of ship money. The survival amongst the Trefusis family papers of a copy of a letter dated 2 February 1637 from the King to the judges concerning ship money, a copy of the King's questions, and the judges' reply, is the sole indication of interest in the case in Cornwall.[83]

Recent historians have challenged the views that the absence of outspoken constitutional opposition to ship money necessarily implies the absence of ideological opposition, and that local opposition was purely a reaction against the amounts demanded and the disruption caused. Rather, they argue that the absence of parliaments throughout the decade deprived the gentry of a forum in which to express ideological grievances. The Privy Council remained the only channel of communication open to the localities, and it would have been reckless to question the constitutional validity of ship money by that means. This 'ensured that opposition was conducted in the language of pure localism'.[84]

It is possible that in Cornwall rating disputes and pleas of poverty and lack of ready money camouflaged strong views on the constitutional basis of ship money. The rival factions of the 1620s had been able to express their views in Parliament, or through Buckingham or Pembroke at Court. Both Buckingham and Pembroke were dead by 1630; Pembroke's successor, Philip, Earl of Pembroke and Montgomery, appears to have been much weaker than his brother; and Bagg's new relationship with Portland did not extend to the Cornish gentry. The loss of access to the Court, together with absence of parliaments, would certainly have reduced or removed opportunities for political expression. It would be reasonable to assume that where ideological opposition to royal policies existed, Cornish gentlemen would have shrouded it with local complaints, rather than risk challenging the King's policies with his own Council.

However, Cornwall had one of the best payment records, and until 1639 Cornish sheriffs encountered no serious or lasting difficulties of the type which occurred from 1635 in Warwickshire, for example.[85] Even if localized complaints did represent ideological grievances, there were relatively few. It is more likely that Cornish people were prepared to accept the King's statement of intent in the ship money writs, and welcomed the fact that at last the government was taking positive action to protect the coast and to quell the pirates.

Piracy had been a major problem throughout the 1620s, and despite a brief lull at the end of that decade, the situation had not improved by the 1630s.[86] The local community remained vitally aware of the inadequacy of coastal defences, and of the need for greater naval protection. The presence of Turkish pirates off the Cornish coast in summer 1636 may have prompted some to question the King's sincerity, and may account for the 'refusers' during Buller's shrievalty. However, after this there were fewer complaints about piracy as the ship money fleet became a regular presence off the coast.[87] In September 1637 Sir Nicholas Slanning, governor of Pendennis castle, made a direct connection between the issues: he claimed that the success of the expedition to Sallee, and the release of many captives, would 'much forward' collection.[88] It can be no coincidence that coastal counties had the best payment records, and that in Sussex, for example, the response to ship money was similarly 'moderate and acquiescent'.[89] In the elections for the Short Parliament in spring 1640 it is significant that while many counties returned gentlemen who had opposed or obstructed collection, Cornwall returned two of the most successful ship money sheriffs, Francis Godolphin of Godolphin and Sir Richard Buller.

6

The Approach of War and Decisions of Allegiance

The Scots Wars and the Short Parliament

The 1639 writ raised ship money to its former level of £5,500, and although the new sheriff, Richard Trevill, employed similarly extreme measures to his predecessor, Francis Godolphin of Treveneage, he managed to collect only £2,700, 51 per cent of his total assessment. He claimed that the sum demanded from Cornwall was proportionately far greater than that from other counties, and that the Cornish were unable to pay it because of a lack of ready money. The assessment had been demanded in the last quarter of the year,

> a time when little money is to be raised in these parts, the general inhabitants being labouring tinners and fishermen, who get very little in the winter season ... The people protest that they have no money, but as soon as they can get it they will pay it.

Trevill protested that he had 'used more than ordinary diligence' in raising the levy, 'whereby I am condemned to be much more forward than former sheriffs in not giving time to the country to provide money'.[1] Initially he had granted warrants to all petty constables, authorizing them to distrain and sell the goods of refusers. This had proved fruitless, so he had twice sent a special messenger to all hundredal constables, demanding the payment of arrears 'in the strictest manner I could . . . upon their utmost perils'. He had also sent them a copy of the King's command concerning collection, so as to brief the petty constables, 'which I hope will be especial motive to further the said service, for certainly it was never hitherto so hard to be effected, which all complain is for want of money'.[2]

Lack of ready money had been raised in 1626 as a reason for not paying the benevolence. However, it had then been linked with demands for a new Parliament, whereas in the 1630s it stood alone. It was a plausible excuse, since the Cornish economy was largely seasonal, and particularly since the financial demands made by ship money were far greater, and reached further down the social scale, than had the parliamentary subsidy.[3] For example, at its peak in 1635–36, the total ship money assessment for Cornwall was three times the value of the 1626 subsidy.[4] Even so, lack of ready money, or even poverty, is insufficient explanation for the sharp decline in and cessation of ship money payments in 1639–40, particularly in view of the county's previous excellent payment record.

Godolphin had encountered problems in collection from late 1638, following the announcement of the King's decision to raise an army to force the new Prayer Book and obedience upon the Scots. The sheriff's difficulties worsened in spring 1639. In February, Pembroke, the lord lieutenant, was ordered to raise 1,500 men, both horse and foot, from the county's trained bands. He was to conduct weekly exercises, and the soldiers were to be ready, at short notice, to march to a rendezvous at York. The cost of maintaining and transporting them was to be met by local coat and conduct money; they were to enter into royal pay only upon arrival at York.[5]

Preparations for the expedition are evident in parish records. For example, the St Breock churchwardens' accounts show unusually high militia expenditure in 1639. The parish constable was paid 21s. for attending the muster, the 'parish soldiers' 3s., and the drummer a further 3s. One Thomas Petegrew was paid 10d. for 'making clean and wearing the armour', 4s.6d. was spent on barrels to hold the powder and on a horse, and one John Bond and his son received 4s.6d. 'for casting of billits'.[6]

In an undated letter, but most likely written in spring 1639, William Coryton informed Sir Thomas Jermyn (who deputized as lord lieutenant after Pembroke's departure to join the King) that one hundred men had already marched north with Sir Nicholas Slanning. The remaining 1,400 had been selected, and were mustered one day every week, 'to the greate chardge of the Countrie of which they much Complaine'. It was hard to provide for the soldiers since coat and conduct money had not yet been collected, and Coryton feared that it could 'be effected but with very great difficulty'. It was increasingly difficult to maintain order and discipline among the unpaid and idle soldiers, and Coryton requested their discharge, or at least their relief from weekly musters, if they were not required immediately. Coryton also complained that this burden had fallen upon him alone, because of the absence from the county of all the other eastern deputies, apart from Sir Reginald Mohun, 'a man of greate age'.[7]

Like other coastal counties, such as Kent, Dorset and Hampshire,

Cornwall expressed unhappiness at the intention to withdraw men and arms from the local militia to fight in so distant a war, leaving the county exposed to external dangers. France, now heavily involved in the Thirty Years War, and Dutch shipping posed a constant threat. In March 1639 the mayor of Plymouth reported the sighting of fifty-six ships off Newhaven, and the rumours that sixteen more were sailing from Holland, and that France was preparing an even larger fleet at Brest and was recruiting sailors at La Rochelle. The mayor told the Council, 'We conceive . . . that there is cause rather to send forces to us than to draw any from us'.[8] Such news and rumours caused equal fear and concern in Cornwall, where many shared the mayor's sentiments. At a general meeting called by Godolphin early in 1639 to settle assessments for the November 1638 ship money writ, 'divers gentlemen of quality and others of good note' asked Godolphin to present their suit to the lord lieutenant and to the Council. They sought assurance that 'in these dangerous and troublesome times' the county would be adequately supplied with powder. The sheriff supported their request and stated that certain places in west Cornwall were so ill provided that 'they lie obnoxious to the fury of an enemy that shall dare to land in these parts'.[9]

The Council asked eighteen leading Cornish gentlemen for their attendance in the north, or alternatively for financial contributions towards the King's journey. Francis Bassett of Tehidy (vice-admiral of north Cornwall) promised a contribution, but Sir Richard Vyvyan of Trelowarren (a deputy) sent an excuse. The remaining sixteen did not reply. These included Sir Reginald Mohun, Sir Richard Edgcumbe, Sir John Trelawny, Sir Richard Buller, Charles Trevanion and William Coryton, all deputies and JPs. Coryton's avoidance is surprising given his activity in raising soldiers for the war. Also named were Nicholas and John Trefusis, Richard Erisey, Thomas Gewen, Edward Coswarth, Ambrose Manaton and John Roe, all JPs, plus 'Mr' Godolphin, 'Mr' Noy and Hugh Boscawen.[10] At least half of these gentlemen were Puritans, and may have sympathized with the Scots, although there is little extant evidence of pro-Scottish sentiment in Cornwall at this stage. There is nothing to link the other 'avoiders' with this sentiment, and it is likely that they regarded the war as remote in distance and interest.

The only known Cornish enthusiast for the first Bishops' War was Bevill Grenvile, who raised a troop of horse, removed his son, Richard, from Oxford to accompany him, and joined the King's army.[11] In Scotland he was attached to Pembroke's royal bodyguard troop.[12] Grenvile resisted advice from Sir John Trelawny to consider his wife and children, and proclaimed:

but S[i]r for my journey it is fixt. I canot contain myself w[i]thin my doors when the K[in]g of En[glan]ds Standard waves in the field upon so just occasion, the cause being such as must make all those that dye in it little inferiour to Martyrs. And for myne owne p[ar]t I desire to acquire an honest name or an hon[oura]ble grave. I never loved my life or ease so much as to shunn such an occasion w[hi]ch if I should I were unworthy of the profession I have held, or to succede those Ances[tors] of mine, who have so many of them in several ages sacrificed their lives for their Country.[13]

Grenvile's 'profession' was the lieutenancy, in which he had succeeded his father as a deputy in 1636.[14] It is unlikely that, when writing of the 'cause' and of the 'just occasion', Grenvile contemplated enforcement of the new Prayer Book in Scotland; he had previously exhibited signs of Puritanism and put a Calvinistic preamble in his will, written just before leaving for Scotland.[15] Rather, he seems to have objected to the Scottish act of rebellion against the anointed King. His letter to Trelawny continued, 'S[i]r the barborous & implacable Enemy (notw[i]thstanding his Ma[jes]ties gracious proceeding w[i]th them) do continue their insolencies & rebellion in the highest degree'. On 15 May 1639, writing from Newcastle to William Morice Esq, Grenvile developed this idea:

our army is not yet very stronge, not such as will become the majestie of soe great a monarch to march with into a country, where he is sure to meete blowes. It hath byn thought impossible that the Scottes could be so impious as to lift their hands against him; but it is now taken for granted that nothinge but force can reduce them to obedience.[16]

Grenvile was knighted by the King at Berwick in the following month.[17]

Francis Godolphin of Godolphin showed much less enthusiasm for the Scots War. In a letter of 8 February 1639, written from London to an unknown correspondent (almost certainly his wife), Godolphin reported the King's intention to have an army of 24,000 foot and 6,000 horse at York by 1 April. He remarked on concern in the capital at the high cost of maintaining an army of that size, but did not express a personal view. Godolphin clearly wanted to avoid involvement:

These considerations are all the intertainement heer, I wish I were well out of them, and then I should next wish myselfe with you, and shall not be easy till I be soe.[18]

Godolphin's younger brother, Sydney, evidently took a different view, since in May 1639 he was present on the Scottish border with Sir Ralph Hopton's troop of the royal bodyguard.[19]

There is little indication that the first Bishops' War prompted the extensive debate or polarization of opinion in Cornwall which Russell and Sharpe have detected in other counties.[20] The King's imminent departure for Scotland was reported in a letter from John Rashleigh to his father, Jonathan, of Menabilly.[21] In March Jonathan Rashleigh's brother-in-law, John Sparke, informed him of the King's safe arrival in York, hoping that the King would return 'w[i]th health and victory'. Sparke added that the Scots had demanded a Parliament in their own country and in England, 'w[hi]ch be for the reforminge and setlying of all questions'. He prayed that God would direct the King to 'grant it', presumably referring to both Parliaments, and suggesting that he perceived Scottish and English problems as interrelated.[22]

In May 1639 the King's 28,000-strong army marched from York to Berwick. However, the royal commanders considered the risks of defeat too great, and the army retreated before a blow was struck. The Poughill churchwardens recorded payment of 9*d*. 'unto five poore soldiers that came out of Scotland' after the withdrawal.[23] The Treaty of Berwick was signed in June, marking the end of the first Bishops' War. However, the Scots continued to challenge royal authority, and in December it was decided to renew the war against them. The King announced his intention of calling an English Parliament to request supply for the war: the writs were issued on 12 February 1640, and Parliament was summoned for 13 April. During the opening months of 1640, Cornish payment of ship money dwindled in anticipation of the Parliament.

The county election, held in March, was not contested, and there is no evidence of the 'anti-Court slogans' which were 'rife' in other counties.[24] As noted above, two of the most successful ship money sheriffs, Francis Godolphin of Godolphin and Sir Richard Buller, were returned for the county. There was, however, a backlash against the duchy in the boroughs, bringing an end to its electoral influence. The duchy Council nominated sixteen candidates for seats in sixteen different boroughs, and asked the mayors of those boroughs to ensure success. Coryton (restored as vice-warden of the stannaries in 1630) and Thomas Gewen (now duchy escheator and feodary) were ordered to assist, and to spare no expense in securing the return of the duchy candidates. However, none of the sixteen was returned for the nominated boroughs, although Sir Richard Wynn, who was nominated for Lostwithiel, was returned by Bodmin.[25] Coryton may have been chosen in place of the original duchy candidate at Grampound, but it appears that he was working in the interest of Pembroke, the lord warden, rather than the duchy Council's.[26] In a few cases others with Court connections were returned in place of duchy nominees. Edward Reade, a courtier, was chosen by Camelford; Fowey returned Edwin Rich, who had no local connections; and Laud's secretary, William Dell, was elected by St Ives, after he had failed to gain a seat at Canterbury.[27]

In rejecting duchy candidates in favour of local men, the boroughs may have been making a purely localist statement against external interference in local elections. Alternatively, if Coryton, the most senior duchy official in the county, was working against the duchy, while advancing the interests of his patron, Pembroke, then the duchy had little prospect of success. In any case, Coryton was no longer trusted by his former associates, and his influence was considerably weaker than in 1626, when he had manipulated the Cornish borough elections on the 3rd Earl of Pembroke's behalf. On 3 March Coryton approached his former ally, Sir Richard Buller, in Pembroke's interest, and requested one of the Saltash seats. Coryton had initially made a direct approach to the Saltash townsmen, who had told him that they had disposed the burgess-ships according to Buller's instructions, with one seat to Sir Richard and the other to his eldest son, Francis. However, since Buller was also standing for the county, Coryton was anxious to know upon whom he intended to confer the second Saltash seat if he were elected knight of the shire. Coryton was aware that his previous conduct had been called into question, but told Buller 'you have no reason I hope to thinke I have or will doe anything contrary to that rule w[hi]ch ought to be observed by every honest man to doe to another as he would be done unto'.[28] This plea was unsuccessful since Buller placed his younger son, George, in the second Saltash seat.

Individual local men may also have been chosen because they represented a certain political or religious stance. If (as seems likely) this were the case, it did not, as Kishlansky has suggested, mark a sudden transformation from consensus politics and uncontested 'selections' to partisan and ideological electioneering.[29] In Cornwall the process of change had begun well before 1640.

Most Cornish borough elections in 1626 and 1628, and even the 1628 county election, did not comply with Kishlansky's unusually narrow definition of a contested election, in which he includes only those where there was a contest on polling day.[30] Nonetheless, partisan electioneering was not uncommon. The local factional situation, dominated first by Pembroke and then by Buckingham, inspired competition for parliamentary seats and the exercise of rival influences over boroughs and (in 1628) the county electorate. This partisan electioneering was not necessarily based in political ideology. Cust has described the forced loan, which was central to the 1628 county election, as an ideological issue, taken up by 'patriots' representing 'the Country' interest against the tyranny of 'the Court'.[31] However, although Eliot and Coryton used 'Country' language, over and above the loan the election was focused on the acquisition or loss of local power and prestige, and on attitudes towards Buckingham and the effect of his policies on Cornwall. Rather, the ideological strand running through Cornish elections and politics between 1626 and 1629 had been religion. Puritanism linked members of the Eliot–Coryton faction, who may have perceived the Duke's military failures as divine judgement upon him, and who opposed his support for anti-Calvinists. Following Buckingham's death, Eliot and Coryton joined with Francis Rous in Parliament in attacking the rise of Arminianism.

A large number of Puritans was returned in spring 1640, many of whom had established a record of opposition to government policies in the 1620s. Possibly Sir Richard Buller was associated more with his anti-government stance of the 1620s than with collection of ship money, and his Puritanism probably won him considerable backing. Buller's two sons, Francis and George, were also elected, for the family borough of Saltash. Another Puritan, Antony Nicoll, the son of Humphrey, the loan refuser, entered Parliament for the first time, representing Bossiney. Two other loan refusers and Puritans, Ambrose Manaton and Nicholas Trefusis, were returned by Launceston and Newport respectively. Coryton was also chosen by Grampound, although his association with Pembroke through the stannaries may have secured his return. Lack of evidence makes it difficult to detect whether these men were returned because of public memory of their earlier anti-government positions, or because of their Puritanism, or simply through their local connections. Puritanism does, however, appear to have been a positive influence. For example, in addition to those Puritans already mentioned, Sir Samuel Rolle (connected with the Bullers through his marriage into the Wise family) was returned at Callington. His brother, John, who was also brother-in-law to Sir Alexander Carew of Antony, and who had resisted tonnage and poundage in 1629, was elected by Truro. John Rolle's partner was the Puritan theologian, Francis Rous, and both probably owed their election to Boscawen influence. Jonathan Rashleigh was returned for Fowey, and John St Aubyn was chosen by Tregony. It is possible that the spring 1640 elections reflected the development of earlier Puritan organization, aligned against anti-Calvinism in its local and national guises. Since ship money was not hated as much in Cornwall as elsewhere, religious changes would have assumed a more dominant position, and Puritans appear to have been the first to organize politically.[32]

The significance of Puritanism (or indeed of a history of opposition to government policies) is to some extent obscured by the strong local connections of these men. For example, the Rashleighs were the principal family in Fowey, and Jonathan Rashleigh had represented the borough in three previous Parliaments. Callington was a Rolle borough, and Sir Samuel Rolle had recently restored the town to prosperity through the yarn trade. Further, Antony Nicoll's family had property interests in Bossiney, and Ambrose Manaton had been recorder of Launceston since 1637.[33]

The circle of Puritans and former oppositionists elected in March 1640 had national connections with others of the same religious and political complexion. Antony Nicoll was John Pym's nephew, and Francis Rous was Pym's step-brother;[34] it is inconceivable that they had not remained in contact during the personal rule. Rous was also connected, through his nephew's marriage, with another leading Cornish Puritan, John Robartes, who in 1634 succeeded his father as 2nd Baron Robartes, and in April 1640 took his seat in the Lords. In 1630 Robartes had married Lucy, daughter of a leading Puritan, Robert Rich, 2nd Earl of Warwick. Warwick had been a loan refuser (and an associate of Eliot), and in the spring 1640 elections in Essex recruited Puritan preachers to commend godly candidates from the pulpit.[35]

The close connection and understanding between Rous and Pym soon became apparent. On 17 April they spoke consecutively in the Commons. Rous mainly confined himself to religious grievances, establishing a theological framework from which his step-brother evolved his own comprehensive account of religious and secular grievances.[36] Rous introduced the subject of Arminianism, and asserted that 'the roote of all our grievances' was 'an intended union betwixt us and Rome'. Rous claimed that 'for the setling of this worke the word puritan is an Essentiall engine', since Arminians had distorted the true meaning of the word 'Puritan', applying it to all mainstream Calvinists, so as to remove them from the central position in the Church of England:

> For this word in the mouth of a drunkard doth meane a sober man, in the mouth of an Arminian, an Orthodox man, in the mouth of a papist, a Protestant. And so it is spoke to shame a man out of all Religion, if a man will bee ashamed to bee saved.

Rous also attacked what he saw as the Arminian hierarchy for enforcing policies without regard for individual conscience. He cited the case of a minister who had been 'suspended, excommunicated, and driven away' from his living for refusing to read the 1633 Declaration of Sports. Rous argued that such policies would alienate all true Protestant ministers, and would precipitate the end of Protestantism in England. He went on to link religious and secular grievances, attacking ship money as designed 'to settle this work of parliament to be made needlesse', and to enable the King to continue the reunion with Rome without parliamentary constraints.[37]

Lord Robartes was appointed to the committee to consider the Book of Common Prayer.[38] On 23 April Rous was named to the committee to choose preachers for the fast and for the communion.[39] A week later the Commons began its consideration of ecclesiastical grievances with discussion of the Laudian altar policy, which Rous equated with idolatry.[40] Rous was also appointed to the committee for the reformation of abuses in ecclesiastical courts.[41]

The King dissolved the Short Parliament on 5 May after only three weeks, exasperated by its reluctance to grant him supply before redress of grievances. Preparations for war continued, however, and on 17 May Charles Trevanion, a deputy, reported to Pembroke that he had given directions for levying coat and conduct money in Cornwall. He had 'sounded the Inclinacon of most men, and found many willinge, but not a few very backwards'. A 'good part' had been collected, but Trevanion requested advice on how to proceed with 'such Refractaryes, as refuse to pay their Rates towards this Service'. This new demand also caused ship money payments to dwindle still further, and ultimately to cease; Trevanion remarked, 'Ship-money is earnestly called for, but more slowly paid than ever'.[42]

The Council ordered Pembroke to raise 1,600 men in Cornwall, with their coat and conduct money, and to prepare them for a general rendezvous, from which they were to march to Newcastle. On 23 May the rendezvous, already postponed to 1 June, was further delayed until 1 July.[43] Trevanion complained to Pembroke on 3 June that he was the only active Cornish deputy; the others had not yet returned from Parliament, so that 'there is not a man yet pressed in this county'. This hindered collection of coat and conduct money, since 'it sticks much in the minds of the country to pay money before the soldiers are pressed'. Of the £430 already collected, £400 had come from the western hundreds (Pyder, Powder, Kerrier and Penwith). Trigg had paid a mere £30, but East, West, Stratton and Lesnewth had paid nothing. Trevanion was sceptical about the 'general cry for the want of money', and believed that if more deputies assisted, 'money might be more plentifully found'.[44]

Trevanion implied a lack of willingness amongst the other deputies, particularly Sir Richard Buller. With reason to believe that Buller had returned from London, Trevanion had requested his assistance with impressment. However, his letters had been returned by Buller's servant, who claimed that his master was not at home.[45] Amongst Buller's papers is a list of reasons against granting supply towards putting down the 'Scots rebellion', in which the Scots are compared with the Huguenots of La Rochelle, whose 'libertie' had been turned into 'slaverie' by King Louis XIII.[46] The author of the document is unknown, and possession of it may denote interest rather than sympathy. If, however, its pro-Scottish sentiments are a true representation of Buller's views during the Short Parliament (which is not unlikely, given his Puritanism) there may have been some justification for Trevanion's implied criticism.

However, Buller claimed that he had not returned from Parliament until 7 June, and that within two days he and Coryton had agreed to impress 800 men in east Cornwall. They had mustered all the trained bands and able-bodied men of the eastern division, had impressed the 800 by 19 June, and had ordered the levying of coat and conduct money in that division. The deputies of the western division had taken similar measures. Buller and Coryton had arranged a general meeting of the deputies at Bodmin on 30 June, and hoped that 'the business will be fully resolved' by then. They complained that impressment had been 'irksome and difficult' because of the many 'pitiful complaints'; the county was 'over-burdened' and had been asked for three times the number of men required from any other county, in addition to the seamen and tinners also pressed.[47]

Almost 1,600 men had been impressed by 1 July, but not without increasing difficulty. The deputies had even been obliged to impress some parish constables 'to enforce them to bring forth their able-bodied men'. Captain Hannibal Bonython of St Mawes castle had obstructed impressment by commanding the men of the four neighbouring parishes 'in a violent way' to attend his muster at the same time the deputies had appointed for their own muster. The deputies urged Pembroke to reduce the unduly large number demanded from Cornwall. They claimed that the imminent departure of so many able-bodied men had aroused great concern in the county, and that tension had been heightened by the presence of sixty Turkish men-of-war off the coast, which had fought with local ships, and had captured inhabitants of Looe, Penzance, and other exposed places.[48]

Writing to Nicholas on 8 July, Francis Bassett (vice-admiral of north Cornwall) proposed that Cornish soldiers be discharged in return for their full coat and conduct money. Bassett asserted that this would 'do His Majesty a special service', since it would enable him to raise men 'in the heart of the kingdom', leaving 'those few of us for the preservation of this poor part, the Turks having lately infested us, and most obvious we are to all other enemies'. Bassett was particularly concerned that the 300 impressed men from Kerrier and Penwith hundreds should be discharged, to relieve the labour shortage in agriculture and mining caused by the impressment:

> I cannot get men half sufficient either for my tillage for next year, or to thresh and make the best profit of what I have of the last. In our tinning, those men now impressed, and those who have fled from the press, have so utterly abandoned those labours and let in the waters . . .

Bassett offered to guarantee full payment of coat and conduct money from those two hundreds if the soldiers were discharged. This, he claimed, would enable him 'to serve with power our Royal master, which shall be ever my passionate desire'.[49]

Following the dissolution of Parliament the King continued to encounter difficulty in financing the war. In July Francis Sawle Esq of Penrice informed his uncle, Jonathan Rashleigh, that the King had seized the bullion in the Tower, 'which is a goode som'.[50] This would have been of particular concern to Rashleigh because of his extensive trade interests. The next month Sawle again commented on the King's impecuniosity and on the City's refusal to assist. In the same letter he also reported on preparations for war, mentioning the power struggle amongst the army officers concerning a replacement for the lord general, the Earl of Northumberland, the King's departure for York, the position of the Scottish army, and the unruly behaviour of English troops billeted in the north.[51]

The Long Parliament

The Scots crossed the Tweed and invaded England on 20 August. After a minor battle at Newburn on the 27th, the English retreated, and the Scots occupied Newcastle. Pressure mounted on Charles to call a Parliament. Elections were held in October, and Parliament was summoned for 3 November. Sir Alexander Carew and Sir Bevill Grenvile were returned, unopposed, for the county. There was, however, considerable competition for borough seats. The duchy nominated eight candidates, all of whom were rejected. Both Coate and Gruenfelder have interpreted this as localist rejection of outside interference.[52] However, it appears that, as in the spring elections, Coryton, the vice-warden of the stannaries, was acting against the interests of the duchy Council in order to gain seats for Pembroke, the lord warden (and lord chamberlain). Pembroke, supported by Coryton, was particularly vigorous in exercising influence in these elections and appears this time to have swayed Sir Richard Buller, since

Edward Hyde, a Pembroke client, took the second Saltash seat.[53] Sir Bevill Grenvile complained of the impossibility of securing a seat for Sir Edward Seymour of Berry Pomeroy, Devon, since Pembroke had written to the boroughs before Grenvile even knew that a Parliament was to be called, and 'such base meanes hath been us[e]d by some ill me[m]b[e]rs in the country as all places were forestalled before I knew of it'.[54]

Coryton had been mayor of Bossiney for a number of years, and was determined to place both borough seats at Pembroke's disposal. Grenvile, who owned land there, wanted one of the seats for Sir Ralph Sydenham of Youlston, near Barnstaple. He proposed that Coryton should have one seat for Pembroke, and that he would have the other for Sydenham, so keeping out Lord Robartes, the third interested party. Coryton, however, would not compromise. According to Grenvile, Coryton supported the custom of election by a select few, since, as mayor, he could command the support of most of the council. Grenvile advanced Sydenham's cause by supporting rival claims for a wider franchise in the borough. He maintained that the election of MPs by nine or ten people 'grieved' the freeholders, who believed that they had equal right to choose. He promised to test their claim in Parliament if they would return his candidate: 'I well know that the opinion of the Par[lia]m[en]t house hath ever been that all inhabitants, being free men, have voice'.[55]

Coryton obtained the writ for the election and 'in a private and unlawfull way' Sir Charles Herbert, Pembroke's kinsman, was returned by the mayor and council. When the freeholders heard of this, they held their own election, and returned Sir Ralph Sydenham (Grenvile's candidate) and Sir John Clotworthy (Robartes' candidate). Grenvile, concerned that Coryton would lead Pembroke to believe that he had opposed his interest, was anxious for the lord warden to know that he had offered to share the seats with Coryton, and that had he not interposed, Robartes' candidates would have won both seats.[56] Grenvile emphasized to Coryton that 'I oppose not my lo[rd]; I oppose a wrongful course and unjust oppression (w[hi]ch hath been long us'd there) for the comon welth sake'.[57]

On 14 November a Commons committee was appointed to investigate complaints against Coryton for using blank indentures and for the undue election of burgesses for Bossiney. As MP for Launceston, Coryton was ordered to withdraw from the House.[58] He admitted that he had brought up a blank indenture and had inserted the names afterwards, and on 7 December the Commons pronounced the Bossiney election void.[59] Writs were issued for a new election, which was held on 22 December. Again, three returns were made, although Sydenham was the only original candidate. One of those returned was Sir Christopher Yelverton of Northamptonshire, the first of the three to arrive at the Commons. He took his seat, but was asked to leave on 12 January 1641, while the House considered the other two returns, which named Thomas Bond and Sir Ralph Sydenham.[60] On 15 February the House declared the election void for a second time, and new writs were issued.[61] After the third election Sydenham and Yelverton took their seats.[62] 'The humble petition of William Coryton Esq' was read in the Commons on 24 June, but on 18 August the House resolved that Coryton should not be admitted to sit as a Member of that Parliament.[63]

The committee for Coryton's business was also instructed to consider allegations of his 'undue proceedings' as vice-warden of the stannaries, contrary to the Petition of Right.[64] These allegations were not confined to Cornwall. Shortly after the opening of Parliament, Sir Thomas Wise, knight of the shire for Devon, presented to the Commons a petition listing his county's grievances, 'amongst w[hi]ch none cries louder for releife than [tha]t of ye Stan[n]aryes', and asked that the petition be referred to Coryton's committee.[65] The committee's responsibilities were further extended to include consideration of Coryton's alleged misdemeanours as steward of the duchy and as deputy lieutenant.[66] The committee was also ordered to investigate the foundations, institution, and jurisdiction of the stannary court of Devon and Cornwall, and to examine the misdemeanours of its officers, and the knights and burgesses of Cornwall were added to it.[67] The bill against oppressions in the stannaries received its second reading on 12 February 1641, and was sent to Coryton's committee.[68] On 16 July, after the bill had been sent to the Lords, the two Cornish peers Robartes and Mohun were appointed to the committee.[69] Mohun's appointment was ironic, since Coryton had instigated the enquiry into Mohun's father's alleged abuse of the stannaries in 1628.

Sir Richard Buller was another accused of using a blank indenture, in his own return for Fowey. He was ordered to withdraw from the House. The committee appointed to consider the case reported that no election had been held, but that Buller's name had been inserted in a blank indenture. However, because 'it appeared not to be with his privity' the committee held it to be 'no misdemeanour in him'. The House resolved that Buller had committed no offence, and issued a new writ for the Fowey election. Buller had returned to the House within two weeks.[70] The contrasting treatment of the Fowey and Bossiney elections suggests that Buller's powerful Puritan friends defended his interest, because they wanted him in the House. The same was apparently true for Pym's nephew, Anthony Nicoll, in the Bodmin election. John Arundell junior of Trerice was returned without question for the first Bodmin seat, and John Bramston of the Middle Temple was elected to the other. However, Nicoll challenged Bramston's election, and although the majority of the committee of privileges upheld it, Pym obstructed publication of its report, and Nicoll was allowed to sit in Bramston's place.[71]

St Germans returned to its first seat Benjamin Valentine, who had previously represented the borough in 1628, and who had been imprisoned in the Tower since 1629 (for his part, with Eliot, in the Commons incident) and had been released only in January 1640.[72] The second St Germans seat was contested between John Moyle junior of Bake and Mr (probably William) Scawen Esq of Molenick, St Germans parish, who claimed to have three or four more scot and lot votes than Moyle. Moyle's father stated that this was irrelevant, since 'tyme out of mynde' all borough inhabitants had held the franchise, regardless of wealth, and even if Scawen were right, and the franchise were more limited, Moyle still had more votes. Buller and his two sons supported Moyle's claim in the House.[73] Although the election had not been decided by 6 January 1641, when it was suggested that Moyle should be allowed to sit until his election was declared void, there is no indication that the matter was pursued further: Moyle continued to sit.[74] This appears to be another example of the godly organizing to secure the return of a Puritan MP.

The Cornish knights of the shire did not arrive at Parliament with a petition of the county's grievances, but Joseph Jane, MP for Liskeard, suggested that the county had high expectations of the Parliament:

> Att the beginninge of this parliam[en]t, Cornwall was of the same complexion, though in a more remisse degree, w[i]th other Counties, who placed much of their happines in yt assemblie . . .[75]

Soon after arriving in Parliament, probably inspired by the reading of so many county petitions in the Commons, Francis Buller asked his constituents of East Looe for a list of their grievances. Their petition has not survived, but in an accompanying letter they added a grievance, not listed in the petition, 'w[hi]ch is concerning the nakedness of our Towne: in the want of ordinance for Defence if Danger should come'. So, whatever other issues concerned them, they remained worried about the inadequacy of the town's defences.[76]

From the opening of Parliament, religious radicals had high hopes of further reforming the Church of England along Puritan lines. Of the Cornish MPs, Francis Rous, again sitting for Truro, was the most enthusiastic supporter of further reformation, and the most active in pursuing it. As in the Short Parliament he attacked the Book of Sports, and on 30 November reported from the committee considering the petition of one Mr Wilson, a minister sequestered from his living for four years for not reading the Book of Sports.[77] Further, Rous opened the debate on the 1640 canons (passed by the convocation of Canterbury after the dissolution of the Short Parliament), and demanded the punishment of the authors.[78]

On 11 December attempts at further reformation were advanced by the presentation to the Commons of a petition signed by 15,000 Londoners, demanding 'root and branch' reform of the Church, and the abolition of episcopacy. In a letter of the same month (probably to his wife) Francis Godolphin of Godolphin, MP for Helston, reported this event:

> The last weeke the Londoners presented a petition to our house of great length, with a roule of fifteen thousand handes to it, wherin complaining of the great pride, cruelty and Popish carriage of Archbishops and Bishops, they desired in conclusion that the order of Bishops might be putt downe and some better government setled by the wisdome of this Parliament.[79]

Godolphin did not openly express a view, but his reference to 'the wisdome of this Parliament' sounds an ironic note; he was not one of the godly, nor was he active in Church reform. However, if this letter was sent to his wife at Godolphin in west Cornwall, it would have informed her, and probably neighbours, friends and relations too of the new demand for the abolition of episcopacy, and of the possible extent of Church reform.[80]

Although less prominent than Rous, other Cornish Puritans promoted further reformation from an early stage. For example, on 19 December Thomas Lower of St Winnow, MP for East Looe, was (with Rous) added to the committee considering the lack of preaching ministers.[81] Further, in February 1641 Sir Richard Buller and Rous were named to the committee for the bill for abolishing superstition and idolatry, which provided for the repositioning of altarwise communion tables, the dismantling of rails, and the removal of pictures and images.[82] In the Lords, Robartes was appointed to the committee for religion, to consider all innovations in the Church.[83] Rous, Sir Richard Buller and Ambrose Manaton were named to the committee for the clerical disabilities bill, designed to prevent clergy acting as JPs.[84] Buller was also appointed to the committee for the bill for reforming abuses in ecclesiastical courts, although nothing more was heard of this bill since it was rendered unnecessary by the Root and Branch bill.[85]

Godolphin's letter of December conveys a sense of the extent and speed of reforms, achieved or planned, in other areas of government. He reported that Archbishop Laud had been accused of high treason, and that Lord Keeper Finch had followed Secretary Windebank into exile. A former ship money sheriff, Godolphin noted that 'the ship shreeves not yet called to accompt will not in their due time be forgotten', and that charges had been made in Parliament against Finch and the other judges in Hampden's case for giving a judgement contrary to the law, and thereby taking away the subjects' property.[86] Joseph Jane, MP for Liskeard, was added to the committee to discover whether the judges in Hampden's case had been influenced into deciding against Hampden, and Lord Robartes was named to the committee for vacating judgement in the case.[87] In June, Sir Richard Buller, another former ship money sheriff, was appointed to the committee for the bill declaring ship money unlawful and void.[88]

Lord Robartes played an active role in preparing the case and proceedings against Thomas Wentworth, Earl of Strafford, the King's leading minister and adviser, who had been imprisoned by Parliament on 11 November 1640. For example, Robartes was named to the committee to take preparatory examinations of witnesses, and to the committee to search for precedents in the manner of proceeding against peers.[89] Strafford's impeachment trial took place in Westminster Hall between 22 March and 10 April. Pym presented the case for the prosecution, and he nominated his nephew, Anthony Nicoll, to be present at the trial.[90]

On 10 April, because of the difficulties in proving the charge of cumulative treason, a bill of attainder was introduced into the Commons, and was passed by the House on 21 April by 204 to 59 votes. Five indigenous Cornish MPs voted against Strafford's attainder. These were the courtier and poet, Sydney Godolphin of Godolphin, MP for Helston, Joseph Jane, MP for Liskeard, 'Mr Edgcumbe' (either Piers, MP for Camelford, or Richard, MP for Newport), and the two MPs for Lostwithiel, brothers-in-law Richard Arundell of Trerice and John Trevanion of Caerhayes, all future royalists.[91] Their names, with others who had opposed Strafford's attainder, were displayed in London, and they were reviled by the mob. For Arundell at least the backlash was not confined to the capital, since Peter Courtney of Trethurfe told Jonathan Rashleigh (MP for Fowey) that:

> I am glad to heare of your good effects agaynst my Lord of Straford but my Cosen Arundel is verye Angrye with his sonne Richard for votinge him not guiltye of high treason.[92]

Strafford's attainder was the first issue on which support for the King, or opposition to Pym's reform programme, was expressed openly by some Cornish MPs. However, Coate's assertion that Strafford's attainder marked the first 'real cleavage' amongst Cornish MPs is misleading.[93] Rival interests had been evident in Cornwall in the spring and autumn elections of 1640. In the opening months of the Long Parliament these competing interests may have been submerged in a common desire to reform the abuses of the 1630s, creating an artificial 'consensus'. However, from the outset that 'consensus' was threatened by the marked contrast between the activity of Puritans and the inactivity of non-Puritans on measures for Church reform. If a 'consensus' existed in November 1640, Puritan pressure for further reformation was the earliest and most important cause of its disintegration. This process was accelerated by Strafford's attainder, as it caused some Cornishmen to move in the opposite direction, but it was a far more gradual and subtle process than suggested by Coate, and the number of MPs involved was still relatively small.

In his next extant letter, written on 10 May 1641, Francis Godolphin reported rumours that Archbishop Laud, Judge Berkeley and Sir John Ratcliffe were to be 'degraded and hanged', and that Strafford was 'to loose his heade within a day or two'. Godolphin recorded some of the events which had preceded the passage of the attainder bill two days before. He mentioned the death the previous day of the Earl of Bedford, 'who should have been Lord Treasurer', an oblique reference to the planned bridge appointments, in which Bedford, Pym and their allies were to have assumed leading positions in the government in exchange for the restoration of the King's finances and Strafford's life. Godolphin also mentioned the army plots, the flight of courtiers Henry Jermyn and Sir John Suckling because of their involvement in the plots, and the rumour that they had tried to involve foreign forces.[94]

On 3 May, in the atmosphere of alarm and anger generated by Pym's revelation of the army plots, MPs agreed to an oath of association for the defence of the King, the Protestant Church, laws and liberties, and privileges of Parliament, to be sworn by all MPs and peers to bind them together against external dangers. All indigenous Cornish MPs took the Protestation in the House, with the sole exception of Francis Godolphin of Treveneage, who had been granted leave of absence 'for some time' on 29 March.[95] Most took the Protestation on 3 May, a few took it later in the month, and both Sir Bevill Grenvile and Richard Erisey, who were absent in May, took it in July.[96] Lord Mohun took the Protestation in the Lords on 24 June, but, although it had been introduced by his allies, and was in line with his Puritan views, Lord Robartes 'positively refused it, alleging there was no law that enjoined it, and the consequence of such voluntary engagements might produce effects that were not then intended'.[97]

In his May letter Godolphin also described 'the May Days' riots, which had erupted on the 3rd, and made a direct link between this popular pressure on Parliament and the passage of the attainder bill:

The citissens are very unquiet and come almost dayly to Whitehall, and Westminster Hall, in great numbers with swords and clubbs, demaunding iustice against my lord of Strafford. The King is to pass tomorrow with the bill for the attainder of the Earle of Strafford . . . The King shed many tears this day, and is extreamly sadd.[98]

Godolphin expressed no personal opinion about Strafford's attainder, but the tone of his account suggests some sympathy with the King. It must be assumed that, unlike his brother, Godolphin voted in favour of the bill, although probably with reservations. Godolphin's apparent ambivalence highlights the confusion experienced by many, and the fluidity of views and political groupings at this stage.

The Trefusis family papers contain a copy of Pym's speech against Strafford of November 1640, and a newsletter dated 25 May 1641, covering similar topics to Godolphin's letter of that month, although with a bias towards the views of the King's opponents. It links Strafford's attainder with religious reform, as part of a political programme, by describing the tension in and around the House in May 1641, and noting the Commons' intention to vote out the bishops 'Roote & Branche, & stick as close to it as ever they did to my Earl of Straffords businesse'.[99]

Lord Robartes clashed with other Cornish Puritans over the bishops' exclusion bill. Robartes supported the majority view of the Lords, that bishops should continue to sit in the House, and on 27 May was named to the committee to prepare the heads for a conference with the Commons about the bill. Francis Rous was appointed to the Commons committee to prepare answers to the Lords' objections, and Robartes reported to the Lords on the conference.[100] However, during the summer Cornish Puritans continued to work together for the reformation of worship and ministers. For example, on 2 June Thomas Lower and Rous were named to the committee for the bill to prevent bargemen and lightermen working on the sabbath, and shortly afterwards Thomas Gewen and Ambrose Manaton were named to the committee for the bill for scandalous ministers, designed to remove unsuitable ministers from the Church.[101] In addition, after the army plots, fears of papist conspiracies heightened, and it was considered essential to take firm action against recusants, and to disarm them, to prevent a future coup. In May Sir Richard Buller and one of his sons (either Francis or George), Francis Rous, and Sir Alexander Carew were named to some committees for anti-papist measures.[102] The next month Robartes was appointed to the committee for the bill for disarming recusants, and at the end of August Sir Alexander and Sir Richard Carew and Sir Richard Buller were named commissioners to disarm recusants in Cornwall.[103]

Cornish Puritans were also involved in Anglo-Scottish relations, and were active in the preparations for peace between the two kingdoms in spring and summer 1641. In April Robartes sat on the Lords committees which discussed the terms of the Treaty of London, including the Scots' desire for religious unity between the two kingdoms.[104] In May and June Sir Richard Buller and Sir Alexander Carew were appointed to a number of committees concerning arrangements for the disbandment of the English and Scottish armies, both of which remained billeted in the north of England.[105] Further, in July Carew, Buller, Ambrose Manaton and Robartes were named to committees to facilitate the payment of billeting money due to the inhabitants of Yorkshire.[106] Buller was also named to the committee for securing the arrears of the Brotherly Assistance due to the Scots, and Carew was appointed to the committee to prepare heads for a conference with the Lords concerning disbandment of the armies.[107] On 19 August Anthony Nicoll was ordered by both Houses to go immediately to the King (who was in Scotland to ratify the Treaty of London) to notify him of their intention to send parliamentary commissioners to join him.[108] Nicoll returned from Scotland later that month with the King's answer, and reported to and managed a conference with the Lords on this matter.[109]

On 1 November Robartes was named to the committee for opening and reading letters containing news of the outbreak of the Irish Rebellion. He reported to the Lords the same day, and was named to the committee to borrow £50,000 from the City for Irish affairs.[110] The next day Robartes was appointed to the committee to draft a Declaration on the state of England and Ireland, and Nicoll was named to the committee for Irish affairs.[111] Exaggerated reports of the massacre of thousands of Protestants by the Catholic rebels inflamed anti-papist hysteria, and on 16 December Francis Rous moved that the Commons should make a contribution to the relief of distressed Protestants who had fled to England from Ireland. He was appointed to collect MPs' voluntary contributions and was named to the committee to consider a bill for a more general contribution towards the relief of Irish Protestant refugees.[112] As a Cornishman, Rous would have been particularly aware of the need for such charity, because of the influx of Irish refugees to Cornwall during the Rebellion.

By the end of 1641 the growing rift between the Commons and the Lords had widened. On 3 December Pym proposed the appointment of a committee to demonstrate to the Lords the value of the bills already passed by the Commons, and to propose that in future the Lords should support these bills. Sydney Godolphin strongly objected to this, and declared that if this were done, 'then the Myner part of the Commons would joyne with the Major part of the Lords and enter into a protestation against them that did it'. Godolphin was ordered to withdraw from the Commons until the House 'had time to consider of his delinquencie', and although the matter was taken no further, Godolphin's actions demonstrated his firm opposition to Pym's policies.[113]

In the same month, George Buller, MP for Saltash, demonstrated his clear support for Pym when he laid the charges against Colonel Thomas Lunsford before the Commons. Lunsford was believed to be an outlaw, 'loose of life', and a crypto-Catholic, and his recent appointment by the King as Lieutenant of the Tower of London was perceived as a threat to the City, and as part of a popish plot. In presenting reasons for Lunsford's dismissal, Buller highlighted the decay of trade, and Lunsford's non-attendance at church while at York.[114] The Trefusis family papers contain a newsletter, dated 28 December 1641, detailing an account of the 'December Days' riots, provoked by Lunsford's appointment, when London citizens again gathered outside the Houses, and apprentices, crying 'No Bishops, No Popish Lords', skirmished with army officers.[115] Robartes was appointed to the committees to investigate the cause of these tumults, and to prepare heads for conference with the Commons about them.[116]

On 3 January 1642 Sir Alexander Carew was teller for the Ayes in the division on whether a committee should be appointed to investigate the King's attempted arrest of Lord Kimbolton and the Five Members. Carew was added to that committee on 28 January when it received information that Sir Nicholas Slanning (MP for Penryn and governor of Pendennis castle) had sent letters and warrants to Sir Francis Bassett, vice-admiral of north Cornwall, informing him that the Five Members were traitors, and urging him to apprehend them. It was also alleged that Slanning had sent similar letters to Cornish JPs at the quarter sessions, and that he had authorized the search of any ship for the Members. Slanning was summoned before the committee, but denied all the charges, claiming that he had merely sent to Cornwall a printed sheet (which he had bought for a penny) which listed the charges against the Members.[117]

Lord Robartes was appointed to committees to consider the attempted arrest, to consider how to vindicate the breach of parliamentary privilege caused by it, and to prepare a draft petition to the King.[118] On 22 March he introduced a bill for vindicating and asserting the privileges of Parliament, lately broken, and was named to the committee for that bill the next day.[119] He also believed that the attorney-general should be punished for impeaching the Five Members, and entered his dissent to three Lords votes against this.[120]

In Cornwall, fears of a Catholic invasion, aggravated by news of the Irish Rebellion, were heightened by the arrival of 800 Irish Catholics, some of whom set up taverns and alehouses. Carew responded to letters of concern by presenting to the Commons an order to restrain English and Irish Catholics from 'going out of this Kingdom . . . into Ireland'; to prevent arms, money, and provisions from going to the relief of the Irish rebels; and

> whereas alsoe divers poore people . . . of the Irishe Nation and Papists have lately come in great numbers out of Ireland into Cornewall Devon and other parts where they have been and are very disorderly, and much terrifie the Inhabitants where they come, and due care is not taken in all places for the suppressing and punishing of them . . . [the Lords and Commons require] . . . that they putt the Lawes in due execution, against such wandring Irishe Papists . . . And that they cause them to be foorthwith Conveyed backe into that Kingdome.[121]

Fears of popish plots, particularly associated with Ireland, continued however. Francis Bassett, vice-admiral of north Cornwall, was especially vigilant. In March he detained a ship and intercepted letters en route from Spain to Ireland, containing valuable information about Catholic plots in those two countries and in Scotland.[122] Two months later Bassett arrested one Ellis Nicholls, suspecting that he was the Irish rebel leader Sir Phelim O'Neill, and claiming that even if he were not O'Neill he was 'a very dangerous Person'. Bassett sent his prisoner to London to appear before the House of Lords, where it transpired that he was in fact the only son of one Mr John Nicholls of Honiton.[123]

On 5 February 1642 the Lords passed the bishops' exclusion bill. By this stage, Robartes had changed his position: he voted for the bill, reported on a conference with the Commons on the King's answer to it, and was named to the committee to draft thanks to the King for his assent.[124] In a letter, presumably written the same month, Francis Godolphin mentioned the passage of this and of the impressment bill, which allowed conscription for Ireland, and limited the King's control of the militia:

> All is likely to be quiet and well heer. The King having gratiously resolved to satisfie the iealousies and distrusts of the people, to putt the militia and forts into such hands as the Parliament shall recommend to him.[125]

Godolphin seems to have hoped that the King's assent to the impressment bill would satisfy Parliament, but his language suggests that he had now placed his own allegiance with the King.

Lord Mohun claimed to have left Parliament at this time:

I had the Honour to sit in Parliament, as a Peer, till about the Beginning of February last, at which Time there was great ado about the getting of your Lordships to agree with the House of Commons in the Militia, where I still gave my Vote according to my Conscience, as long as I could sit there with the Safety of my Person and Honour; which when I could not do, for the Tumults which then swarmed about both Houses of Parliament, I begged Leave of the King for my Absence . . .[126]

Mohun had been granted leave in August 1641, and had been absent at every call of the House from that date, which raises questions over the accuracy of this statement.[127] However, there was a mass exodus of 'royalist' peers from the House in early February, prompted by Parliament's attempts to remove control of the militia from the King's hands, and by intimidation from the London crowds, so the account probably at least reflects Mohun's views.[128]

In April two petitions were sent from Cornwall to Parliament. The first was part of a wider petitioning movement, in which thirty-seven counties petitioned Parliament between December 1641 and May 1642, and which Fletcher has described as 'a remarkable manifestation of the support for Pym's policies in the localities'.[129] Ostensibly sent from 'the Knights, Justices of the Peace, Gentlemen, Ministers, Free-holders and others', the signatories to the first petition were headed by eight Puritan JPs: John Moyle, William Coryton, John and Nicholas Trefusis, Thomas Herle, Thomas Gewen, Ezechiel Grosse of Golden (Coryton's grandson and Francis Buller's father-in-law), and John Carter of St Columb Major (John Moyle's brother-in-law).[130]

The petition opened by praising the achievements of the Parliament, and the subscribers vowed to defend Parliament with their 'Lives and Fortunes'.[131] Religion was the first issue raised: the petitioners advocated the establishment of a form of church government 'agreeable to Gods Word', and the abolition of the liturgy and ceremonies presently in use. They urged the removal of 'unlearned, scandalous or vicious' ministers, and their replacement with those who were 'godly, able and laborious'; and they emphasized the importance of strict observance of the sabbath.

Like petitions from other counties, fear of popery was a central theme. As shown above, in Cornwall this fear was inflamed by the outbreak of the Irish Rebellion, and by the influx of 800 Irish Catholics in January 1642. However, in the petition the Irish situation was not viewed in isolation, but rather as the antecedent of a wider papist design, possibly involving invasion from the continent. Therefore, as well as stressing the urgent need for the relief of Ireland, the petitioners requested the improvement of the county's defences. They urged that the Militia

Ordinance be put into effect: that the captains of the trained bands should be men 'of knowne fidelity, and soundnesse in Religion'; that a county-wide muster should be held; and that the county should be provided with ammunition. They described the decayed state of Pendennis and St Mawes castles, requested their repair and supply, and recommended the fortification of Fowey and Helford. The petitioners also complained that Cornwall was overburdened with impressment compared with other counties; and that the county was taxed more heavily than others. They asked that in future a reasonable proportion of these taxes should be used 'for the ease of their Countie'.[132]

However, the petitioners did not view the papist threat purely in terms of local defence. They also proposed the removal of the King's evil counsellors, who were generally regarded as accomplices to the alleged popish plot, and stressed the necessity of a sound Protestant education for the Prince of Wales. They also emphasized the importance of the bishops' exclusion bill, demanded 'that no Popish Lords may have their Votes in the House of Peeres', and proposed that papists should be confined to the counties in which they resided.

Fletcher has described this countrywide wave of petitioning as 'an authentic expression of deeply felt local opinion', which represented county consensus.[133] However, this does not apply to the Cornish petition. Soon after its presentation, another was sent to the Commons, also from 'the Knights, Esquires, Gentlemen, Ministers, Freeholders, and other Inhabitants, of the County of Cornwall'. The second petition was curiously unsigned. The authors claimed that the previous petition was invalid because it had been rejected by the grand jury at the March assizes and had been laid aside. They further claimed that many of the signatories had since regretted their action, 'wishing back their hands', and that many of the clergy and laity who had signed it were

publike contemners and depravers of the Ceremonies and the Service of the Booke of Common Prayer, by law established, irreverent vilifiers of Gods House, and Church Assemblies in Prayer times, and generally disobedient to Ecclesiasticall Government.

It was alleged that their views did not represent local opinion, and that the majority of Cornishmen 'inoffensively and reverently received and approved' the Book of Common Prayer and the ceremonies.[134]

The second petition also began by commending the work of the Parliament. It requested confirmation of the use of the Book of Common Prayer, and the continuance of episcopal government in the Church. However, it was not anti-Calvinist in tone, and distinguished carefully between individual bishops and the institution of episcopacy. The emphasis was upon orthodoxy, and social and moral order. It stressed the need for adequate maintenance for the parish clergy, in terms of impropriations and tithes, 'so those that Minister at the Altar, may live by the Altar'. The petition also proposed that all clergymen who were found to be 'either Scandalous or not Orthodox' should be reprimanded or removed. Further, it suggested the enactment of a penal law to prevent 'inordinate licenciousnesse', and to punish adulterers; and another law to enforce payment of Church rates.

In other respects the requests made in this petition were broadly similar to those in the previous one. These petitioners too were concerned about the papist threat, and proposed the disarming of recusants, and a Protestant education for recusants' children. They expressed particular concern about the weakness of St Mawes castle, and urged its repair and supply. They too complained of the high subsidies paid by the county 'much above our abilities', and also claimed that Cornwall was over-charged with arms. Further, the petitioners demanded fairer treatment from duchy officials, who had been charging double rents and dues through frequent amercements; and represented the cause of their countrymen who had been captured by Turkish pirates and transported to the Barbary coast. They complained of the poverty caused to the maritime towns by the loss of these men, and requested a guard for the coast to prevent further attack.

The contents of the two petitions were therefore very similar, and the only major difference concerned religion. The authors of the first petition were Puritans, and their demands for further change reflected this. The second group of petitioners, however, were not supporters of Laudian innovations. There is little evidence of support for Laudianism amongst the Cornish gentry, and even those who petitioned in favour of episcopacy hoped that 'the Delinquences of any particular person, may not cause that high and holy Office [of bishop], or Calling, to suffer'. Rather, the second group of petitioners opposed both Laudian excesses and the moves made towards further reformation in 1640–42. In particular, they sought to preserve the use of the Book of Common Prayer and its ceremonies in the parishes. Judith Maltby has labelled such people 'Prayer Book Protestants', conformists (rather than extremists) who sought to regain the initiative for the middle-ground.[135] This suggests that by April 1642 Cornish gentry society was divided between those who favoured further reformation, and those who resisted it. This split was neither Laudian against Puritan, nor royalist against parliamentarian. Further, the terms 'royalist' and 'parliamentarian' cannot confidently be used with reference to any Cornishman until September 1642. By August Coryton was active for the King, but his signature on the Puritan petition shows that in April

1642 the sides were not set for war. Indeed, in neither petition was there a sense of irreversible confrontation, nor any indication of awareness of mutually exclusive support for King or Parliament. In the same paragraph the first petitioners expressed concern for 'his Majesties honour and safety' and 'the Rights and Privilidges of Parliament'; and the second group of petitioners declared their support 'for uniting of his Gracious Majestie and this Honourable Assembly in a mutuall consent and compliancy, as for the unanimous and prosperous proceedings of this Parliament'. The lack of a sense of outright confrontation was common to all the petitions across the country. Fletcher attributes this to the fact that though by this stage the political situation at the centre was determined by the breakdown of trust in the King, the localities had yet to come to distrust Charles I.[136]

Many of the issues raised in the two petitions echoed the grievances of the 1620s. The events of the 1630s and the outbreak of the Irish Rebellion had caused fears of a popish plot and invasion from the continent to grow, but the state of the county's coastal defences had plainly not improved. The work undertaken on Pendennis castle in 1627 had evidently not been completed, since the first petitioners complained that the castle was 'decayed in some of the works, and fortifications, and hath some other works long since begun, but never perfected'. Similarly, they complained that St Mawes castle was 'extremely decayed in Platformes, and Carriages, wants Ordnance, and hath divers unserviceable, is not furnished with any sort of Ammunition'. The request for the fortification of Helford was new, but the fortification of Fowey had been requested as far back as 1625, and on many subsequent occasions. All this, plus the complaint about the continued adverse effect of Turkish piracy upon the maritime towns, shows how little the government had responded (or was perceived to have responded) to the concerns expressed two decades before. Beyond that, Cornish people still considered themselves overburdened with taxes, arms and impressment compared with other counties.

In spring 1642, Cornwall was one of twenty-two counties which circulated petitions in support of episcopacy and the liturgy. The Cornish petition, which was unsigned, was unusual in that it was addressed to Parliament, whereas most of the others were addressed to the King. It took a similar line to the second petition, but raised only religious issues and was rather more aggressive in tone.[137] Equal dismay was expressed at the activities of papists and sectarians, and firm action was demanded against both. The petitioners requested aid for Irish Protestants, and the execution of the penal laws against Catholics. They also demanded action against the 'Scandalous and ill-affected Pamphlets', written and distributed by Puritans, which 'fly abroad in such swarmes . . . able to cloud the pure aire of Truth, and present a darke ignorance to those who have not the two wings of Justice and Knowledge to fly above them'. To combat these dangerous sects, the petitioners demanded the confirmation of the liturgy,

> that you will bee pleased to intimate to the people, your Honourable and wise intentions concerning Divine Service, lest while you hold your peace, some rejecting it in part, others altogether, they vainly conceive you countenance them.

They went on to request the maintenance of episcopacy, although again carefully distinguishing between that institution and the activities of the Arminian bishops ('to continue the reverenced office, and punish the offending persons of Bishops'). The petitioners emphasized tradition, and the fundamental importance of order, conformity, authority and discipline, and asked Parliament to maintain the King's 'just and no way Antilegall Prerogative'.

On 22 May a petition of loyalty was sent from 'the County of Cornwall' to the King, containing 7,000 signatures, headed by those of thirty-six gentlemen and seven clerics, none of whom was a known Puritan. The first signatories were the sheriff, John Grylls Esq of Lanreath, Warwick Lord Mohun, Sir John Trelawny, Sir William Wrey, John Arundell of Trerice, Charles Trevanion, Walter Langdon and Peter Courtney. One surprising signatory was Robert Rous Esq of Landrake, brother of Francis Rous, and both step-brother and brother-in-law to John Pym. In 1629 Rous had upheld government militia policy, and he appears not to have shared the views of his family.[138] Clergy signatories were headed by Obadiah Ghossip, rector of St Tudy, whose patron was Lord Mohun.[139] The petitioners thanked Charles I for his goodness, and promised to defend his person, honour, estate and prerogative 'with their lives and fortunes'. They asked the King 'never to suffer your Subjects to be governed by an arbitrary Government, nor admit an alteration in Religion'. Their main concern was to preserve the established Church from papist and Puritan attack, and they attributed many of Charles' problems to the influence of 'scandalous Pamphlets' and 'seditious Sermons'. However, there was still no suggestion of outright political confrontation: indeed, they went on to 'heartily pray for the reconcilement betwixt your Majesty and your Parliament'.[140]

Fletcher has argued that 'royalism emerged in many counties through conservative petitioning campaigns about the issues of episcopacy and the liturgy'.[141] It is evident from the three Cornish petitions which concerned these matters that while there was no 'royalist party' in Cornwall in May 1642, the perceived papist threat and, in particular, the radical activities of Puritans since November 1640, had together prompted a conservative reaction from a large number of conformists who sought to defend the Book of Common Prayer and its ceremonies from Puritan attack, and to preserve order in the parishes. Through the common political activity of petitioning, necessarily prefaced by discussion, these men acquired a group identity. This group looked to the King for support, and in this respect a form of 'royalist' sentiment was clearly evolving.

The view that Cornish royalism emerged from defence of the established Church and liturgy is supported by Joseph Jane's contemporary account:

> the zelots made upp the body of the rebells, ther zele for the establishe liturgie and the kings cause stirred upp thother . . .[142]

In his analysis of Cornish allegiance, Clarendon further developed this idea, and drew out concerns about the nature and extent of Puritan reforms:

> There was in this county, as throughout the whole kingdom, a wonderful and superstitious reverence towards the name of a Parliament, and a prejudice to the power of the Court; yet a full submission, and love of the established government of Church and State, especially to that part of the Church as concerned the liturgy, or Book of Common Prayer, which was a most general object of veneration with the people; and the jealousy and apprehension that the other party intended to alter it was a principal advancement of the King's service.[143]

It is evident from the petitions that defence of the liturgy and episcopacy was also considered necessary for preservation of the social order. Many believed that Puritan reforms of the Church had gone too far and had undermined discipline and authority, and the group of MPs led by Pym, with whom the Puritans were associated, had caused concern by apparently encouraging popular pressure on Parliament through mob violence. The petition in defence of episcopacy and the liturgy made specific reference to the actions of 'Citizens', and prayed that they might be brought 'into right paths of serving God', so that they would 'bow to Authority, to bee under a Discipline, and live in order'.[144] As with Lord Mohun, mob violence, and fear of its possible repercussions, prompted many gentlemen to defend the King and the Church, which they believed to be the twin bastions of the traditional social order. So, whilst religion was undoubtedly a major influence upon the allegiance of future royalists, concern to defend the liturgy and episcopacy also reflected, to a greater or lesser degree, a concern to maintain social control.

Cornish parliamentarianism, on the other hand, developed from the group identity and activities of the Puritans. Although a minority group, they were well-organized, and secured a substantial number of Cornish seats in the Short and Long Parliaments. Within Parliament they worked together in support of Pym's policies, and particularly for godly reformation of the Church. When war became likely, it was this same group, led by Lord Robartes, Sir Alexander Carew and Sir Richard and Francis Buller, which promoted the parliamentary cause in Cornwall. Joseph Jane, in his royalist-biased account, attributed Cornish parliamentarianism to Puritan-inspired strong leadership from this group:

> the zelots . . . were noe great though a passionate company, some others were ledd by the opinion they had of the wisdome and foresight of particuler men.

Jane believed that 'the Lo[rd] Rob[ar]t[e]s had an influence upon many', and that others followed Sir Richard Buller 'by the knott of alliance', and because of a belief in his son's 'craft', presumably referring to his military ability. Jane also implied that zeal for the parliamentary cause blinded this group to their own weaknesses and to the possibility of defeat:

> Buller, I conceive, lookt only on the strength of the partie, and the succes hoped . . . the rest, I beleeve, led as Carew w[i]th a zele to the parliam[en]t, and [tha]t if it prevayled not, all was lost . . .[145]

However, although the leading Cornish parliamentarians were Puritans, not all Puritans supported Parliament. There were a number of Puritan royalists in Cornwall, most notably Coryton, Jonathan Rashleigh, Ambrose Manaton and (possibly) Sir Bevill Grenville. Coryton had signed the Puritan petition in April, and his patron, Pembroke, supported Parliament. Previously Coryton's Puritan beliefs and his allegiance to Pembroke as lord warden of the stannaries had been the prime influences on his actions, so it must have been expected that he would take Parliament's side. However, Coryton had been humiliated by the Commons in 1640–41 through the investigation into the Bossiney election and his conduct as vice-warden, resulting in his expulsion from the Commons. Bitterness at this treatment is the most likely explanation for Coryton's royalism, particularly since he had been so strongly motivated by bitterness at loss of office in the 1620s. Rashleigh had been granted leave from the Commons in December 1641, and Manaton at the end of February 1642, and neither returned.[146] There is no clear explanation for their royalism, although it is likely that they were more moderate than Rous, Carew and

Buller, and were uncomfortable with the extent of Pym's reforms. Rashleigh does not appear to have been active in the House on any matter. Manaton had been more active, but had not apparently worked for further reformation since his appointment to the committee for the clerical disabilities bill in March 1641.[147]

Preparations for War

During summer 1642 a core of activists on each side, through canvassing and holding meetings, motivated their fellow gentlemen into action. In June the King issued his commission of array for Cornwall. In addition to the sheriff he named twenty-one local gentlemen whom he hoped would support his cause, headed by Warwick Lord Mohun, Sir William Wrey, Sir John Trelawny, Sir William Courtney, Sir Nicholas Slanning, Sir Bevill Grenvile, Sir Peter Courtney, John Arundell junior of Trerice and Charles Trevanion.[148] There are numerous accounts of the efforts of the commissioners of array to rally support for the King. The impression given is of constant activity. In the early summer Warwick Lord Mohun, Sir Nicholas Slanning, Sir Bevill Grenvile and John Arundell junior of Trerice were the most active. They took prompt, decisive action in generating support for the King, and were reported to be 'in their privat Labors and metings very industrious', holding meetings, for example, at Boconnoc (Lord Mohun's house) and at Pendennis castle (where Sir Nicholas Slanning was governor). In September, Sir Richard Buller was informed that Lord Mohun had gone west to visit the Arundells of Trerice and the Coswarths of Coswarth, while Sir Bevill Grenvile had sent a messenger to Mohun.[149]

The commissioners of array also exploited family and friendship connections. For example, on 21 July Lord Mohun wrote to Francis Bassett of Tehidy

> to give you notice that the Commissioners of Array doe meet at Lostwithiell wednesday next, Pray doe mee the honor: to meet your friends Sir Nich: Slanning, Sir Bevill Grenvile & Mr Arundle of Trerise heer a Tuesday, where we shall conferre about some busines concerning setling of this County.[150]

Bassett became an active commissioner of array from August, and it is likely that Mohun's letter, together with a personal appeal from the King, evoking Bassett's duty of loyalty as vice-admiral, was a major influence upon his decision of allegiance.[151] So successful were Mohun and his associates at generating support that by August the number of active commissioners of array had increased considerably, and included John

Grylls (the sheriff), Sir William and Sir Peter Courtney of Trethurfe, William Coryton, Sir Walter Langdon, Samuel Coswarth, and Charles and John Trevanion.

On 27 July the Commons ordered Sir Richard and Francis Buller, Sir Alexander Carew, Francis Godolphin of Treveneage, Richard Erisey, and Thomas Arundell of Duloe to return to Cornwall to execute the Militia Ordinance, which had been passed on 5 March.[152] Their approach was less dynamic than that of the commissioners of array, and they were less persuasive in winning active support. They made direct approaches to individuals, with mixed success. In a number of cases they were too late, sometimes even after the individuals concerned had become active for the King. For example, in August they urged Coryton 'to assist us in the Militia & to oppose the array', but, already active in promoting the array, he gave only a 'shifting answer' to their request.

The militia commissioners' problems were exacerbated by the absence of the lord lieutenant, Lord Robartes, from the county.[153] In August they urged him to return, since 'the executinge of the Comission of the malitia will extremelie suffer without yor presents'. Further, they were apparently concerned with the need to maintain peace in the county, particularly for gathering in the harvest, and told Robartes that they had offered to meet with the commissioners of array 'to preserve thes County from destraction as much as might be and for their piece then and a quiet Harvest', but that the offer had been spurned. It is, however, possible that the offer had been motivated by concern at their opponents' success in recruitment, and a desire to slow them down.[154]

The Launceston assizes, which opened on 5 August, were a watershed in the fortunes of both sides. On 15 July the King had made changes to the Cornish commission of the peace, displacing ten members and adding nineteen others. This was part of an extensive programme of remodelling commissions in many counties, and in all the King removed 177 men whom he perceived as opponents, and added 154 likely supporters, hoping to gain control of county administrations. In Cornwall he removed Lord Robartes, Sir Richard Buller, Francis Buller, John Trefusis, John Moyle, Thomas Gewen, Tristram Arscott, John Carter and Leonard Treise of Treise. Those local gentry added were Lord Mohun, Sir William Wrey, Sir Bevill Grenvile, Sir Peter Courtney, John Arundell junior of Trerice, Piers Edgcumbe, Henry Killigrew of Ince, Francis Godolphin of Godolphin, Walter Langdon, William Glyn, Jonathan Rashleigh and William Pendarves.[155]

This purge greatly strengthened the King's position at the summer assizes. The militia commissioners complained that 'Most of the new Justices are of the Commission of Array, and they go opposite to our

Way'.[156] In his assize sermon, Nicholas Hatch, vicar of Lanteglos-by-Fowey, declared that 'the Militia was in the King', and prayed for his patron, Lord Mohun (now head of the bench), and the sheriff.[157] The judge, Sir Robert Foster, refused the militia commissioners' request to declare the commission of array illegal, and demonstrated his bias by speaking of the array with 'vigor voyce & Rhetorique'. Then, at 10 p.m., Mohun, Slanning, Grenvile, and Arundell, accompanied by Sir William and Sir Peter Courtney, Coryton, John Arundell senior, Francis Bassett, Samuel Coswarth and 'a great Number of their Followers', held a meeting. There the sheriff read the King's Proclamation against the Militia, and the warrant to execute the commission of array. He refused to read the Militia Ordinance, so it was left to the militia commissioners themselves to do so, declaring publicly the illegality of the commission of array.[158] The public declarations for the array from the pulpit, and by the sheriff and the assize judge, undoubtedly gave the royal commissioners an enormous advantage. They now appeared to have the support of the Church, the county administration, and the law—a demonstration of authority and legitimacy of crucial importance in winning further active support for the King. Conversely, the implied illegality of the Militia Ordinance would have made the militia commissioners' task extremely difficult, although they remained optimistic, and told the Speaker that after the assizes

> wee went abroad to understand how our country was possesst, & certainely our Joyrny hither was of high Advantage to hinder their [the Commissioners of Arrays'] proceedings & to gaine an obedience to the Parliament & a benefitt to this much abused county.[159]

On 8 August upon receipt of the militia commissioners' account of the assizes, the Lords summoned Lord Mohun, and the MPs Slanning, Grenvile, John Arundell junior and Sir Peter Courtney as delinquents.[160] The next day the Commons advised the Lords that it had taken action against these MPs, who had been active commissioners of array in Cornwall. The Commons had disabled Slanning from sitting in the House, and had sent for him as a delinquent. It had also summoned the MPs Grenvile and Arundell, together with Nicholas Hatch, the minister who had preached the assize sermon, and the sheriff.[161] They did not appear, but sent a message saying that they were commanded by his Majesty's special command to continue to preserve the peace in his county. Grenvile was disabled from sitting in that Parliament on 19 September, but Arundell was not disabled until January 1644.[162]

Despite the optimism of the commissioners of array, recruitment was slow during August. A muster at Bodmin on the 17th proved very disappointing: even Grenvile managed to raise only 180 men, mostly his own tenants. Indeed, 'there was a great distraccon in Countenance and words that their great expectation fell soe short'. In response, the commissioners of array agreed with their opponents to a cessation for fifteen days from 18 August. This gave the militia commissioners renewed hope (and extra time), and they told Robartes that

> wee all uppon the place doe averr that the reputacon of the Millitia is advanced . . . and growinge and the great sufferance of the Array is apparent and wee are more confident that the Parliament hath a Stronger Interest in this Countye and the greatest power as will appeare with us.[163]

However, when four days later the King raised his standard at Nottingham, signalling the outbreak of war, both sides in Cornwall resumed their preparations for war, heedless of the truce. Grenvile continued to exercise the men he had raised; at Charles Trevanion's suggestion, Robert Rashleigh published a paper against obedience to the Militia Ordinance; and Lord Mohun and the sheriff toured the parishes, raising men and offering them arms.[164]

The event which irrevocably tipped the balance in favour of the King was the arrival of Sir Ralph Hopton in the county on 25 September with 110 horse and fifty dragoons. Joseph Jane believed that the parliamentarians 'would have brought things to a neere poize if the horse had not swayed the scale that came w[i]th the Lord Hopton'.[165]

The parliamentary committee claimed that Hopton's troops had entered the county in a warlike manner, and ordered the trained bands to muster at Bodmin on 28 September to resist them. However, upon Hopton's approach, the parliamentarians retreated from Bodmin to Launceston, and began to fortify it, 'most of the ill affected people of that County, flocking into them'. They also held other parts of east Cornwall, including Saltash, where they erected gates and fortifications. At this stage the parliamentarians still hoped to maintain peace in the county, and sent Sir Alexander Carew and Humphrey Nicoll to treat with Hopton. These negotiations failed, and Hopton advanced to Truro where he met the King's supporters. At this point, from Hopton's own account, it would appear that the county was fairly evenly divided, in topographical terms at least, between the two sides. Hopton remarked that at the end of September, 'Sir Richard Buller and his Confederats had much increased their numbers having drawen to them most of the able men in the East Division of Cornwall', whilst he himself had 'the interest of those well affected Cornish Gentlemen of the Westerne Division'.[166]

At the Michaelmas quarter sessions at Lostwithiel, the parliamentarians presented an indictment against 'divers men unknown' for coming into the county armed, 'contra pacem etc'. In retaliation, the royalists issued bills of indictment against the parliamentary committee, alleging rout and unlawful assembly at Launceston and unlawful attacks on the King's subjects. The grand inquest ordered the sheriff, John Grylls, to raise a *posse comitatus* for dispersing the unlawful assembly at Launceston. Coryton and Manaton, both JPs, were present and, 'being very willing to medyate a right understanding and to prevent the shedding of bloud', were sent to Launceston to invite the parliamentary committee 'to lay down armes, and to prevent further trouble in the country'. These two were both Puritans, and their willingness to mediate may reflect some uneasiness about fighting fellow Puritans, and perhaps a desire for peace. They were unsuccessful, and when the quarter sessions adjourned to Truro, Hopton stood trial for the charges brought against him by the parliamentary committee. The jury acquitted him, and thanked him for coming to the rescue of the county. Warrants were issued immediately to summon the *posse*.

At the same time, also in Truro, during the election for the new mayor, the outgoing mayor clashed with Sir Richard Vyvyan of Trelowarren. Vyvyan stood on the steps of the Town Hall and insisted that the mayor call out the trained bands for the King, arguing that he was legally bound to do so. The mayor disputed this, and refused to act. Vyvyan appealed to the crowd, which had gathered around the Town Hall, to take up arms since 'that they knew not what unlawfull Assemblies were gathered in many parts of the County to the danger of their lives, their wives, and children, if they came not out to assist the Sheriffe and Justices'. The mayor, who plainly favoured Parliament, disputed this too, saying that 'he knew no unlawfull Assemblies to be suppressed'. A few inhabitants proclaimed that 'their Armes should never be carried against the Parliament, they would die rather'. However, Vyvyan's appeal to law and order had won the support of the majority. The new mayor released the town arms, and the following day the trained bands were sent out for the King.[167]

On 4 October 3,000 foot soldiers assembled on Moilesbarrow Down near Lostwithiel. Hopton noted that all of them were raised from western Cornwall, 'most of the easterne part being then under the power of the Committee'. However, the equilibrium had now been upset, since for the second time the force of the law and the county administration was demonstrably behind the royalists. Further, Hopton's *posse* (together with his own troops) vastly outnumbered the parliamentarian forces in the east. Consequently, on 6 October, when Hopton and his 3,000 men advanced on Launceston, Sir Richard Buller and his 700-strong army of occupation retreated. The Cornish parliamentarians withdrew to Devon, where they united with the forces of Sir George Chudleigh.[168]

Hopton now held the Tamar, but was reluctant to advance into Devon. He was disinclined to attack a united parliamentary force; nor could he legally take the *posse* over the county boundary. Further, it was unlikely that its members would agree to fight outside the county. It was at this point that the royalist leaders decided to raise an army of volunteers 'in a formall way'. Grenvile, Slanning, John Trevanion, William Godolphin and Lord Mohun all raised their own foot regiments, and Edward Coswarth raised a troop of dragoons. These regiments were armed partly from those gentlemen's own stores, and partly from the stores of the trained bands.[169] This marked another turning point. The royalists now had the beginnings of an organized and disciplined army, which they could take out of the county, and which was recruited by committed gentlemen specifically for the King's cause.[170]

For the Civil War period, problems in identifying the nature of an individual's allegiance, or his level of commitment, are great. The sources for allegiance are not reliable, especially for royalism, and the problems of classification are immense. Therefore any statistical analysis will inevitably be arbitrary and unsatisfactory. Following Hughes' method, for the purposes of analysis any record of royalism in the Calendar of the Committee for Compounding, the Calendar for the Advance of Money, official reports, or correspondence, has been taken as indicative of some degree of commitment. Some active royalists who managed to avoid sequestration through various means are not listed in the Calendar of the Committee for Compounding, whereas the consistent pleas of innocence from some who were sequestered suggests that they may have been accused unfairly. Similarly, where an individual is recorded as having taken a parliamentary office before 1646, either as a military commander or as a county committeeman, or is recorded as a parliamentarian in official reports or correspondence, he has been classed as a parliamentarian.[171]

There is evidence for the activity of only 45.5 per cent of Cornish gentlemen for either side, although this does not necessarily signify the inactivity of the remainder. Of the 321 heads of gentry families, 91 (28.3 per cent) showed some 'commitment' to royalism, and 52 (16.2 per cent) to parliamentarianism, almost twice as many being royalist as parliamentarian. However, the figures for the greater gentry, for whom a higher proportion of allegiance is known, were slightly more balanced (51 per cent of royalists as opposed to 29.2 per cent of parliamentarians).

Most records necessarily say more about activity than about motivation. Activity for one side or the other does not in itself indicate genuine commitment, nor does it necessarily signify enthusiasm for the war itself. Nor can the fact that two individuals acted in a similar way for the same side be assumed to point to a similar level of commitment. For example, the letters of Sir Bevill Grenvile and Francis Godolphin of Godolphin illustrate different levels of commitment to royalism. Both were active for the King, but whereas Grenvile was extremely enthusiastic and committed from the outset, Godolphin appears to have been a more reluctant participant.

As discussed, in the late 1630s, despite his Calvinist beliefs, Grenvile was active for the King against the Scots, and condemned them for rebelling against their anointed monarch. He was one of the most active commissioners of array in summer 1642, and was quick to raise a regiment when war seemed inevitable. He fought at the Battles of Braddock Down (January 1643) and Stratton (May 1643), and was killed on 5 July 1643 during the Battle of Lansdown. Sir Bevill was intolerant of parliamentarians and neutrals, and was both suspicious and scornful of all negotiations for a political settlement. This uncompromising and rather brutal attitude is vividly expressed in a letter to his wife, written from Bodmin in October 1642:

> for my part I am impatient (as all my honest friends else are) that we did not march presently, to fetch those traitors out of their nest at Launceston, or fire them in it. But some of our fainter bretheren have prevailed so far with the Sheriff, as there is a conference agreed on this day between 6 of a side, to see if they can compose matters.[172]

Again, in March 1643, Grenvile informed his wife that 'there is a cessation agreed on for 20 daies, from whence for my part I looke but for knavery'.[173]

Francis Godolphin of Godolphin was also active in the King's cause, and spent most of the war either in Oxford or on the Isles of Scilly, of which he was governor. Between March and April 1646 he entertained the Prince of Wales and his Council on St Mary's, and on 16 April fled with them to Jersey. However, Godolphin's letters are in complete contrast to Grenvile's. He had not shared Grenvile's enthusiasm for the Scots Wars, and had wished to be at home.[174] Godolphin maintained this somewhat passive attitude, and it was plainly his wish in summer 1642 to abstain from the national conflict. He wrote to his wife (probably from York) in August, saying:

> I suppose every man ought in this distraction, to be provided as well as he can to defende himself and the cause his conscience directs him to defend.[175]

It appears that Godolphin entertained no doubts about which cause he should support, but that he was nevertheless extremely reluctant to take up arms. The frequent hopeful references in his wartime correspondence to settlement negotiations demonstrate his constant longing for peace, and suggest that, although committed to the royalist cause, he was never as convinced as Grenvile about the value of war. Writing from Oxford on 12 February 1643, when the Treaty of Oxford negotiations were in progress, Godolphin remarked that 'there is very great preparation made on the other side, and noe possibility of peace'. A week later he wrote, 'We have sent again to London about a treaty of peace, their answer is hourly expected. I think the hope of peace was never less . . . the preparations for war are very forward'.[176] On 5 March 1644, writing again from Oxford, he reported that, 'We have sent another letter written with the King's owne hand for peace'.[177] Even in 1646, he evidently still hoped for settlement. In a letter of that year, he complained:

> how grosly we are ledd like sheepe to the slaughter . . . All the Kings offers or demaunds are answered with saying the trust reposed in us by the Country will not suffer us to admitt of such conditions.[178]

Sir William Courtney of Saltash sympathized strongly with the parliamentarian cause, but was opposed to the notion of war as a political instrument. Throughout 1641, in his letters to Sir Richard Buller, Courtney frequently expressed his concern for the privileges of Parliament, the liberty of the subject, and the maintenance of the Protestant religion. For example:

> I doe harttely pray to god that he will blesse prottect and kepe this courte of parllement that god may have his true and Righte worshipe and the Kinges subiectes pease for their is no man livinge that hath and do pray for the libertie and equitie of all men in Inglande [more] than mysellfe.[179]

However, the tone of Courtney's letters changed after the outbreak of hostilities. There is no evidence to show that he took up arms, and he appears to have maintained a neutral stance in 1642–43, despite his expressed belief in the parliamentary cause, and his friendship and correspondence with Cornish parliamentary leaders. He firmly believed that the only way to secure Parliament's aims was through peaceful negotiation. In November 1642 he wrote from Saltash to Sir Richard Buller in Plymouth, urging him outte of your wisdome and care of the publlicke good to ende these trobelles by a tretie and not by forse for by a treattie you may preserve the Comones from Ruayne the greatte men theare estattes to them and their posteritie with other benefits to men of all condittions and to the preservatione of Trade the which is the liffe of the Kingdome.[180]

It is clear that one of Courtney's principal concerns about war was the expectation that it would result in the loss of gentry estates. Indeed, it appears that one of the bases of his pacifism was fear of social disorder. For example, in a letter to Sir Richard Buller of 5 August 1641, he stated that if Scottish soldiers were allowed to persist in their iconoclasm, social revolution would ensue:

for I have sine the disposition of men that have armes and strength that the[y] manye times mackes themsellves master of theare offisers and sumtimes offesers sufferes the soullders to be theare masters.[181]

By February 1643, Courtney was extremely pessimistic. Writing to Francis Buller and lamenting the misery which had befallen county, town and parish, he opined that if a settlement were not reached soon, the onset of famine, murder and pestilence was inevitable.[182] By this stage Courtney appears to have been a neuter, ready to co-operate with both sides. After the death of Sir Richard Buller in November 1642, Courtney negotiated with the royalists who were occupying Saltash, so that Sir Richard's body might be transported the short distance across the Tamar from Plymouth to St Stephens by Saltash. He reported to Francis Buller that he had spoken to Sir James Collburne about the matter, but no firm decision could be taken without Hopton's consent. Therefore, Courtney regretted that 'I have noe power to obtane anye thinge more then they ar willinge to grante'.[183]

Few gentlemen defined their allegiance as clearly as Grenvile, Godolphin and Courtney. However, their statements highlight the difficulties of analyzing gentry allegiance, particularly in statistical terms. Although both Grenvile and Godolphin were active for the King, their royalisms were of a wholly different nature, and it is arbitrary to place them in the same category. Courtney was a parliamentarian, but is not known to have been active, and was never enthusiastic about the use of war to achieve Parliament's objectives. He does not fit neatly into any category. Indeed, it seems likely that many, perhaps most, who acted for either side only reluctantly became involved in the war. This does not necessarily imply that they had neutralist, or even localist, views; many simply wanted to avoid being drawn into armed conflict, and feared the consequences.[184] Clarendon recognized the size of this 'group' in his (royalist-biased) description of Cornish gentry allegiance:

> There was a third sort (for a party they cannot be called) greater than either of the other, both in fortune and number, who, though they were satisfied in their consciences of the justice of the King's cause, had yet so great a dread of the power of the Parliament, that they sat still as neuters, assisting neither. So that they who did boldly appear and declare for the King were compelled to proceed with all wariness and circumspection, by the known and well understood rules of the law and justice, and durst not oppose the most extravagant act of the other side but with all the formality that was used in full peace.[185]

Recruitment for both sides was a gradual, cumulative process, and it seems that many made a declaration of allegiance only when there was no alternative. The occupation of a gentleman's parish by troops would have aroused fear for the safety of his person, family, or house, and could have precipitated acceptance of a command for that side. For example, after the retreat of the parliamentarians into Devon in October 1642, the royalists advanced on Millbrook and Mount Edgcumbe, and Piers Edgcumbe of Mount Edgcumbe promptly declared for the King. There is no definite indication of his allegiance or activity before this date, which implies that he became active only when his house was endangered.[186]

These shades of allegiance and commitment emphasize the inadequacy of statistical analysis. However, while taking account of the unreliability of this method, some attempt has been made to compare activists from the two sides. Of known royalists, slightly more lived in west Cornwall than in the east of the county, while slightly more parliamentarians lived in east Cornwall than in the west. Forty-one (45 per cent) known royalists lived in east Cornwall and 50 (55 per cent) in west Cornwall, whereas 31 (60 per cent) of known parliamentarians lived in the east of the county and 21 (40 per cent) in the west. Given the religious differences of the two sides, and Hopton's account of topographical divisions in summer 1642, this weighting towards royalism in west Cornwall and towards parliamentarianism in the east is unsurprising. What is surprising is the relative closeness of the figures: a starker contrast between east and west might have been expected.

The parliamentarians were genenerally wealthier than the royalists. Only 10 per cent of known royalists had a landed income of more than £500 per annum, whereas 30 per cent of parliamentarians fell into this category. Further, about 60 per cent of royalists are known to have had a landed income of less than £500 per annum, compared with about 40 per cent of parliamentarians. The two sides had very similar educational experiences: 52 per cent of known parliamentarians had experienced higher education, compared with 50 per cent of royalists. A few more royalists than parliamentarians had medieval origins in the county, which could suggest that families with deeper roots in Cornwall were more likely to support the King, although again the differences are not sufficiently great as to be conclusive.[187]

Conclusion

Patterns of Continuity and Discontinuity

Graham Haslam has shown how 'benign neglect' followed by 'active dismemberment' during Elizabeth's reign caused the duchy of Cornwall to sink to 'the depths of its fortunes' by 1601. In contrast, after James' accession, inspired by the presence of an heir to the throne and new opportunities for patronage, the duchy rose like a 'phoenix', recovering alienated lands and re-establishing its political power. Dr Haslam has further demonstrated how the duchy became 'a political machine' and how the Prince's Council 'consistently supported the political aims of the early Stuarts'.[1]

This view of the Council's loyalty to the Crown is entirely supported by the findings of the present study. However, for Cornwall, the most significant innovation of the revived duchy was the usurpation of the lord warden's central role in duchy management by the Prince's Council, and the exclusion of the lord warden from the Council.[2] Consequently, with the duchy's political power base fragmented, the lord warden was free to exercise his considerable (albeit curtailed) influence independently of the duchy.

In the elections of 1614 and 1620 Pembroke, the lord warden, was apparently either unable or unwilling to oppose duchy interests, and consequently the Prince's Council achieved considerable electoral success in Cornwall. It was not until 1624 that Pembroke began to exert his electoral influence in Cornish boroughs, and only then prompted by Buckingham's intrusion into the Cornish electoral scene. Although Pembroke was not making a direct challenge to the duchy, his intervention and his mobilization of stannary influence undermined the duchy's position.

In an earlier article, Haslam remarked on the absence of recorded duchy influence for the three remaining elections of the 1620s. He concluded that since the Prince's Council remained in existence after Charles became King, its political activities almost certainly continued too, but stated that it was difficult to determine specific duchy nominees from those Crown and duchy officials returned.[3] The most likely explanation for the 'silence' in the records after 1624 is that duchy interests became subsumed in Buckingham's electoral ambition, which would accord with Haslam's perception of the Prince's Council as 'reliable political allies' of the government.[4] From 1625 the duchy, almost certainly encouraged by the King, apparently gave way to Buckingham in Cornish borough elections and opposed Pembroke's exertion of stannary influence. Former duchy candidates, such as Sir Richard Weston, Sir Francis Cottington and Sir Henry Vane, were Buckingham supporters also, and in 1625 appear to have been returned in Buckingham's interest rather than the duchy's. Weston was again returned for a Cornish seat in Buckingham's interest in 1626, and the Duke placed Cottington at Saltash in 1628.

The Prince's Council resumed its overt political activity in the spring elections of 1640, but experienced a remarkable lack of success. Only one of its sixteen candidates was returned, and he not for the nominated borough. In the autumn elections of that year none of the duchy's eight candidates was successful. Coate attributed this rejection of duchy influence to 'the wish of Cornwall to be represented by Cornishmen', and Gruenfelder has supported her in this view. But, borough franchises were by no means exclusively a gentry preserve, and such a widespread rejection suggests a deep-seated hostility to the duchy in Cornwall.

The rival interest of the stannaries undoubtedly weakened duchy electoral influence. In both 1640 elections Coryton, Pembroke's vice-warden, exerted stannary influence to win seats for the lord warden, and directly opposed the duchy's interests; in the autumn election Pembroke gained seats through personal intervention in several boroughs. Puritans, many with a record of opposition to government policies in the 1620s, and with local connections, gained a large number of returns in both elections. The evidence suggests that of all three factors, this electoral success was founded on Puritan political organization.

Coate stated that the extinction of duchy influence in the borough elections of spring and autumn 1640 'was not a verdict against the duchy as landlord, for its administration was never an issue in the elections'.[5] There is no clear evidence either way, but by spring 1642 the duchy's treatment of its tenants had certainly become a political issue. The second, pro-episcopal, petition from the county in April 1642 prayed:

> that such Dutchey Tenants as within our County pay over their rightfull Rents and Duties unto the Dutchy Officers may not bee doubly charged by Proces out of the Exchequer, as now they are, by extreame and continuall Amercements.[6]

205

Haslam has shown that Charles, as Prince of Wales and as King, used a range of revenue-raising devices to exploit duchy lands fully. These devices were 'unpopular, perhaps profoundly so' and were employed vigorously during the 1630s. If the duchy were perceived as an unfair landlord during the 1630s, and given that this was of sufficient concern to raise in a petition to Parliament in 1642, it would be surprising if such perceptions had no influence upon the borough electorates in 1640.[7]

Further, duchy tenants were unlikely to feel much affection for an unfair landlord; still less would they have been likely to take up arms for one. In his recent study of popular allegiance, Mark Stoyle argued that while this may have been true of some gentlemen it did not apply for 'humbler folk', and he stressed the 'particular affection' of local people to the duchy. However, Stoyle does not explain why tenants should have felt stronger allegiance to the duchy, controlled remotely, as it was, from London, than to local gentry landlords. Nor does he consider the duchy's recent treatment of its tenants; this is particularly surprising as most were of below gentry status.[8] Regarding the duchy's influence on Civil War allegiance Coate's view that 'the fact that a man was a Duchy tenant did not determine his choice [of sides]' would appear more convincing.[9] Consequently, the royalism of duchy tenants should not be taken for granted.

Stoyle is probably right to suggest the importance of the stannaries in providing royalist soldiers.[10] As discussed above, in parliamentary elections the lord warden relied upon the vice-warden's exercise of local power, and in both elections of 1640 Coryton had influenced the borough electorates in Pembroke's interest and against the duchy. In 1642 Coryton (who was not removed from the vice-wardenship, despite the Commons investigation into his conduct) became an active commissioner of array, and may have acted against Pembroke, who supported Parliament. If indeed the vice-warden was influential in this way, the predominance of tin mining in the west might help to explain why popular royalism was stronger there than in the east of the county.

During the second half of the 1620s the effects of Charles' wars with Spain and France, exacerbated by the presence and activities of Turkish pirates, dominated Cornish politics and society. In Russell's view, war raised the 'political temperature' in the country as a whole and was the principal cause of political conflict. War prompted central government to make abnormally heavy demands upon local governors, straining the links between the centre and the localities, and creating a potentially explosive situation. In the 1630s when there were no war pressures, the political temperature dropped; but in 1639–40 the demands of the Scots Wars renewed the strains and caused further political conflict.[11] In Cornwall, the wars of the 1620s certainly raised the political temperature, and aroused anger at the heavy demands being made of the county. But they were not the only cause of political conflict; indeed, they were not so much a cause as a catalyst. The wars created a tense atmosphere in which political conflict could develop, and become inflamed, but the causes of the conflict were more complex.

In Cornwall, political conflict originated in Buckingham's intervention in the borough elections of 1624. Pembroke was prompted to reassert his own political influence as lord warden, which consequently undermined the duchy's electoral position. The greater gentry gradually became polarized into the factions of either Buckingham or Pembroke; connections were forged or strengthened between the peers' local supporters and their non-Cornish clients, some of whom were placed in Cornish seats with local assistance. The process of polarization continued in spring 1625 when Buckingham (now apparently with duchy support) and Pembroke again competed for Cornish seats; it intensified during the autumn and winter of 1625–26 when Sir John Eliot switched his allegiance from Buckingham to Pembroke. This cleared the way for Eliot's rival, Sir James Bagg, to assume a new prominence in his role as the Duke's chief agent in the west. Bagg's scheming and his vitriolic reports to Buckingham did much to stimulate political conflict in the county and to erode the middle ground between the two sides. Bagg employed confrontational language, referring to the Duke's opponents as a 'faction', and attempting to implicate Eliot in an anti-government plot.

The polarization of the greater gentry intensified following Buckingham's purge of his most prominent opponents in summer 1626, and his expulsion of forced loan refusers from office in 1627. The purge was not confined to the Duke's Cornish enemies; Cust has demonstrated its effect in creating rival gentry factions in many counties.[12] In Cornwall, stannary influence was suppressed, and the balance of power on the county Bench and in the lieutenancy was upset. The deputies, now all Buckingham's supporters, encountered widespread opposition when trying to enforce government policies. This opposition was fuelled by the deputies' close association with the Duke, and because many blamed the Duke for the poor conduct of the war.

In this way, military failure and the demands of war on the county aggravated the political conflict. Buckingham's intrusion into Cornish elections had generated the conflict, and his and Bagg's subsequent actions had shaped its development. Those who opposed the Duke were frequently responding to his attempts to raise war finance. For example, Eliot's decision to change his allegiance was apparently provoked by

207

Buckingham's unprecedented request for additional supply from the 1625 Parliament. Eliot feared this would threaten the relationship between the King and the Commons and undermine the principle of parliamentary taxation, but the Duke had requested the money to pay for the Cadiz fleet. Further, the Duke's purge of his opponents was in response to the Commons' impeachment attempt upon him, which had been triggered by the threat of a new war with France, and the Duke's mismanagement of the Spanish war featured prominently in the charges against him. The forced loan originated in the King's urgent need of war revenue independent of Parliament. It is unlikely that the lieutenancy would have become so politicized had this not been a time of war: so, in many ways war provided the pre-conditions for political conflict, if it did not actually cause it.

Cust has emphasized the importance of Parliament's inadequate provision of supply for the wars in feeding Charles' uncertainty about the loyalty of his subjects. Following the impeachment attempt upon Buckingham and opposition to the benevolence in summer 1626, the King and the Duke were convinced that their leading opponents in the Commons were implicated in a 'popular' conspiracy aimed at undermining the monarchy. For this reason they placed great emphasis upon 'loyalty' and 'obedience', and were anxious to defend royal authority from the assaults of 'popularity'. Cust also believes that these views were shared by a number of the King's and Buckingham's supporters at Court and in the country, including Bagg, John Mohun, and other members of their Cornish faction, creating an ideological division between them and their opponents which was 'a more profound cause' of political conflict than were the temporary annoyances caused by the foreign wars.[13]

The proposition that the King and the Duke were motivated by these fears is entirely convincing. However, as discussed in Chapter 3, Bagg's sycophancy and Mohun's overriding desire to control the government of Cornwall make it unlikely that they and their allies genuinely shared these concerns. It is more probable that, out of self-interest and for self-advancement, they adopted language fashionable at Court to exploit the King's and Buckingham's fears. The King's *Declaration* at the end of the 1626 Parliament revealed that he perceived Eliot as a potential leader of the 'ill affected' and the 'multitude' in a conspiracy to undermine the monarchy.[14] Therefore, it would have been apparent to Bagg and Mohun that the most effective means of attacking Eliot was to accuse him and his associates of stimulating 'discontent' among 'unquiet spirits' in their opposition to the forced loan, and in their 1628 election campaign. So, from a Cornish perspective, Court ideology was more a weapon of political conflict than a cause of it.

Cust also presents a rival conspiracy theory, in which 'Country' MPs feared the King's involvement in a popish plot threatening the true Protestant religion and the laws and liberties of Englishmen.[15] It is certainly the case that in attacking the forced loan Eliot and Coryton highlighted its unlawfulness and the threat it posed to liberties. Further, in the 1628 Parliament they linked the effects of the wars, particularly billeting and martial law, with attacks on liberties and property rights, which they connected with the rise of Arminianism, likened to popery. The fact that in the 1629 Parliament Eliot and Coryton joined with Francis Rous in denouncing Arminianism and in drawing out its religious and political implications suggests that they genuinely feared a popish plot. However, before Buckingham's assassination in August 1628 it is difficult to distinguish these fears from dislike of the Duke and bitterness at loss of office. It is important to recognize that for Eliot and Coryton and their associates loan refusal was also a vehicle for expressing personal opposition to Buckingham: both had recently been deprived of their offices at the Duke's hands, and Coryton in particular made plain his bitterness.

* * *

Insofar as there was an ideological division between the two Cornish factions, this was rooted in religion. There was a clear Puritan connection between members of the Eliot–Coryton faction and their supporters; there is no evidence of Puritanism among members of the Bagg–Mohun faction. All of those punished for loan refusal—Eliot, Coryton, Sir Richard Buller, Ambrose Manaton, Nicholas Trefusis and Humphrey Nicoll—were Puritans, and their shared godly perspective may have been influential in their refusal. Eliot and Coryton had attacked Buckingham's military failures in Parliament, and it is possible that they and their supporters perceived these failures as divine judgement upon the Duke, and therefore objected to paying a levy to further the Duke's misguided military ambition.

This Puritan influence remained strong, even after the factional quarrel was extinguished, and was particularly evident in resistance to knighthood composition fines. Trefusis and Manaton again refused to pay, as did John Moyle and William Rous, fellow Puritans and former supporters of the Eliot–Coryton faction. As shown in Chapter 5, resistance to knighthood fines appears to have been Puritan-led, again possibly because the godly objected to repaying debts for disastrous wars which had been the subject of divine judgement. However, Puritans did not always oppose government policy: the seven Puritan JPs who refused to pay knighthood fines were amongst the most zealous in implementing the Book of Orders shortly afterwards, and Manaton was the most active of all. Further, as discussed above, Puritan organization appears to have been responsible for significant election successes in the spring and autumn of 1640. The impression given is of some continuity in Puritan circles between 1626 and 1640, probably stimulated by perceived Laudian excesses during the 1630s.

*　　*　　*

In other respects there was a lack of continuity between 1626 and 1640. During the 1630s the factions which had previously dominated gentry politics disintegrated and political conflict subsided. In part this can be attributed to the end of war. But the absence of parliaments also deprived the gentry of a forum for political expression, and gentry communications with the Court were restricted after Buckingham's assassination in 1628 and Pembroke's death in 1630. Neither Pembroke's successor, Philip, Earl of Pembroke and Montgomery, nor Bagg's new patron, Lord Treasurer Weston, appear to have established close contacts with the Cornish gentry. Without a Court patron, and with Bagg and Mohun estranged, former members of the Bagg–Mohun faction showed little enthusiasm for collecting knighthood fines. Bagg, Sir Bernard Grenvile, Sir William Wrey, Sir Reginald Mohun and Sir Richard Edgcumbe had all died by 1640. Coryton's defection and Eliot's death in the Tower in 1632 removed the focus of the Eliot–Coryton faction. Coryton seems never to have regained intimacy with his former factional colleagues, and Bevill Grenvile became reconciled with his father and with Bagg by 1636. The remainder of the Eliot–Coryton faction and a number of its supporters continued to be united by a Puritan bond.

This picture had changed significantly by 1642. In Parliament between 1640 and 1642 some Cornish Puritans—led in the Commons by Sir Alexander Carew, Sir Richard and Francis Buller, and represented in the Lords by Lord Robartes—acted as a coherent force, working in support of Pym's policies, and particularly for godly reformation of the Church. The extent of these proposed reforms exposed differences between these MPs and their more moderate Puritan colleagues, such as Manaton and Jonathan Rashleigh, and (possibly) Bevill Grenvile. Robartes, Carew and the Bullers formed the nucleus of Cornish parliamentarians in 1642; Manaton and Rashleigh appear ultimately to have found more common ground with conformists who sought to preserve the Book of Common Prayer and its ceremonies, and subsequently they declared for the King. Coryton was another Puritan royalist, but it appears that it was resentment at his treatment by the Commons in 1640–41 that caused him to turn his back on Parliament, despite placing his signature on the Puritan petition in April.

*   *   *

Patterns of Cornish gentry allegiance do not appear to correspond with those of their counterparts in Lincolnshire, Essex and Warwickshire. In these counties Cust found strong links between forced loan refusal, opposition to non-parliamentary taxes in the 1630s, and active parliamentarianism. Some Cornish loan refusers did go on to oppose knighthood composition fines, but this did not automatically lead to support for Parliament. Of the eight leading members of the Eliot–Coryton faction still alive in 1642, five declared for the King and three for Parliament.

Cust also drew attention to a correlation between active supporters of the loan, enforcement of Crown levies during the 1630s, and active royalism. There was certainly more apparent continuity of allegiance amongst the Bagg–Mohun faction, in that the three surviving members —Sir John Trelawny and his younger brother, Edward, and Sir Walter Langdon—all became royalists in 1642. But the number of survivors is too small to draw any significant conclusions, and the link is weakened by the lack of enthusiasm for knighthood fines among this group. The Cornish experience seems to accord more with Russell's view that there was no apparent link between divisions of opinion in the 1620s and the sides of 1642. While there was discontinuity in Cornwall, particularly caused by the death of key figures, an important factor for continuity existed in the form of Puritan organization.[16]

As with Rashleigh and Manaton, for many Cornish gentlemen royalist sentiment developed from their reaction against Puritan extremism. Indeed, although many factors were influential in decisions of allegiance, it appears that Cornish royalism was founded upon a concern to defend the Book of Common Prayer and its ceremonies against Puritan assaults, and to preserve order in the parishes. An explanation for this strong attachment to the established Church may be the apparently limited impact of Arminianism in Cornish parishes. If few real changes had been made during the 1630s, Cornish gentlemen would have been less likely to become alienated from the King, and Puritans may have appeared the greater innovators.

Stoyle's conclusion that religion was the primary influence upon popular allegiance in Cornwall is entirely convincing, particularly given the comparable effect of religion upon greater gentry allegiance. There is no reason to doubt that 'popular puritanism was largely confined to the eastern hundreds', since the most radical Puritan gentry and clergy lived there.[17]

211

The strength of popular royalism in west Cornwall should not be overlooked, particularly in view of the thousands who turned out to support Hopton against Buller and the parliamentarians in September 1642. As with royalist gentry allegiance, and supported by the accounts of Joseph Jane and Clarendon, it is likely that popular royalism was under- pinned by a desire to preserve the established Church.

*　　*　　*

Perceptions of and reactions to religious change appear to have been the principal cause of division among the Cornish gentry in 1642. For many royalists, however, defence of the established Church and liturgy was intrinsically linked with preserving the social order. For others, like Grenvile, these factors were combined with loyalty and honour. For Francis Godolphin an instinctive loyalty to the King overcame reluctance to be involved in armed conflict; for Piers Edgcumbe that factor was the presence of an army in his parish. The parliamentarians appear to have perceived a godly reformation as a sufficient cause, although sometimes this was combined, as it was for Carew, with a 'zele to the Parliament'.

For gentlemen who supported either side in 1642 there were many competing influences, ranging from family, friends, parish and county, to education, officeholding and religion. Some of these influences had remained constant from the 1620s while others had changed; overall the balance had shifted but religion remained the most significant cause of division between members of the Cornish gentry.

Abbreviations

Alumni Cantab: J. Venn and J.A. Venn (eds) *Alumni Cantabrigienses. A biographical list of all known students, graduates and holders of office at the University of Cambridge, from the earliest times to 1900* Part 1 From the earliest times to 1751, 4 vols (Cambridge, 1922–27).

Alumni Oxon: Joseph Foster (ed.) *Alumni Oxonienses: the members of the University of Oxford, 1500–1714; their parentage, birthplace and year of birth, with a record of their degrees, etc* 4 vols (Oxford and London, 1891).

APC: Acts of the Privy Council of England 1618–1631 11 vols (London, 1929–64).

Bellum Civile: Ralph Hopton, *Bellum Civile. Hopton's Narrative of his Campaign in the West (1642–1644) and Other Papers* ed. by C.E.H. Chadwyck Healey, Somerset Record Society, vol. XVIII (1902).

BIHR: Bulletin of the Institute of Historical Research

Birch, *C&T:* Thomas Birch (ed.) *The Court and Times of Charles I* 2 vols (1848).

BL: British Library.

BP: R.N. Worth (ed.) *The Buller Papers* (privately published, 1895).

Carew: Richard Carew, *The Survey of Cornwall* (London, 1769).

CCC: Calendar of the Proceedings of the Committee for Compounding 1643–1660 5 vols (London, 1889–93).

CD 1625: Proceedings in Parliament 1625 ed. by M. Janssen and W.B. Bidwell (New Haven and London, 1987).

CD 1628: Commons Debates 1628 ed. by R.C. Johnson, M.F. Keeler, M.J. Cole and W.B. Bidwell, 6 vols (New Haven and London, 1977–78).

CD 1629: Commons Debates for 1629 ed. by W. Notestein and R.H. Relf (Minneapolis, 1921).

CJ: Journals of the House of Commons vols i and ii.

Clarendon, *History of the Rebellion:* Edward, Earl of Clarendon, *The History of the Rebellion and Civil Wars in England begun in the year 1641* ed. by W. Dunn Macray, 6 vols (Oxford, 1888).

Clarendon, *Tracts:* Edward, Earl of Clarendon, *A Collection of Several Tracts of the Right Honourable Earl of Clarendon, Author of the History of the Rebellion and Civil Wars in England* (London, 1727).

Cornwall Protestation Returns: T.L. Stoate (ed.) *The Cornwall Protestation Returns 1641* (Bristol, 1974).

213

Cornwall Hearth and Poll Taxes: T.L. Stoate (ed.) *Cornwall Hearth and Poll Taxes 1660–1664. Direct Taxation in Cornwall in the Reign of Charles II* (Bristol, 1981).

CRO: Cornwall County Record Office.

CSPD: *Calendar of State Papers Domestic* (London, 1858–97).

DCO: Duchy of Cornwall Record Office.

D'Ewes: Sir Simonds D'Ewes, *The Journal of Sir Simonds D'Ewes. From the first recess of the Long Parliament to the withdrawal of King Charles from London* ed. by W.H. Coates (New Haven, 1942).

DNB: *Dictionary of National Biography* 30 vols (London, 1908–86).

EHR: *English Historical Review.*

Fathers, *The Content of a Wayfaring Man*: John Fathers, *The Content of a Wayfaring Man: And the Accompt Of A Ministers Removall. Two sermons. The one preached at the Morning Lecture in the Citie of London; the other more enlarged in another congregation* (London, 1648).

FitzGeffry, *Elisha*: Charles FitzGeffry, *Elisha His Lamentation, For His Owne, and all Israels losse, in Elijah. The subject of a Sermon, preached at the Funeralls of the Right Worshipfull Sir Anthony Rous, late of Halton in Cornwall, knight* (London, 1622).

FitzGeffry, *Death's Sermon*: Charles FitzGeffry, *Death's Sermon Unto the Living, Delivered at the Funerals of the Religious Ladie Philippe, late Wife unto the Right Worshipfull Sr Anthonie Rous of Halton in Cornwall Knight* (London, 1622).

FitzGeffry, *A Preparative to Repentance*: Charles FitzGeffry, *A preparative to Repentance* (1628).

FitzGeffry, *Dorcas*: Charles FitzGeffry, *The Widower's Tears for the Death of Dorcas* (Fowey, 1631).

FitzGeffry, *The Curse of Corne-horders*: Charles FitzGeffry, *The Curse of Corne-horders: with The Blessing of Seasonable selling* (London, 1631).

FitzGeffry, *Compassion Towards Captives*: Charles FitzGeffry, *Compassion Towards Captives, Chiefly Towards our Bretheren and Country-men who are in miserable bondage in Barbarie* (Oxford, 1637).

Gamon, *Praise of a Godly Woman*: Hannibal Gamon, *The Praise of a Godly Woman. A Sermon preached at the Solemn Funerall of the Right Honourable Ladie, the Ladie Frances Roberts, at Lanhide-rock-church in Cornwall, the tenth of August 1626* (London, 1627).

GEC: G.E. Cockayne, *The Complete Peerage of England, Scotland, Ireland, Great Britain, and the United Kingdom 12 vols* (London, 1910–59).

Gray's Inn Register: Joseph Foster, ed., *The Register of Admissions to Gray's Inn 1521–1889* (London, 1889).

Hall, *Works*: Joseph Hall, *The Works of the Right Reverend Joseph Hall, D.D. Bishop of Exeter and Afterwards of Norwich. A New Edition . . . by Philip Wynter* 10 vols (Oxford, 1863).

HGF: R. Granville, *History of the Granville Family* (Exeter, 1895).

HMC: Historical Manuscripts Commission.

Inner Temple Register: *Students Admitted to the Inner Temple 1547–1660* (1877).

JBS: *Journal of British Studies.*

JRIC: *Journal of the Royal Institution of Cornwall.*

Lincoln's Inn Register: Register of Admissions to the Honourable Society of Lincoln's Inn vol. 1 Admissions 1420–1799 (1896).

LJ: Journals of the House of Lords vols iv. and v.

Middle Temple Register: Register of Admissions to the Honourable Society of the Middle Temple vol. 1 Fifteenth century to 1781 (1949).

NH: Northern History.

Norden: John Norden, *Speculi Britanniae Pars. A topographical and chorographical description of Cornwall* (London, 1728).

P&P: Past and Present.

PJLP: The Private Journals of the Long Parliament 3 January to 5 March 1642 ed. by W.H. Coates, A.S. Young and V.F. Snow (New Haven and London, 1982).

PRO: Public Record Office.

PRO Sheriffs List: *List of Sheriffs for England and Wales from the Earliest Times to AD 1831* PRO Lists and Indexes vol. IX (London, 1898).

PSP: Proceedings of the Short Parliament of 1640 Camden Society, 4th series, vol. 19, ed. by E.S. Cope and W.H. Coates (London, 1977).

Spring: Diary of Sir William Spring (History of Parliament Trust transcript).

TRHS: Transactions of the Royal Historical Society.

V&A: Victoria and Albert Museum.

Vivian, *Visitations of Cornwall:* J.L. Vivian (ed.) *The Visitations of Cornwall . . . of 1530, 1573 and 1620 with additions by J.L. Vivian* (Exeter, 1887).

Walker Revised: A.G. Matthews, *Walker Revised* (Oxford, 1948).

Whitelocke: Diary of Bulstrode Whitelocke (History of Parliament Trust transcript).

Notes

Preface

1. CRO BC/24/2/12, 26; AD 374/9; B 35/44; *Bellum Civile*, pp. 22–23; *HGF*, pp. 249–50; Mary Coate, *Cornwall in the Great Civil War and Interregnum 1642–1660* (Oxford, 1933), pp. 67–69, 81–82.
2. CRO AD 374/9; *Bellum Civile*, pp. 19–22; CRO BC/24/2/49.
3. Coate *Cornwall*, pp. 1–9 and *passim*.
4. Alan Everitt, *The Local Community and the Great Rebellion* (London, 1969), pp. 8, 23. For other examples of the county community school, see D. H. Pennington and I. A. Roots, *The Committee at Stafford, 1643–45* (Manchester, 1957); Alan Everitt, *The Community of Kent and the Great Rebellion, 1640–60* (Leicester, 1966); Alan Everitt, *Change in the Provinces: the Seventeenth Century*, Department of English Local History Occasional Papers, 2nd series, no. 1 (Leicester, 1972); John Morrill, *Cheshire, 1630–60: county government and society during the English Revolution* (London, 1974); Anthony Fletcher, *A County Community in Peace and War: Sussex 1600–1660* (London, 1975); John Morrill, *The Revolt of the Provinces. Conservatives and Radicals in the English Civil War 1630–1650* (London, 1980); Ronald Hutton, *The Royalist War Effort, 1642–1646* (London, 1982).
5. Clive Holmes, 'The County Community in Stuart Historiography' *JBS* vol. XIX, no. 2 (1980), pp. 54–73; Ann Hughes, 'The King, the Parliament, and the Localities during the English Civil War' *JBS* vol. XXIV, no. 2 (1985), pp. 236–63; Ann Hughes, *Politics, society and civil war in Warwickshire, 1620–1660* (Cam- bridge, 1987).
6. Ivan Roots, 'Interest—Public, Private and Communal', in R. H. Parry (ed.) *The English Civil War and After 1642–1658* (London, 1970), pp. 111–22; Hughes, *Warwickshire*, p. xii and *passim*; Ann Hughes, 'Local History and the Origins of the Civil War' in R. Cust and A. Hughes (eds) *Conflict in Early Stuart England. Studies in Religion and Politics 1603–1642* (London and New York, 1989), pp. 229–37.

1: Cornwall and the Cornish Gentry

1. Norden, pp. 3–4.

216

2. Coate, *Cornwall*, p. 1; Carew, pp. 53–54.
3. Daniel and Samuel Lysons, *Magna Britannia: Cornwall* (1814), p. 4; Coate, *Cornwall*, p. 2; John Chynoweth, 'The Gentry of Tudor Cornwall' (University of Exeter Ph.D., 1994), pp. 19–20; Norden, p. 21; Carew, p. 56. For an alternative view of 'Cornish distinctiveness' see Philip Payton, *The Making of Modern Cornwall* (Redruth, 1992).
4. F. J. Levy, 'How Information Spread Among the Gentry, 1550–1640' *JBS* vol. 21, no. 2 (1982), pp. 11–35.
5. CRO R(S) 1036; see also R(S) 1037, 1038.
6. CRO BC/24/4/52.
7. *HGF*, p. 191.
8. *HGF*, p. 221.
9. See Richard Cust, 'News and Politics in Early Seventeenth-Century England' *P&P* no. 112 (1986), pp. 62–69.
10. *CSPD* 1625–1626, pp. 297, 334.
11. Sir John Dodridge, *An Historical Account of the Ancient and Modern State of the Principality of Wales, Dutchy of Cornwall, and Earldom of Chester* (London, 1714), pp. 78–79; Coate, *Cornwall*, p. 10; Graham Haslam, 'Jacobean Phoenix: the Duchy of Cornwall in the principates of Henry Frederick and Charles' in R. W. Hoyle (ed.) *The Estates of the English Crown 1588–1640* (Cambridge, 1992), pp. 274–75.
12. Graham Haslam, 'The Duchy and Parliamentary Representation in Cornwall, 1547–1640' *JRIC* part 3, vol. VIII (1980), pp. 224–28; Haslam, 'Jacobean Phoenix', pp. 270–75.
13. James Whetter, *Cornwall in the 17th Century. An Economic Survey of Kernow* (Gorran, 1974), p. 16; James Whetter, 'The Economic History of Cornwall in the 17th Century' (University of London Ph.D., 1965), pp. 80–83, 102–4; David Cullum, 'Society and Economy in West Cornwall *c.*1588–1750' (University of Exeter Ph.D., 1994), pp. 64–65, 281–83, 290.
14. Coate, *Cornwall*, p. 10; Dodridge, *Duchy*, pp. 93–94; G. R. Lewis, *The Stannaries. A Study of the English Tin Miner* (Cambridge, 1924), pp. 108, 117, 126–29.
15. Revenue from mining often exceeded income from duchy manors. Duchy officers levied duty on each pound of tin presented for weighing and assaying. In addition, a royalty of toll tin was paid for mining on duchy land. Graham Haslam, 'The Elizabethan Duchy of Cornwall: an estate in stasis', in Hoyle (ed.) *The Estates of the English Crown*, pp. 91–92.
16. Haslam, 'Jacobean Phoenix', p. 271; Haslam, 'Elizabethan Duchy', p. 92.
17. For a fuller discussion of the relationship between the duchy and the stannaries see Chapter 3, pp. 72–76, and Chapter 6, pp. 169–70, 175–76.
18. J. C. Sainty, 'Lieutenants of the Counties, 1585–1642' *BIHR* supplement no. 8 (1970), pp. 14–15; *LJ* iv.587b.
19. Carew, p. 86.
20. See Chapter 4, pp. 109–13.
21. See for example *HMC* Salisbury MSS vol. 21, p. 146; *CSPD* 1603–1610, p. 551;

CRO R(S) 1/984; PRO SP16/38/39. See also Anne Duffin, 'The Political Allegiance of the Cornish Gentry *c*.1600–*c*.1642' (University of Exeter Ph.D., 1989), pp. 206–9.

22. The *posse comitatus* was the body of men in the county whom the sheriff could summon to suppress a riot or to defend the county from external attack. L. M. Hill, 'County Government in Caroline England 1625–40' in Conrad Russell (ed.) *The Origins of the English Civil War* (London, 1973), pp. 72–74; Clive Holmes, *Seventeenth-century Lincolnshire*, History of Lincolnshire, 7 (Lincoln, 1980), p. 80; R. H. Silcock, 'County Government in Worcestershire 1603–1660' (University of London Ph.D., 1974), pp. 116, 124–32.

23. Carew, pp. 5–6.

24. Cullum, 'Society and Economy', pp. 277–78.

25. Whetter, *Economic Survey*, pp. 16, 21–25; A. L. Rowse, *Tudor Cornwall. Portrait of a Society* (London, 1957), pp. 36–39, 46–47; Carew, pp. 36–39.

26. Clarendon, *History of the Rebellion*, vol. VI, p. 244.

27. *HGF*, p. 242.

28. Whetter, *Economic Survey*, p. 16; Whetter, 'Economic History', pp. 121–22; Cullum, 'Society and Economy', pp. 283–84.

29. Carew, pp. 6–7; Whetter, 'Economic History', pp. 177–78; Whetter, *Economic Survey*, pp. 107–16.

30. Carew, p. 64.

31. *CSPD* 1611–1618, p. 427.

32. Nikolaus Pevsner, *The Buildings of England: Cornwall* (London, 1951), pp. 74–75.

33. Roger Lockyer, *Buckingham. The Life and Political Career of George Villiers, First Duke of Buckingham 1592–1628* (London, 1981), p. 328.

34. *GEC* vol. 2, p. 36; PRO Sheriffs List; Richard Symonds, *Diary of the Marches of the Royal Army During the Great Civil War* ed. by Charles E. Long, Camden Society no. 74 (1859–1860), pp. 55–56.

35. See Chapter 2, p. 50.

36. *LJ* iv.45b.

37. See Chapter 6, pp. 179–85; John Adamson, 'The Peerage in Politics 1645–49', (University of Cambridge Ph.D., 1986), pp. 75, 290.

38. Coate, *Cornwall*, pp. 139–50.

39. Adamson, 'Peerage in Politics' pp. 115, 123, 152.

40. *GEC* vol. 10, pp. 712–14; *DNB* under John Lord Robartes.

41. *GEC* vol. 9, pp. 25–26; *DNB* under John Mohun; PRO C231 f. 318. I am grateful to Dr John Morrill for pointing out that the grant of a peerage during a father's lifetime was most unusual.

42. *GEC* vol. 9, pp. 26–27.

43. *LJ* iv.249a, 257a.

44. *CSPD* 1641–1643, pp. 386–87.

45. *Bellum Civile*, p. 23.

46. Clarendon, *History of the Rebellion* vol. VI, pp. 245–46.

47. I am grateful to Dr Ronald Hutton for drawing this point to my attention.

48. Coate, *Cornwall*, p. 131; *CCC* II, p. 1504. In 1646 the Parliamentarians sequestered, or confiscated, Cornish royalist estates, and then allowed most royalists to buy them back by paying a composition or fine.
49. *DNB* under Charles Lord Lambert; *GEC* vol. 3, p. 117.
50. *DNB* under Charles Lord Lambert wrongly states that Lambert lived in Ireland from March 1627 onwards.
51. PRO SP16/117/43; *CSPD* 1628–1629, p. 364.
52. PRO C231/4/318; BL Harl. 1622; PRO E163/18/12; SP16/212; C193/13/2; SP16/405; C181/3, 4. Oyer and terminer commissioners were empowered to hear and determine indictments on treasons, felonies, etc.
53. See, for example, Lawrence Stone, 'Social Mobility in England, 1500–1700' *P&P* no. 33 (April 1966), p. 17; also John Morrill, 'The Northern Gentry and the Great Rebellion' *NH* vol. XV (1979), pp. 66–87.
54. For a fuller discussion of the problems and possible methods of 'counting' gentry, see Duffin, 'Cornish Gentry', pp. 26–28; see also J. T. Cliffe, *The Yorkshire gentry, from the Reformation to the Civil War* (London, 1969); B. G. Blackwood, *The Lancashire Gentry and the Great Rebellion, 1640–60* Chetham Society, 3rd series, 25 (Manchester, 1978), pp. 4–5; Morrill, 'Northern Gentry', pp. 66–87.
55. PRO E178/7161; E179/89/324–39; *Cornwall Protestation Returns*; List of Sheriffs; C193/13/1, 2, 3; E163/18/12; BL Harl. 1622; SP16/212, 405; CRO B 35/1; CY 7260; FS3/47/10; Blackwood, *Lancashire*, pp. 4–5; Ann Hughes, 'Politics, society and civil war in Warwickshire, 1620–50' (University of Liverpool Ph.D., 1979), pp. 54–55.
56. Population estimates vary. This figure was calculated by Dr Jonathan Barry for his contribution to the *Historical Atlas of South-West England* ed. R. Kain and W. Ravenhill (forthcoming, Exeter, 1997), using the 1642 protestation returns and the 1676 Compton Census. I am grateful to Dr Barry for this information. T. L. Stoate estimated 128,000, and James Whetter calculated 105,500, both using the protestation returns alone, but with different methods. *Cornwall Hearth and Poll Taxes; Cornwall Protestation Returns*; Whetter, 'Economic History', p. 7.
57. Cited in Blackwood, *Lancashire*, p. 5. Dr Wolffe identified over 2,000 gentry families in Devon, although this figure is rather inflated since she included fathers and sons where both were active in local government between 1625 and 1640. Mary Wolffe, 'The Gentry Government of Devon 1625–1640' (University of Exeter Ph.D., 1992), pp. 4–8.
58. CRO HD/12/25.
59. CRO BW/15/5.
60. CRO CW/GG/35. The tithe—one tenth of the produce of the parish— should, in theory, have been paid to the local clergyman. In this case it had apparently been impropriated by Richard Carew who would have received the tithe contributions himself, and paid the clergyman a fixed sum in return.
61. CRO V/FW/18/6.
62. CRO BW/15/5; HD/12/25; CW/GG/35.

63. Carew, p. 136.
64. Whetter, 'John Rashleigh of Menabilly, Esquire (1554–1624)' *Old Cornwall*, vol. 7, no. 3 (1968), pp. 113–20; CRO R 3609a, 3609b, 3611, 3612, 3613, 3615, 3622, 3671 (Rashleigh marriage settlements); CRO R 5587, 5589 (Rashleigh wills).
65. CRO CN 362, 366, 368, 369, 371.
66. CRO CN 377.
67. Jeanne Stanley, 'The Glory of Golden. An Account of Golden Manor, Probus, and its Owners 1193–1727' *Royal Cornwall Polytechnic Society* (1956), pp. 27–40; H. L. Douch, *The Grosse Family of Norfolk and Cornwall*, (privately published). I am grateful to Mr Douch for allowing me to read this paper.
68. See, for example, CRO HD/12/1–18.
69. CRO EN 2–16; EN II f. 1.
70. CRO EN II ff. 7–8.
71. CRO EN II ff. 2–80.
72. This appears to have been a continuation of the trend in the Tudor period. The number of Cornish gentry families increased from 168 in 1485 to 288 in 1603, and the rate of increase accelerated over the period, principally due to new acquisitions of gentry status. Chynoweth, 'Tudor Gentry', pp. 57–58.
73. Carew, p. 64.
74. Vivian, *Visitations of Cornwall*; Lysons, *Magna Britannia*; Everitt, *Kent*, p. 36; Cliffe, *Yorkshire*, p. 13; Blackwood, *Lancashire*, p. 21; Holmes, *Lincolnshire*, p. 66.
75. Blackwood, *Lancashire*, pp. 21–22; Morrill, *Cheshire*, p. 3.
76. 'Gentry origins' refers either to when a family became established in the county, or to when it acquired gentle status.
77. Everitt, *Kent*, p. 36; Blackwood, *Lancashire*, p. 21. For analysis of gentry origins by hundred, see Duffin, 'Cornish Gentry', pp. 50–51.
78. PRO E179/89/324–39; Morrill, 'Northern Gentry', p. 76 (citing Wanklyn); Lawrence Stone, 'Social Mobility in England, 1500–1700' *P&P* no. 33 (1966), p. 21; Hughes, *Warwickshire*, p. 30.
79. See, for example, J. T. Cliffe, 'The Royalist Composition Papers and the Landed Income of the Gentry: A Rejoinder' *NH*, vol. XIV (1978), p. 168, and Morrill's discussion of Wanklyn in 'The Northern Gentry', p. 75; C. B. Phillips, 'The Royalist Composition Papers and the Landed Income of the Gentry: A Note of Warning from Cumbria' *NH*, vol. XIII (1977), p. 161; Blackwood, *Lancashire*, pp. 115–19; Hughes, 'Politics, society and civil war', p. 58.
80. PRO E179/89/324–39.
81. Blackwood, *Lancashire*, p. 12; Hughes, *Warwickshire*, p. 31; Cliffe, *Yorkshire*, p. 29. Dr Wolffe has noted a 'marked contrast' between the numbers for Devon (59) and for Cornwall (8) in the highest assessment group. However, using her figure of 2,006 gentry families, the percentage of Devonian families in this bracket is 3 per cent, as for Cornwall. This is surprising, but is partially explained by Dr Wolffe's broad criteria in counting gentry. Wolffe, 'Gentry Government of Devon', pp. 31, 4–8.
82. Blackwood, *Lancashire*, p. 12.

83. Cliffe, *Yorkshire*, p. 29.
84. Hughes, 'Politics, society and civil war', p. 61.
85. PRO E179/89/324–39.
86. Chynoweth, 'Tudor Gentry', pp. 24, 88.
87. Figures for the period 1595–1665 have been used to give a more balanced picture.
88. *Alumni Oxon; Alumni Cantab*; Lawrence Stone, 'The Educational Revolution in England, 1560–1640' *P&P* no. 28 (1964), pp. 49–79.
89. The preference for Exeter College, Oxford, was evident amongst the Tudor Cornish gentry, although the numbers attending university were far lower. Chynoweth, 'Tudor Gentry', p. 103. Dr Wolffe found the same overwhelming preference for Oxford, and particularly for Exeter College, amongst the Devon gentry, although her calculations related only to JPs. Wolffe, 'Gentry Government of Devon', p. 32.
90. *Middle Temple Register; Lincoln's Inn Register; Inner Temple Register; Gray's Inn Register.*
91. Morrill, *Revolt of the Provinces*, p. 23; Everitt, *Change in the Provinces*, p. 6; Blackwood, *Lancashire*, pp. 24–25; Victor Morgan, 'Cambridge University and "the Country", 1560–1640' in Lawrence Stone (ed.) *The University and Society* vol. 1 (Princeton, 1974), pp. 183–245.
92. Wilfred Prest, *The Inns of Court under Elizabeth I and the Early Stuarts 1590–1640* (London, 1972), pp. 36–39.
93. Clarendon, *Tracts*, p. 326; Holmes, 'The County Community', p. 59.
94. *HMC* Salisbury MSS vol. XVII, p. 37.
95. Carew, *The True and Ready Way to learn the Latine Tongue* (London, 1654). Carew matriculated at Merton College, Oxford in 1594, and entered the Middle Temple in 1597.
96. Carew, *Latine Tongue.*
97. *HGF*, pp. 205–6.
98. V&A Forster Collection. Sir Bevill to Lady Grace Grenvile, 16 February 1640.
99. *HGF*, pp. 205–6.
100. *HGF*, pp. 209–10. Bevill to Richard Grenvile, *c.* April 1638.
101. V&A Forster Collection. Bevill to Richard Grenvile, 12 January 1639.
102. *HGF*, pp. 210–11.
103. Wilfred Prest, 'Legal Education of the Gentry at the Inns of Court, 1560–1640' *P&P* no. 38 (1967), pp. 22–23, 36.
104. Prest, *Inns of Court*, p. 159.
105. Clarendon, *Tracts*, p. 328.
106. *HGF*, p. 148.
107. Clarendon, *Tracts*, p. 331.
108. Prest, *Inns of Court*, pp. 223–24; Martin Butler, 'Entertaining the Palatine Prince: Plays on Foreign Affairs 1635–1637' *English Literary Renaissance* vol. 13 (1983), pp. 319–44; W. Knowler (ed.) *The Earl of Strafford's Letters and Dispatches* 2 vols (1739), pp. 506–7. For the full story of the masque, see Duffin, 'Cornish Gentry', pp. 68–71.

109. Carew, p. 64; Daniel Defoe, *A Tour Through England and Wales* (London, 1959), p. 234; Everitt, *Change in the Provinces*, pp. 8–11.
110. The figures are for the total number of marriages known, including second or third marriages.
111. The proportion of gentry marriages within the county had, however, fallen since the Tudor period when nearly 80 per cent of gentlemen married Cornish brides. Chynoweth, 'Tudor Gentry', pp. 91–92.
112. Blackwood, *Lancashire*, pp. 25–26; Holmes, *Lincolnshire*, pp. 75–76; G. E. McParlin, 'The Herefordshire gentry in county government, 1625–61' (University of Aberystwyth Ph.D., 1981), p. 25. There was also a 'strong tendency' among the Devon gentry to marry within their own county. Wolffe, 'Gentry Government in Devon', pp. 10–13.
113. For analysis of gentry marriage patterns by hundred see Duffin, 'Cornish Gentry', pp. 74–76.
114. CRO BC/24/4/52.
115. CRO BC/24/4/51–68. For the Puritan dimension to this marriage alliance, see Chapter 2, pp. 56–57.
116. *HGF*, pp. 185–86.
117. See also Ralph Houlbrooke, *The English Family 1450–1700* (London, 1984), p. 88.
118. Lawrence Stone, *The Family Sex and Marriage in England 1500–1800* (abridged edn Oxford, 1979), pp. 37–88.
119. CRO R(S) 1/462. For full discussion of this sermon, see Chapter 2, pp. 48–51. For the Puritan ideal of married love see Alan Macfarlane, *Marriage and Love in England 1300–1840* (Oxford, 1986), p. 181.
120. *HGF*, p. 149.
121. *HGF*, pp. 167–68.
122. *HGF*, p. 190.
123. *HGF*, pp. 214–17.
124. CRO BW/15/5; G 1534, 1535.
125. CRO CW/GG/35; V/FW/10.
126. Carew, pp. 64–65.
127. *HGF*, p. 162.
128. *HGF*, p. 194.
129. *HGF*, pp. 214–17.
130. *HGF*, pp. 186–87.
131. *HGF*, pp. 227–28.
132. *HGF*, pp. 176, 235–36.
133. CRO R 3611, R 3613.
134. See p. 19, above.
135. CRO R(S) 1/16, 1/10, 1/19.
136. CRO R(S) 1/29. Date uncertain but before 1627.
137. Coate, *Cornwall*, *passim*.

2: The Religious Landscape

1. Lysons, *Magna Britannia*, pp. 25–26; Rowse, *Tudor Cornwall*, pp. 141, 149. The deaneries were East, West, Trigg Major, Trigg Minor, Powder, Pyder, Kerrier and Penwith.
2. See below.
3. Jonathan Vage, 'The Diocese of Exeter 1519–1641: a study of Church Government in the Age of the Reformation' (University of Cambridge Ph.D., 1991), pp. 20, 22, 23.
4. This was similar to the position in Warwickshire; see Hughes, *Warwickshire*, p. 62.
5. PRO E179/89/324–339; Robin Clifton, 'Fear of Popery', in Russell (ed.) *Origins*, pp. 152–53.
6. See Chapter 4, p. 119.
7. PRO SP16/11/52, 52I.
8. PRO E179/89/324–339.
9. Coate, *Cornwall*, p. 323.
10. *HMC* Salisbury MSS vol. XV, pp. 124, 178–79.
11. *CSPD* 1603–1610, p. 171.
12. Nicholas Prideaux of Soldon, Devon, and Padstow married Ann, daughter of William Coryton in about 1621. Vivian, *Visitations of Cornwall*, pp. 102, 611.
13. PRO SP14/18/73, 73I, 73II.
14. PRO SP16/118/56; SP16/119/23.
15. PRO SP16/118/35, 35I.
16. PRO SP16/118/56.
17. PRO SP16/119/59.
18. The religious history of this period has been the subject of a lively debate in recent years. My view is based on a reading of the following: Nicholas Tyacke, 'Puritanism, Arminianism and Counter-Revolution', in Russell (ed.) *Origins*, pp. 119–43; Nicholas Tyacke, *Anti-Calvinists* (Oxford, 1987); Nicholas Tyacke, 'The Rise of Arminianism Reconsidered', *P&P* no. 115 (1987), pp. 201–16; Kenneth Fincham, 'Introduction', in Kenneth Fincham (ed.) *The Early Stuart Church, 1603–1642* (London, 1993), pp. 1–22; Kenneth Fincham and Peter Lake, 'The Ecclesiastical Policies of James I and Charles I', in Fincham (ed.) *Early Stuart Church*, pp. 23–50; Peter Lake, 'Calvinism and the English Church 1570–1635' *P&P* no. 114 (1987), pp. 32–76; Peter Lake, 'The Impact of Modern Protestantism' *JBS* vol. 28, no. 3 (1989), pp. 293–304; Anthony Milton, 'The Church of England, Rome, and the True Church: The Demise of a Jacobean Consensus', in Fincham (ed.) *Early Stuart Church*, pp. 187–210.
19. An alternative view to that presented here, by which I am not convinced, argues that both James I and Charles I steered a *via media* between the extremes of Catholic corruption and Puritan excesses, and that the only significant difference between the 1630s and previous decades was the vigour with which this policy was enforced. Charles and Laud are portrayed as conservatives, emphasizing order, obedience and uniformity, in the mode of former monarchs and archbishops, whereas Puritans, rather than

anti-Calvinists, are depicted as the destabilizing force. Peter White, 'The Rise of Arminianism Reconsidered' *P&P* no. 101 (1983), pp. 34–54; Peter White, 'A Rejoinder' *P&P* no. 115 (1987), pp. 217–29; Peter White, 'The *via media* in the early Stuart church' in Fincham (ed.) *Early Stuart Church*, pp. 211–30; G. W. Bernard, The Church of England *c*.1529–*c*.1642' *History* vol. 75, no. 244 (1990), pp. 183–206.

20. Rowse, *Tudor Cornwall*, pp. 338–39.
21. Information on patronage of livings has been taken from the Bishops' Institution Books, supported by the CRO Clergy Index. PRO Institution Books, Series A, 1566–1660, vol. 2; CRO Clergy Index. For comparative examples of patronage see Hughes, *Warwickshire*, pp. 66–68; Fletcher, *Sussex*, p. 72.
22. Fletcher, *Sussex*, p. 63.
23. PRO Prob 11/159/63; CRO AP/P794/1.
24. CRO AP/C278/1.
25. CRO AP/L210/1.
26. CRO AP/S779/1. He was the second son of Thomas St Aubyn Esq of Clowance (died 1626) and younger brother of John (died 1640); Vivian, *Visitations of Cornwall*, p. 438; CRO AP/H95/1.
27. PRO Prob 11/137/63.
28. PRO Prob 11/188/10 (Boscawen); Prob 11/175/144 (Sawle); Prob 11/192/12 (Carew); Prob 11/183/68 (St Aubyn); CRO DDR 5632 (Harris); T789/1 (Trefusis); FS3/792/1 (Gamon).
29. PRO Prob 11/218/161.
30. See Chapter 1, p. 15–17; Duffin, 'Cornish Gentry', pp. 54–55.
31. CRO AP/D349(a)/1; AP/H634/1; AP/Q16/1.
32. CRO DDV/FW/18/5; PRO Prob 11/171/57; CRO V/FN/18/2. By no means all Puritans disapproved of music. Richard Connock's niece, Loveday, daughter of John Connock of Treworgy, was the second wife of Sir Francis Vyvyan. Her father and her brother John were named as overseers of Sir Francis' will.
33. CRO DDR 5605; *Alumni Cantab*, vol. I; Tyacke, *Anti-Calvinists*, p. 49.
34. CRO G 560/1; *DNB* under Thomas Brightman; Cliffe, *Puritan Gentry*, p. 210.
35. Cliffe, *Puritan Gentry*, pp. 125, 130–31; Clare Gittings, *Death, Burial and the Individual in Early Modern England* (London, 1984), pp. 188–97.
36. PRO Prob 11/218/161.
37. Gittings, *Death, Burial and the Individual*, pp. 196–97.
38. PRO Prob 11/188/10.
39. PRO Prob 11/159/48; CRO AP/K88/1.
40. CRO AP/S779/1; AP/T183/1. Tremayne's will, dated 1607 and proved in 1611, included bequests to his godsons John Eliot and John Harris.
41. CRO AP/S779/1; PRO Institution Books, Series A, 1556–1660, vol. 2, under Helston, St Stephens by Saltash, and Maker; Coate, *Cornwall*, pp. 332, 339; CRO AP/B733/1; AP/E170/1; William Lake, *A Complete Parochial History of the County of Cornwall* 4 vols (Truro and London, 1867–72), vol. I, p. 86; vol. II, p. 312; CRO AP/G252/1; AP/H905; *Cornwall Protestation Returns*, p. 172.

42. PRO Prob 11/218/161.
43. FitzGeffry, *Elisha*; FitzGeffry, *Death's Sermon*; CRO R(S) 1/462: FitzGeffry, *Dorcas*.
44. Gamon, *Praise of a Godly Woman*.
45. FitzGeffry, *Elisha*, p. 44.
46. FitzGeffry, *Death's Sermon*, p. 27; CRO R(S) 1/462: FitzGeffry, *Dorcas*. For quotation about Mrs Rashleigh, see p. 32 above.
47. FitzGeffry, *Elisha*, p. 39. There was a strong Puritan influence in Saltash through the combined forces of the Buller and Rous families. Cliffe, *Puritan Gentry*, p. 24.
48. FitzGeffry, *Elisha*, p. 39.
49. CRO R(S) 1/462: FitzGeffry, *Dorcas*.
50. Gamon, *Praise of a Godly Woman*, p. 28.
51. FitzGeffry, *Death's Sermon*, p. 26.
52. CRO R(S) 1/462: FitzGeffry, *Dorcas*.
53. Gamon, *Praise of a Godly Woman*, p. 27.
54. Tyacke, *Anti-Calvinists*, pp. 72–78; *Alumni Oxon*, vol. III.
55. Gamon, *Praise of a Godly Woman*, pp. 27–28.
56. FitzGeffry, *Elisha*, p. 42.
57. Francis Rous, *The Art of Happiness*, Dedication, in *Treatises and Meditations* (London, 1657). After Broadgates, Oxford, Francis was educated at Leiden, where it is likely that he became aware of the views of Arminius. Initially he read law, but later devoted his life to the propagation of the Gospel, and was a prolific writer on religious themes.
58. FitzGeffry, *Elisha*, p. 46.
59. FitzGeffry, *Death's Sermon*, pp. 27–28.
60. CRO R(S) 1/462: FitzGeffry, *Dorcas*.
61. Cliffe, *Puritan Gentry*, p. 122.
62. FitzGeffry, *Elisha*, pp. 47–49.
63. FitzGeffry, *Death's Sermon*, p. 30.
64. Gamon, *Praise of a Godly Woman*, pp. 30, 34–35; Cliffe, *Puritan Gentry*, p. 21.
65. *DNB* under Charles FitzGeffry; *Alumni Oxon*, vol. III.
66. FitzGeffry, *Elisha*.
67. PRO SP16/68/16; E178/7161; Coate, *Cornwall*, p. 32; J. L. Vivian, *The Visitations of the County of Devon* (London, 1895), p. 581; Cliffe, *Puritan Gentry*, p. 58.
68. *HGF*, p. 196.
69. CRO R(S) 1/903; *Cornwall Protestation Returns*, p. 108.
70. CRO R(S) 1/460: FitzGeffry, *A Preparative to Repentance; CD 1629*, p. 129.
71. CRO R(S) 1/17.
72. CRO FS/3/1032.
73. PRO Institution Books, Series A, 1556–1660, vol. 2, under Mawgan-in-Pyder; *DNB* under Hannibal Gamon; CRO FS3/792/1; Hugh Peter, *Digitus Dei or Good News From Holland* (Rotterdam, 1631).
74. Gamon, *Praise of a Godly Woman*, p. A2.
75. The library is still there, in the long gallery. In October 1643 Gamon was

nominated Cornish representative to the Westminster Assembly of Divines, established to recommend a religious settlement to Parliament. Coate, *Cornwall* pp. 327, 336; *Walker Revised*, p. 97.

76. CRO R(S) 1/461: Hannibal Gamon, *God's Smiting to Amendment, or Revengement. With Preservatives against Revolting. In a sermon preached at the Assises in Launceston, the 6 of August, 1628* (London, 1629).

77. PRO Institution Books, Series A, 1566–1660, vol. 2, under St Stephens by Saltash; Fathers, *The Content of A Wayfaring Man*, p. 45.

78. PRO SP16/385/32.

79. *Cornwall Protestation Returns*; CRO BC/24/4/27.

80. John Fathers, *The Strife of Brethren and a Treaty for Peace. Two Sermons. The one, Preached at the Morning Lecture in the Citie of London: The other, More inlarged in another Congregation* (London, 1648).

81. Fathers, *The Content of a Wayfaring Man*, pp. 71–72.

82. CRO BC/24/2/1; BC/24/1/43; BC/24/2/90.

83. CRO BC/24/4/12.

84. CRO BC/24/4/49.

85. CRO BC/24/4/50.

86. M. F. Keeler, *The Long Parliament, 1640–1641. A Biographical Study of its Members* (Philadelphia, 1954), p. 121; Cliffe, *Puritan Gentry*, p. 31; Vivian, *Visitations of Cornwall*, p. 57; R. Havenden (ed.) *The Visitation of Kent, taken in the years 1619–1621 by John Philpott* Harleian Society, vol. XLII (London, 1898).

87. Keeler, *Long Parliament*, p. 398.

88. Keeler, *Long Parliament*, p. 398; *Alumni Cantab*, vol. I; Cliffe, *Puritan Gentry*, pp. 92, 98.

89. CRO BC/26/18/10–65 (Wise wardship correspondence); Keeler, *Long Parliament*, p. 398; Vivian, *Visitations of Cornwall*, p. 392.

90. Vivian, *Visitations of Devon*, p. 791; Keeler, *Long Parliament*, p. 327.

91. Cliffe, *Puritan Gentry*, p. 58; Vivian, *Visitations of Cornwall*; Vivian, *Visitations of Devon*, p. 654.

92. *DNB* under William Cotton; *HMC* Salisbury MSS vol. X, pp. 450–51; vol. XI, p. 26.

93. *DNB* under William Cotton; Vage, 'Diocese of Exeter', p. 253; Fincham and Lake, 'Ecclesiastical Policies', in Fincham (ed.) *Early Stuart Church*, p. 25.

94. *HMC* Salisbury MSS vol. XVIII, pp. 297–98.

95. Vage, 'Diocese of Exeter', pp. 260–64.

96. Vage, 'Diocese of Exeter', p. 253; Fincham, 'Episcopal Government, 1603–1640' in Fincham (ed.) *Early Stuart Church*, pp. 75–76; Fincham and Lake, 'Ecclesiastical Policies' in Fincham (ed.) *Early Stuart Church*, pp. 26–27.

97. Vage, 'Diocese of Exeter', pp. 255–56, 253.

98. Vage, 'Diocese of Exeter', pp. 256, 500.

99. CRO H251/1, 2, 3.

100. *DNB* under Matthew Sutcliffe; Vage, 'Diocese of Exeter', pp. 266, 269; PRO Prob 11/137/63.

101. *DNB* under Valentine Carey; Vage, 'Diocese of Exeter', pp. 292–93. Vage

denies the existence of anti-Calvinism in the Jacobean Church, and claims that Carey's was a strategic rather than a doctrinal appointment.

102. Tyacke, *Anti-Calvinists*, p. 193.
103. *DNB* under Valentine Carey; Vage, 'Diocese of Exeter', pp. 324–25, 327.
104. CRO R(S) 1/903.
105. CRO P162/5/1.
106. CRO P126/4/1.
107. CRO P192/5/2.
108. Vage, 'Diocese of Exeter', pp. 327–28; *DNB* under Valentine Carey.
109. Fincham, 'Episcopal Government, 1603–1640' in Fincham (ed). *Early Stuart Church*, p. 70; Fincham and Lake, 'Ecclesiastical Policies' in Fincham (ed.) *Early Stuart Church*, p. 39; Tyacke, *Anti-Calvinists*, p. 168.
110. Hall, *Works*, vol. I, p. xlv.
111. Hall, *Works*, vol. VIII, p. 740.
112. Hall, *Works*, vol. I, p. xliii.
113. Hall, *Works*, vol. VIII, p. 631.
114. Fincham, 'Episcopal Government, 1603–1640' in Fincham (ed.) *Early Stuart Church*, p. 86.
115. Hall, *Works*, vol. VIII, p. 631. *The Old Religion: A Treatise, wherein is laid down the true state of the difference betwixt the Reformed and Roman Church.*
116. Fincham, 'Episcopal Government, 1603–1640' in Fincham (ed.) *Early Stuart Church*, p. 86.
117. Tyacke, *Anti-Calvinists*, p. 215.
118. Hall, *Works*, vol. I, p. xlvi. Some caution is required in interpreting this account as it was given by Hall in his own defence during the attack on episcopacy in the 1640s and therefore may be coloured by hindsight.
119. CRO Eliot Letterbooks, vol. 10, ff. 18–18v., 19.
120. CRO Eliot Letterbooks, vol. 10, f. 20; John Forster, *Sir John Eliot: A Biography 1590–1632* 2 vols (London, 1864), vol. II, p. 430.
121. Hall, *Works*, vol. I, p. xlvi.
122. Hall, *Works*, vol. I, p. xlvi; *DNB* under Joseph Hall.
123. William Laud, *The Works of William Laud* ed. by W. Scott and J. Bliss, 7 vols (Oxford, 1847–60), vol. V, pp. 325, 335, 343, 352, 357, 369.
124. Fincham, 'Episcopal Government, 1603–1640' in Fincham (ed.) *Early Stuart Church*, p. 86.
125. CRO P126/4/1; P162/5/1; PD 322/2–3; P192/5/2.
126. Tyacke, *Anti-Calvinists*, p. 215.
127. Pevsner, *Cornwall*, p. 30; Lake, *Parochial History of Cornwall*, vol. III, p. 46. For the Mohuns' political ascendancy, see Chapter 3.
128. CRO P162/5/1.
129. CRO P192/5/2.
130. CRO P126/4/1. Cowling's patron was Sir Shilston Calmady of Wembury, whose son, Josias, married Thomasine, daughter of Sir Richard Buller, and Sir Shilston took up arms for Parliament in 1642. Cowling was ejected from the living in 1646 and restored in 1660. PRO Institution Books, Series A,

1566–1660, vol. 2, under Liskeard; Vivian, *Visitations of Devon*, p. 130; Coate, *Cornwall*, p. 43; *Walker Revised*, p. 95.

131. See Plate 5, p. 65.
132. Lake, *Parochial History of Cornwall*, vol. II, pp. 405–8; Pevsner, *Cornwall*, pp. 215–16, 86–87, 70.
133. CRO PD 322/3; P 19/5/7–11; P170/5/1.
134. CRO P126/4/1.
135. CRO PD 322/2–3.
136. CRO P162/5/1.
137. CRO P192/5/2.
138. CRO P170/5/1.
139. CRO P126/4/1; P162/5/1; P192/5/2.
140. CRO PD 322/3; P126/4/1; P19/5/9–10.
141. CRO P126/4/1; P162/5/1; PD 322/2–3.
142. CRO P126/4/1.
143. CRO P192/5/2; Lake, *Parochial History of Cornwall*, vol. II, p. 5.
144. CRO P214/5/1.
145. CRO P170/5/1; PRO Bishops Institution Books, Series A, 1556–1660, vol. 2, under Padstow; *Walker Revised*, p. 99; J. H. Matthews, *A History of the Parishes of Saint Ives, Lelant, Towednack and Zennor, in the County of Cornwall* (London, 1892), pp. 59–60.
146. Tyacke, *Anti-Calvinists*, pp. 212–14; CRO P162/5/1; P126/4/1.
147. Fincham, 'Episcopal Government, 1603–1640' in Fincham (ed.) *Early Stuart Church*, pp. 84, 86.
148. Hall, *Works*, vol. I, p. xlvi.
149. See Plate 6, p. 69–70.
150. CRO P126/4/1; B/Lisk/268–288; P170/5/1; PD 322/2–3.
151. CRO H251/1, 2, 3; PRO Prob 11/145/43.
152. George Lewis, *A Life of Joseph Hall, D.D., Bishop of Exeter and Norwich* (London, 1886), pp. 292–93; Vage, 'Diocese of Exeter', pp. 376–77.
153. Lewis, *Hall*, pp. 293–94; Vage, 'Diocese of Exeter', pp. 376–77.
154. Hall, *Works*, vol. I, p. xlvii; Tyacke, *Anti- Calvinists*, pp. 238–42.
155. Hall, *Works*, vol. IX, pp. 142–44; vol. VIII, pp. 278– 81; vol. VIII, pp. 281–84.
156. Hughes, *Warwickshire*, p. 85.

3: The Political Landscape

1. See Mark Kishlansky, *Parliamentary Selection. Social and Political Choice in Early Modern England* (Cambridge, 1986).
2. *HMC* Salisbury MSS vol. II, p. 405; Rowse, *Tudor Cornwall*, p. 94; PRO SP14/16/27; SP14/48/116; Robert Ruigh, *The Parliament of 1624. Politics and Foreign Policy* (Harvard, 1971), p. 128.
3. Haslam, 'The Duchy', p. 238; Haslam, 'Jacobean Phoenix', p. 271.
4. Thomas Moir, *The Addled Parliament of 1614* (Oxford, 1958), p. 48; Haslam, 'The Duchy', p. 240; John Gruenfelder, *Influence in Early Stuart Elections*

1604–1640 (Columbus, 1981), pp. 86–87; *DNB* under Sir Robert Naunton, Sir Henry Vane.
5. DCO 'Letters and Warrants, 1620–1621', f. 39.
6. The six were: Sir Edward Coke, privy councillor (nominated Bossiney, returned Liskeard); Sir Thomas Trevor, solicitor-general to the Prince (nominated West Looe, returned Saltash); William Noy, Cornish lawyer (nominated Fowey, returned Helston); Heneage Finch, Prince Charles' serjeant-at-law (nominated Helston, returned West Looe); Sir Henry Vane, duchy councillor (nominated Liskeard, elected Lostwithiel); Edward Salter, duchy manorial steward (nominated Plymouth, returned Liskeard). DCO 'Letters and Warrants 1620–21', f. 39; Haslam, 'The Duchy', pp. 238–39.
7. PRO SP16/117/55; *APC* 1619–1621, pp. 84, 136, 225. Coryton had not sat in Parliament before, and did not stand for election to any seat in 1621.
8. PRO SP14/117/55. There is no apparent explanation for this animosity between Sir Reginald and John Mohun in 1620.
9. Sir Richard Weston, chancellor of the exchequer (Bossiney), Sir Thomas Trevor, solicitor-general (Saltash), Sir John Walter, attorney-general (East Looe), William Noy Esq (Fowey), Sir Francis Crane (Launceston). DCO 'Burgesses for Parliament 1623–1624', f. 33; Gruenfelder, *Early Stuart Elections*, p. 89.
10. Sir John Hobart (nominated West Looe, returned Lostwithiel); Sir Thomas Carey (nominated Grampound, returned Helston); Sir Francis Cottington (not nominated for a Cornish borough, returned Camelford). *DCO* 'Burgesses for Parliament 1623–1624', f. 33; Gruenfelder, *Early Stuart Elections*, p. 89.
11. Gruenfelder, *Early Stuart Elections*, p. 89.
12. James Derriman, *Killigarth. Three Centuries of a Cornish Manor* (privately published, Morden, 1994), p. 26.
13. Haslam, 'The Duchy', p. 241; Ruigh, *1624 Parliament*, p. 130; Gruenfelder, *Early Stuart Elections*, pp. 90, 129.
14. *HMC* 12th Report, Coke MSS, p. 157; Gruenfelder, *Early Stuart Elections*, p. 129; *DNB* under John Coke.
15. Conrad Russell, *Parliaments and English Politics 1621–1629* (Oxford, 1979), pp. 147–48.
16. Russell, *Parliaments*, p. 174; *CJ* ii.723a, 725a; Spring, p. 49.
17. For the case of the pirate Nutt, see Forster, *Eliot*, vol. I, pp. 44–86.
18. Forster, *Eliot*, vol. I, pp. 196–97.
19. Ruigh, *1624 Parliament*, pp. 80, 35, 181; Forster, *Eliot*, vol I, p. 123; Russell, *Parliaments*, p. 174.
20. PRO SP16/521/19.
21. PRO C219/39/1/22. Arundell's daughter, Anne, married Trevanion's son and heir, John, in 1630. Vivian, *Visitations of Cornwall*, p. 502.
22. *DNB* under Sir Edwin Sandys; Russell, *Parliaments*, p. 212.
23. *CD 1625*, p. 693.
24. *CD 1625*, p. 672.

25. *CD 1625*, p. 692. George Chudleigh and Nicholas Kendall were also returned for Lostwithiel.
26. Keeler, *Long Parliament*, p. 359. Keeler believed Thomas to be Mohun's secretary or solicitor. Sir Reginald and John Mohun had apparently settled their earlier differences.
27. PRO SP16/1/25.
28. *CD 1625*, p. 519 (*Negotium Posterorum*, p. 102).
29. *CD 1625*, p. 520 (*Negotium Posterorum*, p. 105).
30. *CD 1625*, p. 520 (*Negotium Posterorum*, p. 105).
31. *CD 1625*, p. 520 (*Negotium Posterorum*, p. 106).
32. *CD 1625*, pp. 412, 416.
33. *CD 1625*, p. 416.
34. As prestmaster and victualler, Bagg was responsible for impressing men for naval service, and for supplying stores to naval vessels. PRO SP16/1/69.
35. PRO SP16/12/95 Eliot to Conway, 31 December 1625.
36. PRO SP16/523/77; Russell, *Parliaments*, pp. 255, 267.
37. PRO SP16/523/77.
38. PRO SP16/523/77.
39. Russell, *Parliaments*, pp. 269, 263–66, 279–81.
40. Russell, *Parliaments*, pp. 289–90; Whitelocke, p. 156.
41. Russell, *Parliaments*, p. 301.
42. Whitelocke, p. 215.
43. Whitelocke, p. 376; S. R. Gardiner (ed.) *Constitutional Documents of the Puritan Revolution 1625–1660* (Oxford, 1889, repr. 1979), pp. 16–17.
44. Russell, *Parliaments*, p. 304.
45. Forster, *Eliot*, vol. I, p. 547.
46. Russell, *Parliaments*, pp. 306–7; Forster, *Eliot*, vol. I, pp. 553, 559.
47. *HGF*, p. 161.
48. *HGF*, p. 161.
49. Russell, *Parliaments*, p. 326; Birch, *C&T*, vol. I, p. 132.
50. Somerset RO, Phelips MSS DD/PH 219/66.
51. Forster, *Eliot*, vol. II, pp. 27–28.
52. Richard Cust, 'Charles I and a draft Declaration for the 1628 Parliament' *BIHR* vol. 63, no. 151 (June 1990), p. 156.
53. PRO SP16/31/2.
54. PRO SP16/36/37; Forster, *Eliot*, vol. II, pp. 27–28. For a discussion of the benevolence see Chapter 5, pp. 146–47.
55. PRO SP16/37/91.
56. PRO SP16/60/75.
57. PRO SP14/117/55; SP16/521/19; see pp. 73–74 above.
58. Eliot and Coryton were imprisoned in London from April 1627 to January 1628 for their refusal to pay the loan. Curiously, there is no other record of Arundell's refusal and he was never punished.
59. BL Harl. MSS 39 ff. 413r.–14.
60. PRO SP16/68/16.

61. PRO SP16/74/78.
62. PRO SP16/68/16 Buckingham to Nicholas; SP16/74/43I Bagg to Nicholas, 28 August 1627.
63. PRO SP16/68/16; SP16/68/25 Bagg to Nicholas, 28 June 1627.
64. PRO SP16/68/16.
65. PRO SP16/68/25.
66. *HGF*, p. 163.
67. PRO SP16/60/75 Bagg to Buckingham, 20 April 1627.
68. PRO SP16/64/26 Bagg to Buckingham.
69. Forster, *Eliot*, vol. II, p. 38.
70. PRO SP16/84/93 Bagg to Buckingham, 17 November 1627.
71. PRO SP16/87/11.
72. Richard Cust, *The Forced Loan and English Politics 1626–1628* (Oxford, 1987), pp. 209–10.
73. Forster, *Eliot*, vol. I, p. 142; vol. II, pp. 204–205.
74. Cust, *Forced Loan*, p. 202.
75. Cust, 'Draft Declaration', p. 156.
76. PRO SP16/60/75 (Arundell); SP16/74/43I; *HGF*, p. 163 (Grenvile); SP16/521/19 (Trevanion).
77. PRO C219/41B/135.
78. PRO SP16/96/36. John Trelawny married Elizabeth, daughter of Sir Reginald Mohun. Vivian, *Visitations of Cornwall*, pp. 325, 476.
79. PRO C193/12/2.
80. PRO SP16/106/14I.
81. PRO SP16/106/14I.
82. PRO SP16/106/14I; SP16/96/36.
83. PRO SP16/96/48I.
84. PRO SP16/96/36. The success of this measure is unknown.
85. *CD 1628* vol. II, pp. 33, 35.
86. PRO SP16/106/14; *CD 1628* vol. 2, pp. 33–34; *HMC* Hervey MSS, p. 62.
87. PRO SP16/96/36.
88. PRO SP16/96/48.
89. *CD 1628* vol. II, p. 375.
90. Birch, *C&T*, vol. I, p. 332; Cust, *Forced Loan*, p. 313.
91. PRO SP16/106/14I.
92. *CD 1628* vol. II, pp. 29, 31, 33–34, 41. The ringleaders were the nine signatories of the offending letters, being Sir Reginald Mohun, Sir William Wrey, Sir Bernard Grenvile, John Trelawny, Sir Richard Edgcumbe, John Mohun, Walter Langdon, Richard Trevanion and Edward Trelawny.
93. PRO SP16/471/69.
94. *CJ* i.895b–896a; *CD 1628* vol. III, pp. 367–68.
95. *CD 1628* vol. III, pp. 368, 370, 380.
96. *CD 1628* vol. III, pp. 376, 381.
97. *CD 1628* vol. III, pp. 368, 381.
98. *CD 1628* vol. III, p. 389.

99. *CD 1628* vol. III, pp. 391–94, 388 (Mr Littleton's speech).
100. PRO SP16/106/14I.
101. Cust, *Forced Loan*, p. 212.
102. PRO SP16/106/14.
103. Forster, *Eliot*, vol. II, p. 280; *Alumni Cantab*, vol II, under Walter Langdon; Vivian, *Visitations of Cornwall*, pp. 564, 476; Birch, *C&T*, vol I, pp. 373–74. Edward Trelawny alone did not receive an honour, perhaps because he was a younger son.
104. *CD 1628* vol. III, p. 370, n. 20; *LJ* iii. 788.
105. PRO SP16/96/36.
106. CRO EL/564 Mohun case papers; *CD 1628* vol. II, p. 404.
107. *CD 1628* vol. II, p. 479; vol. III, pp. 623, 625–26, 631–34; vol. IV, pp. 3–12; Forster, *Eliot*, vol. II, pp. 284–304.
108. *CD 1628* vol. IV, p. 6.
109. *CD 1628* vol. IV, pp. 4, 9; CRO EL/542/1, 2, warrant for the arrest and imprisonment of William Mayowe, 1626, warrant to the keeper of Launceston gaol. Both documents were signed by Mohun, Trelawny and Langdon, and it was ordered that Mayowe should appear before them at Trelawne (Trelawny's house) before being taken to Launceston. Clearly the authors of the letters opposing Eliot's and Coryton's candidature in 1628 had worked closely together for some time.
110. Forster, *Eliot*, vol. II, p. 285; *CD 1628* vol. III, p. 625; vol. IV, p. 5.
111. Forster, *Eliot*, vol. II, pp. 287–88; G. C. Boase and W. P. Courtney *Biblioteca Cornubiensis* 3 vols (London 1874–1882), vol. III, p. 1157; PRO Institution Books, Series A, 1566–1660, vol. II, under St Mellion. Eliot left Dix £10 in his will of 1630. CRO EL/572/27.
112. Forster, *Eliot*, vol. II, pp. 289–90.
113. Forster, *Eliot*, vol. II, pp. 296–300; *CD 1628* vol. IV, pp. 5–6, 9–10.
114. *CD 1628* vol. IV, pp. 3, 23, 324–25.
115. PRO SP16/118/37.
116. *CD 1628* vol. VI, p. 216; Harold Hulme, *The Life of Sir John Eliot 1592–1632. Struggle for Parliamentary Freedom* (London, 1957), p. 240.
117. CRO Eliot Letterbooks, vol. 2, f. 1r., endorsed 'S[i]r W[illia]m Cortney's discoursse at Cuttenb[eke] aft[e]r dinner 2 July 1628'.
118. PRO SP16/37/91 Bagg to Buckingham, 16 October 1626.
119. Cust, *Forced Loan*, pp. 212–13.
120. PRO SP16/37/91; Forster, *Eliot*, vol. II, p. 290; CRO Eliot Letterbooks, vol. 2, f. 1r.
121. PRO SP16/37/91.
122. PRO SP16/96/36 Bagg to Buckingham, 17 March 1628.
123. PRO SP16/118/37.
124. PRO SP16/96/36.
125. PRO SP16/96/36; SP16/100/47.
126. *CD 1628* vol. II, p. 33.
127. *CD 1628* vol. III, pp. 53–54.

128. For the effect of defence problems on Cornwall see Chapter 4.
129. *CJ* iv. 876a, 879a.
130. *CD 1628* vol. IV, pp. 215, 217.
131. *CD 1628* vol. IV, pp. 281–83.
132. *CD 1628* vol. IV, p. 280. Coat and conduct money was levied from local populations to clothe, pay and transport soldiers to other parts of the country.
133. Russell, *Parliaments*, pp. 342–49.
134. Forster, *Eliot*, vol. II, p. 124.
135. Russell, *Parliaments*, pp. 358–59.
136. *CD 1628* vol. III, pp. 24–25.
137. *CD 1628* vol. III, pp. 307–8; J. P. Kenyon, *The Stuart Constitution 1603–1688. Documents and Commentary* (Cambridge, 1986), pp. 83–84.
138. Forster, *Eliot*, vol. II, pp. 128–29.
139. *CD 1628* vol. IV, p. 115.
140. *CD 1628* vol. IV, p. 254.
141. *CD 1628* vol. IV, p. 321.
142. Russell, *Parliaments*, pp. 393–96.
143. 'Arminianism' rather than 'anti-Calvinism' was the term used in the debate.
144. *CD 1629*, p. 12.
145. *CD 1629*, pp. 12–14.
146. *CD 1629*, pp. 24–28.
147. *CD 1629*, pp. 24–28.
148. *CD 1629*, pp. 33–34.
149. *CD 1629*, p. 18.
150. *CD 1629*, p. 121.
151. *CD 1629*, p. 176.
152. *CD 1629*, p. 52.
153. *CD 1628* vol. IV, p. 9n.; Christopher Thompson, 'The Divided Leadership in the House of Commons in 1629', in Kevin Sharpe (ed.) *Faction and Parliament. Essays on Early Stuart History* (London, 1985), p. 251; *CJ* iv.921a. For Rolle's Cornish Puritan connections, see Chapter 2, p. 57.
154. *CD 1628* vol. IV, p. 61.
155. S. R. Gardiner, *History of England from the Accession of James I to the Outbreak of the Civil War 1603–1642* 10 vols (New York, 1965), vol. VII, pp. 67–71; *CD 1628* vol. IV, p. 255.
156. *CD 1629*, pp. 102–3.
157. *CD 1629*, pp. 101–3.
158. *CSPD* Addenda 1625–49, p. 374.
159. PRO C231/4; *CSPD* 1628–29, pp. 495, 527; CRO CY 7241; PRO C231/5/25.
160. See Chapter 4.
161. *CSPD* 1629–1631, pp. 249, 455–56; *CSPD* Addenda 1625–49, p. 374; PRO SP16/119/59; SP16/150/74.
162. See Forster, *Eliot*, vol. II, pp. 528–29, 567, 623–29.
163. *HGF*, p. 179.

164. *HGF*, p. 181.
165. Coryton's inclusion in the list of commissioners for knighthood composition fines, despite his earlier staunch forced loan refusal, also indicates a shift in his position. See Chapter 5, p. 153.
166. *HGF*, p. 182.
167. *HGF*, pp. 183–84.
168. Vivian, *Visitations of Cornwall*, p. 502; *HGF*, pp. 185–86. For more detail on these marriage negotiations, see Chapter 1, p. 31–32.
169. *HGF*, pp. 184–85.
170. *HGF*, pp. 214–17.
171. Gardiner, *History of England*, vol. VIII, p. 89. For an account of Weston's ascendancy see Kevin Sharpe, *The Personal Rule of Charles I* (New Haven and London, 1992), pp. 145–53.
172. *CSPD* 1635, p. 29; 1636–1637, pp. 388–89; *CD 1628* vol. II, p. 370; PRO SP16/101/47.
173. *Strafford Letters*, vol. I, pp. 426, 336.
174. *CSPD* 1635, p. 29.
175. *CSPD* 1637, p. 260. I am grateful to Dr Andrew Thrush for several useful discussions about this case, and for showing me an early draft of his views on it. However, I cannot agree with Dr Thrush's belief in Bagg's innocence.
176. *Strafford Letters*, vol. I, p. 337; Gardiner, *History of England*, vol. VIII, p. 89.
177. *Strafford Letters*, vol. I, p. 377.
178. Sharpe, *Personal Rule*, pp. 148, 177–78. This division may have had more to do with the personal hostility between Laud and Cottington, and with Laud's dislike of Portland and Cottington's regard for him, than with the justice of the case.
179. Gardiner, *History of England*, vol. VIII, pp. 89–91; *Strafford Letters*, vol. I, p. 489.
180. Derriman, *Killigarth*, pp. 27–29.
181. *HGF*, p. 191.
182. *HGF*, p. 137 Bevill Grenvile to Revd Ralph Byrd, June 1636.
183. *HGF*, p. 192.
184. *HGF*, p. 194; Vivian, *Visitations of Cornwall*, p. 564.
185. *CSPD* 1637–1638, p. 604.
186. *CSPD* 1638–1639, p. 158.
187. PRO SP16/436/33.
188. A third inquisition, held on 24 April 1641 at Bodmin by the sheriff, Francis Wills, attached a further charge of £3,000 to Killigarth in respect of money owed to the Crown on a recognizance made in 1626 for collection of the western impositions. *CSPD* 1640, p. 356; PRO SP16/438/48; Derriman, *Killigarth*, pp. 31–32; PRO E367/565, 656; SP23/185/119, 120, 121, 122, 129; E368/685/28. I am very grateful to Mr James Derriman for drawing these documents to my attention and for kindly providing me with transcripts.

4: Local Government and Defence

1. Sharpe, *Personal Rule*, pp. 431–34; Hughes, *Warwickshire*, p. 51; Fletcher, *Sussex*, p. 128. JPs were advised of their duties by publications such as Dalton's *The Countrey Justice*. Michael Dalton, *The Countrey Justice* (1619; repr. 1973) cited in Wolffe, 'Gentry Government in Devon', p. 67.
2. Carew, *Cornwall*, p. 88.
3. See, for example, FitzGeffry, *The Curse of Corne-horders*. This sermon is analyzed on p. 116 below.
4. Rowse, *Tudor Cornwall*, p. 84. Rowse does not specify whether these figures represent the whole commission, including the great officers of state and non-resident peers, but for the purposes of this analysis it is assumed that the figures are all-inclusive.
5. See Appendix 1. PRO SP14/33; C193/13/1. The figures include the great officers of state and non-resident peers. Anthony Fletcher, *Reform in the Provinces. The Government of Stuart England* (New Haven and London, 1986), p. 8.
6. Fletcher, *Reform in the Provinces*, p. 6; B. W. Quintrell, 'The Making of Charles I's Book of Orders', *EHR* vol. 95 (1980), p. 559.
7. PRO C231/4/55.
8. The new appointments are recorded in the Crown Office Docquet Book 1615–1629. PRO C231/4.
9. Barnes, *Somerset*, pp. 42–43.
10. PRO C193/13/1.
11. Twenty-six new appointments were made between 1617 and 1622, but five of these were not subsequently named on the 1622 commission, and one (Francis Godolphin Esq) was admitted twice (in 1618 and 1620). A further eight appointments were made between 1623 and 1625. In total these numbered thirty-four. All are recorded in the Crown Office Docquet Book 1615–1629. PRO C231/4.
12. For an analysis of Cornish gentry wealth see Chapter 1, pp. 24–25.
13. In 1608 55 per cent of JPs lived in west Cornwall and 42 per cent in the east of the county. In 1622 this position was reversed, with 54 per cent of JPs living in east Cornwall and 41 per cent in the west.
14. The same applied in Warwickshire. See Hughes, *Warwickshire*, pp. 51–52.
15. Charles Lord Lambert (1623), Richard Erisey Esq of Erisey (1624), Robert Rous Esq of Landrake (1624), Edward Trelawny Esq of Bake (1624), Joseph Borlase Esq (1625), Samuel Pendarves Esq (1625), Anthony Pye Esq (1625) and John Mohun Esq of Boconnoc (1625). The last was probably a political appointment due to the influence of the Duke of Buckingham.
16. For the interrelationship between politics, religion, and local government, see Fletcher, *Reform in the Provinces*, Chapter 1. Fletcher observed that 'There was no way of keeping politics out of local government' (p. 1).
17. For appointments see Crown Office Docquet Book 1615–1629. PRO C231/4.
18. See Appendix 1. PRO E163/18/12. Of the twenty-two, eighteen were survivors from the 1622 commission, and four had been appointed between 1623 and 1625.

19. Fletcher, *Reform in the Provinces*, p. 8.
20. Hughes, *Warwickshire*, p. 53; Fletcher, *Sussex*, p. 129.
21. Fletcher, *Sussex*, p. 130; PRO C231/4.
22. See Chapter 3, pp. 82–84, and Chapter 5, p. 151.
23. PRO C231/4; C231/5/25; SP16/190/2I; SP16/212.
24. Fletcher, *Reform in the Provinces*, p. 9; CRO C231/5/232. Langford was replaced by George Hele Esq of Whitstone (in the hundred of Stratton), who was added to the commission the same day.
25. See, for example, Gardiner, *History of England*, vol. VII, p. 160; Barnes, *Somerset*, p. 173.
26. Paul Slack, 'Books of Orders: The Making of English Social Policy, 1577–1631' *TRHS* 5th series, vol. 30 (1980), pp. 1–22; Quintrell, 'Book of Orders', pp. 553–72.
27. Sharpe, *Personal Rule*, p. 456.
28. Slack, 'Books of Orders', *passim*; Quintrell, 'Book of Orders', *passim*; Sharpe, *Personal Rule*, pp. 456–61.
29. Quintrell, 'Book of Orders', p. 572.
30. Slack, 'Books of Orders', pp. 1–2.
31. See Todd Gray (ed.) *Harvest Failure in Cornwall and Devon. The Book of Orders and the Corn Surveys of 1623 and 1630–1* Sources of Cornish History 1 (Redruth, 1992). See, for example, PRO SP16/175/35.
32. Slack, 'Books of Orders', pp. 1–2, 5, 13.
33. Quintrell, 'Book of Orders', p. 569, n. 2.
34. PRO SP16/191/46.
35. PRO SP16/225/3.
36. PRO SP16/237/41.
37. PRO SP16/289/58, 64.
38. Quintrell, 'Book of Orders', p. 569.
39. PRO SP16/247/61; SP16/248/70.
40. Of the twenty-two eastern reports the others were fairly evenly divided: four from Stratton and Lesnewth respectively, and three from Trigg and West respectively. Had the western justices been as assiduous as the eastern JPs, Cornwall would have been in the top five counties for volume of certificates returned.
41. FitzGeffry, *The Curse of Corne-horders*, pp. A2–A3.
42. FitzGeffry, *The Curse of Corne-horders*, p. 1.
43. FitzGeffry, *The Curse of Corne-horders*, p. 48.
44. FitzGeffry, *The Curse of Corne-horders*, p. 49. FitzGeffry's use of the word 'Deacon' has Presbyterian overtones.
45. FitzGeffry, *Compassion Towards Captives*, Dedication, p. 2. Perhaps FitzGeffry was referring to the non-Puritan JPs who responded to the Book of Orders, such as Sir William Wrey and Sir Richard Edgcumbe.
46. Barnes, *Somerset*, pp. 304–6.
47. Hughes, *Warwickshire*, p. 58.
48. See Appendix 1.

49. CRO CY 7260.
50. PRO SP16/32/61; SP16/33/11.
51. Forster, *Eliot*, vol. II, pp. 27–28; PRO SP16/68/25; SP16/74/34. Buller, a member of the Eliot–Coryton faction, claimed to have paid the forced loan.
52. Lindsay Boynton, *The Elizabethan Militia 1558–1638* (London, 1967), pp. 209–14; *CSPD* 1603–1610, p. 109; 1610–1618, p. 182; 1611–1618, p. 258.
53. *APC* 1623–25, p. 8.
54. Boynton, *Elizabethan Militia*, pp. 327–41; *CSPD* 1619–1623, p. 178; 1619–1623, p. 179; 1636–1637, p. 276. This document, the petition of Arthur Hill to the Privy Council, is wrongly dated in the Calendar as ?1636. It quite clearly refers to the case of 1620 when the persons involved and the facts of the case were the same.
55. Boynton, *Elizabethan Militia*, pp. 246–55; Barnes, *Somerset*, pp. 244–47.
56. PRO SP16/19/105.
57. PRO SP16/33/111 deputy lieutenants of Cornwall to the Earl of Pembroke, 15 August 1626.
58. PRO SP16/33/111.
59. PRO SP16/33/111.
60. PRO SP16/33/111 Cornish deputies to Pembroke.
61. PRO SP16/32/61; SP16/88/53; *CSPD* Addenda 1625–1649, p. 249; *APC* 1626, pp. 331–33.
62. Boynton, *Elizabethan Militia*, p. 270.
63. Forster, *Eliot*, vol. II, pp. 27–28; PRO SP16/74/34; SP16/68/16, 25.
64. PRO SP16/147/14 Sir Bernard Grenvile to Sir James Bagg, 19 July 1629. In contrast, the deputy lieutenants of Devon remained conscientious in mustering and training troops throughout the period 1625–40. Wolffe, 'Gentry Government in Devon', pp. 192–209.
65. Fletcher, *Sussex*, pp. 187–88.
66. *CD 1628* vol. II, p. 90. A remarkably similar situation existed in Somerset, where Sir Robert Phelips led factional opposition to the deputy lieutenants in the county, and questioned their authority in the Commons in 1628. Barnes, *Somerset*, pp. 265–66.
67. PRO SP16/147/83.
68. PRO SP16/147/46.
69. Robert Rous was the second son of Sir Anthony Rous of Halton and his first wife, Elizabeth. This made him John Pym's step-brother. Rous married Jane Pym, daughter of Alexander Pym, and through this became John Pym's brother-in-law also.
70. PRO SP16/166/52, 52I.
71. Roberts appears in this series of documents variously as 'yeoman' and 'gent', but it is likely that he was the same John Roberts listed as 'gent' of Landrake parish in the 1641 subsidy roll.
72. PRO SP16/166/52I; SP16/166/54; *APC* May 1629–May 1630, pp. 379–80.
73. PRO SP16/166/54; *CSPD* 1629–1631, p. 255; PRO SP16/166/55; *APC* May 1629–May 1630, pp. 379–80.

74. *APC* May 1629–May 1630, pp. 379–80.
75. CRO FS/3/47/21; PRO SP16/150/74.
76. PRO SP16/150/74.
77. Barnes, *Somerset*, pp. 265–66.
78. Carew, p. 84.
79. Russell, *Parliaments*, p. 326; Barnes, *Somerset*, pp. 263–80. Barnes has shown that similar problems applied in Somerset where Pembroke was also lord lieutenant.
80. CRO P162/5/1.
81. CRO DPP 19/5/8.
82. *APC* 1623–1625, p. 499; PRO SP16/1/69; *APC* 1625–1626, pp. 42–44, 171–72; *CSPD* 1625–1626, pp. 103, 105.
83. *APC* 1623–1625, pp. 486–87.
84. *APC* Jan–Aug 1627, p. 212; *CSPD* 1627–1628, pp. 374, 301, 419; PRO SP16/86/27.
85. PRO SP16/88/46. The response to this petition is unknown.
86. PRO SP16/100/40, 47.
87. *APC* 1625–1626, pp. 56–57. The soldiers outnumbered Plymouth's population of about 8,000 or 9,000. Wolffe, 'Gentry Government of Devon', p. 212, and pp. 210–38 for the effect of these measures upon Devon and its gentry governors.
88. PRO SP16/3/101.
89. PRO SP16/4/149.
90. PRO SP16/3/101.
91. *APC* 1625–26, p. 318.
92. *APC* 1625–26, p. 416.
93. *CSPD* 1625–1626, pp. 78, 172; PRO SP16/29/46; CRO P126/4/1. There had been deaths from plague and spotted fever in Plymouth since May 1625; by the return of the fleet in December there was a full-scale outbreak of plague in the town. Wolffe, 'Gentry Government of Devon', pp. 212, 216.
94. CRO B/LISK/281.
95. CRO P126/4/1.
96. *APC* 1626, pp. 216–19.
97. *APC* 1627, p. 85.
98. *APC* Sept 1627–June 1628, pp. 127–28; *CSPD* 1627–1628, p. 451; PRO SP16/86/27.
99. *APC* Sept 1627–June 1628, pp. 155, 181, 235, 299.
100. PRO SP16/88/46. The petition is undated and unsigned. It was almost certainly composed in late 1627. The author is unknown, but the style is eloquent, suggesting an educated hand.
101. In 1628 the churchwardens of Poughill in north Cornwall paid 4*d*. 'for a prayer for the fleet'. This suggests public awareness of the position. CRO P192/5/2.
102. PRO SP16/81/41 Drake to Nicholas, 14 October 1627. Drake was a Devonian ally of Bagg, and in 1626 was appointed to the Admiralty Commission to investigate Eliot's conduct as vice-admiral of Devon.

103. *HMC* 12th Report, Coke MSS, p. 329. Bagg to Sir John Coke, October 1627.
104. The named commissioners were Charles Lord Lambert, Sir Reginald Mohun, Sir Bernard Grenvile, Sir Richard Edgcumbe, Sir William Wrey, Sir Richard Buller, Sir Robert Killigrew, Sir Francis Vyvyan, Sir Francis Godolphin, Sir James Bagg, John Mohun and Charles Trevanion.
105. PRO SP16/86/27 Bagg to Buckingham, 7 December 1627.
106. *CD 1628* vol. III, pp. 4, 7.
107. David Hebb, *Piracy and the English Government 1616–1642* (Aldershot and Brookfield, 1994) pp. 10–15, 204–208; Ralph Davis, 'England and the Mediterranean 1570–1670', in F. J. Fisher (ed.), *Essays in the Economic and Social History of Tudor and Stuart England in honour of R. H. Tawney* (Cambridge, 1961), pp. 127–30; J. C. Appleby, 'English privateering during the Spanish and French Wars, 1625–30' (University of Hull Ph.D., 1983), pp. 27, 35.
108. CRO B/LISK/271, 272.
109. CRO P162/5/1; PD 322/2.
110. PRO SP16/1/69.
111. PRO SP16/4/149.
112. PRO SP16/4/149.
113. PRO SP16/5/6.
114. David Hebb, 'The English Government and the Problem of Piracy, 1616–42 (University of London Ph.D, 1985), p. 264; Hebb, *Piracy*, pp. 199–201.
115. PRO SP16/5/36.
116. PRO SP16/5/36.
117. *CSPD* 1625–1626, p. 86.
118. *CSPD* 1625–1626, p. 89. The identity of 'Munnigeesa' is unknown.
119. Russell, *Parliaments*, pp. 215, 217, 227–29; Russell, 'Parliament and the King's Finances' in Russell, (ed.) *Origins*, pp. 104–6.
120. PRO SP16/27/73.
121. PRO SP16/31/35I.
122. PRO SP16/27/54; *CSPD* 1625–1626, pp. 356, 418, 439.
123. *CSPD* 1628–1629, p. 397.
124. *CSPD* 1629–1631, p. 44; CRO PD 322/3.
125. *CSPD* 1636–1637, p. 60.
126. CRO B/LISK/288.
127. CRO P126/4/1; DPP 19/5/8; FitzGeffry, *Compassion Towards Captives*.
128. Hebb, *Piracy*, pp. 237–65.
129. *CSPD* 1637, p. 430.
130. PRO SP16/12/78, I, II. The list of signatories was headed by John Treffry, Jonathan Rashleigh, Robert Rashleigh Gent, and the Revd Ralph Byrd (Sir Bernard Grenvile's friend).
131. PRO SP16/19/105.
132. PRO SP16/19/105.
133. PRO SP16/27/73.

134. See, for example, *CSPD* 1625–26, p. 124; *HMC* 12th Report, Coke MSS, p. 264.
135. PRO SP16/40/29.
136. PRO SP16/10/69.
137. PRO SP16/25/105.
138. PRO SP16/49/6.
139. *CSPD* 1628–1629, p. 218; Addenda 1625–49, p. 22; *HMC* Salisbury MSS vol. XXII, p. 54; *CSPD* 1627–1628, pp. 127, 515, 547.
140. *APC* 1626, p. 393.
141. *APC* January–August 1627, p. 22.
142. *APC* January–August 1627, p. 64.
143. *CSPD* 1628–1629, p. 154.
144. *CSPD* 1627–1628, p. 79 John Tresahar to Conway.
145. *CSPD* 1627–1628, p. 123; *APC* January–August 1627, pp. 64–65.
146. PRO SP16/73/49.
147. *CD 1628* vol. IV, pp. 146, 202, 216–17.
148. *CD 1628* vol. IV, p. 253.
149. See *CSPD* 1637–1638, pp. 260–61 Sir Francis Godolphin to the Privy Council, 16 February 1638.

5: The Impact of Arbitrary Taxation

1. CRO RP 1/8 Request for privy seal loan, addressed to James Praed of Lelant Gent.
2. Cust, *Forced Loan*, pp. 35–39; Hughes, *Warwickshire*, p. 94.
3. CRO CY 7287.
4. PRO SP16/11/64.
5. CRO R(S) 1/987. Rashleigh's privy seal letter was dated 8 November 1625, and requested the sum of £40, which he paid on 10 January 1626. CRO R(S) 1/1109.
6. See, for example, CRO R(S) 1/987; CY 7288.
7. See Chapter 3, p. 76.
8. CRO CY 7288.
9. CRO CY 7286; PRO E401/2586 'Register of Privy Seal Loans, 1625–1626, Cornwall'.
10. Cust, *Forced Loan*, pp. 32–34.
11. PRO SP16/37/50.
12. Cust, *Forced Loan*, pp. 96, 95, 98.
13. PRO SP16/36/37.
14. The King articulated this view in his *Declaration* at the dissolution of the 1626 Parliament. See Chapter 3, p. 92.
15. Cust, *Forced Loan*, p. 99.
16. PRO SP16/37/91.
17. PRO C193/12/2. See Appendix 3.
18. See Chapter 4, p. 130.

19. PRO SP16/54/20.
20. *APC* 1627, p. 108.
21. PRO SP16/56/31.
22. PRO SP16/68/16; SP16/73/103.
23. PRO SP16/73/49.
24. PRO SP16/60/75.
25. Cust, *Forced Loan*, p. 166.
26. For a record of their dates and places of imprisonment, see *CD 1628* vol. I, p. 64.
27. Forster, *Eliot*, vol. II, p. 92.
28. Forster, *Eliot*, vol. II, pp. 90–91.
29. 'A Relation of soe muche as passed Betwene the Lordes of the Councell and Mr Corinton, at the Councell Table touchinge his Refusall to Contribute to the Lones he beinge then Prisoner in the Gatehowse at Westminster in Aprill 1627' BL Harl. MSS 39 ff. 412r.–13. See also Cust, *Forced Loan*, pp. 169–70.
30. BL Harl. MSS 39 f. 413.
31. BL Harl. MSS. 39 ff. 413r.–14.
32. Cust, *Forced Loan*, p. 168. Dr Cust has found that twenty copies of the 'Petition' and three copies of 'The Relation' survive. For Bagg's interpretation of Eliot's motives, see Chapter 3, pp. 85–86.
33. This is intrinsically linked with the development of political factions in Cornwall, and is analyzed in that context in Chapter 3, pp. 78–102.
34. *HGF*, p. 163.
35. PRO SP16/68/25.
36. PRO SP16/68/16.
37. PRO SP16/74/78.
38. PRO SP16/72/57; C231/4.
39. Wolffe, 'Gentry Government in Devon', pp. 139–40; Cust, *Forced Loan*, pp. 122–26.
40. Dr Cust suggests a possible link between loan refusal and Puritanism, and the identity of the Cornish refusers would appear to support this view. Cust, *Forced Loan*, p. 320.
41. H. H. Leonard, 'Distraint of Knighthood: the Last Phase, 1625–41' *History* vol. 63 (1978), pp. 23–26.
42. Leonard, 'Distraint of Knighthood', p. 25.
43. PRO E178/7161.
44. *APC* June 1630–June 1631, p. 32.
45. See p. 102. *APC* June 1630–June 1631, p. 32; PRO SP16/187/18.
46. PRO E178/89/310; E178/7161; Leonard, 'Distraint of Knighthood', p. 29.
47. PRO E178/7161.
48. PRO E178/89/310.
49. PRO E178/7161.
50. Trefusis and Erisey were two of the five JPs who had been active in attempting to collect the benevolence in summer 1626. See above p. 146.

51. PRO SP16/187/18.
52. PRO E407/35.
53. PRO SP16/239/59; SP16/242/64.
54. PRO E401/1920, 1922.
55. Gardiner, *Constitutional Documents*, pp. 105–6.
56. Peter Lake, 'The Collection of Ship Money in Cheshire During the Sixteen-Thirties: a Case Study of Relations between Central and Local Government' *NH* (1981), pp. 54–57; Barnes, *Somerset*, p. 208.
57. M. D. Gordon, 'The Collection of Ship Money in the Reign of Charles I' *TRHS* 3rd series, vol. IV (1910), pp. 146–47.
58. Gordon, 'Ship Money', pp. 141–62.
59. PRO SP16/302/86.
60. *CSPD* 1634–1635, p. 244.
61. PRO SP16/302/86.
62. *CSPD* 1635–1636, p. 149.
63. *CSPD* 1635–1636, p. 149.
64. *CSPD* 1635–1636, p. 569.
65. PRO SP16/336/45.
66. *CSPD* 1636–1637, p. 82.
67. *CSPD* 1636–1637, p. 435.
68. CRO HD/13/75.
69. CRO BO/21/23/1–4: 'Cornwall. A list of the Rates for the busines of Shipping Annis 1636 et 1637'. See Appendix 4.
70. CRO BO/21/23/1–4.
71. CRO BO/21/23/1–4.
72. CRO CN 1931/1.
73. *CSPD* 1639, p. 62.
74. *CSPD* 1639, p. 63.
75. PRO SP16/424/43 Godolphin to Nicholas, 21 June 1639.
76. *CSPD* 1639, p. 62.
77. *CSPD* 1638–1639. p. 429.
78. PRO SP16/444/44.
79. *CSPD* 1639, p. 63.
80. The composition of this shortfall was Bodmin £30; Lostwithiel £8; St Mawes £4; Bossiney £14; Camelford £4; Callington £3. PRO SP16/444/44.
81. Gordon, 'Ship Money', p. 142. The other eight counties were Cheshire, Derbyshire, Lancashire, Monmouth, Sussex, Anglesea, Glamorgan and Radnor.
82. Coate, *Cornwall*, p. 22.
83. CRO T.CP13. The Trefusis papers contain a number of copy letters and newsletters, mainly from an anti-government stance, which chart many of the important contemporary issues.
84. Morrill, *Revolt of the Provinces*, pp. 24–28; Hughes, *Warwickshire*, pp. 99–100, 105, 109–12; Lake, 'Ship Money in Cheshire', pp. 44–71, especially p. 70.
85. Hughes, *Warwickshire*, pp. 105–8.

86. See Chapter 4, pp. 134–39.
87. Sharpe, *Personal Rule*, pp. 594–96.
88. See Chapter 4, pp. 138–39.
89. Fletcher, *Sussex*, p. 208. See also Wolffe, 'Gentry Government in Devon', p. 174.

6: The Approach of War and Decisions of Allegiance

1. *CSPD* 1639–1640, p. 590.
2. *CSPD* 1640, p. 317.
3. Lake, 'Ship Money in Cheshire', p. 61.
4. CRO BO/21/23/1; PRO E179/88/293; E179/89/304–12.
5. *CSPD* 1638–1639, pp. 513–14; CRO RP 1/10. Dr Wolffe has shown that Sir John Pole, sheriff of Devon 1638–39, faced similar problems in collection because of the dual demands of ship money and the Scots War. Wolffe, 'Gentry Government of Devon', pp. 184–86.
6. CRO P19/5/10.
7. PRO SP16/458/87. This document is incorrectly dated in the Calendar as ?June 1640.
8. Sharpe, *Personal Rule*, p. 812; *CSPD* 1638–1639, p. 563.
9. *CSPD* 1639, p. 62.
10. John Rushworth, *Historical Collections* 8 vols (London, 1721–1722), vol. III, pp. 911–13.
11. *HGF*, pp. 217–22.
12. Keeler, *Long Parliament*, p. 195.
13. *HGF*, p. 213.
14. See Chapter 3, p. 106.
15. The preamble reads: 'And first I commend my soule into the hands of Almightie God, my Maker and Redeemer, in full assurance that all my sinnes are washed away by the precious blood of Jesus Christ my Saviour, who is the Lambe of God that taketh away the sinnes of the world, and that at the last day I shall be presented to him without spot, and received into his kingdom of Glorye, there to live evermore'. *HGF*, pp. 214–17.
16. *HGF*, pp. 217–18.
17. *HGF*, pp. 221–22.
18. CRO RP 1/10.
19. Keeler, *Long Parliament*, p. 188.
20. Conrad Russell, *The Fall of the British Monarchies 1637–1642* (Oxford, 1991), pp. 86–87; Sharpe, *Personal Rule*, pp. 813–23.
21. CRO R(S) 1/1038.
22. CRO R(S) 1/1036.
23. CRO P192/5/2.
24. Richard Cust, 'Politics and the Electorate in the 1620s' in Cust and Hughes (eds) *Conflict*, p. 153.

25. Haslam, 'The Duchy', p. 242; Coate, *Cornwall*, pp. 23–24; Gruenfelder, *Early Stuart Elections*, p. 184.
26. CRO BO/23/63/1.
27. Gruenfelder, *Early Stuart Elections*, p. 184.
28. CRO BO/23/63/1.
29. Kishlansky, *Parliamentary Selection*, pp. 105–11.
30. Kishlansky, *Parliamentary Selection*, pp. 74–75, 109; Cust, 'Politics and the Electorate', p. 135, & n. 4.
31. Cust, 'Politics and the Electorate', pp. 134–67.
32. See, for example, Russell, *Fall of the British Monarchies*, pp. 94–95. However, Russell says that, because of their organization and commitment, the Puritans were 'the first beneficiaries of this shift towards partisan politics' in 1640.
33. Keeler, *Long Parliament*, pp. 327, 285, 266.
34. Vivian, *Visitations of Cornwall*, pp. 344, 413.
35. *DNB* under John Robartes; Sharpe, *Personal Rule*, p. 853.
36. Judith Maltby (ed.) *The Short Parliament (1640) Diary of Sir Thomas Aston* Camden Society, 4th series, vol. 35 (London, 1988), pp. 8–10; Russell, *Fall of the British Monarchies*, p. 106; Sharpe, *Personal Rule*, p. 865.
37. *PSP*, pp. 145–48. See also, Maltby (ed.) *Short Parliament*, p. 7. Russell, *Fall of the British Monarchies*, pp. 105–6.
38. *LJ* iv.58a.
39. *CJ* ii.9b.
40. Russell, *Fall of the British Monarchies*, p. 114.
41. *CJ* ii.17b.
42. PRO SP16/456/64.
43. *CSPD* 1640, p. 210.
44. *CSPD* 1640, p. 264.
45. *CSPD* 1640, p. 264.
46. *BP*, p. 27.
47. *CSPD* 1640, pp. 321–22.
48. *CSPD* 1640, pp. 437–38.
49. *CSPD* 1640, pp. 456–59.
50. CRO R(S) 1/1039.
51. CRO R(S) 1/1040.
52. Coate, *Cornwall*, p. 24; Gruenfelder, *Early Stuart Elections*, p. 196.
53. Russell, *Fall of the British Monarchies*, pp. 214–15.
54. *HGF*, p. 235. Seymour was selected knight of the shire for Devon in these elections. Keeler, *Long Parliament*, pp. 42, 337.
55. *HGF*, pp. 233–34.
56. *HGF*, pp. 233–34.
57. *HGF*, p. 233.
58. *CJ* ii.29a. Coryton's former ally, Ambrose Manaton, was named to that committee.
59. *CJ* ii.46b, 47a.
60. *CJ* ii.66a, b, 68a.

61. *CJ* ii.86a.
62. Keeler, *Long Parliament*, p. 38.
63. *CJ* ii.184a, 261b.
64. *CJ* ii.29a.
65. *BP*, pp. 138–39; Keeler, *Long Parliament*, pp. 41, 327. Wise was a cousin and close friend of the Bullers. His brother-in-law was Sir Samuel Rolle, who helped to draft and signed the petition, and who was himself brother-in-law to Sir Alexander Carew, knight of the shire for Cornwall.
66. *CJ* ii.46b, 47a.
67. *CJ* ii.57a, b.
68. *CJ* ii.83b.
69. *LJ* iv.316b.
70. Another Puritan, Jonathan Rashleigh, was returned for the first Fowey seat, and the town had shown strong Puritan inclinations. See Chapter 2, pp. 52–54. *CJ* ii.29a, 32a, b.; Keeler, *Long Parliament*, p. 39.
71. Keeler, *Long Parliament*, p. 38; *DNB* under Anthony Nicoll.
72. Keeler, *Long Parliament*, pp. 39, 370.
73. *BP*, pp. 30–31. Scot and lot was a tax levied by boroughs upon their members in proportionate shares for the defraying of borough expenses. Therefore, it is fair to assume that scot and lot voters were those who paid for this tax.
74. Keeler, *Long Parliament*, p. 40.
75. Bodleian Library Clarendon MSS 26, f. 163.
76. *BP*, p. 29.
77. *CJ* ii.39a.
78. Russell, *Fall of the British Monarchies*, p. 231.
79. CRO RP 1/10–11.
80. For news dissemination see Chapter 1, p. 3.
81. *CJ* ii.54b.
82. *CJ* ii.84b; Russell, *Fall of the British Monarchies*, pp. 337–38.
83. *CJ* ii.174a 1 March 1641.
84. *CJ* ii.99a 8 March 1641.
85. *CJ* ii.128b 27 April 1641; Russell, *Fall of the British Monarchies*, p. 226.
86. CRO RP 1/10–11.
87. *CJ* ii.47b; D'Ewes, p. 124; *LJ* iv.156a.
88. *CJ* ii.181b.
89. *LJ* iv.103b, 115b.
90. *CJ* ii.115a, b.
91. Three non-indigenous MPs for Cornish constituencies also voted against the attainder bill. These were Sir Nicholas Slanning (Penryn), George Parry (St Mawes), and Robert Holborne (Michell). All became royalists. *Verney Papers, Notes of Proceedings in the Long Parliament* Camden Society (London, 1845), pp. 57–58.
92. CRO R(S) 1/35. 'My cosen Arundell' was John Arundell of Trerice, the former member of the Eliot–Coryton faction, who had a history of opposition to government policies. However, John Arundell supported the King in 1642.

93. Coate, *Cornwall*, pp. 27–28.
94. CRO RP 1/11; Russell, *Fall of the British Monarchies*, pp. 293–94.
95. *CJ* ii.113b.
96. *CJ* ii.133b, 136b, 142a, 149a, 231b, 201a.
97. *LJ* iv.284b; Clarendon, *History of the Rebellion*, vol. III, p. 187.
98. CRO RP 1/11.
99. CRO T.CP16, 19.
100. *LJ* iv.258b; *CJ* ii.165b; *LJ* iv.265a.
101. *CJ* ii.165b, 211a, 14 June 1641; Russell, *Fall of the British Monarchies*, pp. 338–39.
102. *CJ* ii.136b, 139a.
103. *LJ* iv.306b, 385a, 30 August 1641.
104. *LJ* iv.222b, 224a.
105. *CJ* ii.152a, 170a, 188b.
106. *CJ* ii.196a, 215a; *LJ* iv.329a.
107. *CJ* ii.239a.
108. *CJ* ii.263a, 264a; *LJ* iv.371b.
109. *CJ* ii.276a; *LJ* iv.383a.
110. *LJ* iv.416b, 417a, b.
111. *LJ* iv.419a; *CJ* ii.202a.
112. *D'Ewes*, pp. 170, 296; *CJ* ii.344b, 350a.
113. *D'Ewes*, p. 228 & n.
114. *D'Ewes*, pp. 339 & n., 340.
115. CRO T.CP20.
116. *LJ* iv.491a, 492b, 493a.
117. *D'Ewes*, p. 15; *PJLP*, pp. 208 & n. 12, 210 & nn, 26, 27, 214, 220; *CJ* ii.401b, 432a.
118. *LJ* iv.501a, 518a, 649a.
119. *LJ* iv.660a, 665a.
120. *LJ* iv.645a, b.
121. *PJLP*, pp. 217 & n. 6, 219, 176, 179; *CJ* ii.404a; *LJ* iv.549a, b; CRO T.CP23.
122. *PJLP*, pp. 292, 303, 459 & n. 30, 460, 499 & n. 5.
123. *LJ* v.70b, 241b.
124. Russell, *Fall of the British Monarchies*, p. 471; *LJ* iv.570b, 581a.
125. CRO RP 1/12.
126. *LJ* v.363. This was Mohun's reply in September 1642 to the Lords' summons to answer for his 'high Contempts' in leaving Parliament, and for executing the commission of array.
127. *LJ* iv.340a, 443b, 571b, 693a, 718b; v.8a.
128. Anthony Fletcher, *The Outbreak of the English Civil War* (London, 1981), pp. 242–43; Russell, *Fall of the British Monarchies*, pp. 470–71.
129. Fletcher, *Outbreak*, pp. 191–92.
130. Bodleian Library Rawlinson MSS C.789, f. 56r.
131. BL E143 (19).
132. BL E143 (19); Fletcher, *Outbreak*, pp. 210–13.

133. Fletcher, *Outbreak*, pp. 192–94.
134. BL E150 (28) p. 40.
135. Judith Maltby, "'By this Book"; Parishioners, the Prayer Book and the Established Church', in Fincham (ed.) *Early Stuart Church*, pp. 115–37.
136. BL E143 (19); E150 (28) p. 40; Fletcher, *Outbreak*, pp. 223–26.
137. Fletcher, *Outbreak*, p. 284; BL E150 (28) p. 37.
138. See Chapter 4, pp. 123–24.
139. PRO Bishops Institution Books, Series A, 1566–1660, under St Tudy.
140. BL E150 (28) p. 32; Rushworth, *Historical Collections*, vol. IV, pp. 638–39; Coate, *Cornwall*, p. 356. Only the thirty-six signatures referred to survive.
141. Fletcher, *Outbreak*, p. 283.
142. Bodleian Library Clarendon MSS 26, f. 163.
143. Clarendon, *History of the Rebellion*, vol. II, p. 448.
144. BL E150 (28) p. 37.
145. Bodleian Library Clarendon MSS 26, f. 163.
146. *CJ* ii.164b, 460b.
147. *CJ* ii.99a.
148. Northants RO, Finch Hatton MSS 113.
149. CRO BC/24/2/12. 26; CRO AD 374/9.
150. CRO B 35/44.
151. CRO B 35/4.
152. *CJ* ii.694.
153. Robartes was appointed lord lieutenant by Parliament on 26 February 1642. PRO C231/5/508.
154. CRO BC/24/2/13.
155. PRO C231/5/529.
156. *LJ* v.275a, b.
157. For the Mohuns' connection with Lanteglos-by-Fowey see Chapter 2, p. 63. PRO Bishops Institution Books, Series A, 1566–1660, under Lanteglos-by-Fowey; *Cornwall Protestation Returns*, p. 162; Lake, *Parochial History of Cornwall*, vol. III, p. 46.
158. CRO AD 374/9; BC/24/2/12; Coate, *Cornwall*, p. 34.
159. CRO AD 374/9.
160. *LJ* v.271b.
161. *LJ* v.275a.
162. *CJ* ii.772a; Coate, *Cornwall*, p. 376.
163. CRO BC/24/2/20.
164. CRO BC/24/2/20, 22; Coate, *Cornwall*, p. 35.
165. Bodleian Library Clarendon MSS 26, f. 163.
166. *Bellum Civile*, pp. 19–20. For the formation of the Cornish county committee and its initial instructions from Parliament, see *CJ* ii.694, 732; C. H. Firth and R. S. Rait, *Acts and Ordinances of the Interregnum, 1642–60* (London, 1911) 3 vols, vol. I, p. 53.
167. BL E124 (20) 'New News From Cornwall', 27 October 1642; Coate, *Cornwall*, p. 36.

168. *Bellum Civile*, pp. 20–22.
169. *Bellum Civile*, pp. 22–23.
170. John Morrill discussed this in a general sense in his article 'The Religious Context of the English Civil War', *TRHS* 5th series, vol. 34 (1984), p. 177.
171. Hughes, *Warwickshire*, pp. 158–62.
172. V&A Forster Collection.
173. *HGF*, p. 255. This cessation, involving Devon and Cornwall, was proposed to Hopton by the Puritan and parliamentarian, Nicholas Trefusis, and was negotiated by six commissioners from each side. It expired on 22 April 1643. Coate, *Cornwall*, pp. 54–55.
174. CRO RP 1/10.
175. CRO RP 1/13.
176. CRO RP 1/15, 1/16.
177. CRO RP 1/17.
178. CRO RP 1/23.
179. CRO BC/24/2/6.
180. CRO BC/24/2/48.
181. CRO BC/24/2/11.
182. CRO BC/24/2/55.
183. CRO BC/24/2/49.
184. For a discussion of neutralism see Fletcher, *Outbreak*, pp. 380–404; Ann Hughes, 'Local History and the Origins of the Civil War' in Cust and Hughes (eds) *Conflict*, p. 237.
185. Clarendon, *History of the Rebellion*, vol. II, p. 448.
186. *Bellum Civile*, p. 23.
187. Thirty-nine royalists (42.9 per cent) and eighteen parliamentarians (34.6 per cent) had medieval origins.

Conclusion: Patterns of Continuity and Discontinuity

1. Haslam, 'Elizabethan Duchy', pp. 109–11, & *passim*; Haslam, 'Jacobean Phoenix', pp. 263–73, 295, & *passim*.
2. Haslam, 'Elizabethan Duchy', p. 92; Haslam, 'Jacobean Phoenix', p. 271; Haslam, 'The Duchy', pp. 230–31, 237–38.
3. Haslam, 'The Duchy', p. 242.
4. Haslam, 'Jacobean Phoenix', p. 296.
5. Coate, *Cornwall*, p. 24.
6. BL E150 (28) p. 40.
7. Haslam, 'Jacobean Phoenix', pp. 294–95.
8. Stoyle, *Loyalty and Locality. Popular Allegiance in Devon during the English Civil War* (Exeter, 1994), p. 237.
9. Coate, *Cornwall*, p. 32.
10. Stoyle, *Loyalty and Locality*, p. 237.
11. Russell, *Parliaments*, pp. 70–84, 323–40.
12. Cust, *Forced Loan*, p. 318 & *passim*.

13. Cust, *Forced Loan*, pp. 326–28, 201–18.
14. Cust, 'Draft Declaration', pp. 156–57.
15. Cust, *Forced Loan*, p. 328.
16. Russell, *Parliaments*, pp. 426–28; Cust, *Forced Loan*, pp. 333–35.
17. Stoyle, *Loyalty and Locality*, p. 237.

Appendices

Appendix 1
Size of the commission of the peace 1608–36[1]

Date	Gentry JPs
April 1608–1611[2]	30
November 1621–July 1622[3]	39
October 1626[4]	22
February 1632[5]	29
July 1634–c. August 1638[6]	23–29
July 1636[7]	24

1. The list does not include great officers of state nor non-resident peers. However, it does include the semi-resident peer, Charles Lord Lambert, and non-resident clerics from the diocese of Exeter. The location of sources and guidance on their dates was obtained from T.G. Barnes and A. Hassell Smith, 'Justice of the Peace from 1588–1688—a Revised List of Sources' *BIHR* vol. 32 (1959), pp. 221–42.
2. PRO SP14/33. List drafted 19 April 1608 shortly before the death of Lord Treasurer Dorset, and corrected by the Crown office on 20 May following the appointment of the new Lord Treasurer, Salisbury. Further corrected to 1611.
3. PRO C193/13/1. Liber pacis or Crown office entry book.
4. PRO E163/18/12. List of justices of the peace.
5. PRO SP16/212. Liber pacis.
6. PRO C193/13/2 Liber pacis. Corrected to at least August 1638. The name of Sir James Bagg, who died 26 August 1638, is crossed out, and 'morte' written alongside his name. The second figure is a maximum, including those whose names were crossed out by 1638.
7. PRO SP16/405. Liber pacis.

Appendix 2
The Composition of the 1622 commission of the peace[1]

	Hundred where resident	Age in 1622	Educational background	Wealth exceeding £1,000 pa	Origin of bride(s)	Originlage of family	Religious allegiance	Factional allegiance 1626–28	Civil War allegiance
i) JPs who were also named in the 1608 commission									
Sir Reginald Mohun	West	58	—	Y	1: Elsewhere 2: Devon 3: Devon	Medieval	? Arminian	Buckingham–Bagg	dead
Sir William Wrey	East	—	—	Y	Devon	Later 16th century	? Roman Catholic	Buckingham–Bagg	dead
Nicholas Prideaux	Pyder	72	—	?	1: Devon 2: Cornwall	Medieval	? Puritan	—	dead
Christopher Harris	West	31	Oxford/ Lincoln's Inn	Y	Cornwall	Later 16th century	?	dead	dead
John Arundell of Trerice	Pyder	46	Middle Temple	Y	1: Cornwall 2: Devon	Medieval	Calvinist Episcopalian	Eliot–Coryton	Royalist
Thomas St Aubyn	Penwith	79	—	Y	Devon	Medieval	Puritan	dead	dead
Arthur Harris	Penwith	61	—	Y	Devon	Later 16th century	?	—	dead
Edward Coswarth	Pyder	—	—	Y	Cornwall	Medieval	?	—	—
John Rashleigh	Powder	67	Oxford	Y	Cornwall	Early 16th century	? Puritan	dead	dead
John Roscarrock	Trigg	—	Oxford	N	—	Medieval	?	—	dead
Richard Trevanion	Powder	—	—	N	Cornwall	Medieval	Puritan	—	dead
Thomas Tubb	Powder	—	—	N	—	—	?	—	—

ii) JPs who were newly appointed in 1622

Hugh Boscawen	Powder	43	Oxford/Middle Temple	Y	Devon	Medieval	Puritan	—	dead
Sir Richard Edgcumbe	East	51	—	Y	1: Devon 2: Elsewhere	Medieval	?	Buckingham–Bagg	dead
Sir Robert Killigrew	Kerrier	42	Oxford	Y	Elsewhere	Medieval	Arminian	Buckingham–Bagg	dead
John Wood	—	—	—	—	—	—	—	—	—
Charles Trevanion	Powder	28	Oxford	Y	Elsewhere	Medieval	?	Eliot–Coryton	Royalist
William Coryton	East	43	—	Y	Devon	Medieval	Puritan	Eliot–Coryton	Royalist
Sampson Manaton	East	—	—	N	Devon	Medieval	?	—	—
Walter Langdon	West	23	Cambridge	Y	1: Cornwall 2: Devon	Later 16th century	?	Buckingham–Bagg	Royalist
Charles Roscarrock	Trigg	30	Cambridge Inner Temple	Y	Cornwall	Medieval	?	—	dead
John Trelawny	West	30	Oxford	Y	Cornwall	Medieval	?	Buckingham–Bagg	Royalist
Thomas Arundell	West	—	—	Y	Devon	Medieval	?	—	Parliamentarian
Samuel Rolle	East	34	Oxford/Inner Temple	N	1: West Country 2: Devon	—	Puritan	—	Parliamentarian
Thomas Wyvell	East	—	—	N	1: Cornwall 2: Cornwall	Later 16th century	?	—	—
John Moyle	East	30	Oxford/Inner Temple	Y	Devon	Medieval	Puritan	Eliot–Coryton	Parliamentarian
Nicholas Trefusis	East	32	Lincoln's Inn	N	Cornwall	Medieval	?	Eliot–Coryton	Parliamentarian
Francis Godolphin of Treveneage	Penwith	34	Oxford/Middle Temple	Y	Cornwall	Medieval	Puritan	—	Parliamentarian
Sir John Eliot	East	30	Oxford	Y	Cornwall	Early 16th century	Puritan	Eliot–Coryton	dead

Name	Region	Age	University/Inn		Marriage	Family antiquity	Religion	Faction	
John St Aubyn	Penwith	45	Oxford/Middle Temple	Y	Cornwall	Medieval	Puritan	—	dead
Ambrose Manaton	East	—	Lincoln's Inn	N	Cornwall	Medieval	Puritan	Eliot–Coryton	Royalist
Francis Vyvyan	Kerrier	46	Oxford/Middle Temple	Y	1: Cornwall 2: Cornwall	Medieval	? Puritan	—	dead
John Chamond	Stratton	72	Oxford	—	—	—	?	dead	dead
John Trefusis	Kerrier	35	Oxford/Lincoln's Inn	Y	Cornwall	Medieval	? Puritan	—	dead
Sir Richard Buller	East	43	Middle Temple	Y	Elsewhere	Early 16th century	Puritan	Eliot–Coryton	Parliamentarian
Sir Nicholas Lower	East	46	Oxford	Y	—	Medieval	? Arminian	—	Royalist
Francis Godolphin	Kerrier	44	—	Y	Unmarried	Medieval	?	—	dead
Reskymer Bonython	Kerrier	—	—	Y	—	Early 16th century	?	—	—
William Rous	East	27	Oxford/Middle Temple	Y	Cornwall	Later 16th century	Puritan	Eliot–Coryton	dead

1. PRO C193/13/1. The table extends only to local gentry JPs. It is based on Hughes' methodology, but examines the 1622 commission only, and list religious, political and factional criteria in addition to social characteristics.

Appendix 3
Forced Loan Commissioners, Cornwall *c.* March 1627[1]

Name	Hundred	JP	Refuser
(i) Non-Cornishmen			
Thomas Coventry, Kt, Lord Keeper	—	Y	N
James Earl of Marlborough	—	Y	N
Henry Earl of Manchester	—	Y	N
Edward Earl of Worcester	—	Y	N
George Duke of Buckingham	—	Y	N
William Earl of Pembroke	—	Y	N
Edward Earl of Bedford	—	Y	N
Theophilus Earl of Suffolk	—	Y	N
Sir John Walter, Chief Baron	—	Y	N
Sir John Denham, one of the Barons	—	Y	N
Daniel Price, Dean of Hereford	—	Y	N
William Parker, Master of the Chancery	—	Y	N
Charles Lord Lambert		Y	N
Sir James Bagg	—	N	N
(ii) Cornishmen			
Richard Lord Robartes	Powder	N	N
Sir Reginald Mohun Kt & Bt	West	Y	N
Sir Bernard Grenvile Kt	Stratton	N	N
Sir Robert Killigrew Kt	Kerrier	Y	N
Sir Richard Edgcumbe Kt	East	Y	N
Sir Richard Buller Kt	East	Y	Y
Sir William Wrey Kt	East	N	N
Sir Nicholas Lower Kt	East	Y	N
Sir Francis Godolphin Kt	Kerrier	Y	N
Sir Francis Vyvyan Kt	Kerrier	N	N
John Mohun Esq	West	Y	N
Bevill Grenvile Esq	Stratton	N	Y
Richard Edgcumbe Esq	Powder	N	N
John Trelawny Esq	West	Y	N
Charles Trevanion Esq	Powder	Y	N

Arthur Harris Esq	Penwith	Y	N
Francis Bassett Esq	Penwith	N	N
Charles Roscarrock Esq	Lesnewth	Y	N
John Trefusis Esq	Kerrier	Y	N
Walter Langdon Esq	West	Y	N
Richard Trevanion Esq	Powder	Y	N
Thomas Wyvell Esq	East	Y	N
Nicholas Trefusis Esq	Kerrier	Y	Y
William Rous Esq	East	Y	N
Richard Erisey Esq	Kerrier	Y	N
Ambrose Manaton Esq	East	Y	Y
Edward Trelawny Esq of Bake	East	Y	N
John Moyle Esq	East	Y	N
Hugh Boscawen Esq	Powder	N	N
Sampson Manaton Esq	East	N	N
Humphry Nicoll Esq	Trigg	N	Y

1. PRO C193/12/2.

Appendix 4
Buller's List of Ship Money 'Refusers', 1637[1]

Hundred	Parish	Name	Arrear
East			£ s. d.
	South Petherwin	Mr John Clobery	00.02.03
	South Petherwin	Mr Richard Eliot	00.02.03
	St Thomas by Launceston	Baronet Drake	00.16.00
	St Stephen by Launceston	Baronet Drake	00.17.00
	Egloskerry	Mr Nevill Bligh	00.10.06
	Egloskerry	— Denning	00.14.00
West	Cardinham	Mr Gennis of Bodmin	00.10.00
	Morval	Francis Buller Esq	01.10.00
Lesnewth	Altarnun	Mr Barrett	02.00.00
	Poundstock	Mr Mawpowder in Devon	03.00.00
	Warbstow	Mr Eliot & Mrs Moulsworth	03.00.00

255

	Treneglos	Mr Eliot & Mrs Moulsworth	00.10.00
Trigg	St Kew	Mr John Vivian	00.13.00
	St Kew	Mr Roules	00.01.00
	St Kew	Mr Godolphin	00.01.00
	Bodmin	Mr William Prust	00.09.04
	Bodmin	Mrs Anne Robins	00.06.08
Stratton	Launcells	Mr Porter	03.06.08
	North Tamerton	Abdell Vosper	00.14.00
	North Tamerton	Edmund Heydon	00.01.06
	Week St Mary	Mr Clifton	00.14.00
	Boyton	Henry Kemp	00.14.00
	Bridgerule	Mr Sampson Heale	00.08.06
Pyder	Newlyn	John Arundell	05.07.04
	Newlyn	Sampson Coswarth	01.15.04
	Newlyn	Nicholas Leverton	00.04.00
	Colan	Edward Coswarth	03.13.00
	Colan	Colan Bluett	01.00.00
	St Columb Major	Mr Legg	03.00.00
	St Eval	Mr Ceely	00.09.00
	Lanhydrock	Mr William Speccott	01.00.00
Powder	Ladock	Sir William Courteney	03.06.08
	Ladock	Peter Courteney	02.14.00
	Ladock	Harman Browne	00.06.00
	Lanlivery	Mr Walter Kendall	01.18.00
	Lanlivery	Mr Taprell	00.03.00
	Lanlivery	Thomas Strong	00.01.00
	Kea	Sam Spry	00.05.00
	Kea	William Jennens	00.01.00
	Kenwyn	George Spry	01.10.00
	Kenwyn	John Arundell	00.14.00
	St Allen	Mr John Arundell	00.18.00
Kerrier	Cury	Renatus Bellott	00.19.00
	Cury	Thomas Cossen	00.10.00
	Cury	John Sparnon	00.00.09
Penwith	none	none	none
Corporation	Tintagel and Trevena	Mr William Scawen	00.10.00

1. CRO BO/21/23/1–4.

Bibliography

1. Unpublished Primary Sources

I. Public Record Office

C181/3, Crown Office Entry Book 1620–1629.
C181/4, Crown Office Entry Book 1629–1634.
C181/5, Crown Office Entry Book 1635–1645.
C193/12/2, List of commissioners for the forced loan, 1626–27.
C193/13/1, Liber Pacis c.July 1622.
C193/13/2, Liber Pacis c.July 1634.
C231/4, Crown Office Docquet Book 1615–1629.
C231/5, Crown Office Docquet Book 1629–1643.
E163/18/12, Liber Pacis October 1626.
E178/7161, Schedule of compositions for fines for not receiving the order of knighthood at the coronation of Charles I.
E179/88/293, 1625 Lay Subsidy Roll, Penwith and Kerrier.
E179/89/307–312, 1626 Lay Subsidy Roll, Cornwall.
E179/89/324–335, 1641 Lay Subsidy Roll, Cornwall.
E331, Bishops Institution Books, Series A, 1566–1660, vol. 2.
E401/2586, Register of Privy Seal Loans, 1625–1626, Cornwall.
E401/1917–1925, Exchequer Receipt Books, including knighthood composition payments.
E407/35, Book of compositions for not taking the order of knighthood 1630–1632.
PROB 11, Prerogative Court of Canterbury, wills.
SP14, State Papers, James I.
SP16, State Papers, Charles I.

II. British Library

Additional MSS, 12,511: Sir John Eliot's Petition from the Gatehouse concerning the forced loan.
Additional MSS 30,926: Examination of Sir John Eliot, 1629.
Harleian MSS, 39, ff. 410–415: Privy Council's examination of William Coryton for refusal to pay the forced loan.
Harleian MSS 1622: Liber Pacis January 1626.

257

III. Bodleian Library
Clarendon MSS 26.
Rawlinson MSS C.789.

IV. Victoria And Albert Museum
Forster Special Collection: Letters of Sir Bevill Grenvile.

V. Duchy of Cornwall Record Office
Letters and Patents 1620–1621.
Letters and Warrants 1620–1621.
Burgesses for Parliament 1623–1624.

VI. Cornwall County Record Office
AD/374, Cornish Militia Commissioners to Speaker, House of Commons.
AP, Probate Records.
B/BOD, Bodmin Mayors' Accounts.
B/LA, Launceston Mayors' Accounts.
B/LISK, Liskeard Mayors' Accounts.
B/PEN, Penryn Mayors' Accounts.
BC, BW, CW/GG, HD, Buller of Shillingham papers.
B, Bassett of Tehidy papers.
CN, Carlyon of Tregrehan papers.
CY, Coryton of West Newton Ferrers papers.
EN, Enys of Enys papers.
G, Gregor of Trewarthenick papers.
P19/5/7–14, St Breock Churchwardens' Accounts.
P36/8/1, St Columb Major Green Book.
P126/4/1, Liskeard Churchwardens' Accounts.
P132/5/1, St Mabyn Churchwardens' Accounts.
P144/5/3/8–10, Menheniot Churchwardens' Accounts.
P162/5/1, St Neot Churchwardens' Accounts.
P170/5/1, Padstow Churchwardens' Accounts.
P192/5/2, Poughill Churchwardens' Accounts.
P221/5/10–12, St Thomas by Launceston Churchwardens' Accounts.
P214/5/1, St Stephens by Saltash Churchwardens' Accounts.
PD322/2–3, Camborne Churchwardens' Accounts.
R, R/S, Rashleigh of Menabilly papers.
RP, Penrose papers (letters of Francis Godolphin of Godolphin).
T, Tremayne of Heligan papers.
TF, Treffry of Place papers.
V, Vyvyan of Trelowarren papers.
FS/3/47, Papers of Robert Bennet of Lawhitton.
T.CP, Trefusis of Trefusis papers.

VII. Royal Institution of Cornwall
Henderson Collection.

VIII. Somerset Record Office
Phelips Manuscripts.

IX. Northamptonshire Record Office
Finch Hatton Manuscripts.

X. History Of Parliament Trust (transcripts)
Diary of Sir William Spring.
Diary of Bulstrode Whitelocke.

2. Printed Primary Sources

Acts and Ordinances of the Interregnum, 1642–60 ed. by C.H. Firth and R.S. Rait, 3 vols (London, 1911).
Acts of the Privy Council of England 1618–1631 11 vols (London, 1929–64).
Birch, Thomas (ed.) *The Court and Times of Charles I* 2 vols (1848).
Bruce, John (ed.) *Verney Papers. Notes of Proceedings in the Long Parliament* Camden Society, 1st series, vol. 31 (London, 1845).
Calendar of the Proceedings of the Committee for the Advance of Money 1642–1656 3 vols (London, 1888).
Calendar of the Proceedings of the Committee for Compounding 1643–1660 5 vols (London, 1889–93).
Calendar of State Papers Domestic (London, 1858–97).
Carew, Richard, *The True and Ready Way to Learn the Latine Tongue* (London, 1654).
Carew, Richard, *The Survey of Cornwall* (London, 1769).
Clarendon, Edward Earl of, *A Collection of Several Tracts of the Right Honourable Earl of Clarendon, Author of the History of the Rebellion and Civil Wars in England* (London, 1727).
Clarendon, Edward Earl of, *The Continuation of the Life of Edward Earl of Clarendon, Lord High Chancellor of England, and Chancellor of the University of Oxford; from the Restoration in 1660, to his Banishment in 1667* (Oxford, 1827).
Clarendon, Edward Earl of, *The History of the Rebellion and Civil Wars in England begun in the year 1641* ed. by W. Dunn Macray, 6 vols (Oxford, 1888).
Cockburn, J.S. (ed.) *Western Circuit Assize Orders 1629–1648. A Calendar* Camden Society, 4th Series, vol. 17 (London, 1976).
Commons Debates 1625 ed. by M. Janssen and W.B. Bidwell (New Haven and London, 1987).
Commons Debates 1628 ed. by R.C. Johnson, M.F. Keeler, M.J. Cole and W.B. Bidwell, 6 vols (New Haven and London, 1977–78).
Commons Debates for 1629 ed. by W. Notestein and R.H. Relf (Minneapolis, 1921).
Defoe, Daniel, *A Tour Through England and Wales* (London, 1959).
D'Ewes, Sir Simonds, *The Journal of Sir Simonds D'Ewes. From the first recess of the*

Long Parliament to the withdrawal of King Charles from London ed. by W.H. Coates (New Haven, 1942).

Fathers, John, *The Content of a Wayfaring Man: And the Accompt Of A Ministers Removall. Two sermons. The one preached at the Morning Lecture in the Citie of London; the other more enlarged in another congregation* (London, 1648).

Fathers, John, *The Strife of Brethren and a Treaty for Peace. Two Sermons. The one, Preached at the Morning Lecture in the Citie of London: The other, More inlarged in another Congregation* (London, 1648).

FitzGeffry, Charles, *Elisha His Lamentation, For His Owne, and all Israels losse, in Elijah. The subject of a Sermon, preached at the Funeralls of the Right Worshipfull Sir Anthony Rous, late of Halton in Cornwall, knight* (London, 1622).

FitzGeffry, Charles, *Death's Sermon Unto the Living, Delivered at the Funerals of the Religious Ladie Philippe, late Wife unto the Right Worshipfull Sr Anthonie Rous of Halton in Cornwall Knight* (London, 1622).

FitzGeffry, Charles, *A preparative to Repentance* (1628).

FitzGeffry, Charles, *The Widower's Tears for the Death of Dorcas* (London, 1631).

FitzGeffry, Charles, *The Curse of Corne-horders: with The Blessing of Seasonable selling* (London, 1631).

FitzGeffry, Charles, *Compassion Towards Captives, Chiefly Towards our Bretheren and Country-men who are in miserable bondage in Barbarie* (Oxford, 1637).

Foster, Joseph (ed.) *The Register of Admissions to Gray's Inn 1521–1889* (London, 1889).

Foster, Joseph (ed.) *Alumni Oxonienses: the members of the University of Oxford, 1500–1714; their parentage, birthplace and year of birth, with a record of their degrees, etc* 4 vols (Oxford and London, 1891).

Gamon, Hannibal, *The Praise of a Godly Woman. A Sermon preached at the Solemn Funerall of the Right Honourable Ladie, the Ladie Frances Roberts, at Lan-hide-rock-church in Cornwall, the tenth of August 1626* (London, 1627).

Gamon, Hannibal, *God's Smiting to Amendment, or Revengement. With Preservatives against Revolting. In a sermon preached at the Assises in Launceston, the 6 of August, 1628* (London, 1629).

Gardiner, S.R., *Constitutional Documents of the Puritan Revolution 1625–1660* (Oxford, 1889; repr. 1979).

Grosart, Alexander B. (ed.) *De Jure Maiestatis or Political Treatise of Government (1628–30) and the Letter-Book of Sir John Eliot (1625–1632)* 2 vols (London, 1882).

Hall, Joseph, *The Works of the Right Reverend Joseph Hall, D.D. Bishop of Exeter and Afterwards of Norwich. A New Edition . . . by Philip Wynter* 10 vols (Oxford, 1863).

Havenden, Robert (ed.) *The Visitation of Kent, taken in the years 1619–1621 by John Philpot* Harleian Society, vol. XLII (London, 1898).

Historical Manuscripts Commission 12th Report, Coke MSS; Salisbury MSS; Hervey MSS.

Hopton, Ralph, *Bellum Civile. Hopton's Narrative of his Campaign in the West (1642–1644) and Other Papers* ed. by C.E.H. Chadwyck Healey, Somerset Record Society, vol. XVIII (Taunton, 1902).

Journals of the House of Commons vols i and ii.

Journals of the House of Lords vols iv. and v.

Knowler, W. (ed.) *The Earl of Strafford's Letters and Dispatches* 2 vols (London, 1739).

Laud, William, *The Works of William Laud* ed. by W. Scott and J. Bliss, 7 vols (Oxford, 1847–60), vol. 5.

List of Sheriffs for England and Wales from the Earliest Times to AD 1831 PRO Lists and Indexes vol. IX (London, 1898).

Maltby, Judith (ed.) *The Short Parliament (1640) Diary of Sir Thomas Aston* Camden Society, 4th Series, vol. 35 (London, 1988).

New News From Cornwall BL E124 (20).

Norden, John, *Speculi Britanniae Pars. A topographical and chorographical description of Cornwall* (London, 1728).

Peter, Hugh, *Digitus Dei or Good News From Holland* (Rotterdam, 1631).

Proceedings of the Short Parliament of 1640 Camden Society, 4th Series, vol. 19, ed. by E.S. Cope and W.H. Coates (London, 1977).

Register of Admissions to the Honourable Society of Lincoln's Inn vol. 1 Admissions 1420–1799 (London, 1896).

Register of Admissions to the Honourable Society of the Middle Temple vol. 1 Fifteenth century to 1781 (London, 1949).

Rous, Francis, *Treatises and Meditations* (London, 1657).

Rushworth, John, *Historical Collections* 7 vols (London, 1659–1701).

Stoate, T.L. (ed.) *The Cornwall Protestation Returns 1641* (Bristol, 1974).

Stoate, T.L. (ed.) *Cornwall Hearth and Poll Taxes 1660–1664. Direct Taxation in Cornwall in the Reign of Charles II* (Bristol, 1981).

Students Admitted to the Inner Temple 1547–1660 (London, 1877).

Symonds, Richard, *Diary of the Marches of the Royal Army During the Great Civil War* ed. by Charles E. Long, Camden Society, 1st Series, no. 74 (London, 1859–60).

The humble Petition of the Gentlemen, and other of the Inhabitants of the County of Cornwall BL E150 (28), p. 37.

The humble Petition of the Knights, Esquires, Gentlemen, Ministers, Freeholders, and other Inhabitants of the County of Cornwall BL E150 (28), p. 40.

The humble Petition of the Knights, Justices of the Peace, Gentlemen, Ministers, Freeholders and others of the County of Cornwall BL E143 (19).

The Private Journals of the Long Parliament 3 January to 5 March 1642 ed. by W.H. Coates, A.S. Young and V.F. Snow (New Haven, 1982).

Thurloe, John, *A Collection of the State Papers of John Thurloe 1638–[1660], published from the originals . . . also . . . letters and papers from the Library at Lambeth [Palace]: prefixed by the Life of Mr Thurloe . . . the whole digested into an . . . order of time* ed. by Thomas Birch, 7 vols (London, 1742).

To the Kings most Excellent Maiestie. The humble Petition of the County of Cornewall BL E150 (28), p. 32.

Venn, J. and Venn, J.A. (eds) *Alumni Cantabrigienses. A biographical list of all known students, graduates and holders of office at the University of Cambridge, from the earliest times to 1900* Part 1 From the earliest times to 1751, 4 vols (Cambridge, 1922–27).

Vivian, J.L. and Drake, H.H. (eds) *The visitation of the county of Cornwall, in the year 1620* Harleian Society, vol. IX (London, 1874).

Vivian, J.L. (ed.) *The Visitations of Cornwall . . . of 1530, 1573 and 1620 with additions by J.L. Vivian* (Exeter, 1887).
Vivian, J.L. (ed.) *The Visitations of the County of Devon* (London, 1895).
Worth, R.N. (ed.) *The Buller Papers* (privately published, 1895).

3. Published Secondary Sources

Ashton, Robert, *The English Civil War. Conservatism and Revolution 1603–1649* (London, 1978).
Ball, J.N., 'Sir John Eliot and Parliament, 1624–1629' in Sharpe (ed.) *Faction and Parliament*, pp. 173—207.
Barnes, T.G. and Hassell Smith, A., 'Justices of the Peace from 1588–1688—a Revised List of Sources' *Bulletin of the Institute of Historical Research* vol. XXXII (1959), pp. 221–42.
Barnes, T.G., *Somerset 1625–1640. A County's Government During the Personal Rule* (Oxford, 1961).
Bernard, G.W., 'The Church of England c.1529–c.1642' *History* vol. 75, no. 244 (June 1990), pp. 183–206.
Blackwood, B.G., *The Lancashire Gentry and the Great Rebellion, 1640–60* Chetham Society, 3rd series, vol. 25 (Manchester, 1978).
Boase, G.C. and Courtney, W.P., *Biblioteca Cornubiensis* 3 vols (London, 1874–82).
Boase, G.C., *Collectanea Cornubiensia* (Truro, 1890).
Boynton, Lindsay, 'Billeting: the example of the Isle of Wight' *English Historical Review* vol. 74 (1959), pp. 23–40.
Boynton, Lindsay, *The Elizabethan Militia 1558–1638* (London, 1967).
Butler, Martin, 'Entertaining the Palatine Prince: Plays on Foreign Affairs 1635–1637' *English Literary Renaissance* vol. 13 (1983), pp. 319–44.
Campbell, Mildred, *The English Yeoman Under Elizabeth and the Early Stuarts* (New Haven, 1942).
Cliffe, J.T., *The Yorkshire gentry, from the Reformation to the Civil War* (London, 1969).
Cliffe, J.T., 'The Royalist Composition Papers and the Landed Income of the Gentry: A Rejoinder' *Northern History* vol. XIV (1978), pp. 164–68.
Cliffe, J.T., *The Puritan Gentry* (London, 1984).
Clifton, Robin, 'Fear of Popery' in Russell (ed.) *Origins*, pp. 144–67.
Coate, Mary, *Cornwall in the Great Civil War and Interregnum 1642–1660* (Oxford, 1933).
Cockayne, G.E., *The Complete Peerage of England, Scotland, Ireland, Great Britain, and the United Kingdom* 12 vols (London, 1910–59).
Collinson, Patrick, *The Religion of Protestants. The Church in English Society 1559–1625* (Oxford, 1982).
Cope, Esther S., *Politics Without Parliaments 1629–1640* (London, 1987).
Cust, Richard, 'A list of commissioners for the forced loan of 1626–7' *Bulletin of the Institute of Historical Research* vol. LI, (1978), pp. 199–206.

Cust, Richard, 'Charles I, the Privy Council, and the Forced Loan' *Journal of British Studies* vol. 124, no. 2 (April 1985), pp. 208–35.

Cust, Richard, 'News and Politics in Early Seventeenth-Century England' *Past and Present* no. 112 (1986), pp. 60–90.

Cust, Richard, *The Forced Loan and English Politics 1626–1628* (Oxford, 1987).

Cust, Richard, 'Politics and the Electorate in the 1620s' in Cust and Hughes (eds) *Conflict*, pp. 134–67.

Cust, Richard, 'Charles I and a draft Declaration for the 1628 Parliament' *Bulletin of the Institute of Historical Research* vol. 63, no. 151 (June 1990), pp. 143–61.

Cust, Richard and Hughes, Ann (eds) *Conflict in Early Stuart England. Studies in Religion and Politics 1603–1642* (London and New York, 1989).

Davis, Ralph, 'England and the Mediterranean 1570–1670' in F.J. Fisher (ed.) *Essays in the Economic and Social History of Tudor and Stuart England in honour of R.H. Tawney* (Cambridge, 1961), pp. 117–37.

Derriman, James, *Killigarth. Three Centuries of a Cornish Manor* (privately published, Morden, 1994).

Dictionary of National Biography 30 vols (London, 1908–86).

Dodridge, Sir John, *An Historical Account of the Ancient and Modern State of the Principality of Wales, Dutchy of Cornwall, and Earldom of Chester* (London, 1714).

Douch, H.L., *The Grosse Family of Norfolk and Cornwall* (privately published).

Duffin, Anne, 'The Defence of Cornwall in the Early Seventeenth Century' in Robert Higham (ed.) *Security and Defence in South-West England Before 1800* (Exeter, 1987), pp. 69–77.

Everitt, Alan, *The Community of Kent and the Great Rebellion, 1640–60* (Leicester, 1966).

Everitt, Alan, *The Local Community and the Great Rebellion* (London, 1969).

Everitt, Alan, *Change in the Provinces: the Seventeenth Century* Department of English Local History Occasional Papers, 2nd series, no. 1 (Leicester, 1972).

Fincham, Kenneth, 'The Judges' Decision on Ship Money in February 1637: the Reaction of Kent' *Bulletin of the Institute of Historical Research* vol. LVII (1984), pp. 230–37.

Fincham, Kenneth (ed.) *The Early Stuart Church, 1603–1642* (London, 1993).

Fincham, Kenneth, 'Introduction', in Fincham (ed.) *Early Stuart Church*, pp. 1–22.

Fincham, Kenneth, 'Episcopal Government, 1603–1640' in Fincham (ed.) *Early Stuart Church*, pp. 71–91.

Fincham, Kenneth and Lake, Peter, 'The Ecclesiastical Policies of James I and Charles I' in Fincham (ed.) *Early Stuart Church*, pp. 23–50.

Fletcher, Anthony, *A County Community in Peace and War: Sussex 1600–1660* (London, 1975).

Fletcher, Anthony, *The Outbreak of the English Civil War* (London, 1981).

Fletcher, Anthony, 'The Coming of War' in Morrill (ed.) *Reactions*, pp. 29–49.

Fletcher, Anthony, 'Debate, Parliament and People in Seventeenth-Century England' *Past and Present* no. 98 (1983), pp. 151–55.

Fletcher, Anthony, 'National and Local Awareness in the County Communities' in Howard Tomlinson (ed.) *Before the English Civil War* (London, 1983), pp. 151–74.

Fletcher, Anthony, *Reform in the Provinces. The Government of Stuart England* (New Haven and London, 1986).

Forster, John, *Sir John Eliot: A Biography 1590–1632* 2 vols (London, 1864).

Gardiner, S.R., 'Notes by Sir James Bagge on the Parliament of 1626' *Notes and Queries* 4th series, vol. 10 (1872), pp. 325–26.

Gardiner, S.R., *History of England from the Accession of James I to the Outbreak of the Civil War 1603–1642* 10 vols (New York, 1965).

Gittings, Clare, *Death, Burial and the Individual in Early Modern England* (London, 1984).

Gordon, M.D., 'The Collection of Ship Money in the Reign of Charles I' *Transactions of the Royal Historical Society* 3rd series, vol. IV (1910), pp. 141–62.

Granville, R., *History of the Granville Family* (Exeter, 1895).

Gray, Todd (ed.) *Harvest Failure in Cornwall and Devon. The Book of Orders and the Corn Surveys of 1623 and 1630–1* Sources of Cornish History 1 (Redruth, 1992).

Gruenfelder, J.K., *Influence in Early Stuart Elections 1604–1640* (Columbus, 1981).

Harris, G.L., 'Medieval Doctrines in the Debates on Supply, 1610–1629' in Sharpe (ed.) *Faction and Parliament*, pp. 73–103.

Haslam, Graham, 'The Duchy and Parliamentary Representation in Cornwall, 1547–1640' *Journal of the Royal Institution of Cornwall* part 3, vol. VIII (1980), pp. 224–42.

Haslam, Graham, 'The Elizabethan Duchy of Cornwall, an estate in stasis' in Hoyle (ed.) *The Estates of the English Crown*, pp. 88–111.

Haslam, Graham, 'Jacobean Phoenix: the Duchy of Cornwall in the principates of Henry Frederick and Charles' in Hoyle (ed.) *The Estates of the English Crown*, pp. 263–96.

Hebb, David, *Piracy and the English Government 1616–1642* (Aldershot and Brookfield, 1994).

Hibbard, Caroline, *Charles I and the Popish Plot* (North Carolina, 1983).

Hill, Christopher, 'Parliament and People in Seventeenth-Century England' *Past and Present* no. 92 (1981), pp. 100–24.

Hill, Christopher, 'A Rejoinder' *Past and Present* no. 98 (1983), pp. 155–58.

Hill, L.M., 'County Government in Caroline England 1625–40' in Russell (ed.) *Origins*, pp. 66–90.

Hirst, Derek, *The Representative of the People? Voters and Voting in England under the Early Stuarts* (Cambridge, 1975).

Hirst, Derek, 'Revisionism Revised: Two Perspectives on Early Stuart Parliamentary History . . . The Place of Principle' *Past and Present* no. 92 (1981), pp. 79–99.

Holmes, Clive, *Seventeenth-century Lincolnshire* History of Lincolnshire, vol. 7 (Lincoln, 1980).

Holmes, Clive, 'The County Community in Stuart Historiography' *Journal of British Studies* vol. XIX, no. 2 (1980), pp. 54–73.

Houlbrooke, R., *The English Family 1450–1700* (London, 1984).

Hoyle, R.W. (ed.) *The Estates of the English Crown, 1588–1640* (Cambridge, 1992).

Hughes, Ann, 'Warwickshire on the eve of the Civil War: A "County Community"?' *Midland History* vol. VII (1982), pp. 42–72.

Hughes, Ann, 'The King, the Parliament, and the Localities during the English Civil War' *Journal of British Studies* vol. XXIV, no. 2 (1985), pp. 236–63.

Hughes, Ann, *Politics, society and civil war in Warwickshire, 1620–1660* (Cambridge, 1987).

Hughes, Ann, 'Local History and the Origins of the Civil War' in Cust and Hughes (eds) *Conflict*, pp. 224–53.

Hughes, Ann, *The Causes of the English Civil War* (Basingstoke and London, 1991).

Hulme, Harold, *The Life of Sir John Eliot 1592–1632. Struggle for Parliamentary Freedom* (London, 1957).

Hutton, Ronald, *The Royalist War Effort, 1642–1646* (London, 1982).

Hutton, Ronald, 'The Royalist War Effort' in Morrill (ed.) *Reactions*, pp. 51–66.

Keeler, M.F., *The Long Parliament, 1640–1641. A Biographical Study of its Members* (Philadelphia, 1954).

Kenyon, J.P. (ed.) *The Stuart Constitution 1603–1688. Documents and Commentary* (Cambridge, 1966).

Kishlansky, Mark, *Parliamentary Selection. Social and Political Choice in Early Modern England* (Cambridge, 1986).

Lake, Peter, 'The Collection of Ship Money in Cheshire During the Sixteen-Thirties: a Case Study of Relations between Central and Local Government' *Northern History* vol. 17 (1981), pp. 44–71.

Lake, Peter, 'Calvinism and the English Church 1570–1635', *Past and Present* no. 114 (1987), pp. 32–76.

Lake, Peter, 'The Impact of Modern Protestantism' *Journal of British Studies* vol. 28, no. 3 (July 1989), pp. 293–304.

Lake, William, *A Complete Parochial History of the County of Cornwall* 4 vols (Truro and London, 1867–72).

Leonard, H.H., 'Distraint of Knighthood: the Last Phase, 1625–41' *History* vol. 63 (1978), pp. 23–37.

Lewis, George, *A Life of Joseph Hall, D.D., Bishop of Exeter and Norwich* (London, 1886).

Lewis, G.R., *The Stannaries: A Study of the English Tin Miner* (Cambridge, 1924).

Levy, F.J., 'How Information Spread Among the Gentry, 1550–1640' *Journal of British Studies* vol. 21 (1982), pp. 11–35.

Lockyer, Roger, *Buckingham. The Life and Political Career of George Villiers, First Duke of Buckingham 1592–1628* (London, 1981).

Lysons, Daniel and Samuel, *Magna Britannia: Cornwall* (1814).

Macfarlane, Alan, *Marriage and Love in England 1300–1840* (Oxford, 1986).

Maltby, Judith, ' "By this Book": Parishioners, the Prayer Book and the Established Church', in Fincham (ed.) *Early Stuart Church*, pp. 115–37.

Matthews, A.G., *Walker Revised* (Oxford, 1948).

Matthews, J.H., *A History of the Parishes of Saint Ives, Lelant, Towednack and Zennor, in the County of Cornwall* (London, 1892).

Miller, Amos C., *Sir Richard Grenville of the Civil War* (London, 1979).

Milton, Anthony, 'The Church of England, Rome, and the True Church: The Demise of a Jacobean Consensus', in Fincham (ed.) *Early Stuart Church*, pp. 187–210.

Moir, Thomas, *The Addled Parliament of 1614* (Oxford, 1958).

Morgan, Victor, 'Cambridge University and "the Country", 1560–1640' in Lawrence Stone (ed.) *The University and Society* vol. 1 (Princeton, 1974), pp. 183–245.

Morrill, John, *Cheshire, 1630–60: county government and society during the English Revolution* (London, 1974).

Morrill, John, 'The Northern Gentry and the Great Rebellion' *Northern History* vol. XV (1979), pp. 66–87.

Morrill, John, *The Revolt of the Provinces. Conservatives and Radicals in the English Civil War 1630–1650* (London, 1980).

Morrill, John (ed.) *Reactions to the English Civil War 1642–1649* (London and Basingstoke, 1982).

Morrill, John, 'The Church in England, 1642–9' in Morrill (ed.) *Reactions*, pp. 89–114.

Morrill, John, 'The Religious Context of the English Civil War' *Transactions of the Royal Historical Society* 5th series, vol. 34 (1984), pp. 155–78.

Oliver, S. Pasfield, *Pendennis and St Mawes: An historical Sketch of Two Cornish Castles* (Truro, 1875).

Payton, Philip, *The Making of Modern Cornwall* (Redruth, 1992).

Peck, Linda Levy, ' "For a King not to be bountiful were a fault": Perspectives on Court Patronage in Early Stuart England' *Journal of British Studies* vol. 25, no. 1 (1986), pp. 31–61.

Pevsner, Nikolaus, *The Buildings of England: Cornwall* (London, 1951).

Phillips, C.B., 'The Royalist Composition Papers and the Landed Income of the Gentry: A Note of Warning from Cumbria' *Northern History* vol. XIII (1977), pp. 161–74.

Pounds, Norman J., *The Parliamentary Survey of the Duchy of Cornwall* Devon and Cornwall Record Society, new series, vols 25 and 27 (Torquay, 1982–84), 2 parts.

Prest, Wilfred, 'Legal Education of the Gentry at the Inns of Court, 1560–1640' *Past and Present* no. 38 (1967), pp. 20–39.

Prest, Wilfred, *The Inns of Court under Elizabeth I and the Early Stuarts 1590–1640* (London, 1972).

Quintrell, B.W., 'The making of Charles I's Book of Orders' *English Historical Review* vol. 95 (1980), pp. 553–72.

Richardson, R.C., *The Debate on the English Revolution* (London, 1977)

Roberts, Stephen, *Recovery and Restoration in an English County: Devon Local Administration 1646–1670* (Exeter, 1985).

Roots, Ivan, *The Great Rebellion 1642–1660* (London, 1966; revised edn Stroud, 1995).

Roots, Ivan, 'The Central Government and the Local Community' in E.W. Ives (ed.) *The English Revolution 1600–1660* (London, 1968), pp. 34–47.

Roots, Ivan, 'Interest—Public, Private and Communal' in R.H. Parry (ed.) *The English Civil War and After 1642–1658* (London, 1970), pp. 111–22.

Rowe, Violet, 'The Influence of the Earls of Pembroke on Parliamentary Elections, 1625–41' *English Historical Review* vol. 50 (1935), pp. 242–56.

Rowse, A.L., *Tudor Cornwall. Portrait of a Society* (London, 1957).

Ruigh, Robert E., *The Parliament of 1624. Politics and Foreign Policy* (Harvard, 1971).

Russell, Conrad (ed.) *The. Origins of the English Civil War* (London, 1973).

Russell, Conrad, 'Parliament and the King's Finances' in Russell (ed.) *Origins*, pp. 91–116.

Russell, Conrad, 'Parliamentary History in Perspective 1604–1629' *History* vol. 61 (1976), pp. 1–27.

Russell, Conrad, *Parliaments and English Politics, 1621–9* (Oxford, 1979).

Russell, Conrad, 'The Nature of a Parliament in Early Stuart England' in Tomlinson (ed.) *Before the English Civil War*, pp. 123–50.

Russell, Conrad, *The Causes of the English Civil War* (Oxford, 1990).

Russell, Conrad, *The Fall of the British Monarchies 1637–1642* (Oxford, 1991).

Sainty, J.C., 'Lieutenants of the Counties 1585–1642' *Bulletin of the Institute of Historical Research* special supplement, no. 8 (May 1970).

Sharpe, Kevin, 'The Personal Rule of Charles I' in Tomlinson (ed.) *Before the English Civil War*, pp. 53–78.

Sharpe, Kevin (ed.) *Faction and Parliament. Essays on Early Stuart History* (London, 1985).

Sharpe, Kevin, 'Crown, Parliament and Locality: Government and Communication in Early Stuart England' *English Historical Review* vol. CI (1986), pp. 321–50.

Sharpe, Kevin, *The Personal Rule of Charles I* (New Haven and London, 1992).

Slack, Paul, 'Books of Orders: The Making of English Social Policy, 1577–1631' *Transactions of the Royal Historical Society* 5th series, vol. 30 (1980), pp. 1–22.

Stanley, Jeanne, 'The Glory of Golden. An Account of Golden Manor, Probus, and its Owners 1193–1727' *Royal Cornwall Polytechnic Society* (1956), pp. 27–40.

Stone, Lawrence, 'The Educational Revolution in England, 1560–1640' *Past and Present* no. 28 (1964), pp. 41–80.

Stone, Lawrence, *The Crisis of the Aristocracy, 1558–1641* (Oxford, 1965).

Stone, Lawrence, 'Social Mobility in England, 1500–1700' *Past and Present* no. 33 (1966), pp. 16–55.

Stone, Lawrence, *The Family Sex and Marriage in England 1500–1800* (abridged edn Oxford, 1979).

Stoyle, Mark, *Loyalty and Locality. Popular Allegiance in Devon during the English Civil War* (Exeter, 1994).

Swales, R.J.W., 'The Ship Money Levy of 1628' *Bulletin of the Institute of Historical Research* vol. 50 (1977), pp. 164–76.

Thompson, Christopher, 'The Divided Leadership in the House of Commons in 1629' in Sharpe (ed.) *Faction and Parliament*, pp. 245–84.

Tomlinson, Howard (ed.) *Before the English Civil War. Essays on Early Stuart Politics and Government* (London, 1983).

Tyacke, Nicholas, 'Puritanism, Arminianism and Counter-Revolution' in Russell (ed.) *Origins*, pp. 119–43.

Tyacke, Nicholas, *Anti-Calvinists. The Rise of English Arminianism c.1590–1640* (Oxford, 1987).

Tyacke, Nicholas, 'The Rise of Arminianism Reconsidered' *Past and Present* no. 115 (May 1987), pp. 201–16.

Underdown, David, 'The Problem of Popular Allegiance in the English Civil War' *Transactions of the Royal Historical Society* 5th series, vol. 31 (1981), pp. 67–93.

Vage, J.A., 'Ecclesiastical discipline in the early seventeenth century: some findings and some problems from the archdeaconry of Cornwall' *Journal of the Society of Archivists* vol. VII, no. 1 (1982), pp. 85–105.

Whetter, James, *Cornwall in the 17th Century. An economic survey of Kernow* (Gorran, 1974).

Whetter, James, 'Cornish trade in the 17th Century: an analysis of the Port Books' *Journal of the Royal Institution of Cornwall* new series, vol. IV, part 4 (1964), pp. 388–413.

Whetter, James, 'John Rashleigh of Menabilly, Esquire (1554–1624)' *Old Cornwall* vol. 7, no. 3 (1968), pp. 113–120.

White, Peter, 'The Rise of Arminianism Reconsidered', *Past and Present* no. 101 (1983), pp. 34–54.

White, Peter, 'A Rejoinder' *Past and Present* no. 115 (May 1987), pp. 217–29.

White, Peter, 'The *via media* in the early Stuart church' in Fincham (ed.), *Early Stuart Church*, pp. 211–30.

Williams, F.B., *Index of Dedications and Commendatory Verses in English Books Before 1641* (London, 1962).

Wood, Anthony, *Athenae Oxonienses. An exact history of all the writers and bishops who have had their education in the University of Oxford. To which are added the Fasti, or annals of the said University* 4 vols (London, 1813–20).

4. Theses

Adamson, J.S.A., 'The Peerage in Politics 1645–49' (University of Cambridge Ph.D., 1986).

Appleby, J.C., 'English privateering during the Spanish and French wars, 1625–30' (University of Hull Ph.D., 1983).

Chynoweth, John, 'The Gentry of Tudor Cornwall' (University of Exeter Ph.D., 1994).

Cullum, David, 'Society and Economy in West Cornwall c.1588–1750' (University of Exeter Ph.D., 1994).

Cust, Richard, 'The Forced Loan and English Politics, 1626–8' (University of London Ph.D., 1984).

Duffin, Anne, 'The Political Allegiance of the Cornish Gentry c.1600–c.1642' (University of Exeter Ph.D., 1989).

Hebb, David, 'The English Government and the Problem of Piracy, 1616–42' (University of London Ph.D., 1985).

Hughes, Ann, 'Politics, society and civil war in Warwickshire, 1620–50' (University of Liverpool Ph.D., 1979).

McParlin, G.E., 'The Herefordshire gentry in county government, 1625–61' (University of Aberystwyth Ph.D., 1981).

Morrill, John, 'The Government of Cheshire During the Civil Wars and Interregnum' (University of Oxford D.Phil., 1971).

Morton-Thorpe, A.M., 'The Gentry of Derbyshire, 1640–1660' (University of Leicester M.A., 1971).

Phillips, C.B., 'The gentry in Cumberland and Westmorland, 1600–65' (University of Lancaster Ph.D., 1973).

Silcock, R.H., 'County Government in Worcestershire 1603–1660' (University of London Ph.D., 1974).

Wanklyn, M.D.G., 'The King's Armies in the West of England, 1642–46' (University of Manchester M.A., 1966).

Whetter, James, 'The Economic History of Cornwall in the 17th Century' (University of London Ph.D., 1965).

Williams, J.R., 'County and Municipal Government in Cornwall, Devon, Dorset and Somerset 1649–1660' (University of Bristol Ph.D., 1981).

Wolffe, Mary, 'The Gentry Government of Devon 1625–1640' (University of Exeter Ph.D., 1992).

Vage, J.A., 'The Diocese of Exeter 1519–1641: a study of Church Government in the Age of the Reformation' (University of Cambridge Ph.D., 1991).

Index

anti-Calvinism, 38, 42, 59, 62–64,
66–67, 71, 98, 99, 100–1, 116,
171, 187
Arminianism, 42, 46, 50, 52, 59–61,
99–102, 171–72, 190, 209, 211
Arscott, Tristram, of Launcells, 114,
122, 194
Arundell,
of Duloe, Thomas, 194
of Lanherne, Sir John 39–40, 54
of Trerice,
family, 22, 193
Ann, 31, 104, 156
John, sen., 24, 31, 34, 73–74,
76–77, 83, 87–89, 97, 104, 107,
111–12, 124, 149, 156–57, 160,
190, 195
John, jun., 177, 193–95
Mary, 31, 104
Richard, 180
assizes, 6, 17, 55, 84, 91, 104, 113,
187, 194–95

Bagg, Sir James, of Saltram, 5, 10, 34,
74, 77–80, 82–83, 85–89, 91–96,
102, 104–7, 111, 121–22, 125–28,
131, 133–35, 144, 147–49, 151,
153, 162, 207–8, 210
Bagg-Mohun faction, 88–90, 92–93,
96, 102, 104, 111, 117, 121, 124,
127, 133, 156, 209, 210, 211
Basill, Edward, vicar of Fowey, 53, 59
Bassett, of Tehidy,

family, 22
Sir Francis, 5, 126, 136, 148, 167,
174–75, 184–85, 193, 195
Thomas, 141
Bastard, of Duloe,
Joseph, 154–55
William, 128
Bedford, Francis Russell, Earl of, 122,
123, 181
benevolence, 82, 146–47, 165, 208
Bennett, Robert, of Lawhitton, 124
billeting, 97–98, 118, 120, 127–33,
139, 145, 148–49, 151, 209
Billings, Richard, duchy feodary, 73
Bodmin, 8, 13, 34, 52, 109, 122, 130,
146, 153, 174, 196, 199
Bonython, of Carclew,
Hannibal, governor of St Mawes
castle, 174
John, deputy governor of Pendennis
castle, 3, 136, 139
Alice, 18
Book of Common Prayer, 67, 173,
187–88, 191, 210, 211
Book of Orders, 113–17, 155, 209
Borlase, of Newlyn-in-Pyder
family, 39
Nicholas, 13, 41, 102, 125
Boscawen, of Tregothnan,
Hugh, sen., 24, 44, 47, 57, 158–60,
167
Hugh, jun., 57
Bossiney, 4, 13, 72, 172, 176

270